The Begums of Bhopal

The Begums of Bhopal

A Dynasty of Women Rulers in Raj India

Shaharyar M. Khan

I.B.Tauris Publishers
LONDON • NEW YORK

Published in 2000 by I.B.Tauris & Co Ltd
Victoria House, Bloomsbury Square, London WC1B 4DZ
175 Fifth Avenue, New York NY 10010
Website: http://www.ibtauris.com

Reprinted 2000

In the United States and Canada distributed by St. Martin's Press
175 Fifth Avenue, New York NY 10010

Copyright © Shaharyar M. Khan, 2000

The right of Shaharyar M. Khan to be identified as the author of this work has been asserted by the author in accordance with the Copyright, Designs and Patents Act 1988.

All rights reserved. Except for brief quotations in a review, this book, or any part thereof, may not be reproduced, stored in or introduced into a retrieval system, or transmitted, in any form or by any means, electronic, mechanical, photocopying, recording or otherwise, without the prior written permission of the publisher.

ISBN 1-86064-528-3

A full CIP record for this book is available from the British Library
A full CIP record for this book is available from the Library of Congress

Library of Congress catalog card: available

Typeset in Bookman Old Style by A. & D. Worthington, Newmarket
Printed and bound in Great Britain by Mackays of Chatham plc, Chatham, Kent

Contents

List of illustrations	vi
Preface	vii
Prologue	ix
Map of Bhopal	xi

1.	Dost Mohammad Khan – Founder of Bhopal, 1672–1728	1
2.	The 'reign' of Mamola Bai, 1728–95	30
3.	The Siege of Bhopal	52
4.	Qudsia Begum, 1819–37	70
5.	Sikandar Begum, 1847–68	90
6.	Shahjehan Begum, 1868–1901	119
7.	Sultan Jahan Begum, 1901–26	154
8.	The Bhopal Succession Case	188
9.	The Begums – A final assessment	214

Epilogue	230
Appendices	235
Bibliography	253
Bhopal rulers and British officials	260
Genealogical tree of the Orakzai Pathans of Tirah	262
Reigns of Bhopal rulers	263
Glossary	264
Index	267

Illustrations

1. Dost Mohammad Khan. Founder of the State.
2. Dost's tomb. Headstone in English, installed around 200 years after his death.
3. The author praying at the derelict tomb of Yar Mohammad Khan at Islamnagar, December 1998.
4. Ginnor Fort, 1998.
5. Shahzad Masih (Balthazar de Bourbon).
6. Sarkar Dulhan smoking a hookah with her 'slave' Sheeda.
7. Raisen Fort with one of the water reservoirs (non-perennial).
8. Qudsia Begum.
9. Sikandar Begum flanked by her Chief Minister, Maulvi Jamaluddin, and Army Chief, Mattu Khan.
10. Shahjehan Begum.
11. Siddiq Hassan.
12. The derelict Taj Mahal.
13. Portrait photograph of Sultan Jahan, London 1926.
14. Sultan Jahan Begum with the Viceroy, Lord Minto, Lady Minto and grandchildren, Bhopal 1911.
15. Sultan Jahan Begum with eldest granddaughter, Abida Sultaan, London 1926 (during succession case).
16. Hamidullah Khan, last Nawab.

Preface

I wrote *The Begums of Bhopal* as a family history. The book was not intended to be a definitive history of Bhopal, as I am neither historian nor author, but a career diplomat who retired in 1994 as Pakistan's Foreign Secretary. It all began with my mother showing me the first draft of her memoirs. She was the last heir apparent of Bhopal before it merged into the Indian Union in 1947. I told her that she was engaged in writing two separate books – the history of Bhopal and her own remarkable life. 'Then you finish the first part,' she replied. 'I am not of an age to go traipsing around libraries and peering through microfilms.'

I took up the challenge about six years ago, first reading all the books, documents and manuscripts on Bhopal's history that were available in my mother's library. I then spent long hours in the British Library scouring through confidential reports on Bhopal by British civil servants. The more I studied these documents the more I realized that an objective history of Bhopal had never been written. The Begums had written – and had commissioned state archivists to compile – highly subjective histories of Bhopal in which battles lost, sovereignty surrendered and character deficiencies of the rulers were conveniently omitted. I realized that in trying to present an objective history of Bhopal, I would be treading fresh ground and might ruffle a few family feathers.

Bhopal's history is extraordinary because of the unique phenomenon of four Muslim women rulers successively governing the state in their own legal, constitutional right for over a century. Bhopal was the second largest princely Muslim state (after Hyderabad), had a Hindu population of 90 per cent and was surrounded by aggressive, covetous neighbours. How did these Begums govern the state in the chaotic, anarchic times of post-Moghul India, belonging, as they did, to conservative Islamic tradition? I hope this book provides some of the answers.

My mother and I emigrated to Pakistan in 1950 when I was a boy of 16. She has been my main inspiration and guide in writing this book. She is steeped in the family's history and has lovingly preserved books, documents and rare manuscripts relating to Bhopal in her library. She has also recorded her impressions of Bhopal's history on tape as related to her by her grandmother, Sultan Jahan Begum, and old civil servants, family members and retainers whose recall went back to Sikandar Begum's golden era in the mid-nineteenth century.

After completing my research, I returned briefly to Bhopal last winter to immerse myself in the mists of our history swirling across the ruined forts, the decaying palaces and the tombs of my forebears. I took with me Manish Swarup, the brilliant photographer of the *Hindustan Times*, whose images are included in this book. I also consulted sages and old historians, notably Sahabzada Sikandar Mohammad Khan, Umrao Doulah's great-grandson, and Tayyaba Bi who have made the study of Bhopal's history a life-long passion. I owe them a deep debt of gratitude.

I must also express my sincere appreciation to my son Ali and his wife Mariyam who have helped me tremendously in researching rare documents and manuscripts. My profound thanks also go to Amsale Retta in Rwanda where I was the UN Secretary General's Special Representative between 1994 and 1996, Zahir ul Haq Khan, Abdur Rahman and Rashed Malik from Pakistan who typed out the manuscript in Kigali, Islamabad and Paris while my young colleague Khayyam Akbar did most of the computer work. A special vote of thanks goes to Shri Digvijay Singh, the Chief Minister of Madhya Pradesh, for his courtesy in helping me tour the historic sites of Bhopal and also to Professor R.K.S. Chauhan, Vice Chancellor of Vikram University, Ujjain, who procured for me the invaluable unpublished treatise on Bhopal by Dr O.P. Malhotra.

Finally, I would like to express my deep appreciation to Alison Worthington for her meticulous and highly professional editing of the manuscript, to Dr Lester Crook for his wise and experienced advice in organizing the historical context of my research and to I.B.Tauris for their support and enthusiasm in publishing the book.

Since I began my research the book has become more than a challenge. It is almost an obsession – a debt to be repaid to 14 generations of my forebears that began the saga of Bhopal with the advent of that brave, pioneering buccaneer Dost Mohammad Khan, and saw four Begums rule the state for 107 years. I have enjoyed writing this book for my mother and, in becoming an amateur historian, I have learnt more about statecraft than in 40 years of diplomacy.

Prologue

In 1707, before Dost Mohammad Khan arrived in Malwa, central India (see map), Bhopal was a small village on the banks of the River Banganga. An old fort, lying in ruins, was testimony to Bhopal having known more prosperous times in the distant past. The earliest reference to Bhopal is traced to AD 640 when it was ruled by the Parmar dynasty. In fact, Bhopal derives its name from one of its Hindu rajas named Bhoj who dominated the region during a lengthy reign beginning in 1018. According to legend, Raja Bhoj contracted leprosy and was advised by his *sanyasis* (Hindu soothsayers or astrologers) to build a lake that drew water from 365 rivers and then to bathe in its holy water. Raja Bhoj duly built a dam that led to the formation of a lake stretching across 200 square miles. This lake was named Bhoj-tal (literally Bhoj's lake). Bhojtal became corrupted to Bhojpal and then to Bhopal.

Situated in the Vindhya mountains with several rivers criss-crossing through lush forests, Bhopal was located in a particularly picturesque and fertile region. The climate was temperate, making Bhopal an attractive prize for competing warlords. According to historical accounts, Raja Bhoj's death led to decline and, sometime in the thirteenth century, the dam was destroyed by the local ruler, Hoshang Alap Khan, draining out the famous lake and leaving the fort in ruins. Hoshang Alap Khan reasoned that the lake had led to the region being infested with wild beasts and was the cause of pestilence. Thereafter, the local population, which consisted of indigenous Gonds[1] and Bhils, was dominated by a succession of warlords who were either local chieftains (gond-rajas) or Aryan invaders like Rajput chiefs or Muslim commanders who briefly governed the region, usually as *sanad* (title) holders on behalf of the more powerful overlords and emperors operating from Delhi, Agra, Rajputana or Bundelkhand.

Apart from its rich and fertile agriculture, Malwa was a central crossroad of trade between India's east and west coasts and also between north and south. It was also strategically situated in terms of military routes. The fact that in the second century BC, Buddhists had built their stupa at Sanchi (supposedly the Tropic of Cancer bisects the stupa) testifies to the importance of the region from earliest times.

---

[1] Gonds and Bhils were the Dravidian (non-Aryan) population settled in the region. More detail on the background of the Gonds may be found in Appendix 2. Gond-rajas were warlords of the Gonds.

By the time Dost set foot in Malwa Bhopal, despite its natural beauty and its fertility, had been reduced to ruin and decay. His arrival saw a revival of Bhopal's fortunes from a village of barely 20 families to a vibrant city state that developed its own culture, ethos and tradition under the Orakzai-Afghan dynasty dominated by the four famous Begums of Bhopal. The state was formed in 1715 and became one of India's leading princely states with a 19-gun salute. After Hyderabad, it was the most important Muslim state in India. The state lasted 230 years until independence in 1947 when its 13th ruler, Hamidullah Khan, signed the merger agreement with the newly independent Indian Union.

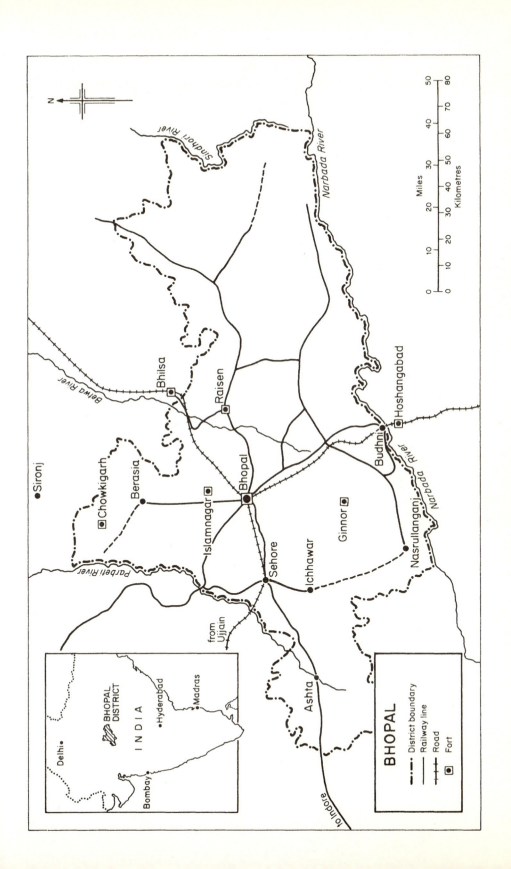

1

Dost Mohammad Khan Founder of Bhopal 1672–1728

The early days

The story of Bhopal begins with Sardar[1] Dost Mohammad Khan, founder of the state and of the Bhopal dynasty. Born around 1672[2] in Tirah, a village in the tribal area on the border between today's Pakistan and Afghanistan, Dost was the son of Sardar Nur Mohammad Khan,[3] a Pathan nobleman who belonged to the Mirazi-khel[4] clan of the Orakzai tribe.[5] Near the turn of the century, Dost was a strapping, handsome, brash and ambitious young man. Like all Pathan noblemen, he had been brought up in the warrior tradition of his clan and now, in the flush of young manhood, Dost was an expert horseman, hunter and swordsman. He had received a smattering of religious education through a succession of *imams* (Islamic clerics) but the most important element of Dost's upbringing was the inculcation of a rigid code of ethics that is, even today, part of Afghan tradition.

In Tirah, as in all Afghanistan, every young man was aware of the glory and riches of the Great Moghul Empire which had reached its zenith in India by the turn of the seventeenth century under its sixth Emperor, Aurangzeb. The Moghul emperors, as indeed the earlier Muslim rulers that had crossed into India through Afghanistan from central Asia, had relied on the brave, sturdy and martial Afghan tribesmen to form the backbone of their armies to fight, conquer and eventually consolidate their rule over India.

---

[1] A sardar is a clan chief.
[2] Controversy on the dates relating to Dost and his son Yar – the first two Nawabs of Bhopal – is assessed in Appendix 1.
[3] See genealogical table on p 262.
[4] Mirazi-khel is probably a corruption of Mir Aziz Khel.
[5] The Orakzai tribe was itself a sub-tribe of the Gorran tribe of Pathans and migrated from Iran to Afghanistan in the seventh century (see Appendix 3).

By the end of the seventeenth century, generations of Afghan travellers who had found fortune in the service of the Moghul kingdom carried home images of grandeur, fortune and glory. In Tirah, as in most villages of Afghanistan, the glitter of the Moghul Empire beckoned every young man. Being exceptionally gifted in physique, personality and the martial arts, Dost's only ambition was to enlist in Aurangzeb's army and make his future, like many others before him, in the service of the Moghul Empire. Perhaps he could command a company, defeat the 'infidels' in battle, earn a handsome salary, claim a booty of jewels and gold sovereigns, even end up as governor of a province. In any case, the parched, rocky terrain of Tirah offered no challenge or hope for a young man.

Around 1697, Dost was in his mid-20s and a brash, dare-devil, buccaneer of a character. He was restless and ready to seek his fortune by crossing the Khyber Pass into India, but family links had held him back in Tirah. Dost was engaged to Mehraj Bibi, apparently an attractive and high-born girl from a neighbouring Orakzai clan, but later the two families had decided to betroth Mehraj Bibi to one of Dost's cousins because they felt that Dost was too rough and aggressive a character. Either because of the insult or because he was in love with Mehraj Bibi, Dost created a rumpus and killed his cousin. He then virtually forced marriage on Mehraj Bibi. As a result, both families shunned and ostracized Dost for this act of passion and vengeance. Dost thus became even more determined to leave his tense, brooding surroundings to seek his fortune in India and though his father tried to dissuade his son from leaving Tirah and wandering away into the sunset, Dost had made up his mind. One night, Dost saddled the strongest horse in the stable, tied his scabbard around his waist, thrust some sovereigns in his pocket and galloped away in the dead of night to seek his fortune in the distant land of India.[1]

Dost headed first for Jalalabad (not the Jalalabad in Afghanistan, but a town 100 miles north-west of Delhi) where he knew that Afghan relatives had settled. Across the Khyber Pass, through the rugged mountains of today's North-West Frontier and into the verdant plains of the Punjab, Dost Mohammad Khan rode a trail that had been crossed by generations of Afghans before him. He found kinsmen in various *serais* (wayside lodgings) where he stayed, so that neither food nor custom nor language was totally alien to him. Several weeks after he left Tirah, Dost found his kinsmen in Lohari, a suburb of Jalalabad.[2] The family of Sardar Jalal Khan welcomed the young Pathan as the son of a fellow tribal sardar and soon Dost had found himself a temporary shelter from where he could take stock, survey the scene and decide on when and how to make the next move towards fulfilling his ambition.

---

[1] The exact date of Dost's arrival in India is not known. Chroniclers have given different dates for his journey to Jalalabad in Uttar Pradesh (formerly United Provinces) ranging between 1696 and 1703. It is established that Dost arrived in India during the final years of Emperor Aurangzeb's reign. Thus the dates given in the books by the Begums, i.e. during Bahadur Shah's reign, are patently wrong.
[2] Lohari/Jalalabad were subsequently identified as Thana-Ghaon in Saharanpur district of Uttar Pradesh. It lies 30 miles south of Saharanpur and 20 miles east of Deoband.

Sardar Jalal Khan's family was related to Dost's family and, in fact, Sardar Jalal Khan was the *Mansabdar* (Moghul official) of Lohari, his family having been settled in Lohari for several generations as *zamindars* (land-owners). Dost adjusted quickly to his new environment and was soon hunting, riding and frolicking with family members of his own age. Being young and bursting with life, Dost formed an attachment with one of the young house-maidens. One day, when Sardar Jalal Khan was celebrating a birthday feast, a quarrel over the girl broke out between Dost and one of Jalal Khan's sons. Dost was attacked with a bow and arrow by his opponent. Retaliating, he plunged a dagger into his young rival's heart, killing him instantly.[1] Dost realized at once the magnitude of his crime. In a few seconds of mad jealousy, he had killed a scion of the noble family that had treated him as their own. He had betrayed their trust and now, true to Pathan tradition, the family would not rest until the slain youth had been avenged. As much through fear for his life as shame at his ingratitude to the Jalal Khan family, Dost realized that his only option was to flee. In a flash, facing the greatest crisis of his young life, Dost gathered his belongings, stuffed a sack with dried chickpeas and galloped away in a cloud of dust as fast as his faithful steed could carry him.

Dost was now in a frenzy. He imagined the entire Jalal Khan family, traumatized by his treachery, setting off in a posse to pursue him and to seek immediate vengeance. They were familiar with the terrain, the roads, the hideaways. They would track him down by seeking the help of local villagers who had known this noble Afghan family for a long time. As he coaxed his horse to go faster and faster from his imagined pursuers, Dost's world came tumbling down around him. Instead of easing himself comfortably into the Moghul Emperor's service through Afghan family connections, he was now an unknown fugitive in an alien land with no friends. The only family he knew, he had betrayed in a fit of passion, and retribution was perhaps only a few minutes away. He thought he could hear the sound of hooves pursuing him as he galloped through the brushwood. All Dost knew was that Delhi lay about 100 miles south-east and, looking up at the sky, he headed frantically towards a city in which he hoped he could find cover and sanctuary.

On and on he sped, his face covered with dust, his lips parched, his dress stained with the blood of the youth he had killed. After almost six hours at a constant gallop, Dost's favourite horse, faithful to his master to the last, collapsed and died. Dost was devastated. To a brash soldier of fortune, a favourite horse was his most trusted friend. Carrying him across from Tirah to Jalalabad, sharing his adventures in *shikar* (hunting safari), now sensing the crisis faced by his master, the steed had given the last ounce of life to him. Dost wondered if it was Allah's punishment for his crime. But this was no time for sentiment, there was no turning back; he had to go forward and, throwing his sack of chickpeas across his shoulder, Dost continued his journey on foot.

---

[1] *Dost's Diary (Roznamcha).*

Dost reached Karnal, 30 miles west of Delhi[1] haggard, bedraggled, hungry and totally anonymous. The journey on foot had, at least, camouflaged him from his pursuers who were obviously looking for a tall, young horseman. Dost describes in his *roznamcha* (diary) that not having eaten for days, pursued by imagined or real avengers, penniless and virtually bereft of all hope, he stood in front of a *nan-bai*'s stall (a roadside bakery) waiting for an opportunity to snatch a loaf and some eggs to satisfy his hunger. While he waited for the baker's eye to be diverted, a kindly old man with a flowing grey beard approached Dost, stopped, looked him over and in a cultured Persian accent, asked, 'Are you not Dost Mohammad Khan of Tirah?'

Dost knew that he had been cornered. Even in the bazaar of a metropolis near Delhi, camouflaged in torn clothes, without a horse, his avengers had found him through their network of informers. There was no way out now but to surrender. In a second, his whole life and his ambitions flashed before him: his comfortable home in Tirah; his upbringing as the scion of a noble family; the supremacy of his race and religion; visions of a successful career as a soldier in the Moghul army, covering himself with the glory of conquest; of jewels and gold sovereigns; of the power that derives from courage and conquest, of which he knew he was capable; of marriage to a fair Afghan bride but dalliance with the swarthy, bare-midriffed, gentle women of India who seemed to have a knowledge of love and carnal satisfaction that the simple and shy Afghan women could never imagine. All these hopes lay shattered in his mind as he answered truthfully, 'Yes, sir, I am Dost Mohammad Khan of Tirah.'

'Don't you recognize me, my son? I am Mullah Jamali of Kashgar. I taught you the Quran when you were a young boy in Tirah. I recognized you by your exceptionally handsome bearing and I wondered what you were doing in this wretched state in the bazaars of Delhi.' Dost embraced his long-lost teacher whom he now recognized. His relief at meeting an acquaintance in this vast land, when all seemed lost, was overwhelming. He wondered if Divine destiny had ordained this extraordinary coincidence. Dost was given shelter by the kindly Imam who, like many educated persons of his ilk, had also left Afghanistan to seek a better life under the shade of the Moghul Empire.

Mullah Jamali had founded a *madrasa* (religious school) in Delhi and soon Dost was given food, clothes, shelter and breathing space to collect his thoughts, recharge his batteries and revive the vision with which he had set forth from Tirah and which had so abruptly and almost tragically been destroyed in Jalalabad.

Dost stayed in Mullah Jamali's house for nearly a year. He soon realized that the Moghul Empire had passed its zenith and under Aurangzeb's iron-fisted and fanatical rule was beginning to show signs of decline and creaking strain. Aurangzeb was in his 80s, campaigning mostly in the south, leaving his sons in Delhi squabbling openly for influence and power. His trusted Muslim governors – Afghans, Turks,

---

[1] Delhi was known by its Moghul name, Shahjehanabad, at the time.

central Asians – were also looking to their own resources to secure power as the Moghul Empire tottered and Aurangzeb's health began to fade. In the west and south, the Marhattas were successfully leading a revolt, while in the north and centre the Rajputs, who had so skilfully been won over by Akbar the Great through marriage and compromise, were resurgent again in their traditional domains.

Significantly, the European powers had recognized in India their jewel in the East and their impressive sea-power saw them consolidate their footholds around the coastal periphery of India. The Portuguese had been the first to arrive followed by the Dutch, but it was the French and the British that were now the major contenders for influence. At the turn of the seventeenth century, the East India Company had planted itself firmly on the seaboard of Madras and Bengal. The French had occupied Pondicherry, while the Portuguese were ensconced in Goa, Daman and Diu.

Dost Mohammad Khan had been brought up in the single-dimensional, wild-west culture of Tirah. Since arriving in India, he had observed with wide-eyed fascination the magnificence of the Moghul capital and the kaleidoscope of different religions, cultures and *mores*. During his stay in Delhi, the young Afghan had greatly enhanced his learning and education, not through the study of Mullah Jamali's books but by a sharp observation of all the new influences around him.

In Delhi, Dost had stood awe-struck by the spectacular monuments that the Moghul emperors had built. He roamed the streets of Delhi, dazzled by the mosaic of differing cultures. He prayed at the magnificent Juma Masjid and stood, overwhelmed, on the banks of the Jamuna River, contemplating the beauty of the Taj Mahal. He walked about in the beautiful gardens of Delhi and Agra, climbed the Qutub Minar and marvelled at the roads that the Muslim emperors had built. Above all, he felt the power of belonging to the ruling class of Muslim central Asians flowing through his veins: a class that had dominated the Sub-Continent for centuries and whose zenith had been achieved during the Moghul rule that began 200 years and six emperors earlier.

Dost also became aware of the civilizing influences of Muslim culture – the poetry, mysticism, calligraphy, music and the beautiful gardens that seemed part of the Moghul Islamic tradition. He witnessed the glittering, shimmering grace of the Delhi aristocracy, beautiful women in muslin dresses and sparkling jewels being carried in palanquins by liveried footmen. He sat in on the poetry sessions that were a special pastime for the Muslim gentry. Sporting contests included great wrestling matches with famous grapplers from far and wide pitched in combat before large crowds gathered around *akharas* (wrestling pits). There were *qawwals*[1] who sang in praise of saints like Nizam-ud-Din Aulia and Amir Khusrau. Earthy nautch girls gyrated in the red-light areas, but Dost also witnessed the vivid art of the classical kathak

---

[1] *Qawwali* was invented by the fourteenth-century genius and sage, Amir Khusrau. It is performed by *qawwals* (groups of singers) who render songs with an Islamic motif, in a rhythmic beat. The nearest equivalent in the west to *qawwals* is gospel singers. Internationally, the best-known *qawwals* were Nusrat Fateh Ali and Party.

dancers. In the afternoons, the sky would be littered with colourful paper kites, heavy bets being placed on their aerial jousts. The Muslim gentry of Delhi were consummate gamblers. They would gamble on cock fights, quail fights and dog fights. The more refined would play chess and go on shikar, while their scions mastered the art of tent-pegging, archery and fencing. All this was part of a Muslim culture with its meat-oriented cuisine, its Turkish, central Asian form of dress and its Arabo-Persian oriented language. Their women lived in separate, exclusive quarters in their homes and ventured out only under veils and *burqas*.[1]

Dost's eyes had also been opened to another culture – the Hindu civilization – which had existed in India for centuries before the Muslim invaders set foot and eventually colonized practically the whole of India. Dost appreciated the difference, diversity and depth of this alien culture. The Hindu temples were magnificent, architecturally different to the mosques, dominated by idols of various gods. Dost quickly recognized the caste system among the Hindus with the privileged Brahmin class, the noble Rajputs who were the defenders of the realm, the Banias who were the merchants, the Kshatris, the Gonds and the Bhils who were the tillers of the soil, and the untouchables who performed the menial tasks. The Hindu civilization appeared to have liberated its women who moved freely in the bazaars and highways dressed in white muslin saris, their navels bare, their long black hair falling to their waists. In some of the temples, Dost had seen images of women depicted in the nude. There were goddesses of evil and good, of fire and water. In the Buddhist and Jain temples, he saw carvings that appeared to be profane and yet were the subject of prayer and obeisance. Animals, like cows, monkeys and peacocks were also venerated and worshipped.

These different civilizations were like circles that existed separately, linking only occasionally. The happier occasions were usually at festival time such as Eid when Hindus would offer sweets to their Muslim neighbours and the elegant Hindu festivals like Diwali (festival of lights) in which Muslims would participate, from a respectful distance; the more sombre ones when, for instance, Aurangzeb had defiant Hindus publicly trampled to death by his elephants.

Dost Mohammad Khan's education in understanding his new, rich, multi-faceted environment had been eager and intensive. But perhaps the most important lesson that he absorbed was from the life of his idol – the Emperor Aurangzeb. The height of Moghul power had been achieved in the lifetime of this last great Moghul Emperor. Aurangzeb was a pious man to the point of fanaticism. He was an ascetic, a servant of Allah. Yet, the pursuit of conquest and power had seen Aurangzeb imprison his own father, torture and blind his brothers and commit numerous acts of treachery and deceit. Dost also heard stories of how Akbar the Great, the third Moghul Emperor, had married Rajput wives to pacify and win over his opponents. All these lessons Dost had absorbed sitting at the feet of the wise old Imam.

---

[1] A burqa is a tent-like dress that covers a woman's body from head to foot with only a slit at eye-level.

After spending almost a year at Mullah Jamali's madrasa, Dost was ready, both mentally and physically, to step out into the arena and create a brave new world for himself. To this young Afghan, the glory of his race, his religion and his culture was symbolized by the majestic reign of the Moghuls. They were invincible, supreme in the world, and this sense of power and belonging strengthened his desire to serve in the Moghul forces. In fact, enlisting in Aurangzeb's army became an obsession.

Try though he might to influence young Dost to take up the study of Islam as a career, Mullah Jamali failed to divert his young protégé from his original aim of joining the Moghul army. Dost was now ready to take the first step and with the help of the kindly Mullah, who gave him a horse and five *ashrafis* (gold coins), Dost took his leave and enlisted with Mir Fazlullah, Aurangzeb's Keeper of Arms. The young Afghan now embarked on his chosen career as a soldier and steadily scaled the lower rungs of the ladder to establish himself as a courageous fighter and a born leader of men.

Around 1704, Dost was given his first test when he was ordered to quell a rebellion by Governor Tardi Beg who was commanding a sizeable force in Bundelkhand. Dost proceeded to Gwalior at the head of a loyal Moghul regiment and engaged in battle with Tardi Beg's forces which were commanded by the fearsome general, Kashko Khan, who had gained the reputation of a ruthless tyrant. The battle went badly for the imperial forces and soon Dost had sword wounds lacerated across his body. Seeing his force in disarray, Dost decided that his only hope was to go for the jugular. He gathered his lance and charged Kashko Khan's elephant. Dost's attack was met by Kashko Khan's guards and one of the *mahawats* (elephant riders) actually pierced Dost with his sword. Undaunted, Dost continued his assault and, according to his diary, he was ensnared by the elephant in its trunk. Dost wriggled free and, mounting the elephant, decapitated Kashko Khan with one stroke. The death of the general at the hands of his adversary led to the surrender of Tardi Beg's force and Dost returned to Delhi in triumph, delivering the decapitated head of his vanquished opponent to Mir Fazlullah.[1]

Shortly after this daring and successful encounter, Mir Fazlullah arranged for Dost to be presented to the Emperor. Aurangzeb had decided to return to Delhi in 1705, after spending 21 years in Deccan trying to consolidate the Moghul conquest of the south. Dost Mohammad Khan, now 33 years old, records in his diary that his regiment was summoned to the presence of the Emperor who inspected the unit at Aurangabad. Dost states that though wizened and bent, Aurangzeb had an awesome presence that made him tremble with trepidation. Looking through the ranks, the Emperor spotted Dost and commanded, 'You, young Rohilla,[2] come and present yourself to me.' He then turned to Mir Fazlullah and declared, 'He seems to be a strong and handsome lad with a noble mien. Make sure he is well treated and is given an appropriate command.'

---

[1] *Dost's Diary (Roznamcha).*
[2] Rohilla was a term used for Afghans who had settled in the northern regions of India.

Aurangzeb then took two fistfuls of ashrafis and thrust them into Dost's hands. Dost states that he was overwhelmed by the Emperor's kindness and conveyed his undying loyalty to him. Clearly, Dost had made an impression on Aurangzeb who had probably been briefed by Mir Fazlullah to look out for the sturdy, handsome Afghan.

Dost soon enhanced his reputation and earned his spurs as an intrepid fighter, a charismatic leader and, true to his Pathan tradition, a loyal selfless standard-bearer of the Moghul Emperor. Promotion was swift. Dost was given a high military rank and was assigned to Malwa – the geographical centre and crucial heartland of India where north and south, east and west cross, almost equidistantly.

Geographically, Malwa stretches across the central plateau of India which, during the British period, was known as Central India and Central Provinces. Today, it is the area covered by Madhya Pradesh. At the time, its main inhabitants were the indigenous Gonds and Bhils who had settled in the region for centuries. Superimposed over this indigenous population were the martial Rajputs who had extended their control from Rajputana towards Malwa. More recently, the Marhattas – equally martial and wilier than the noble Rajputs – had reached out from the Western Ghats towards Malwa so that the Marhatta feudal chieftains – Holkar of Indore, Scindia of Gwalior, Gaekwad of Baroda and Bhonsle of Nagpur – operating under the overall control of the *Peshwa*, the powerful Chief Minister of the Marhatta kingdom in Poona, were beginning to exert a significant influence in the region.

Dost found Malwa to be a rich, verdant and picturesque land. The Vindhya mountains were interlaced with beautiful rivers, natural lakes and valleys. The forests were deep, with every kind of wildlife, tigers, bears, leopards, crocodiles, deer, sambar (elk), nilgai (blue bull),[1] cheetal (spotted deer) and wild buck.[2] The soil was fertile as water was plentiful. The famous Buddhist stupa at Sanchi was testimony to the fact that several earlier civilizations had found Malwa climatically congenial, fertile and accommodating. Malwa was rich and relatively prosperous. It was a cross-roads for trade and also of military routes between the north and south, east and west of India. Artisans and craftsmen had settled in Malwa, with cottage industries flourishing in towns like Sironj where the finest muslin in India could be found. The French traveller and chronicler, Tavernier,[3] described Malwa in the following terms:

> Cloth of the finest texture was woven here. There is made at Sironj, a variety of muslin which is so fine that when it is on the person you see all the skin as though it were uncovered. The merchants are allowed to export it and the governor sends all of it for the great Moghul's seraglio and for the principal countries. From this muslin the Sultanas and the wives of the great nobles make for themselves shifts and garments for the hot weather and the king and nobles enjoy seeing them wearing those fine shifts and cause them to dance in them. Malwa is rich in agricultural wealth too, producing large

---

[1] Indian equivalent of African kudu.
[2] World records for size of antlers for both sambar and cheetal were once held in Bhopal.
[3] The author recently met in Paris Senator Tavernier who is the direct descendant of the famous French traveller and historian.

quantities of the higher crops, such as opium, sugar-cane, grapes, musk, melons and betel-leaf.[1]

As Dost and his armed contingent reached Malwa, news of revolts all over the land was coming thick and fast, playing havoc with loyalty and discipline in his army. In Malwa, Aurangzeb was replacing one governor after another in rapid succession, one of whom was his grandson – Bedar Bakht – who decided to return to base even before he reached the province. As Dost reached Bhilsa, news came of Aurangzeb's death on 20 February 1707. Fast on its heels came further news of in-fighting between Aurangzeb's sons and the eventual collapse of central authority. Dost was approached for allegiance by two of Aurangzeb's warring sons but replied that, having taken the loyal oath to the Emperor, he could not raise his sword against one of his sons on behalf of another. In Malwa itself, the Muslim feudal chiefs, the Hindu Rajputs and Marhattas began to agitate for power – each seeking alliances within or outside the province. The central power of the Moghul Empire had collapsed and revolts erupted in all the major domains of the Empire. Malwa remained the coveted strategic region and now the contending pulls from the resurgent Rajput chieftains, the powerful Marhattas and the remnants of the Moghul Empire became an added dimension in the Malwa syndrome. Racked by pillage, loot, plunder and disarray, Malwa entered a stage of chaos and degenerating civil strife.

Aurangzeb's death marked the steep decline and fall of the great Moghul Empire that was comparable to its Roman equivalent. Against the backdrop of gruesome and macabre intrigues among Aurangzeb's offspring, the central edifice of power began to crumble rapidly, unleashing warlords, big and small, attempting to grab power, territory and loot. Thus soon after 1707, the whole of India was convulsed in a whirlpool of disorder, chaos and frenzy that endured for over a century. It was in these tumultuous times that adventurers like Dost Mohammad Khan staked their claims to principalities that they carved out for themselves through courage, charisma and abundant treachery. Some survived the ensuing convulsions to emerge independent. Others were submerged in the flood-tide of power play until the British emerged dominant towards the beginning of the nineteenth century.

Bhopal – The foundation

In this bloody and fissiparous melee, Dost realized that only the fittest could survive. Accordingly, he and his loyal men, now reduced to 50 of his Afghan kinsmen who owed personal allegiance to Dost, became predatory foragers in the jungles of Malwa. His links with the central Moghul power in Delhi became increasingly tenuous and Dost headed a band of mercenaries who were solicited by various feudal barons for protection. Dost and his men fought many a battle, partly as an act of survival against marauding warlords and partly as protectors of local

---

[1] *Travels in India*, as quoted in Raghubir Sinh, *Malwa in Transition*.

chieftains who provided them with finance and security. Dost's prowess as a military tactician, a fearless fighter and leader continued to grow so that, within a year of Aurangzeb's death, his reputation had spread across Malwa. Untethered from links with the central command, Dost and his men knocked about central India in search of plunder and security.

Dost first attached himself to the Raja of Sitamau. He then sought employment with Mohammad Farooq, Governor of Bhilsa and later with Diye Bahadur, the Moghul Deputy Governor of Malwa. Finally, he was employed by Raja Anand Singh Solanki of Mangalgarh, a Rajput chieftain who needed protection against covetous neighbours. Soon afterwards, Anand Singh died, but his mother, the Dowager *Rani* (queen), had taken a great liking to Dost and asked him to continue protecting Mangalgarh, a request that he willingly accepted. Accordingly, around 1708 Dost was appointed *mukhtar* (guardian) of Mangalgarh with the task of protecting the Dowager Rani and her estate.

During his service as protector of Mangalgarh, Dost married Fatah Bibi, a Rajput girl, from the Mangalgarh royal household. Apart from Mehraj Bibi, Dost married several other wives, but Fatah Bibi, who converted to Islam, was the love of his life. She brought finances for Dost which he later used to pay for the lease of Berasia. She even paid ransom money for Dost when he was imprisoned by his own mutinous soldiers during an unsuccessful raid on Gujrat.

Fatah Bibi was the first woman in the Bhopal family to play a significant role in the affairs of the state. Her background is not fully recorded but it is evident that she was a Rajput from the Mangalgarh family. Chroniclers of the Bhopal family, who were devout Muslims, tended to ignore, erase and even destroy evidence of non-Muslim blood flowing into the Bhopal dynasty. Therefore, while these chroniclers took great pains to describe in detail the lineage of various Muslim families that married into the Bhopal family, there is a meaningful silence – a vacuum – concerning the background of Fatah Bibi and later of Mamola Bai. Fatah Bibi was no ordinary woman. She was spirited, wise and courageous. She accompanied Dost everywhere on horseback, at battle fronts, on shikar and on his wanderings along the lakes, mountains and rivers of Malwa. She became Dost's inseparable partner, soulmate and inspiration.

For the next few years, Dost based himself in Mangalgarh and operated mainly as a mercenary and hired protector for anyone who was prepared to pay the price. He had built up a fearsome reputation in the region and was capable of extreme daring, noble chivalry and the most deceitful treachery! In an age of plunder and anarchy, all was fair. During this period he won more battles and skirmishes than he lost, but after a couple of years marauding through the jungles of central India, Dost arrived at two fundamental decisions.

First, he decided that instead of latching himself on as a mercenary to various benefactors, he needed to carve out a small fiefdom for himself. He liked the region, had got to know its nooks and crannies and its people, and therefore decided to drop anchor in Malwa. His first step, around 1709, was to take on the lease of Berasia, a small *mustajiri* (rented estate) 22 miles north of Bhopal.[1] The lease was given by Taj Mohammad Khan, a Moghul fief-holder who preferred to live in Delhi, for an annual payment of 30,000 rupees. Dost then set about organizing his little fiefdom in his own style, appointing Maulvi Mohammad Saleh as *Qazi* (Islamic judge), building a mosque and a fort and giving several administrative assignments to trusted Afghan lieutenants who had faithfully stuck it out with him. This was, in fact, the first step in the foundation of what eventually became the state of Bhopal.

Secondly, Dost knew that though most of his men were Afghans, they were not from his own tribe and, in a world of treachery and deceit, they could just as easily betray him and fight for a more powerful feudal baron. In fact, they had shown their treacherous inclinations when Dost unsuccessfully forayed into Gujrat and, after losing the battle with the Marhatta warlord, was imprisoned by his own soldiers, who released him only after his devoted wife, Fatah Bibi, paid the ransom. Dost realized that in order to survive and be master of his own domain, he needed to have his own family surround and support him. He therefore decided to persuade, cajole and entice his clan in Tirah to join him on his epic adventure in Malwa.

There are two versions of how Dost persuaded his father, brothers, wife and Mirazi-khel tribesmen to join him in Malwa. The first and more romantic version recounts Dost deciding personally to visit Tirah to persuade his family, leaving Fatah Bibi to literally hold the fort in his absence. For four long months while Dost was away in Tirah, Fatah Bibi courageously kept control in Berasia at a time of general pillage and strife.

The second and more probable account is that Dost sent a personal messenger to Tirah who eventually persuaded Nur Mohammad Khan and around 50 Mirazi-khel tribesmen to make the trek to Bhopal on horseback.

Thus, one day around 1712, a phalanx of 50 Mirazi-khel tribesmen, fiercely loyal to the young Pathan and his family, together with his father, wife and five brothers, rode into Berasia to the sound of welcoming drums and joyous celebration. This event saw a new chapter being written in Bhopal's history as these Mirazi-khel tribesmen became the pioneer settlers of Bhopal. They were called the Barru-kat Pathans of Bhopal (literally the shrub dwellers) who initially made their homes with thatched reeds. It was they who fought for, made sacrifices for and loyally served Dost Mohammad Khan and his descendants to become the original pioneering families of Bhopal. Apart from his father and Mehraj Bibi, five of Dost's brothers joined him in Bhopal. They were Sher, Alif, Shah, Mir Ahmad and Aqil. All except Aqil died in battle.

The presence of his kinsmen gave Dost a new strength and vision to spread his influence and power. He could now rely totally on a group of men who had to sink or swim with him as they had cut their moorings

---

[1] See map on p xi.

from Tirah. Bolstered by the support of his Barru-kat kinsmen, Dost began to strike out boldly to expand his influence and domain.

At the time, the headlong lust for power recognized no ethnic or religious affinities as Rajput fought Rajput, Marhatta schemed against Marhatta and Afghan battled Afghan. It was, therefore, entirely plausible that a Hindu Rajput chieftain should seek the protection of Muslim Afghan mercenaries against other Rajputs. Soon, the Rani of Mangalgarh's Rajput neighbours banded together against the growing power of the Rani and, led by the *Thakur* (Chief) of Parason, the Rajput chieftains gathered for battle.[1]

The Rajputs treated war as a sport, like cricket, to be played according to established traditions of the game. They were noble, chivalrous and played the game like gentlemen. At Parason, battle raged for several days without either side making significant gains. However, the festival of Holi was at hand and the Thakur sent word that he wanted a truce to celebrate the festival. Dost agreed, but he also knew that during Holi, the Hindus would celebrate with abandon, flagrantly getting drunk and letting their hair and their guard down. While the festival was at its height, Dost first sent a spy dressed as a beggar to the Rajput camp and, being informed of drunken revelry, attacked the Rajputs late at night and routed his unsuspecting enemy in a treacherous, murderous raid. Dost was no cricketer and played to win by hook or by crook.

Typical of Dost's campaign to enlarge and consolidate his domain was an incident in which he agreed to negotiate a treaty with Narsingh Rao Chauhan, a neighbouring Rajput chief. Both sides agreed to meet at Jagdishpur, 20 miles south of Berasia, with 16 aides on each side. Dost pitched a tent on the banks of the River Thal and after a congenial and sumptuous lunch that he had arranged, stepped outside to order the delicacy of *itr* and *paan* (perfume and betel leaf). This was the signal for Dost's soldiers who had been hidden in a nearby thicket to rush the tent, cut its ropes and murder the unsuspecting Rajputs. So gruesome was the slaughter that the river went red with the blood of the victims. To this day, it is known as the Halali (kosher) river after the slaughter of the Rajputs. Dost celebrated his success by renaming Jagdishpur Islamnagar and soon strengthened the fort, making it his headquarters. Several years later in 1722, Dost repeated this treacherous stratagem with his cousin, Diler Mohammad Khan, who had come to Dost with a proposal to share his newly acquired domain.

In another encounter, the powerful Rajput general and Moghul Subedar,[2] Diye Bahadur, defeated Dost's army which turned and fled, leaving its leader and a few valiant loyalists to fight it out against the superior force. Dost lost one of his brothers in the battle, was badly wounded himself and taken prisoner. True to Rajput tradition, he was well treated and when restored to health, presented before Diye Bahadur. Dost recounts in his diary that he was overwhelmed by the kindness and treatment shown to him by the victorious commander. Evidently im-

---

[1] *Dirafshe-Shaukat.*
[2] Subedar was equivalent to a governor.

pressed by Dost's bravery, Diye Bahadur inquired if he would join his forces. Dost, having expressed deep gratitude to his host, declined. Diye Bahadur then asked what the prisoner intended doing if he were released. Dost replied, 'I shall fight your forces in battle again.' For this insolent reply, Dost expected to be put to death or thrown into a dungeon, but he records that Diye Bahadur thought for a moment, then with a smile on his face replied, 'All right, you are a brave man. I shall set you free and we shall do battle in 40 days.' Such was the chivalry of the time that Dost was given a horse on which he gratefully rode back home. Several months later, Dost raised a force and defeated Diye Bahadur in an encounter.

During these turbulent times, Dost's reputation as a fearless and intrepid commander grew with every passing day. In describing his regular skirmishes, Dost records in his diary that a force was sent from Delhi to quell the Rajput rebellion that was taking place in Malwa. Dost was torn between his loyalty to the distant Moghul Court and his commitment to the local Rajput chieftains to whom he had given his allegiance.

Eventually, Dost sided with the Rajputs and in the ensuing battle was wounded and lost consciousness. His men fled, abandoning their leader for dead. Long past midnight, on a silent, eerie battleground strewn with dead bodies, Dost recounts in his diary that he regained consciousness when predatory jackals began nibbling at his extremities. He barely managed to shrug them off when he heard another man, lying a few yards away, moaning loudly and calling for help. Obviously, he too was badly wounded. Dost raised his voice and said to the wounded man, 'Why are you moaning so loudly? It is not becoming of a warrior to cry out like this. Grieve silently, like a man, and take what is coming to you as God's verdict with dignity.' The young man answered Dost by saying, 'I'm not crying out because of my wounds. I'm only trying to scare off the jackals eating away at my entrails. In any case I'm dying of thirst. Can you help me?' Dost could not rise from his prone position but he had some water left in his *mushuk* (leather water-carrier). He summoned enough strength to push the bag with his lance towards the wounded soldier who drank avidly from it.

At dawn, a posse of soldiers from the victorious army began scouring the battle-field evidently looking for one of their leaders. They came upon the very soldier that Dost had first admonished for cowardly behaviour and then saved by giving him water. He was obviously an important man as the soldiers, on finding him alive, made a great fuss of him. Before the rescue party could put him on a stretcher, the young man told the soldiers that their first duty was to help the brave man lying a few yards away, who had saved his life. Accordingly, Dost too was rescued by the soldiers who belonged to the opposing army. The person that he had saved turned out to be Sayyed Hussain Ali Barha, the younger of the Sayyed brothers who were now the power behind the throne in the Moghul Court at Delhi.

Dost Mohammad Khan recuperated under the care of Sayyed Hussain Ali Barha who recalled the earlier friendship that Dost had formed with his elder brother, Sayyed Abdullah Barha. Fate had led them to being opponents on the battle-field but now, restored to health, Sayyed Hussain Ali pleaded with Dost to join him and his brother, offering to make him governor of Allahabad. Dost was grateful but declined, explaining that he had too many roots in Malwa. Hussain Ali reluctantly agreed. Dost was given some gold sovereigns, a sword and a band of horses as he took leave of his friend and rode back to Mangalgarh to resume his loyal guardianship of the Rani who was overjoyed to see him return. Friendship and loyalty to the Sayyed brothers was later to place Dost in the dilemma of deciding whether to side with the Sayyeds, acting in the name of the Moghul Emperor, or with the Nizam, once the Emperor's most trusted aide but now in open revolt against the Moghul Court. Dost's decision to throw in his lot with the Sayyeds had far-reaching consequences for Bhopal.

Shortly after his return to Mangalgarh, the Rani who had adopted Dost as a son died. As there was no direct heir, Dost, having redeemed his pledge of loyalty to the Dowager Rani, considered himself absolved of any further fidelity to Mangalgarh. He plundered the treasury and took over the jewels and gold coins that belonged to the Rajput principality.

With the help of his family and the loyal support of the Barru-kat Pathans, Dost continued his campaign to carve out a fief – a state – which would become his kingdom. The ferocity with which Dost waged his campaign saw him annex vast tracts of territory, many *jagirdars* (landed gentry) and zamindars accepting subjugation without a fight. Dost was brave and ferocious in battle but magnanimous with the vanquished because he realized that he needed to gain the loyalty and respect of the indigenous Hindu population. During this period, Dost extended his domain over the *parganas* (districts) of Doraha, Sehore, Ichawar, Ashta and Shujalpur. In these campaigns Dost lost two of his brothers, all killed in battle. His father, Nur Mohammad Khan, had died in 1715 soon after arriving in Berasia.

Dost's next encounter, perhaps the most daring of his entire career, was against Mohammad Farooq, Governor of Bhilsa, who had betrayed Dost's trust by imprisoning his men and confiscating his belongings. When confronted, Farooq pleaded that he had learnt that Dost had died in battle. He released Dost's men but gave back only half the confiscated chattels, thereby earning the hostility of the young Pathan. Enmity between the two had risen to the point where a battle became inevitable and the two armies faced each other near Bhilsa with Farooq heading a force of 40,000 Marhatta and Rajputs against Dost's 5000 loyal Afghans, aided by some straggling Rajput support. The battle was predictably one-sided. Dost lost a brother, Sher Mohammad Khan, and despite a courageous rearguard action, defeat stared him in the face by dusk. As his defeated army fled in retreat, Dost, accompanied by a few of his most loyal comrades, managed to hide in a thicket until they could see the enemy rejoice on the battleground at their victory. In accordance with tradition, the kettle-drummers were summoned and began playing out the victory beat for Farooq's army. Dost then clad himself in the uniform of one of his slain opponents and, camouflaging himself with a scarf and a low-slung helmet, unobtrusively approached the elephant which carried the victorious leader. The din of the drums, the noise of the cheering army and the stupor of victory allowed Dost and his posse to come closer and closer to the elephant and, as twilight led to nightfall, Dost moved stealthily behind the leading elephant while the victorious troops celebrated by looting and pillaging. In a trice, he mounted the howdah and through his phenomenal strength managed silently to kill the guard who stood behind his master. Dost then thrust a dagger into Farooq but propped him up with his arms – while Farooq's army continued to celebrate with loot and plunder and the drums resounded in a frenzied beat of victory. As Farooq's elephant entered the Bhilsa Fort with his body standing erect, the whole populace gathered to welcome its conquering hero when, suddenly, his dead corpse was flung at the crowd, with Dost daringly claiming victory. This dramatic act totally numbed the populace who saw their leader ignominiously flung from the howdah and Dost claiming victory. The daring Pathan had lost the battle, but by a remarkable feat of raw courage had saved the day.

Dost's final consolidation and annexation of Bhopal came about through a fairy-tale romance which belongs to the realm of legend but is, in fact, a true story. Around the lake of Bhopal, the population consisted mainly of Gonds and Bhils. The Gonds had several warlords – gond-rajas – each vying for supremacy. One of these gond-rajas was Nizam Shah who emerged as the strongest among the competing warlords and took for his wife Kamlapati, a woman of luminous beauty and unmatched talents. She was not only lovely in appearance but was educated, refined and superbly talented in the arts. Rani Kamlapati became the subject of praise, poetry and eventually of legend for her beauty and grace.

The legend of Rani Kamlapati describes her as more beautiful than a *pari* (heavenly fairy), more graceful than a doe, more delicate than a rose. On moonlit nights, she would emerge from her waterside palace and swim in the lake, carried afloat by a lotus flower and attended by 500 maidens following her in rowing boats. The legend has it that when her husband was poisoned, Rani Kamlapati took all her worldly belongings, her jewels, her gold sovereigns and drowned herself in the lake. To this day, every child in Bhopal is brought up singing the ditty:

Taal hai to Bhopal taal
aur sab hain talayyen
Rani thi to Kamlapati
aur sab hain gadhayyen

If there ever was a lake, it is the Bhopal lake
All others are mere ponds
If there ever was a queen, it was Kamlapati
All others are mere cattle [literally she-donkeys!]

garh hai to Ginnor garh
aur sab hain garhaiyyen
raja tha to Ramchandar
aur sab hain rajayyen

If ever there was a fort, it was Ginnor Fort
All others are mere (hilltop) shacks
If ever there was a king, it was Ramchandar[1]
All others are mere princelings[2]

The reality regarding Kamlapati was not far removed from the legend. In fact, she was immensely talented and beautiful. She was the daughter of Chaudhri Kirpa-Ramchandar and married Nizam Shah, a prominent Gond warlord, as one of his seven ranis. Nizam Shah's supremacy over rival gond-rajas was due both to the extraordinary wisdom and farsightedness of his favourite queen and to the fact that he had succeeded in capturing the virtually impregnable fort of Ginnor. Located 46 miles east of Bhopal, Ginnor Fort was built at the summit of a steep 2000-foot rock. The fort had sheer cliff drops on each side and was surrounded by thick forest in which wild beasts prevented human habitation. Only one narrow path led up to the fort so that it was easy to defend. Incredibly, a natural underground spring gave Ginnor all the water that it needed so that the fortress was a relatively comfortable abode as well as almost impossible to penetrate. Nizam Shah increased the fort's security by building two ramparts which formed its outer and inner rings. From this impregnable eyrie, Nizam Shah was able to dominate his rivals and became the supreme power among the Gonds. Kamlapati first took up residence in Ginnor but later, Nizam Shah built her a palace by the riverside in Bhopal.[3]

One of Nizam Shah's rivals for power among the Gonds was a young relative, Alam Shah, the Gond-Raja of Chainpur-Bara. This ambitious young man not only coveted Nizam Shah's status as the most powerful gond-raja but had become totally obsessed by the beauty of Rani Kamlapati. It is likely that having access to Nizam Shah's household, Alam Shah declared his feelings to the Rani but was rejected by her. Undeterred, the young pretender continued to make lustful advances towards Kamlapati and, not being able to gain her by fair means, managed to inveigle Nizam Shah into partaking of a feast given in his honour. Nizam Shah was poisoned and died immediately, leaving his domain and his beautiful widow at the mercy of this unscrupulous villain.

Kamlapati felt deeply insecure at this sudden, tragic death of her husband, and though immensely popular with her people, was suddenly vulnerable and needed protection. She immediately invited Dost Mohammad Khan to her palace and, offering him one lakh of rupees,[4] asked if he would avenge her honour against the Raja of Chainpur-Bara and act as her protector. Coming as it did from a woman of extraordinary beauty and grace, Dost immediately accepted the offer, whereupon

---

[1] Kamlapati's father.
[2] Razia Hamid and Sultan, *Nuqoosh-e-Bhopal*.
[3] Only the small lake existed in Bhopal at the time. The Big Lake came into being 50 years later when Chottey Khan dammed the Banganga river and created an artificial lake. Even today, the two lower storeys of Kamlapati's seven-storey palace stand submerged under the Big Lake.
[4] A lakh is a unit of 100,000.

Kamlapati tied a *rakhi* (a cotton bracelet) on Dost's wrist – a Hindu custom in which a woman selects a man to be her eternal brother.

Dost kept his word. He attacked the Gond-Raja of Chainpur-Bara, defeated his force and slew him. Kamlapati was deeply grateful to Dost but did not have the lakh of rupees that she had promised. Instead, she paid him half the sum and gifted the village of Bhopal in lieu of the remainder. This was the beginning of Bhopal becoming the capital of Dost's domain, though it was not until the reign of Faiz Mohammad Khan, Dost's grandson, that the capital was formally moved from Islamnagar to Bhopal.

Dost continued to give full protection to Kamlapati who reigned peacefully and successfully over her Gond kingdom for a decade. Dost was now the most powerful figure in the region and, given Kamlapati's benign support, Dost was able to extend his control over the Gond population during Kamlapati's reign. Historians and chroniclers are agreed that Dost gave loyal support to Rani Kamlapati and her son Nawal Shah until she died. They differ on the reasons for his loyalty. Some state that Dost was totally enchanted with Kamlapati whose charms were irresistible. Others believe that Dost was faithful to the tryst of the rakhi and though treachery and betrayal were part of Dost's armoury, he kept his word to two vulnerable women who had sought his protection, the Rani of Mangalgarh and Rani Kamlapati.

When Rani Kamlapati died in 1723, Dost's contract with the family was at an end. As with Mangalgarh, Dost took over the palace, the jewels and precious items that had belonged to the Rani. He feigned allegiance to Nawal Shah who still controlled the impregnable fortress at Ginnor. Then, in a brilliant, treacherous manoeuvre he placed 100 of his soldiers dressed up as women to be carried up to the fortress in *dolis* (palanquins carried by porters) that were normally used for transporting sick women and children. At the gate Nawal Shah's unsuspecting guards let the dolis through into the fortress where Dost's soldiers fought and defeated Nawal Shah's force. Nawal Shah was killed and Dost took over the strategic fort of Ginnor, consolidating his control over the southern region of Bhopal. Typically, Dost was fair and humane towards his new subjects, treating the gond-ranis (princesses) of the region with honour and respect.

Four-power rivalry for control of Malwa

The collapse of the Moghul Empire after Aurangzeb's death had been one of the most gruesome, venal and horrifying spectacles in history. Immediately after Aurangzeb's death, his surviving sons, betraying each other at every possible turn, engaged in brutal fratricide. Eventually, the 64-year-old eldest son, Muazzam, survived the mayhem and was installed as Emperor Bahadur Shah. This bloodletting was predictable as Bahadur Shah's father, Aurangzeb, grandfather, Shahjehan, and great-grandfather, Jahangir, had all imprisoned, tortured, blinded and murdered their fathers, brothers and sons to secure their thrones. It was the events that followed the death of Bahadur Shah that made the earlier blood-baths and treachery appear mundane.

Bahadur Shah died on 28 February 1712. Immediately after his death, his four sons squared up to battle for the coveted throne. The two youngest brothers were won over by the eldest, Jahandar Shah, into jointly opposing the second son, Azim-us-Shan, who had the stronger force. A battle took place in which Azim's forces lost. Azim-us-Shan drowned in the River Jhelum when his elephant was shot and went berserk, plunging into the quicksand. Jahandar then treacherously turned on the brothers who had supported him. He first blinded his mother for favouring a rival son and then poured molten lead into the eardrums of his unfortunate brother. Later, Jahandar had him strangled while the other brother was put to death by more conventional means. Emperor Jahandar did not live long to enjoy the fruits of his treachery. Within a few months of proclaiming himself Emperor, he was assassinated by the increasingly influential Barha Sayyed brothers, Abdullah and Hussain Ali, who were now the main power-brokers behind the Moghul throne. The Sayyed brothers then propped up the murdered Azim-us-Shan's son, Farrukhsiyar, on the throne, who promptly paraded the streets of the capital with the severed head of his uncle, Emperor Jahandar, trailing behind him on a donkey.

All these grotesque events took place in 1712, and on 9 January 1713 Farrukhsiyar began a seven-year reign that for devilish cunning, shameless venality and sheer villainy would make the Boyars and Ottomans appear like junior mafiosi. Among his numerous dastardly acts, Farrukhsiyar began plotting the downfall of his main supporters, the Sayyed brothers. He made treacherous deals with his opponents, frequently arranging the assassination of his own commanders as a pay-off. Eventually, Farrukhsiyar's villainy proved too much for the Sayyed brothers who, discovering his treachery, blinded the monarch on 25 February 1719, but felt it expedient to continue propping him up as emperor. In a bizarre, almost ghoulish turn of events, the Moghul Court was presided over by a monarch who had been blinded by his main benefactors. Even this dreadful punishment did not prevent Farrukhsiyar from engaging in further deceit until, on 19 April 1719, while he was in camp, leading a force towards the Deccan, Sayyed Abdullah personally strangled the Moghul Emperor to death.

This gruesome *grand guignol* did not end on this horrific note as the Sayyed brothers, seeking to install pliant emperors on the throne, produced two consumptive youths – sons of the murdered Emperor Jahandar – the first drugged to his eyeballs and the second a transvestite whose main pastime was to dance the kathak with his accompanying eunuchs. Both these youths died within months of being crowned and a fourth emperor, Mohammad Shah, was installed on the throne in 1720. Suprisingly Mohammad Shah held on till 1748 and his main achievement was to turn the tables on the Sayyed brothers. Hussain Ali was assassinated in 1722 and Abdullah locked in prison where he was poisoned to death in 1724.

Macaulay describes the Moghul Empire's appalling descent into this surrealistic horror in the following words:

> A succession of nominal sovereigns, sunk in indolence and debauchery, sauntered away life in secluded palaces, chewing bhang, fondling concubines and listening to buffoons. A succession of ferocious invaders descended through the western passes to prey on the defenceless wealth of Hindostan ... and every corner of the wide Empire learned to tremble at the mighty name of the Marathas ... Whenever their kettle-drums were heard, the peasant threw his bag of rice on his shoulder, hid his small savings in his girdle and fled with his wife and children to the mountains or the jungles, to the milder neighbourhood of the hyena and the tiger.
>
> Wherever the Viceroys of the Moghul retained authority they became sovereigns. They might still acknowledge in words the superiority of the house of Tamerlane; as a Court of Flanders or a Duke of Burgundy might have acknowledged the superiority of the most helpless driveller among the later Carlovingians. In truth, however, they were no longer lieutenants removable at pleasure but independent hereditary princes.[1]

In the period after taking on the lease of Berasia, Dost took advantage of the power vacuum in Malwa to build the foundations of his state. Fortunately for him, the four major powers in India were not, as yet, willing or able to exercise actual control over Malwa, though each in turn claimed long-distance sovereignty over this coveted province. These four powers were the Moghul Court itself, Nizam-ul-Mulk, the Rajputs and the Marhattas.

The Moghul Court

The Moghul Court, despite murderous internecine intrigue and a succession of weak, decadent emperors, retained an aura of power and authority based on over 200 years of magnificent rule. This power was exercised by ambitious courtiers who used their influence over weak and debauched Moghul monarchs in whose name edicts were issued. So great was the prestige and momentum generated by the Moghul Court that a succession of power-wielders invariably sought to rule through the *firmans* (edicts) of the Moghul Court. These puppet-masters were not limited to courtiers like the Sayyed brothers, but extended to the Emperor's opponents, like Nadir Shah, the Marhattas, the Nizam and later the British, who sought to rule India in the name of the Moghul Emperor.

The Nizam

The second focal point of power in India was Chin-Qilich Khan, Asaf Jah, Nizam-ul-Mulk, whose family originated from Samarkand. Asaf Jah was a loyal, upright and highly accomplished aide of Aurangzeb. Through dedicated service, he had been elevated to the highest rank in the

---

[1] As quoted in Bamber Gascoigne, *The Great Moghuls*.

administration as Nizam-ul-Mulk and had a significant force under him. In fact, Asaf Jah had combined closely with the Sayyed brothers to support Bahadur Shah's campaign for succession. As the Sayyed brothers' influence grew, differences and suspicion developed between them and the Nizam. When Farrukhsiyar ascended the throne, the Sayyeds managed to persuade the Emperor to post the Nizam to distant governorates and conspired to have his force defeated in battle by opponents who were surreptitiously given support. The Nizam survived these treacherous stratagems and eventually decided, in disgust, to detach himself from the Moghul Court. He removed himself to the south with the Emperor's firman of governorships of Malwa and the Deccan. It was an open secret, however, that the Nizam intended to set up his own independent state in the region. Thus by 1720, the two Muslim power blocks – the Moghul Court and the Nizam – were ranged against each other with only a veneer of cordiality between sovereign and governor.

The Rajputs

The two remaining contenders for power, both Hindu, were the Rajputs and the Marhattas. The Rajputs operated mainly in Rajasthan and central India but were never sufficiently united to become an important unified force. The famous Rajput houses of Udaipur, Jodhpur, Jaipur and Mewar had, over the centuries, sent their weaker family members to preside over the smaller principalities of Malwa. Thus, unlike the great houses of Rajputana, Malwa had seen the emergence of smaller Rajput states that the senior Rajput rulers aimed to rule by proxy. This system did not work, partly because it was too unwieldy and partly because the Rajput states could never combine cohesively under a single leader. Thus, divided and lured by one side or the other, the Rajputs failed to achieve their full potential in seizing the initiative from a decaying centre. Religious affinities seemed to count for little as the Muslim Emperor or Nizam frequently sought and gained the support of Hindu princes against other Rajputs or Marhattas. Surprisingly, in the shifting sands of short-lived alliances between these four major power blocs, the least frequent were those between the co-religionists, the Hindu Rajputs and Marhattas or the Muslim Emperor and the Nizam.

The Marhattas

The fourth and most vibrant claimants to power were the Marhattas, operating mainly from the south-west. Sivaji, the supreme guerilla, had severely undermined the last years of Aurangzeb's rule and had given the Marhattas a vision of power and supremacy over the whole of India. After Sivaji's death, there was a brief decline but his daughter-in-law, Tara Bai, and grandson, Shahu, had again lit the flame of glory in the hearts of the Marhatta people. The Marhattas had their own warlord houses in the Scindia of Gwalior, the Holkar of Indore, the Bhonsle of Nagpur and the Gaekwad of Baroda who were frequently jostling for power among themselves. Fortunately, Shahu, who was recognized as the titular head of the Marhattas, found in his new Peshwa, Balaji Rao Viswanath – a Koncan Brahmin – a man of unique foresight, ability and wisdom. Peshwa Balaji Rao set about uniting the Marhattas and organizing their administration, army and finances in such a way that by 1715 the Marhatta resurgence had become a reality. Clearly, the Marhattas were set on dominating not only the south-western and central region but, eventually, the whole of India in order to exorcise the subjugation that they had suffered for centuries at the hands of Muslim invaders. In contrast to other contenders for power who were beset by intrigue, decay and internecine rivalries, the Marhattas were determined, focused and united under the leadership of Peshwa Balaji Rao.

Balaji Rao was a brilliant tactician, a wise statesman and a genius at organizing finances. Though not a great general (it was said that the Peshwa had to be held down on his horse by two footmen), he was a crafty military strategist who realized that the Marhatta goals of dominating India could only be achieved through healthy financing, unity among the senior Marhatta houses and temporary agreements with potential rivals for power against a common enemy. Thus, the Peshwa allied himself with the Nizam against the Moghul Court even though it was clear that they were the principal rivals for power in central and south India. Balaji Rao died in 1720, but the Marhatta revival was continued by his brilliant son, Baji Rao, who was as good a military strategist as he was an administrator.

As far as the control of Malwa was concerned, the Moghul Court was too degenerate and corrupt to exercise real sovereignty over a distant province except in name. Worthless firmans were issued in the name of the Emperor which everyone recognized as a charade. The powerful states of Rajputana preferred to attempt ruling by proxy, nominating surrogate weaklings as local feudal chiefs in Malwa. The Rajputs were, in any case, too divided and too easily lured by promised alliances to provide an effective challenge for power. The Nizam, who had formally been made governor of Malwa, operated from his new stronghold in the Deccan, but was not sufficiently entrenched to foray out of his own territory. The Marhattas also claimed sovereignty over Malwa, but the Peshwa had his sights set on major campaigns in the north and preferred to claim the *chauth* (a tax representing a quarter of the revenue) in order to build up his army through a viable financial base. Thus each one of these four major powers claimed sovereignty and periodically appointed governors to Malwa. However, except for occasional punitive raids against a particularly rebellious local feudal baron, they preferred to claim sovereignty by remote control.

This policy suited the emergent states of Malwa, like Bhopal, as they could consolidate their own control over their domains while keeping the larger powers at bay by paying their chauth and periodically doffing their hats in recognition of distant sovereignty. Dost was particularly adept at this game as he made a point of acknowledging allegiance to the Moghul

Court by sending gifts and letters to the Emperor. To the Marhattas, Dost regularly paid the chauth on the understanding that they would not interfere in the exercise of governance in his territory. It was against this background that Dost established control, order and governance over the newly founded state of Bhopal.

In the first quarter of the eighteenth century, the European powers were still entrenched along the Indian seaboard, but were beginning to match their strength against each other and against local chieftains. In Bengal, Madras and on the western coast the British were locked in a battle for supremacy with the French. European influence remained restricted to the coastal region until the 1740s when it began to spread inland during the second half of the century.

At this point of time, in the early 1720s, Bhopal was a village with a population of around 1000, lying on the banks of the Banganga river which flowed into a natural lake (the Old Lake). Surrounded by hills, valleys and lush jungles, it was a particularly beautiful spot. Islamnagar was Dost's capital where he had enlarged the fort and built a small palace for himself. Bhopal lay five miles south and, particularly after Rani Kamlapati had ceded her palace and territory to Dost, became increasingly important.

By 1723, 16 years after arriving in Malwa, Dost had transformed his status from that of a mercenary to that of a ruler of a state. He had achieved this primarily through incredible daring, astute military prowess and skilful statecraft. He was supported by his doting, affluent wife and by a loyal band of Barru-kat Pathans. He now displayed the normal trappings of governance found in a fledgling, feudal state such as raising an army, levying taxes, appointing a Qazi and other administrators, building forts and mosques, having his name mentioned in the Friday *khutba* (sermon), operating from a capital (Islamnagar) and generally holding sway over a population that consisted mainly of Gonds and Bhils. The conduct of relations with neighbouring feudal states, large and small, was also part of Dost's newly acquired status. All state documents were written in Persian and soon Dost assumed the title of Nawab and sought recognition from the corrupt and degenerate Moghul Court by sending expensive gifts, like an elephant, and fawning letters of allegiance to the titular Emperor in Delhi. In 1717, the Emperor Farrukhsiyar conferred the title of 'Nawab Diler Jang' on Dost, probably on the recommendation of his friends, the Sayyed brothers.

A typical trait of Dost's Afghan upbringing was his reluctance to assume the title of Nawab while his father and elder brother were present in Berasia. Even though Dost had been the unquestioned leader, strategist and pathfinder for his family, his filial reverence to his elders made him hesitate to assume formal leadership. Eventually, however, Dost's father and elder brother insisted at a family caucus that Dost should assume the title of Nawab.

One day, Dost and Fatah Bibi rode out on one of their long rambling shikar treks into the forest. After several hours in the heat, they found themselves in a wooded glade near Bhopal on the banks of the river. It was a beautiful, shady spot where Dost and Fatah Bibi decided to dismount, rest and wait for the geese and duck that Dost was fond of shooting. Not a soul was about and the silence of the forest was disturbed only by the hum of insects and the gentle nibbling of the horses, grazing a few feet away from the reclining couple. Sunset was followed by twilight which gave way to a starlit night. A little later, Fatah Bibi asked Dost to tie the horses on the other side of the thicket. Later still, Dost fell asleep and dreamt that an old saint had asked him to build a fort. He woke up and told Fatah Bibi of his dream. She made him swear to build a fort on the same spot.

This was the origin of the Fatahgarh Fort near the village of Bhopal. Thus, in 1722, Dost laid the foundation of the fort with his own hands and soon a magnificent fortress was erected, named Fatahgarh Fort after his beloved wife. Fatahgarh Fort's first stone was laid by Qazi Mohammad Moazzam of Raisen, a revered scholar who later became Qazi of Bhopal. Dost, Fatah Bibi and the Barru-kat Pathans then helped to build the fort with their bare hands. Eventually, it encircled the village of Bhopal, connecting its rampart with the old fort of Bhopal. Six gates – named after each day of the week – were built and also Bhopal's first mosque – the Two-and-a-Half-Step Mosque in the fort itself. The fort was strengthened and improved over the years to the extent that it had a sundial. Dost also acquired and kept in the fort a remarkable copy of a handwritten Quran with a Farsi (Persian) translation which had pages five feet in length and two and half feet wide.[1] Throughout its history, the Fatahgarh Fort never fell to an invader. In fact, five forts played an important part in Bhopal's early history: the Fatahgarh Fort in Bhopal itself, the fort at Islamnagar which frequently served as the alternate capital and the forts of Raisen, Chowkigarh and Ginnor.

Dost and his family gradually began to use the Fatahgarh Fort as their main bastion and the rapid construction of a high protective wall built around the fort area saw Bhopal develop from a village into a town. Islamnagar continued, however, to serve as the capital.

Although having a fearsome reputation as a fighter, Dost was fair, even humane towards his subjects, bringing about improvements in their economic and social status. He ensured peace, stability and fair governance for the people. For the remaining years of his life, Dost attempted to consolidate his rule over Bhopal. The Marhattas were his greatest threat, but had set their sights on conquering the weak and vulnerable centre in Delhi so that a major attack on a local opponent was not imminent. In any case, they preferred to receive revenue. Dost felt he could handle the Rajputs and, during one of his subjugating forays, he won over the local Hindu chieftain of Shujalpur, Bijjeh Ram, who decided to join Dost rather than fight him. Bijjeh Ram was made *Dewan* – or Chief Minister – of the state and served Dost and two succeeding nawabs with devotion and wise council. No doubt being Hindu, he helped Dost in winning over his population and in keeping hostile

---

[1] The sundial can be seen in the garden of Bhopal's Flagstaff House. The Quran was presented by Nawab Hamidullah Khan, the last Nawab of Bhopal, to the Al-Azhar University in Cairo in 1948. It is kept in the Al-Azhar University Museum.

neighbours at bay. Bijjeh Ram's contribution to the foundation of the state of Bhopal, working loyally at Dost's side, needs to be given due recognition.

For Dost, the rivalry between the Moghul Court and the Nizam placed him in an acute dilemma. The Nizam was strong and well armed. He had passed through Bhopal on his way down to the Deccan with an impressive show of force. Cannons, elephants, horses, musketry and a large, trained army had left a deep impression on the Bhopalis. On the other hand, Dost not only owed nominal allegiance to the Moghul Emperor, but the clinching factor was his personal friendship with the Sayyed brothers. Threatened at the local level by Marhattas and Rajputs, Dost decided to align himself with Delhi and allowed his brother, Mir Ahmad, to fight alongside Dilawar Ali Khan who had been set up by the Moghul Court to ambush the Nizam on his way to the Deccan. Dilawar lost the Battle of Burhanpur in 1720, earning for Bhopal the Nizam's hostility. Mir Ahmad was killed in battle.

In view of the growth of the Peshwa and the Nizam's power in the south and their open defiance of the Moghul Court, the hostility between the Sayyed brothers and the Nizam reached a point where a showdown became inevitable. Emperor Mohammad Shah was prevailed upon to march down to the south and subjugate his opponents. As in the past, the Moghuls managed to align some Rajput chieftains to their cause and a vast unwieldy force was collected to march towards the Deccan.[1] Confronted by a common enemy, the Nizam and Peshwa Baji Rao joined in an unholy alliance against the Moghul Emperor.

On 19 June 1720, in the ensuing battle at Khandwa, the Moghul army was defeated by the combined forces of the Nizam and the Marhattas. Mohammad Shah retreated to Delhi while Dost earned the wrath of the Nizam and the Peshwa for opposing them. However, for the present, the Nizam was too preoccupied with consolidating his base in Deccan to react immediately against Bhopal and returned to Hyderabad.

By 1723, Dost's fortunes had reached their apogee. He was in his 50s and in his prime. He controlled vast tracts of territory and had been formally recognized by the Moghul Emperor as 'Nawab Diler Jang'. He had a force of 10,000 soldiers, artillery, elephants and cavalry. He headed an administration with all the trappings of state power and had managed through statecraft and military campaigns to keep Rajput and Marhatta predators at bay. Dost, with his devoted Fatah Bibi by his side, was now ready to consolidate his hold on his new-found state. So far, the adventures of this brave Afghan buccaneer had resulted in a remarkable success story.

Bhopal submits to the Nizam

Then started the decline. From 1723 onwards until his death in 1728, Dost faced increasing difficulty in ruling his state because both the

---

[1] Typically of the prevailing court intrigues, the Emperor and his mother kept sending secret letters to the Nizam telling him that they were being forced into a war with him!

Nizam and the Peshwa were unforgiving and hostile to him and were reaching out towards Malwa as the coveted gateway to the conquest of the north. The victorious Nizam had been too preoccupied with deciding whether to consolidate in the Deccan or to return and rule as the Moghul Emperor's Chief Minister. He briefly returned to Delhi in 1722 but disgusted, a second time, by Court intrigues in Delhi, the Nizam took the former course and decisively defeated the Moghul surrogate, Mubariz Khan in the Battle of Shakarkhelda in 1724. The Nizam was again assisted by his great rival in the south, Peshwa Baji Rao, who fought in league with the Nizam against the Moghul Emperor's force. Having established complete control over Malwa and the south and having received the Emperor's reluctant benediction, the Nizam returned to Bhopal to settle scores with Dost.

Wisely, Dost did not resist for long. Initially, he fortified himself in Islamnagar, but after a brief siege agreed to a truce with the Nizam. Dost saw discretion as the better part of valour. Taking on the Nizam's forces would have been suicidal and, even if he had resisted, it would only have weakened both sides, allowing the Marhattas to take advantage. Accordingly, Dost arranged a sumptuous welcome banquet for Nizam and billeted his force on a lush hillock, since christened Nizam-*tekri* (hillock). In the truce agreement, Dost acknowledged the Nizam's superiority, ceded territory including Islamnagar Fort, paid a tribute of ten lakhs of rupees with a promise of a second instalment later, presented him with an elephant and gave up his 14-year-old son and heir, Yar Mohammad Khan, as hostage. This was a defeat for Dost and for Bhopal in which major concessions were made without battle being engaged. The Nizam assumed sovereign control over Bhopal, appointing Dost as his own *killedar* (fort commander), while Dost was reduced to running the remainder of his state, virtually on behalf of the Nizam. The event showed that Dost was now a mellower, wiser and more compliant personality, willing to recognize the writing on the wall and ready to concede in order to preserve and consolidate. It indicated a maturing of Dost's character.

The remainder of Dost's life was spent in attempting effective governance of the state that covered 7000 square miles – the size of Wales, El Salvador or Israel – but had been severely truncated to pacify the Nizam and the Marhattas. Before Dost died in March 1728, the Nizam and Peshwa were openly vying for supremacy in Malwa and the Deccan. The last years of Dost's life had seen him hang on perilously to the state that he had founded with such valour and sacrifice. He had ceded territory, given up his son as hostage, paid tribute, offered gifts and bowed reverentially to the superior force of the Nizam. Dost's forbearance and compromise barely managed to keep his state afloat.

Dost encouraged Muslim intelligentsia, scholars, teachers, artists, etc to settle in Bhopal. Thus, apart from the Barru-kat Pathans, Bhopal became a welcoming beacon for Yusufzais, Feroze-khel and Rohelas who brought their typical Afghan/Pathan culture to Bhopal. Following in their wake, came non-Pathan Muslims who found Bhopal congenial, welcoming, egalitarian and well administered. The real incentive for these eminent outsiders to settle in Bhopal was the security, harmony and justice that Dost promised and provided in his new state. Among these theologians and literati were Mohammad Muazzam Sumbhuli, Qazi of Raisen, Mullah Ahmad Deccani and Rustam Ali Sirhindi who wrote a chronicle of the times, describing Bhopal's ambience in the following words:

> Bhopal genuinely deserves to be called a bastion of peace. Dost's encouragement of religious scholarship and learning led to scholars and theologians from all over India gathering in Bhopal. They regularly dine at Dost's table, leading to the enhancement of learning and culture. Due to their [Dost and his son's] humility, bravery and tolerance, Bhopal's internal conditions are peaceful. Justice and fair play prevail throughout the realm so that the tiger and the goat drink from the same watering hole.[1]

In his final years, after Fatah Bibi's death, Dost appears to have inclined towards religious devotion, seeking inspiration from *sufis* (Islamic mystics) and saints. Increasingly shunning material benefits, he veered towards spiritualism. Mellowed in character, he would severely admonish his brother Aqil for desecrating a Buddhist statue in Sanchi. Dost died of an illness in March 1728 at the age of around 56. He was survived by six sons, Yar, Sultan, Sadar, Fazil, Wasil and Khan Bahadur, and five daughters, from several wives. As testimony to his extraordinary life as a fighter, he had 30 wounds on his body. He was buried in Fatahgarh Fort beside his devoted wife Fatah Bibi.

Dost – An assessment

Dost started life as a dare-devil adventurer, a buccaneer, but emerged as a charismatic leader with unique qualities of valour and statesmanship. The real foundation of Dost's accomplishments must lie in his incredible bravery and physical strength that were apparent in his turning certain defeats into incredible victories against, for instance, Mohammad Farooq and Tardi Beg. Dost was also capable of nobility and chivalry, especially towards the weak, as he demonstrated with Kamlapati and the Rani of Mangalgarh. He was equally capable of the most devilish stratagems and appalling treachery when facing an enemy in battle, sparing no mercy even to his cousins. The night attack against the Holi revellers of Parason or the slaughters under collapsed tents at Jagdishpur were part of Dost's armoury that considered every means, fair or foul, to be part of the legitimacy of war. Towards the end of his life, Dost had mellowed, wisely compromising with the Nizam and the Marhattas in order to preserve the remains of his kingdom that he had won against such amazing odds. Ten years earlier, he would have fought his corner till death and destruction.

Dost was a tall, well-built and exceptionally handsome man. He wore a dashing beard which he dyed red with henna as he began to grey. He

---

[1] Rustam Ali Sirhindi, *Tahrikh-i-Hindi*, as quoted in William Hough, *A Brief History of the Bhopal Principality of Central India*.

loved shikar and particularly enjoyed shooting duck, wild fowl and geese. In his diet, he preferred roast guinea fowl and duck. He avoided sweets and as part of his battle-discipline, would fast for days during which he would only take *nan* (flat bread) and water. Dost said his prayers regularly and sought the company of theologians and sufis who were often invited to break bread with him at table. Dost invited scholars, *hakeems* (oriental doctors) and men of learning to settle in Bhopal and gave them jagirs as an inducement. Dost loved to say the *azan* (call to prayer) which he would perform in a particularly melodious voice. Dost always went out of his way to help the poor, especially the families who had lost their bread-winner in battle. He also enjoyed listening to tales of past history. This was a special art of the times and various story-tellers earned their living by recalling tales of mythology, history and religion. Dost was an expert horseman and, though travelling occasionally on an elephant, accompanied by the ceremonial scarlet sun-screen and drums,[1] he preferred to ride and even to race on horseback.

Dost's several marriages are only vaguely chronicled. Clearly, his first wife was Mehraj Bibi from whom he had four children, but Yar was not one of them. Dost's favourite wife was the Rajput, Fatah Bibi of Mangalgarh. She is reported to have been childless and adopted a son whom the couple named Ibrahim Khan. Dost is also recorded as having married Kunwar Sardar Bai, the daughter of Anand Singh – another Rajput – from whom he had further offspring. A third Hindu wife was presented to Dost as a prize of conquest by the zamindar of Kaliakheri. This lady, Jai Kunwar (later called Taj Bibi) bore him three further children. It is not clear which of these wives gave birth to Dost's 'son and heir', Yar Mohammad Khan, who became Bhopal's second Nawab. He was not Mehraj Bibi's son, nor was he Fatah Bibi's, as she died childless. Some chroniclers have referred to Yar Mohammad Khan as illegitimate and it is likely that Yar was born of a Muslim wife or consort soon after Dost came to Malwa and before Mehraj Bibi joined her husband from Tirah. In any case, Yar was the first-born male and obviously regarded as Dost's chosen heir.

Dost's life was an extraordinary odyssey of achievement against impossible odds. At critical moments, circumstances favoured him but he also made his luck by his remarkable courage, his military prowess and his charismatic leadership. Lesser men could never have created a Muslim state with a 90 per cent Hindu population, and surrounded by a sea of Rajput and Marhatta adversaries. Apart from his personal qualities, Dost's decision to persuade his clansmen to migrate from Tirah to Bhopal was a major factor in the founding of the state. The Barru-kat pioneers were fiercely loyal to Dost and provided an impregnable shield to the defence of the state. In 1815, three generations later, it was the same Barru-kat Pathans who helped Dost's great-grandson, Wazir, save Bhopal from annihilation. Dost, though ruthless and even treacherous

---

[1] A scarlet sun-screen was considered the symbol of the ruler. Among Muslims, another symbol of sovereignty was for the ruler's name to be mentioned by the Imam at Friday prayers.

with his enemies, had learnt the art and of statecraft and diplomacy from the time spent in Delhi with Mullah Jamali. He not only married Hindu wives but treated his Hindu subjects with humanity, justice and dignity. His most accomplished Dewan was also a Hindu, Bijjey Ram.

Of course, the power vacuum and strife that developed in Malwa – as indeed in the whole of India – after Aurangzeb's death, helped Dost to create a permanent niche for himself. Accordingly, Dost's most successful efforts to gain territory were achieved in the first ten years of his reign. From 1723 onwards, first the Nizam and then the Marhattas took up cudgels with him and began their domination of Bhopal. Thus, in the later period of his life, Dost had to hand over his son as a hostage, cede forts and territory, and regularly pay tribute in order to preserve the kernel of his state.

Recognizing a superior force and keeping it at bay were qualities of diplomacy and statesmanship that Dost had acquired late in life. A decisive factor in the preservation of the state was that the Marhattas decided, as a policy, not to establish an administrative structure in territories over which they had acquired supremacy. Instead, they preferred to acquire financial tribute and material that would help build up their war machine in pursuit of the conquest of India's northern heartland, on which the Peshwa had set his ambitions. Raghubir Sinh describes this policy succinctly in the following terms:

> This fluid condition of Malwa afforded excellent opportunity to local adventurers and powerful zamindars as well as to the former Moghul grantees. They seized the chance, and seeing that the Marhattas were too strong for them to oppose, they agreed to pay money tributes and went on strengthening their own hold over their possessions. Slowly these States crystallised into political entities, and taking advantage of the situation their rulers formed full-fledged States. Thus, the Marhattas inadvertently helped the rise and strengthening of a new factor in Malwa, which was later to prove a source of real danger to their domination over the province, and this process went on unchecked even after 1765.[1]

Another important factor in Dost's success was his ability to consolidate his post-conquest authority by enlightened, humane and just governance, so that he won over the sympathy of his Hindu subjects. Due to his inspirational leadership, Bhopal became known for its fair governance, its tolerance and harmony between Hindus and Muslims and for its spirit of liberal egalitarianism. In assessing Dost's extraordinary achievements, the supportive role of Fatah Bibi, his wife, soulmate and constant companion needs to be underlined. Fatah Bibi was more than a devoted wife. She financed Dost's leasing of Berasia – the first block in the foundation of Bhopal. She was his counsellor and horseback companion on the battle-field and on shikar. She helped build the fort in Bhopal by laying the stones with her bare hands, alongside her husband. Dost was devoted to Fatah Bibi and named the fort after her as also Bhopal's formal ensign which, to this day is called the 'Fatah-nishan'.

---

[1] *Malwa in Transition.*

At Dost's death, the contrast between the Muslim cultures of the magnificent Moghul Court in Delhi and the emerging state of Bhopal could not have been more poignant. The Moghul Court was pervaded with an air of decadence, venal intrigue and a succession of debauched, eccentric emperors who were surrounded by flatterers, buffoons, pimps, courtesans and eunuchs. They lived in unbelievable splendour, whiling away their time on shikar, among their vast harems and in the pursuit of inane and kinky pleasures. A typical illustration of the decaying moral fibre in the Moghul Court was Emperor Mohammad Shah hiding in his harem when the severed head of his former patron, Sayyed Hussain Ali Barha was brought to him. The Emperor was duly located in the harem and forced back, cringing and squealing, by Hussain Ali's killers. Bhopal, in sharp, contrast, was robust, ascetic and virile. Dost was tough but fair in his governance. He was also tolerant. He respected scholars and writers, deliberately promoting harmony between the Pathan settlers and the local Hindu population. Dost provided Bhopal with an ethos of Muslim culture by encouraging education, literature and research. He welcomed Muslim scholars and sufis to Bhopal and also musicians, craftsmen, hakeems and poets. These qualities were hallmarks that successive rulers attempted, with varying degrees of success, to emulate.

So ended the epic adventure of Sardar Dost Mohammad Khan. Starting as a young, bright-eyed soldier of fortune in the Moghul army, he became an intrepid mercenary in the jungles of Malwa as the Moghul Empire collapsed about him. Gaining a foothold in Berasia, Dost gathered his clan around him and through courage and stealth, statesmanship and treachery carved out a state for himself. He held firm against onslaughts from the Marhattas, the Rajputs and Muslim chieftains like the Nizam and won over the respect of his mainly non-Muslim subjects. On his death, he bequeathed a state and a dynasty that lasted 240 years.

2

The 'reign' of Mamola Bai 1728–95

Yar Mohammad Khan
Second Nawab, 1728–42

When Dost died in March 1728, his eldest son and heir, Yar Mohammad Khan, was 18 years old and had been a hostage of the Nizam of Hyderabad for four years. With the passage of time, the initial hostility between the Nizam and Dost had mellowed and the Nizam, with an eye to cultivating a Muslim ally against the Marhattas, had taken pains to provide his young hostage with an appropriate upbringing as heir to the Nawab of Bhopal. Far from being dismissed to a distant dungeon in chains, Yar was given a thorough grooming as the prospective heir to the throne. He was taught Urdu and Farsi by three learned imams who had accompanied him from Bhopal, learnt to fence, ride, swim and was generally tutored in the craft of combat and leadership.

As soon as the Nizam learnt of Dost's death, Yar was despatched to Bhopal at the head of a 400-strong detachment from the Nizam's army. Asaf Jah also invested Yar with the title of 'Nawab and Amir', conferring on him the historic fish ensign (Mahi-Marateb) which remained Bhopal's emblem to the end. Chroniclers describe Yar's return to Bhopal 'at the head of drumbeaters, banner holders, elephants, palanquins, umbrellas, a charger and a sun-screen'.

Yar Mohammad Khan returned to Bhopal to find that his only surviving uncle, Aqil Mohammad Khan, backed by the Barru-kat high command of Dost's army, had installed his eight-year-old half-brother, Sultan Mohammad Khan, as the Nawab. The news of Yar's arrival on the outskirts of Bhopal ran feverishly through the town and Bhopal's populace warmly greeted Yar as Dost's rightful successor. In a brief skirmish, Yar's supporters which included the Nizam's detachment and were led by Bijjey Ram, routed Sultan's henchmen whereupon Sultan's mother wisely advised her son to accept Yar's claim in return for a substantial jagir. Yar Mohammad Khan's right to succeed as Nawab of Bhopal was based neither on being Dost's eldest son, as he was, nor on commanding a superior force, but as the nominee of the Nizam who was the all-powerful overlord (sanad-holder) of the state. The legality of succession was thus established as the will of the suzerain power, the Nizam, with the consent of the court nobles. Yar Mohammad Khan became the second Nawab of Bhopal at the age of 18 on 30 August 1728.

Yar Mohammad Khan then set about asserting his authority in Bhopal. In this task, he benefited from the foundation and momentum provided to the state by his father, the basic unity within the Pathan ranks and their pioneering spirit that was still at a high pitch. At his side was the loyal Dewan, Bijjeh Ram, whose mature and far-sighted counsel helped Yar to establish himself. Aqil and his nephew Sultan were pensioned off with jagirs and Bijjey Ram reappointed Dewan. Yar was fortunate in that, at the time, the Marhattas and the Nizam were openly squabbling for control over Malwa. Peshwa Baji Rao was gradually gaining ground over the beleaguered Nizam, pushing him towards reconciliation with Emperor Mohammad Shah in Delhi.

Mamola Bai, 1715-95

During one of these victorious campaigns, Yar Mohammad Khan came across a beautiful and accomplished lady named Mamola Bai who was 'surrendered' to him as part of the spoils of victory. Chroniclers of Bhopal's history – mainly the Begums themselves – have for reasons already stated cast a veil over the origins of Mamola Bai. There is no doubt, however, that she was a Hindu and probably a Rajput, belonging to the household of one of the Rajput thakurs that were defeated by Yar. Some writers state that she was the daughter of the Rajput Raja of Kotah. Others indicate that Mamola Bai was a 'Brahmin lady from northern India'. She is recorded as having died childless.

Unquestionably, Mamola Bai was the first woman to exercise a dominant influence in Bhopal's history, first, as Yar's wife and subsequently as the 'mother' of his sons Faiz and Hayat who succeeded him as the third and fourth Nawabs of Bhopal. Mamola Bai ruled Bhopal in the name of her two stepsons – Faiz, a religious recluse and Hayat, an ineffectual weakling – and effectively governed the state for a span of 50 years until her death in 1795 at the age of around 80. At a time when Bhopal's ruling family had no dominant male personality at its helm, Mamola Bai managed to hold the state together against pressures from within as well as from rapacious neighbours.

Yar married Muslim wives from within his family from whom he had five sons: Faiz, Hayat, Saeed, Husain and Yasin. Mamola Bai is repeatedly referred to as their stepmother and as having 'failed to produce a child from her womb'. In fact, Faiz was born in 1731, a year after Yar married Mamola Bai so that Yar would have cohabited with a Muslim Begum simultaneously with his Hindu consort.

Of course, keeping more than one wife was not uncommon, especially for the Muslim gentry, but it was evident that Mamola Bai assumed a leading role in Yar's court soon after she became his consort. She converted to Islam – but never adopted a Muslim name as was the custom when Muslims took Hindu wives – and was widely acclaimed for her wisdom and compassion for the poor. She built three mosques in Bhopal which were recognized as her contribution to the teaching of Islam.

Marhatta domination of Malwa

The Nizam–Peshwa rivalry enabled Yar to recover some of Bhopal's lost territories and to reassert his authority over the domain that his father had conquered. The Marhattas were too preoccupied, however, with their major campaign against the Nizam – and eventually against the Moghul Court – to be diverted by Yar's local pinpricks. Nevertheless, by December 1736, Peshwa Baji Rao had decided to gain control over the whole of Malwa and invaded Bhopal with a significant force. Yar attempted a defence but was overwhelmed by the superior Marhatta force and obliged to submit to a treaty with Peshwa Baji Rao in which he acknowledged Marhatta supremacy, ceded territory, paid an annual grant of five lakhs of rupees and promised cavalry and men to the Marhatta army.

These gains by the Marhattas in Malwa led to the reconciliation between the Moghul Court and the Nizam in Delhi who saw a common threat to their power base. The Nizam was despatched with a vast force which converged on Bhopal where battle was to be engaged. The Nizam occupied Raisen Fort and waited for Moghul reinforcements to arrive while the Peshwa mounted his famous guerilla tactics, aimed at starving out the Nizam's unwieldy force.

Seeing the Nizam and the Moghul Emperor reconciled, Yar began to play a highly dangerous and duplicitous game with both warring opponents. He first sided with the Nizam by assuring him of the Bhopal army's support and refused to fulfil his treaty obligations with the Peshwa. Then, when he saw the beleaguered Nizam's force in despair and no sign of Moghul reinforcements, he secretly began repaying his dues to the Peshwa.

Meanwhile, Peshwa Baji Rao, following in the footsteps of Sivaji, adopted the famous Marhatta guerilla tactics of harassment through light cavalry attacks, raising a siege and preventing rations reaching the beleaguered army. Several weeks later, the Nizam's forces were desperate. They began eating artillery oxen and boiling leaves to survive. During the siege, the Nizam's Rajput and Jat allies deserted him and eventually the Nizam's force emerged from Raisen to engage in battle and was roundly defeated in Bhopal. On 6 January 1738 the Nizam, writing in his own hand, signed a peace treaty with the Peshwa Baji Rao at Doraha-Serai, near Bhopal, in which he ceded Malwa, acknowledged Marhatta sovereignty over the territory between the Narbada and Chambal rivers and promised to pay 50 lakhs of rupees in reparations. The Nizam was then allowed safe passage back to Hyderabad.

The victorious Peshwa Baji Rao stayed on in Bhopal for three weeks, flaunting his dominance and relishing the luxury and beauty of the surroundings, to the obvious chagrin of the Barru-kat Pathans. Yar had affected a neutrality between the Nizam and the Peshwa, but it was evident that the sympathy and covert support of the Bhopalis lay with the Nizam. Yar then entered into another treaty with the Marhattas in which he agreed to pay tribute, provide food, cavalry and troops and to pay taxes to the Peshwa. In effect, the agreement recognized that the Peshwa had replaced the Nizam as the overlord of Bhopal, of course acting under the imprimatur of the hapless Moghul Emperor.

Masters of Malwa and the south, the Marhatta confederacy was bristling with power and ready to embark on its ultimate ambition of controlling the northern heartland of India when, in 1739, they were stopped in their tracks by the lightning invasion from Persia of Nadir Shah. He defeated Emperor Mohammad Shah and sacked Delhi, killing 20,000 citizens in a day. Fearing an attack towards the south, the Marhattas dug in across the Narbada river but the dreaded confrontation never took place. Nadir Shah, having plundered the riches of the Moghul Empire, including the Peacock Throne and the Kohinoor Diamond, returned to Persia leaving a deflated Moghul Emperor in charge. However, the psychological impact of Nadir Shah's invasion left the Marhattas stunned and undecided. Hardly had they recovered from Nadir Shah's invasion than Peshwa Baji Rao died in 1740, leaving the Marhattas in a state of internal turmoil. His son Balaji Rao II succeeded him, but did not possess the charismatic qualities of his father. Balaji Rao II was not a military strategist like his father, but proved to be a wily politician and diplomat. Temporarily, therefore, the Marhattas looked inwards to set their house in order.

In 1741, Balaji Rao II had recovered sufficient Marhatta strength to persuade the Moghul Court to legalize Marhatta supremacy over Malwa. The Peshwa then signed a formal treaty with Yar in which Bhopal recognized Marhatta sovereignty and agreed to pay annual tribute of 3½ lakhs of rupees and provide elephants, cavalry and grain in return for Yar being allowed to retain governance over his domain. This arrangement suited the Marhattas who required financing for the *putsch* towards Delhi and were, therefore, disinclined towards administrative governance of Malwa. It provided Yar opportunity and space to win back some of the territory that had been gnawed away from Bhopal by Marhatta and Rajput chieftains in the final years of Dost's reign.

During Yar's reign, the Marhatta campaign to dominate the north was put on hold for a few years. Briefly the Rajputs, under the charismatic leadership of Jai Singh, again became players in the power game. Jai Singh also wanted to control Malwa and aligned himself with each major power at different times, but never realized his ambition. Eventually, the Marhatta Confederacy overcame the shock of Nadir Shah's invasion and Baji Rao's death. They began again to assert themselves in south and central India, this time under the leadership of Shahuji's nephew, Raghunath Rao, and his cousin, the brilliant general Sudashiv Bhau.

Thus, Yar Mohammad Khan's 14-year reign saw Bhopal genuflect deeper towards the Marhattas with peace being achieved at the cost of territory and finances. Yar Mohammad Khan died of an illness in 1742 at the relatively young age of 32. He was buried at Islamnagar. Yar's reign had seen Bhopal barely keep its head above water. There was no high intrigue in the family and even the dominant presence of an outsider, Mamola Bai, had been a pacifying rather than an exacerbating influence on the scene in Bhopal – the lull before the storm.

Faiz Mohammad Khan
Third Nawab, 1742–77

Yar Mohammad Khan's death led to another major confrontation between family aspirants to the title. His quixotic and mercurial half-brother, Sultan Mohammad Khan, made a second attempt to claim the *gaddi* (throne). Aligned with ambitious and disenchanted members of the family, Sultan and his younger brother Sadar seized Fatahgarh Fort and sought the support of neighbouring Marhatta kingdoms, promising them one of Bhopal's five main forts in return. Mamola Bai faced the revolt from Islamnagar, her first internal crisis in Bhopal, with calm and equanimity. She proclaimed Yar's 11-year-old eldest son, Faiz Mohammad Khan, as the Nawab and, with the help of the loyal and capable Chief Minister Bijjeh Ram, rallied the rump of Bhopalis towards supporting legality and legitimacy. Ironically, the Hindu convert Mamola Bai and her chief adviser Bijjeh Ram, another Hindu, were invoking the Islamic tenets of legitimacy in favour of Mamola Bai's 11-year-old stepson against the claims of Dost Mohammad Khan's second son, Sultan!

At the head of the loyalist force was Bijjeh Ram, now into his third generation of service with the Bhopal Nawabs. He collected a force of 5000 soldiers and a confrontation took place around the Eidgah Hill which, looking back, seems to have ended up in comic mayhem rather than an organized battle. In this melee, Sultan's motley force charged about the town taking swipes at anyone in sight. He was then tricked by the Marhatta representative, Holas Rai, to allow the Marhattas entry into the fort from which Sultan's forces were immediately locked out. It was no surprise, therefore, that Sultan lost. He, along with Sadar, surrendered and sought pardon from Mamola Bai which was granted on condition that the brothers renounce, forever, their claims to the title. The defeated aspirants readily agreed and retired to the neighbouring state of Kurwai. Thus Mamola Bai (now 27 years old) had moved quickly and effectively to defuse the crisis on her husband's death and had successfully won her first battle, installing her stepson, Faiz, as the third Nawab of Bhopal.

From early childhood, Faiz Mohammad Khan devoted himself to prayer and meditation. Faiz was an imposing figure, almost seven feet tall with arms so long that they stretched down to his knees. He was no barnstorming fanatic but a benign, saintly man who became the epitome of piety, tolerance and goodness. As Faiz's devotion to Sufic Islam grew, his interest in statecraft and worldly affairs declined so that, even in his lifetime, Faiz willingly transferred affairs of state to his stepmother and achieved the status of a saint. His reputation of holiness and benevolence travelled quickly across the state and beyond, with both Muslims and Hindus paying homage to his memory. Even today, Faiz Mohammad Khan's *Urs* (annual religious festival) is celebrated by the Muslims and Hindus of Bhopal.

As Faiz withdrew behind a veil of devotion, the Dowager Mamola Bai assumed effective governance of the state in the name of her stepson. It was she who took decisions on military campaigns, the conferment of jagirs, the collection of taxes, the appointment of administrators and, above all, the conduct of relations with neighbouring states.

By 1745, Peshwa Balaji Rao II who was a financial genius but not an enthusiastic general, had decided to consolidate his hold in Malwa. He invaded territories that Yar had eaten into around the time that Nadir Shah had sacked Delhi and the death had occurred of Peshwa Baji Rao. Against a formidable force led by the Marhatta general, Daulat Rao Scindia, the Bhopal forces retreated from Bhilsa Fort which they handed over to the Marhattas. Mamola Bai advised restraint and on 2 March 1745 a treaty was signed between Faiz and the Peshwa in which almost half of Bhopal's territories were surrendered. The Peshwa was also provided with financial and material assistance, in return for which Faiz was permitted to rule in his truncated state and allowed to claim the important fort of Raisen. The Marhattas had been encouraged to take this initiative by Wasil Mohammad Khan, Yar's brother, who hoped that the Marhattas would seat him on the Bhopal gaddi. The 1745 treaty, in fact, led to the consolidation of the Mamola–Faiz rule in Bhopal because Wasil was dismissed with only a few villages in compensation while Bhopal enjoyed a decade of peace from the Marhattas who had set their sights on building up finances for the thrust towards Delhi.

Given the nod by the Marhattas, Mamola Bai personally supervised the siege and takeover of Raisen Fort which was under nominal Moghul control. In a deft diplomatic manoeuvre, she sent the trusted Bijjey Ram to the Imperial Court in Delhi with a message to the Emperor stating that she had acted to save Raisen Fort from the killedar's impending treachery. Emperor Alamgir II, realizing that he was faced with a fait accompli, decided to grant Nawab Faiz Mohammad Khan the formal title to the fort.

The political scene in India in the 1750s

By the turn of the half-century, a significant change had occurred in the balance of power in India. The Moghul Court's impotence was now apparent. Like the Wizard of Oz, the Emperor made loud, frightening noises and affected a grandeur that fooled nobody. The Court's only asset was a fading memory of supreme power which the real wielders of authority exploited to the hilt. Like a railway wagon carrying a load of circus animals, the Moghul emperors were pulled in various directions by the locomotives of real power to parade their act before a once reverential public.

After Jai Singh's death, the Rajputs also faded from the scene, racked as they traditionally were by divisions of ultra-proud, warrior chieftains who refused to accept another's authority. The Nizam of Hyderabad too, now old and infirm, had been severely reduced in strength and prestige by his defeat at the hands of the Marhattas in 1738. He handed over control of Malwa and adjacent territories to the Peshwa and recoiled back into his shell, no longer a threat to Marhatta supremacy; he died in 1748.

Thus, by the 1750s the Moghul Court, the Nizam of Hyderabad and the Rajputs were on the decline.

Ascendant and increasingly powerful were the Marhattas and the British. The Marhattas had recovered from the slump following Peshwa Baji Rao's death and the psychological impact of Nadir Shah's invasion of the north. The Marhatta Confederacy was headed by Peshwa Balaji Rao II, but real power had moved into the hands of the military leaders, Sudashiv Bhau, Dattaji Scindia and Malhar Rao Holkar. By the 1750s, Marhatta power was resplendent again, dominating Malwa and the south and ready to fulfil its cherished ambition of planting its standard in Delhi. In 1755, the Confederacy began its move northwards to achieve its ultimate ambition of conquering the northern heartland of India.

By the 1750s, the British, under Robert Clive, Admiral Watson and Sir Eyre Coote, succeeded in getting the better of their European rivals, the French. Scarred and indignant at the humiliation of events like the Black Hole of Calcutta, they began their march inland from their coastal bastions that they held to protect their trade. From 1750 onwards, British sea-power, superior military prowess and cunning leadership led to the defeats of indigenous rulers, notably at the Battle of Plassey in 1757 after which the East India Company began assuming a growing importance in the power play that unfolded on the mainland of the Sub-Continent in the second half of the eighteenth country.

By the mid-1750s, a third important player emerged on the north-western horizon of India. Ahmad Shah Abdali, like Nadir Shah before him, controlled Iran and Afghanistan and was finding it profitable to make periodic invasions into northern India, plunder its riches and return home, leaving behind governors and surrogates to maintain order on his behalf. The Marhattas saw in Ahmad Shah Abdali their major rival for power in India. For them, the spectre of seven centuries appeared to be emerging again when a succession of Muslim invaders entered India from the north-west, plundering and dominating the whole of the land. The Marhattas were determined not to allow history to repeat itself and by 1760, the Bhau had captured Delhi, replaced one degenerate Moghul emperor with another and even moved into Lahore.

Far from home and running short of funds, against the advice of his Rajput and Jat allies, the arrogant Bhau plundered the jewels and ornaments of the Moghul Court, defacing the mosques and shrines that the Moghuls had built in Delhi and Agra. He desecrated the Moti Masjid and converted its jewelled decorations into booty. This domination of the north by the Marhattas had a profound impact on the divided and somewhat degenerate Muslim hierarchy who now looked to Ahmad Shah Abdali as their saviour. For a change, the Muslim chieftains and general public buried the hatchet of internecine division and pledged their support to their liberator, Ahmad Shah Abdali.

As the Marhattas and the Afghan invaders squared up for battle, the Muslim states and Rohilla power-barons of northern India sent their forces in support of Ahmad Shah Abdali as the integrity of these Muslim states depended on the defeat of the Marhattas. In 1760, the Bhau had marched his huge Marhatta force through Bhopal. The Bhau summoned Nawab Faiz Mohammad Khan to Bhilsa to seek support for his campaign against Abdali. Faiz declined, leaving the Bhau furious and declaring openly that he would wreak vengeance on Bhopal, after defeating Abdali. Having conveyed this threat, the Bhau proceeded northwards to engage in battle with the Muslim invader. It is sometimes suggested that a Bhopali contingent fought alongside Abdali at the Battle of Panipat in 1761, but even though Faiz was hostile to the Marhattas and prayed openly for Abdali's success, Bhopal's forces could not have been present at Panipat because it was not possible for them to cross Marhatta-held territory.

In January 1761, the mother of battles took place, again at Panipat.[1] The Marhattas were supported by Suraj Mal Jat of Bharatpur and by some Rajput princes who viewed Abdali's invasions as a repetition of foreign Muslim dominance over India. Far from home, short of supplies and in dire need of financing, the truculent Bhau declined the advice of his strongest ally, Suraj Mal Jat, not to engage Abdali in fixed combat and to rely on their traditionally successful strategy of guerilla warfare.

The third Battle of Panipat began on the morning of 13 January 1761. The Bhau placed himself in the centre of his huge force along with the Peshwa's son, the 19-year-old Vishvas Rao – a handsome, Apollo-like figure – by his side. On his right flank were the armies of rivals Malhar Rao Holkar and Jankoji Scindia.[2] On the Bhau's left was Damaji Gaekwad and the 'renegade Muslim' general, Ibrahim Khan Gardi who had learnt French military strategy from General Bussy in the Deccan. Against all advice, the Bhau had brought women, children, servants and non-combatant retainers into the battle zone. Ahmad Shah Abdali's force was lighter and relied on swift cavalry attacks mounted on their superior Turki horses. Ahmad Shah Abdali also placed himself in the centre of his force along with his Chief Minister Shah Wali Khan and was flanked by Najib-ud-Daulah and Shuja-ul-Daulah along with the Rohilla forces that had allied themselves with Ahmad Shah.

Battle began at dawn and by afternoon it was hand to hand. At one point, the Marhattas appeared on the verge of victory, but Abdali's capacity to counter attack led to the Marhatta centre giving way. The Bhau died bravely in combat and suddenly the mighty Marhatta force

---

[1] Two earlier defining battles in Indian history had taken place at Panipat, in 1526 and 1556, leading to Moghul domination of India.
[2] Jankoji was the hereditary ruler but his uncle Dattaji was the guardian and power behind Scindia. Dattaji was killed in battle in 1760. Jankoji then took over control.

turned and fled. A huge massacre followed, leading to one of the defining events in Indian history.

The Marhattas suffered a shattering defeat that saw their dream of domination over the whole of India's crash in ruins. The damage to the Marhatta cause was as much psychological as military and they returned homewards, a broken and dispirited force. Sudashiv Bhau, Vishvas Rao – the Peshwa's young son, Jankoji Scindia and the leading Marhatta generals were killed in battle. Only Malhar Rao Holkar and Damaji Gaekwad along with Scindia's deputy, Mahadji, survived as the Marhattas retreated in disarray, mercilessly pursued by Abdali's forces. The Peshwa, who had been waiting at Bhilsa for the clarion call of victory, could not believe the news of the Marhatta defeat until he saw the remnants of his routed army. He turned back to Poona broken and mortified, dying a few months later. He was succeeded as Peshwa by Madhav Rao who proved to be the weakest in four generations of Peshwas. Temporarily, Bhopal had been saved from the Marhatta threat as their armies retreated homewards to lick their wounds. Many people in Bhopal ascribed their salvation from the Marhatta threat to the prayers of the saintly Nawab, Faiz Mohammad Khan.

Ironically, the victorious Ahmad Shah Abdali did not stay on to enjoy the fruits of victory. Like Nadir Shah before him, he returned home leaving the Moghul Emperor, Shah Alam II, in charge. Ahmad Shah Abdali was an Afghan of the Durrani tribe. One hundred and fifty years after the Battle of Panipat and 11 generations later, Maimoona Sultan, a direct descendant of Ahmad Shah, was to marry Hamidullah Khan, the last Nawab of Bhopal. Shah Alam, like all Moghul emperors after Aurangzeb, was in no way capable of asserting his authority and soon after the Battle of Panipat, the only power that was vibrant, focused and united began asserting its domination over the whole of India. Panipat had opened the door for the British to fill the power vacuum.

Dissent and intrigue

As Bhopal breathed a sigh of relief, Mamola Bai strengthened her hold on the levers of power and regained some territories ceded earlier to the Marhattas. The external threat to Bhopal had temporarily subsided but now problems from within began to surface. Dissent and intrigue emerged from the ranks of the ruling family in Bhopal. It is reasonable to assume that the Barru-kat Pathans, who considered themselves the pioneers and defenders of the state, became increasingly concerned at the arrogation of power by two Hindu outsiders: the faithful Chief Minister Bijjeh Ram and the convert Dowager Mamola Bai. No doubt intrigues began to play on the theme that Hindu Raj was dominating the scene in Bhopal at the expense of Muslim Pathan rule. These conspirators evidently played on the sensitivities of Dost Mohammad Khan's immediate family members, convincing them of their superior claims to the title compared with the reclusive Faiz and the power-sharing duo of Mamola Bai and Bijjeh Ram.

These intrigues came to a head after the death, in 1762, of the wise and loyal Bijjeh Ram. His son, Ghansi Ram, succeeded him as Dewan but, unlike his father, proved to be a bigoted Hindu who brought Muslim–Hindu tension into the open. Soon after he took over, Ghansi Ram was murdered by a Pathan. His successor, Izzat Khan, was poisoned by a courtesan and the third Minister, Kesari Lall, met a similarly violent end when his house was blown up by dynamite after he was accused of having illicit relations with an Afghan girl. Thus, within a short span of time, three ministers had met violent deaths indicating a seething, fractious period in the state. Bhopal had thus entered a dangerous period of violence that was producing tension and disarray from within. Eventually, Mamola Bai appointed Faiz's youngest brother, Yasin, as Dewan, keeping the administration entirely within the family.

In Poona, following the disaster of Panipat, the new Peshwa and his brother Raghunath Rao were at loggerheads and fighting each other. The Bhau and senior Marhatta leaders had perished at Panipat, leaving Malhar Rao Holkar and a severely wounded Mahadji Scindia to rally the Marhattas. So began the emergence of Holkar, Bhopal's neighbour, as a leader of the Marhattas. By 1766, Malhar Rao Holkar was also dead, succeeded by his infant son but with his widow, Ahliya Bai, acting as the powerful regent. Neighbouring Bhopal and Indore were now both effectively run by two women acting in the name of their sons. Under Ahliya Bai, who was sympathetic to Mamola Bai, the threat from Holkar evaporated leaving the young Mahadji Rao Scindia as the rising star in the Marhatta firmament.

By 1775 the Marhatta states had recovered from their defeat at Panipat and the four kingdoms – Gwalior, Indore, Baroda and Nagpur – began to flex their muscles independently and separately. They had postponed the goal of conquering Delhi and concentrated on controlling Malwa and the south. In 1776 the Peshwa entered Bhopal with a large force. Again, Mamola Bai wisely advised restraint and ceded five districts along with the Hoshangabad Fort. Satisfied, the Peshwa left Bhopal, content with territory and tribute. Marhatta domination of Bhopal that had begun in the final year of Dost's reign was now almost complete, with the Bhopal *riasat* (princely state) barely capable of keeping its nose above water.

Hayat Mohammad Khan
Fourth Nawab, 1778–1807

At the age of 46, the revered, saintly Faiz Mohammad Khan developed the illness of dropsy. He died on 12 December 1777. His reign had lasted 35 years during which he took scant interest in the affairs of state, leaving Mamola Bai in charge of navigating the ship of state through turbulent waters. The capital had been moved from Islamnagar to Bhopal and Faiz is recorded as having stepped out of his palace only once during his entire reign of 35 years. He was buried near Kamlapati's palace beside his real mother. Faiz died childless, leaving behind a widow, Saleha Begum, better known as Bahu Begum, a spirited, defiant, outgoing woman who was not prepared to play second fiddle after her husband's death.

Sensing another crisis of succession, the 62-year-old Mamola Bai again moved quickly. Even before the traditional 40-day mourning (*chehlum*) was completed, she declared her second stepson, Faiz's younger brother, Hayat Mohammad Khan, as the fourth Nawab of Bhopal on 3 January 1778. Hayat was 43 years old when he ascended the throne, a weak, indolent, corpulent, pleasure-loving character who could not aspire to the reverence in which his brother had been held.

Hayat's accession to the gaddi sparked another crisis for Mamola Bai. Faiz's widow, Bahu Begum, refused to accept Hayat's accession and began a revolt in which she was supported by members of Dost Mohammad Khan's descendants. Bahu Begum, who detested Mamola Bai, perceived that by placing her weak, indolent 'son' on the gaddi, Mamola Bai was seeking to perpetuate her Hindu-oriented reign in Bhopal. Bahu Begum began holding court at her husband's *mazar* (tomb) and set up a parallel government in Islamnagar. For three years, she regularly held *durbars* (royal courts, formal assemblies) as an act of defiance against the rule of Mamola Bai. Typically of Bhopal's history, two women headed rival cabals vying for power in the state.

Bhopal was now effectively split in two: the Dowager Mamola Bai operating from Fatahgarh Fort in the name of Hayat, while Bahu Begum held court in Islamnagar about five miles away, taunting, cajoling and urging her husband's cousins to uphold the honour of Dost Mohammad Khan's heritage. Mamola Bai temporized and requested Bahu Begum, as a compromise, to nominate any of Yar's brothers as the Nawab while Bahu Begum acted as regent. In fact, Hayat Mohammad Khan offered to step down to pacify the tempestuous Bahu Begum.

General Goddard[1] passes through Bhopal, 1778

By the time Hayat became the fourth Nawab of Bhopal, the British had established a firm hold over India's heartland. Clive's extraordinary odyssey in India had ended in suicide and in 1774 Warren Hastings, another controversial figure, had been appointed the first British Governor-General of India. Britain's main rivals for power were the Marhattas and the French with whom they were engaged in mortal combat across India's mainland. Against this background, in November 1778, an event took place which would have a profound effect upon Bhopal's history. General Thomas Goddard and his doughty regiment arrived in Bhopal on his epic march across the breadth of India. It was the first time that the British had attempted to create a transcontinental link between its strongholds on India's eastern and western shores. Goddard's march is part of British history in India. Goddard had fought his way past hostile opponents, both Hindu and Muslim, who had harassed him all the way

---

[1] Thomas Goddard was a colonel in 1778 and was later promoted to the rank of general.

into Malwa. He was beleaguered, exhausted and short of money and rations when he entered the unknown territory of Bhopal.

Goddard's famous march across India was conceived as an attempt by the East India Company, acting under Warren Hastings' instructions, to suppress the Marhatta threat in the west. A large British force was prepared to trek across from Calcutta to Bombay to confront the Marhatta confederacy. Initially, the force was commanded by Colonel Leslie but he was relieved of his charge and his deputy Colonel Thomas Goddard replaced him. Goddard reached Bhopal on 20 November 1778.

Evidently, the wily and far-sighted Mamola Bai recognized in Goddard a glimmer of hope in her efforts to keep predatory neighbours at bay. She was aware of the growing influence of British power in Bengal, Oudh, Bombay and the south and must have concluded that by aligning her beleaguered state with this emergent power, she could bolster Bhopal's independence against Marhatta domination. Despite the hostility of the local population, Mamola Bai ensured that Goddard's men were given a warm welcome in Bhopal. They were securely billeted in Raisen Fort, given rations, treated with courtesy and allowed to rest and recuperate from their arduous trek. This unexpected act of hospitality left a deep impression on General Goddard and gained for Bhopal the lasting gratitude of the British East India Company.

Goddard was highly appreciative of Mamola Bai's gesture and conveyed to his superiors the importance of maintaining a close relationship with this fragile Muslim state that was surrounded by neighbours who were vying with the British for power and influence in the control of India. Goddard's visit to Bhopal struck the first chord in Britain's relationship with Bhopal that became a recurrent theme in Bhopal's efforts to maintain its independence.

Chottey Khan, 1780–94

Shortly after she became Yar Mohammad Khan's consort, Mamola Bai, known in Bhopal as Manji Saheba (revered mother), decided to adopt, convert and groom four Hindu boys. The first was a Gond, and the second and third were Aheer. The fourth, a Brahmin, was given the name of Chottey Khan. By 1780, he was an adult and beholden to Manji Saheba. After the violent deaths of three ministers in quick succession, Mamola Bai decided to play her trump card and appointed Chottey Khan as her Chief Minister on 17 November 1780. Chottey Khan immediately brought the fraying social and administrative structure of Bhopal under control. He proved to be an able administrator, implementing reforms, bolstering the administration and suppressing dissent from within. To Mamola Bai, Chottey Khan's steadying influence provided the stability in the state that had been absent since the death of Bijjeh Ram.

Chottey Khan was an astute, crafty and unscrupulous political tactician. He reorganized the army and recruited an effective police force which included an intelligence department that kept the Chief Minister fully informed of threats and intrigues. He posted police officials to the rural districts and appointed representatives – diplomatic emissaries – to the neighbouring states of Gwalior, Indore and Baroda. Chottey Khan encouraged trade from Bhopal by extending facilities to merchants. He also built roads, extended Bhopal's suburbs and built a dam on the Banganga river so that Bhopal had another artificial lake to augment its water supply and enhance its scenic beauty. He built several bridges across the rivers that flowed through Bhopal. Chottey Khan strengthened the Fatahgarh Fort and ensured that Bhopal's mosques were properly administered. He encouraged poets, authors and religious scholars to settle in Bhopal so that Bhopal began to reflect the Muslim cultural ambience of Delhi in the north and Hyderabad in the south. Above all, Chottey Khan's 14-year stewardship of the state saw Bhopal enter an era of development, stability and contentment.

Chottey Khan's ruthless but effective administration was seen as a major challenge by Bahu Begum who taunted Shareef Mohammad Khan, Dost's grandson by stating, 'If I was a man, I would never allow this Brahmin slave to rule over the family of Dost Mohammad Khan.' She then promised him funds to raise an army against the Mamola–Hayat–Chottey axis. Shareef set to work in earnest, galvanizing his cousins to support him, urging the Barru-kat Pathans to demonstrate their loyalty to Dost and rallying Pathan recalcitrants to overthrow the Hindu Raj being supported by Mamola Bai and her protégé, Chottey. Having raised an army of 5000, Shareef asked Bahu Begum for the promised financing. She failed to deliver. Shareef withdrew in disgust and with this non-event, Bahu Begum's alternative government began to falter until it no longer posed a threat to Hayat.

Bahu Begum's life represents an extraordinary odyssey of compassion, betrayal and retribution. Saleha – Bahu Begum – was the daughter of the traitor Wasil Mohammad Khan who had conspired with the Peshwa to invade Bhopal and wrest the throne from his nephew, Faiz Mohammad Khan. The Peshwa's force subsequently invaded Bhopal, but Mamola Bai advised restraint and negotiation. Eventually, she agreed to cede almost half of Bhopal's territory to the Marhatta chief who allowed Mamola and Faiz to preside over a truncated Bhopal. In this arrangement, Wasil the traitor lost out as the Peshwa declined to place him on the Bhopal gaddi. From that point onwards, Wasil's fortunes declined sharply. Despised in Bhopal and shunned by the Marhattas, Wasil fell into penury and dire straits, dying shortly afterwards in misery. Mamola Bai took pity on his widow, Izzat Begum, and eight-year-old daughter Saleha, and brought them back to Bhopal, providing them with a subsistence and raising little Saleha under her own guidance. Saleha was then married off to the young Nawab Faiz Mohammad Khan and was known as Bahu Begum.

Instead of showing gratitude towards her mother-in-law, Bahu Begum became increasingly truculent and hostile to Mamola Bai who had saved her from misery and brought her up in her own palace. Eventually, on her husband's death, Bahu Begum defied her stepmother-in-law, set up a separate court and ran a parallel government. She conspired with other family members to rise against the Mamola–Hayat axis, but failed to deliver the finances that would have fuelled an armed insurrection. Bahu Begum's decline began immediately after this let-down.

Chottey Khan continued, however, in his aggressive, uncompromising pursuit of Hayat's rivals with the objective of permanently undermining their strength. The focal point of the opposition had now moved from Bahu Begum to Shareef Mohammad Khan himself. Shareef had seven brothers and a brave, handsome adolescent son, Wazir Mohammad Khan. Shareef, having assumed the mantle of the main opposition to Hayat, was duly banished from Bhopal. He withdrew to adjacent Rajput territory where he was welcomed and given support with a view to harnessing this powerful ally in the pursuit of the break-up of Bhopal. Shareef again set about raising an army in preparation for a showdown with Hayat's forces. Once he had raised a fighting force, Shareef's first act of defiance was to capture the fort of Ginnor which meant that the gauntlet had been flung down against the Mamola–Hayat–Chottey axis ruling Bhopal.

The Battle of Phanda, 1787

The showdown came on 24 February 1787, when both sides squared up for battle at a village called Phanda, eight miles west of Bhopal. This battle was one of the fiercest in the annals of Bhopal's history. Shareef led his army with his seven brothers, while his young son Wazir was given the responsibility of protecting the women and children of the family at the nearby village of Ashta. Chottey Khan had the support of loyalist Pathans, some Rajput and Sikh mercenaries and Bhopal's regular army. It was a battle for power between contending members of Dost's family, except that Bhopal's army was led by a Brahmin convert loyal to his adopted Rajput mother. While the two armies prepared for battle at Phanda, Hayat remained ensconced in his palace in Bhopal, comforted by his regular attendants of mullahs, soothsayers, eunuchs and courtesans.

At Phanda, the earth trembled with the thunder of gun-fire, the sound of galloping hooves, the shrill trumpeting of attacking elephants, the clash of swords and the thud of spears. It was a bloody, ruthless battle in which Shareef's rebel forces were defeated. Brave and courageous to the last, Shareef and his brothers stood their ground and all except one, Kamil, were slaughtered. So vicious was the battle and so deep the hostility that Chottey Khan's victorious army severed the heads of the six brothers – Dost's grandsons – and carried them home on swords to Hayat's palace.

This display of gory arrogance by Chottey Khan was deeply disturbing for Hayat, not only because such displays were against the family tradition, but also because they indicated a mean, vicious streak in Chottey Khan's character. An assumption of complete control over the state, especially as Mamola Bai was now ageing and losing her grip on power, was also a source of alarm for Hayat and the loyalists who had supported him against Shareef.

Typical of Chottey Khan's astute governance was his handling of the Pindara threat which had been wreaking havoc across north and central India. The Pindaras[1] were a band of marauding Muslims who had terrorized the region by their ferocious onslaughts. They attacked Bhopal but were contained and eventually bought off by Chottey Khan so that they agreed not to threaten Bhopal again.

For the next seven years after the Battle of Phanda, Chottey Khan assumed increasing power. Hayat and his mother, now into her 70s, recognized, as so often in history, that their humble, unctuous, adopted 'slave' had assumed the role of a Frankenstein who paid scant respect to the wishes of the Nawab or his mother. He was particularly vindictive towards the wives of the former Hindu Dewans, Bijjeh Ram and Himmat Rai, turning them out of their homes into forced exile. Chottey Khan's arrogant and ruthless exercise of power saw him oppress the Pathan families that had been the backbone of the Bhopal state. Even the loyalist Barru-kat Pathans who had sided with Chottey against Shareef at the Battle of Phanda were now, like Hayat, aghast at Chottey Khan's arrogance. Chottey Khan realized that he had taken on the wrath of all Barru-kat Pathans and that all of Dost Mohammad Khan's family, except Hayat, had become his bitter enemies. Chottey Khan knew that he was the target of numerous assassins who saw in him a non-family usurper of power.

Then suddenly in 1794 Chottey Khan died. Soon afterwards, in 1795, the 80-year-old Manji Mamola Bai also died so that within the space of two years, the rule of the two Hindu converts to Islam who had effectively governed the state in the name of reclusive, titular nawabs was at an end. The steadying influence of Mamola Bai that had preserved Bhopal's sovereignty and independence was gone. So was the firm grip on the administration by Chottey Khan which had also been a major factor in Bhopal's stability. The stage was set for intrigue, dissent and decline.

Mamola Bai – An assessment

Unquestionably, Manji Mamola Bai was Bhopal's first de facto woman ruler. She reigned for over 50 years, as Yar's consort and later as the power behind the throne of her two stepsons, the reclusive Faiz and the indolent Hayat. Mamola's rule coincided with the period when Bhopal was subservient, first to the Nizam and later to the Marhattas. Despite its being virtually a vassal state, Mamola managed to retain basic minimal independence for Bhopal so that, after the turn of the century, it was able to reassert itself as an independent princely state. Mamola's wise and far-sighted navigation of Bhopal's destiny during these difficult and uncertain times was thus a major achievement. In fact, it was Mamola Bai who first recognized the importance of seeking British support against the irredentist pressures from her neighbours by

---

[1] See Appendix 4.

providing General Goddard with a warm welcome during his cross-country march in 1778.

Unlike Fatah Bibi who had been wooed and won over by Dost, Mamola Bai came to Yar as part of the spoils of conquest. She has been described as a remarkably talented woman of matchless beauty, and obviously possessed remarkable traits of character. As soon as she became Yar's consort, Mamola Bai assumed a dominating influence in Yar's court through her wisdom, compassion and strength of character. Some chroniclers, like Malcolm, have stated that Yar never formally married Mamola, but this may have been due to her being a Hindu who later converted to Islam. There is no doubt, however, that Mamola became Yar's principal consort and adviser. Mamola is said never to have had issue from Yar and yet her life was spent ensuring that her stepsons succeeded Yar as the third and fourth Nawabs of Bhopal, often against violent claims from other contenders of Dost's offspring. Indian history is replete with Hindu wives making extraordinary sacrifices for their husbands and it falls entirely within the realm of credibility that Mamola dedicated herself to ensuring that the sons of her husband from Muslim wives should succeed Yar to their rightful heritage. As Yar's dowager and the dominant personality in his court, Mamola assumed full charge of the state and it was she who appointed ministers and ordered military campaigns against Faiz's uncles Sultan and Sadar. It was she who decided to placate the Marhattas through negotiations and to introduce a system of administration that was fair and just. It is testimony to her skilful exercise of power that, once the initial threat from the family to Faiz's assumption of the gaddi had been neutralized, there was no major threat to Faiz's reign from within.

It is evident that the majority Hindu population of Bhopal, as indeed the neighbouring Hindu chieftains, welcomed the fact that the effective ruler of Bhopal was a Rajput princess, albeit converted to Islam, assisted by a Hindu Chief Minister, Bijjeh Ram, while Faiz and Hayat were the nawabs in name. The Muslim gentry of Bhopal, and especially the Barrukat Pathans, were obviously won over by Manji Saheba's personality, her devotion to her stepsons' cause and her effective exercise of power in safeguarding Bhopal's territorial integrity. The fact that she built three mosques and took a leading role in social welfare activities endeared her to the people of Bhopal. Mamola Bai was known for her benevolence, charity and kindness especially to the poor. Chroniclers record that she would not eat her evening meal until she was satisfied that no one went hungry in her state. She was also a courageous woman who led from the front. When she decided to occupy the Raisen Fort which was held by a Moghul appointee, Mamola Bai led the Bhopal force herself on horseback and succeeded in defeating the Moghul force. Later, she showed herself to be a diplomat and a stateswoman by sending emissaries and gifts to the Moghul Emperor, eventually persuading him to formally assign Raisen to Bhopal.

So revered was she by the Muslims of Bhopal that when she fell seriously ill and went into a coma, a Muslim saint, Shah Ali Shah, announced that he would ask Allah to take ten years off his life and spare hers. In strains of Babar circling Humayun's dying body,[1] the saint went into seclusion to pray for Mamola Bai's revival. On the seventh day of prayer, Shah Ali Shah died and Mamola Bai recovered to widespread rejoicing. To this day, the island on the lake where Shah Ali Shah is buried retains his name and an annual Urs is attended by pilgrims from far and wide.

Mamola Bai's greatest contribution to the foundation of the state was her decision to establish the first cooperative links with the British by providing relief and succour to General Goddard when he passed through Bhopal in 1778. These links were strengthened by succeeding rulers, but it required immense farsightedness – or perhaps sheer instinct – to recognize the advent of an emergent political force that would eventually provide Bhopal with support and security to exist as an independent state. Mamola Bai's decision to help Goddard against the general trend of public opinion required courage and far-sight, qualities that enabled her to navigate Bhopal through the most turbulent waters during the 50 years of chaos and mayhem in India following the collapse of the Moghul Empire.

An intriguing trait in Mamola Bai's character is revealed by her decision to adopt four Hindu boys and convert them to Islam. Was this done to demonstrate to her Muslim constituents that she was the servant of Islam, like her sons Faiz and to a lesser degree Hayat? Or was the adoption a deep-laid plan to groom a Hindu-born adopted son to wield power under her guidance? This, in fact, is the course that subsequent events took when her fourth adopted son, Chottey Khan, a born Brahmin, was appointed Dewan by Mamola Bai and exercised complete power in Bhopal for 15 years. Mamola Bai must have known that both her sons, Faiz and Hayat, were either unwilling or incapable of exercising power as rulers. This Brahmin convert soon became an aggressive, dynamic and ruthless administrator of the state. Chottey Khan built bridges and moats around the city. He introduced a modern system of administration and taxation. He organized an efficient armed force that was well paid and he improved the hygiene, communications and educational system of Bhopal. Chottey Khan's significant contribution to Bhopal under Mamola Bai's benevolent guidance cannot be denied by Muslim chroniclers who have tended to take a negative view of his ambitious and eventually disloyal character. But an objective assessment leads to the conclusion that during his tenure, there was an all-round improvement in the administration, facilities, security and quality of life in Bhopal. In his history of Bhopal,[2] Major William Hough described Mamola Bai in the following words:

> From the account given of her conduct, under the most trying circumstances, it seems difficult to pronounce whether she was most remarkable for the humanity of her disposition, or the excellence of her judgement. She was beloved and respected by all. Her memory is still cherished by the natives, both Hindu and Mahomedan, of Bhopal, and it is consoling to observe, in the example of her life, that, even amid scenes of violence and crime, goodness and virtue, when combined with spirit and sense, maintain that superiority which be-

---

[1] The first Moghul Emperor Babar, on finding his son Humayun dying of high fever, decided to pray, calling to Allah to take his life and spare his son's. After Babar had circled Humayun's comatose body seven times, Humayun recovered while Babar fell ill and died soon afterwards.
[2] A *Brief History of the Bhopal Principality of Central India.*

longs alone to the higher qualities of human nature; and which, without these, can be permanently conferred by neither title nor station.

The greatest tribute paid to Mamola Bai's humanity and caring dedication to the poor came from Pir[1] Ghous Ahmed Shah Gailani, a direct descendent of one of Islam's most revered saints, Pir Abdul Qader al-Gailani. Pir Ghous Ahmed Shah declared Mamola Bai to be Rabia Basri[2] the Second and had his declaration formally attested by the Moghul Emperor.[3] Mamola Bai was buried in Ginnor Fort.

Mamola Bai's extraordinary de facto reign of nearly 50 years came to an end when both she and Chottey Khan died within a year of each other. There is no question that the first real woman ruler of Bhopal was Manji Mamola Bai, the Hindu princess who governed in the name of her two stepsons and who consolidated Dost's foundations of Bhopal by remarkably astute, enlightened and effective rule over the state. It was Mamola Bai who gave Bhopal stability and effective government. She consolidated the rule of the Bhopal nawabs over a territory whose sovereignty and independence was brittle and fragile. She encouraged harmony between the Muslim elite and the majority Hindu subjects and, above all, managed to placate predatory neighbours to prevent them from undermining Bhopal's sovereignty. She employed tact and diplomacy in keeping internal and external threats at bay and had the farsightedness to recognize that the British were a growing power that could help Bhopal safeguard its independence against hostile neighbours. There can be no doubt that Mamola Bai played a central role in consolidating the foundations of the state of Bhopal and deserves to be recognized as the first Begum of Bhopal.

Dissent and decline

Immediately after Mamola Bai's death, a vacuum developed because Hayat was weak, reclusive, decadent and a known failure. The real contenders for power, his cousins, had either been killed or banished into exile. Hayat, therefore, retained his titular hold on the state while every kind of intrigue and strife began to surface.

On Chottey Khan's death, his son Amir was appointed Dewan. He and his brothers soon came out in the family's true colours. They conspired with Bhopal's enemy, the Scindia Marhattas, and when their conspiracies were discovered, Amir raided the treasury and, making off with 1½ lakhs cash, took refuge with Daulat Rao Scindia. Recognizing Hayat's weakness, and bereft of the guiding influences of Manji Mamola Bai and Chottey Khan, the neighbouring states again began to cast acquisitive eyes towards Bhopal.

Fortunately for Bhopal, the Marhatta kingdoms were themselves in disarray. In Poona, the Peshwa had thrown himself from the top of his

---

[1] A pir is a Muslim saint or religious leader.
[2] Rabia Basri was regarded as one of the most saintly women of Islam.
[3] The original document is in the possession of the author's mother, Princess Abida Sultaan.

palace in a fit of despair with the royal household. The same year, 1794, Mahadji Scindia died and was succeeded by his great-nephew Daulat Rao. In 1795, Ahliya Bai died in Indore, unleashing a murderous struggle for power in the Holkar family. Daulat Rao Scindia and Raghoji Bhonsle were locked in a major struggle for power with the British which left them little time and energy to address the problem of Bhopal. Nevertheless in 1796 Amir persuaded Daulat Rao Scindia to invade Bhopal with a force of 49,000. Hayat was in no position to take on the Marhatta forces and conceded the forts of Hoshangabad and Raisen. As a result, the Marhattas appointed Himmat Rai as Dewan who became the effective administrator of Bhopal. The prestige and honour of the state was now at its lowest ebb, with Hayat a virtual prisoner and the state occupied and, for the most part, run by Marhatta nominees.

Hayat now realized the folly of having opposed his cousin Shareef and his family. Without the guiding hand of his 'mother', the state was drifting into division and strife. Its administration had been taken over by outsiders who were not even Muslims, let alone Pathans. He deeply regretted having banished Shareef's courageous son, Wazir Mohammad Khan, into exile where he had built up a reputation as a brave swordsman, intrepid fighter and a worthy descendant of Dost Mohammad Khan. Hayat silently wished Wazir would return and help him defend the state.

A complicating factor in Hayat's desire to seek a reconciliation with the remnants of Dost's family was the emergence of his eldest son, Ghous Mohammad Khan, as heir apparent. Ghous, like his father, was a decadent, pleasure-seeking wastrel, whose ambition was focused on the licentious pursuit of women. In 1794, Ghous was married off to Zeenat Begum who had been brought up by Hayat and his favourite wife, Asmat, in the palace. Zeenat was a spirited girl whose mother had died soon after childbirth and whose father, a Barru-kat general, had been killed soon afterwards while leading a Bhopal force against a Marhatta invasion in Sehore. Zeenat had three children from Ghous – Moiz, Gohar Ara (later known as Qudsia Begum) and Faujdar. Zeenat remained loyal to Bhopal's ruling family even though Ghous indulged himself by keeping a harem of numerous wives, courtesans and casual pick-ups. Ghous fathered 16 legitimate children and about 40 outside wedlock.

At this time, when Bhopal's fortunes were at their nadir, a handsome young man, riding on a horse with its tail cut off, arrived at the gates of Bhopal's fort. He was Wazir Mohammad Khan who had learnt of Bhopal's travails and had arrived to bury the hatchet with his cousin and save Bhopal from annihilation. Wazir had been banished by Chottey Khan after the Battle of Phanda and had taken up service with a Rajput chieftain, Hati Singh, for whom he distinguished himself as a noble, fearless warrior. Later, Wazir was employed by the Nizam of Hyderabad where he enhanced his reputation further as a leader and military tactician. Hayat embraced Wazir and wanted to appoint him Dewan and Commander-in-Chief of the army in place of Himmat Rai. However, Hayat was opposed by his son Ghous who recognized in Wazir a threat to his power and influence. Accordingly, Wazir was not given office but allowed to stay in Bhopal where his stature and following among the public increased with every passing day. Pressurized by his wife Asmat and his son, Hayat then decided to send for another cousin, Murid Mohammad Khan, son of the conspirator Sultan Mohammad Khan, as a replacement for Himmat Rai.

Murid's entry into Bhopal on 20 May 1796 saw the arrival of an unctuous, reptilian villain capable of unbelievable treachery. Murid arrived, accompanied by 1000 followers, ostensibly to loyally serve the Nawab and the state after the trauma of Hindu Raj. On entering Bhopal territory, he vowed to expiate all non-family influences and to redeem Dost Mohammad Khan's honour. In a theatrical display of religious incantations, Murid pretended to humble himself at the graves of his ancestors where he wailed and cried in a prayer that lasted several hours. He then proceeded to the palace to prostrate himself before the Nawab and his wife Asmat. Murid was described as having the mien of a usurer and soon he had ingratiated himself into the household of Hayat and Asmat, who foolishly saw in this vile conspirator the saving spirit of Bhopal. So deeply did Murid ingratiate himself with Hayat that Ghous was temporarily relegated to a secondary position in the exercise of power.

Murid was sworn in as Chief Minister in 1796. He soon embarked on a policy of high spending which initially impressed the Bhopali people. The armed forces' pay was raised, promises were made to the civil servants and a programme of public works implemented. Murid knew that the treasury could not sustain this high expenditure and soon began to put pressure on the jagirdars to contribute to state finances. When they declined, they were put in prison and tortured and their families harassed.

Within a year, Murid's mask was lifted, revealing his true face. Secretly, he made a deal with the Pindaras and gave away tracts of Bhopal territory. Meanwhile, the army, not having been paid, mutinied, which made Murid pressurize the nobles even further. By now, the Marhatta threat began to loom even larger, and so Murid sought a private meeting with Asmat in order to raise finances to defend Bhopal.

Asmat was Hayat's favourite wife. She was the daughter of a musician and not part of Bhopal's gentry. Asmat was, however, beautiful, accomplished and assertive so that she soon assumed a dominating influence in Hayat's court. Chroniclers likened her role to that of Noor Jahan with the Emperor Jahangir.

After Mamola Bai's death, Asmat had become the effective ruler of Bhopal, taking all decisions in the name of her husband and with the advice of her favourite eunuch and constant companion, Gulab Khwajah. On 30 December 1797 during this period of turmoil, Asmat sat behind a curtain in the private quarters of her palace, while Murid pleaded with her to provide jewellery and cash so that the Marhattas could be opposed. Asmat declined and asked Murid to raise funds through taxes. Furious, Murid pulled out a dagger, tore down the curtain and attacked the defenceless Asmat. She ran upstairs screaming for help, but Murid grabbed her and killed her with vicious dagger thrusts while his accomplices murdered her protecting eunuch, Gulab Khwajah. Murid then plundered the cash and jewels from Asmat's house.

Asmat's household was stunned by the sudden, brutal murder of the Begum, but the spirited Zeenat raised the alarm and called out the guards. His treachery exposed, Murid announced that he had been put up to murdering Asmat by her stepson, Ghous. However, no one believed Murid, whose villainy was now completely unmasked. He then declared open rebellion against Hayat and took over the Fatahgarh Fort. From there, he sent a message to the Marhatta leaders, offering his support to them and inviting them to take over Bhopal. Meanwhile, Hayat realizing Murid's treachery and that he had murdered his favourite wife, at last summoned Wazir Mohammad Khan to save Bhopal from Murid's villainy.

Wazir, loyal and patriotic to Dost's memory, responded immediately to Hayat's desperate call. He gathered a force of about 1000 tribesmen, entered Bhopal across the Pukka Bridge Chottey Khan had built and effectively took charge of the state. Wazir immediately set about recovering Hoshangabad Fort, occupied by the Nagpur Marhattas; after a fierce battle, he led his force with remarkable valour and recaptured the fort. Meanwhile, Murid sent messages to General Bala Rao Anglia of Gwalior, who was governor of Sironj, and to Raghuji Bhonsle of Nagpur to support his insurrection against the Bhopal Nawab. Bala Rao sent a force to Murid with a condition that one of the two major forts be handed over to him. Desperate, Murid agreed to transfer Islamnagar to Bala Rao. He set out for Islamnagar to hand over the fort personally to Bala Rao, leaving a Marhatta contingent in Fatahgarh palace to watch over Hayat and Ghous, who were placed under house arrest.

On reaching Islamnagar, Murid was refused entry into the fort by Moti Begum, Hayat's spirited sister, whose guards attacked Murid. Thwarted by this brave woman, Murid now turned to Raisen and, after securing it, made good his promise to the Marhattas by surrendering Raisen to General Bala Rao. Murid was now ready for the final act of treachery against the state, the Nawab and his own family. He conspired with the Marhattas and raised a force of 40,000 and set out to besiege the Fatahgarh Fort. The die was cast. Murid had the support of Gwalior, Nagpur and the Pindara Amir Khan of Tonk, while Hayat was supported by Wazir and Kuli Khan, the Jagirdar of Ambapani, who had earlier conspired with Najaf to end Chottey Khan's rule.

The siege of Fatahgarh Fort was bravely resisted by Wazir and ended with Bala Rao withdrawing, unwilling to engage in a murderous battle with the Bhopalis, at least for the present. Shortly afterwards, Bala Rao discovered that Murid had lied and cheated on him also, with the result that the allies fell out. Bala Rao imprisoned Murid in Sironj where he committed suicide by swallowing diamond dust, perhaps the only courageous act in his life. So deep was Bala Rao's suspicion of Murid's capacity for treachery that, fearing Murid was faking death, he did not allow his corpse to be buried until it actually began to decompose. Murid is buried in Sironj and so detested is his memory by Bhopalis that legend makes it incumbent on a Bhopali to strike his grave with a shoe five times instead of praying for his salvation.

In the 70 years after Dost's death, Bhopal had barely managed to maintain its independence. From the halcyon days of Dost's daring adventures which led to the founding of the state, Bhopal had first to bow to the superior force of the Nizam and then to the Peshwa. Fortunately for Bhopal, Mamola Bai's far-sighted diplomatic skills saw her cede territory in order to retain a modicum of self-rule. The Battle of Panipat saved Bhopal from total Marhatta domination, but the Marhatta overlords Scindia and Bhonsle continued to threaten Bhopal's independence and had often to be bought off by the surrender of territory and forts and the payment of tribute. When Mamola Bai and Chottey Khan died leaving Bhopal in the hands of two decadent nawabs – Hayat and Ghous – the state began to slide back into dissent, intrigue and weakness. It would have sunk without trace but for the advent of a figure as brave, capable and charismatic as Dost Mohammad Khan in the person of his great-grandson, Wazir Mohammad Khan.

3

The Siege of Bhopal

Having successfully repulsed the Marhattas and overcome Murid's villainous machinations, Wazir was acknowledged as the de facto ruler of Bhopal. Immensely brave, chivalrous, humble and a true stalwart, Wazir symbolized the best of Dost Mohammad Khan's legendary personality. Wazir was appointed Dewan and Commander-in-Chief by Hayat in 1797 to massive rejoicing among the people of Bhopal. Wazir's reputation as an intrepid fighter, natural leader and loyal supporter of the Bhopal ruling family meant that the people of Bhopal, its feudal gentry and even his adversaries recognized him as the real power in Bhopal. Only his loyalty and innate nobility prevented him from actually taking over the title of Nawab. As Wazir's reputation grew so too did, in inverse proportion, the jealousy and insecurity of Hayat and Ghous.

Wazir soon set about repairing the damage of Hayat's feeble regime by recovering the territories that had been frittered away during Hayat's rule. The administration was geared up, the morale of the army raised to a high pitch, and the vicious palace intrigues scotched under a firm and enlightened leader. From the edge of the precipice, Wazir had hauled Bhopal back to respectability in the eyes of its own people, its neighbours and the British East India Company, who began to take notice of this maverick Muslim state surrounded by Rajput and Marhatta neighbours.

Between 1801 and 1807 when Hayat died, Wazir engaged in a vigorous campaign to recover the territories and forts that the weak rulers of Bhopal had ceded to its neighbours. Wazir's efforts were partially successful, but inevitably aroused the hostility of his two powerful neighbours, the chieftains of Gwalior and Nagpur. In 1804, Daulat Rao Scindia formally claimed Bhopal as a tributary, a claim that was staunchly denied by Wazir with the support of the British who were locked in a struggle for supremacy in the region with the Marhattas. Wazir thus began negotiations with the British for a treaty that would give Bhopal protection again its neighbours. These negotiations became protracted because Ghous, the heir apparent, was amenable to striking treacherous deals with Gwalior and Nagpur, leaving the British unsure of Bhopal's commitment to resisting Marhatta power. Ghous's treachery is described by Major William Hough as follows:

So eager was this prince to ruin Vizier Mahomed, that he engaged to surrender the fort of Islamnuggur, pay four lakhs of rupees in cash, and present an annual tribute of 50,000 to Sindiah, with 11,000 rupees to his public officers. Having consented to these terms, he proceeded to Bhopal, after being invested with an honorary dress by Dowlut Rao Sindiah, whose ostensible support he seems to have thought sufficient to maintain him in power; nor does he appear to have met with any opposition on the part of Vizier Mahomed. But what could Vizier Mahomed do while the Nawab was alive, and the son was permitted to exercise the powers of Nawab: and the minister had not always possessed the full executive authority.[1]

Ghous Mohammad Khan
Fifth Nawab, 1807-27

Hayat died on 17 November 1807, aged 73, after a fairly inglorious reign of 29 years. He was succeeded 18 days later by his spoilt and decadent heir, Ghous, as the fifth Nawab of Bhopal. It was not long before Ghous's deep-seated hostility towards Wazir came to the surface. Soon after his *gadda-nashini* (coronation), Ghous struck a number of treacherous deals with Rajput neighbours and Nagpur Marhattas, secretly ceding parts of Bhopal territory to them. Ghous then banished Wazir from Bhopal.

Rather than cause a family crisis and risk an internecine war that could be ruinous for Bhopal, Wazir rode quietly away on his tail-less horse, Pankhraj, to take up residence in the fort of Ginnor. His was an act of supreme dignity and sacrifice which, nevertheless, plunged the people of Bhopal into despair because Wazir, alone, had the leadership and charisma to defend the state against its powerful neighbours.

Ghous's weakness and constant bargaining with his Marhatta neighbours soon led to Raghuji Bhonsle seizing his opportunity to overwhelm Bhopal. He sent a force of 40,000 under his able general, Sadiq Ali, who took over Bhopal and demanded that Ghous hand over Wazir and his wife as hostages. Ghous agreed to hand over Wazir, but refused to give up Wazir's wife. Sadiq Ali decided, instead, to take Ghous's son Moiz and returned to Nagpur leaving an occupying force in Bhopal with Ghous a virtual prisoner. No sooner had Sadiq Ali left than Wazir swooped down from Ginnor and, in a lightning assault, routed the Nagpur force and resumed governance of Bhopal. Wazir then accused Ghous of supreme treachery and the wretched Nawab passed the blame on to his Hindu advisers. Exacting exemplary punishment, Wazir had two of these advisers, Munshi Suraj Mal and Bani Lal, stuffed into cannons as human cannon-balls and blown to smithereens. The remaining traitors, Lalji Mustafa and Lala Roop Chand, were trampled to death by elephants in full public view. Ghous's humiliation was complete and he was banished to Raisen, never to exercise executive authority again, but still retaining his title as the Nawab of Bhopal.

The Marhattas were, of course, furious at Wazir's presumptuous counter-attack. Accordingly, Gwalior and Nagpur resolved, jointly, to

---

[1] *A Brief History of the Bhopal Principality of Central India.*

defeat Wazir and to carve up the state between themselves. By 1812, the die was cast as the joint armies of Scindia and Bhonsle were ready for their onslaught on Bhopal. As the Marhatta peril mounted through threats and impossible demands, a deep sense of foreboding and despair overcame the people of Bhopal.

During these years, Wazir passed through a harrowing time in attempting to keep the state intact against predatory onslaughts from powerful neighbours and vicious intrigue at home. Both Hayat and, after his death in 1807, Ghous were titular nawabs who were weak, indolent and treacherous. Ghous, in particular, conspired with the Marhattas to 'rid Bhopal of Wazir's menace' and frequently bartered away forts and large tracts of Bhopal territory to curry favour with Gwalior and Nagpur. Holkar, which had not threatened Bhopal during Ahliya Bai's lifetime, once she had died also joined in attempts to subjugate Bhopal. Moreover, the powerful Pindaras were a menace to be contended with. Wazir battled away bravely against these threats, sometimes compromising with one or two of his opponents to gain time and breathing space for the defence of his state. Fortunately for Bhopal, the two major Marhatta states, Scindia and Holkar, were engaged in a murderous battle for supremacy during a 20-year war that saw them virtually bleed each other to death. For Bhopal, the greater threat came from Daulat Rao Scindia of Gwalior and Raghuji Bhonsle of Nagpur. By 1812, Gwalior and Nagpur had decided to join hands to, once and for all, jointly overcome Wazir's resistance and to carve up Bhopal between them.

During this period, Wazir sought Bhopal's salvation in British support, recognizing their growing power and the fact that the Marhattas constituted the major threat to their supremacy in India. Accordingly, he sent endless messages to the Governor-General and to British army commanders soliciting a treaty of friendship. The British were initially inclined to respond to Wazir's entreaties but drew back from committing their support, partly because they did not entirely trust Wazir and partly because they still hoped to neutralize the Marhattas by compromise. When Gwalior and Nagpur invaded Bhopal in 1812, Wazir stood virtually alone as the British had not decided on signing an alliance with Bhopal.

Thus, in October 1812, as the vast Marhatta armies converged on Bhopal, its people faced the greatest crisis in Bhopal's history since Dost Mohammad Khan had, almost 100 years earlier, hoisted the Bhopal ensign on the Islamnagar Fort. The defining test of Wazir's mettle, and indeed of Bhopal's survival, had come. Seeing Bhopal re-emerge as a major state in the region and despairing of Bhopal's earlier propensity to destroy itself through division and intrigue, the neighbouring states of Gwalior and Nagpur joined hands to provide the coup de grace.

The Siege of Bhopal, 1812–13

The Siege of Bhopal is an epic in its history and deserves a detailed account as it symbolized the extraordinary resilience and spirit of the people of Bhopal, especially its women.

On 15 October 1812, the joint force of Gwalior and Nagpur, numbering 82,000, marched towards Bhopal under the famous Scindia General, Jagua Bapu. He was joined by a Nagpur force under the Muslim General Sadiq Ali. Wazir could muster only 11,000 able-bodied fighters made up of Bhopal's Pathan army, Rajput allies, Sikh mercenaries and Pindari fighters from neighbouring Tonk. Rather than seek an open battle, Wazir wisely ordered the closure of the gates to the Fatahgarh Fort with the entire population of Bhopal seeking shelter within. Jagua Bapu, his second-in-command General Kachua and Sadiq Ali decided to encircle the fort and lay siege to it. The siege endured for nine months[1] with life inside the fort becoming desperate to the point of capitulation. Almost every day, the Marhattas would attempt entry by storming the gates or stealthily throwing rope ladders over the walls at night to scale the walls of the fortress. Day and night, the men and women of Bhopal resisted these efforts by pouring boiling water on the attackers and meeting them with a barrage of rocks and stones. Women, often dressed up as men, would appear on the ramparts to mislead the besieging force into believing that the fort was defended by more men than was actually the case.

A few weeks into the siege, Wazir's allies, the Rajput, Sikh and some Pindari forces decided to quit and withdraw from the fort. The Bhopal force, consisting mainly of Afghans, was now reduced to 6000. Later still, hunger, deprivation and hardship led to Ghous's resistance giving in. Wazir negotiated a safe passage for this idle and worthless ruler to occupy a house outside Bhopal where he resided in relative comfort, accompanied by his retinue of eunuchs and courtesans. It is a measure of Ghous's value that the besieging force saw no advantage in taking him hostage. Surprisingly, Ghous's first wife Zeenat and her eldest daughter Qudsia[2] did not accompany him and bravely decided to stay on in the fort to rally their people in resisting the siege.

There were a number of occasions when the Marhatta forces almost succeeded in gaining entry into the fortified area. On one occasion, the Budhwara gate was attacked and the guards eliminated. The gateway was forced open but Sardar Bakhshi Bahadur Khan, the Commander-in-Chief and most loyal of all the Barru-kat Pathans, assisted by a few soldiers, fought a rearguard action. The women of Bhopal joined in and began stoning and pouring boiling water on the invaders. When Wazir was informed of the incursion, he rushed to Bakhshi Bahadur's help and managed to throw out the Marhatta invaders. It was a narrow escape in which Sardar Bakhshi Bahadur was severely wounded, but the breach had been prevented.

The siege endured week after week, month after long month. While the Marhatta armies waited patiently for the inevitable capitulation, the besieged Bhopalis were given to eating leaves and boiling shoe leather for nourishment. The main source of food came from the loyal Rajput

---

[1] Some chroniclers state that the siege lasted six months.
[2] Qudsia's real name was Gohar Ara. She later assumed the name of Qudsia by which she is referred to throughout this book.

zamindars Ratan Singh and Aman Singh who, under the cover of darkness, would bring cartloads of grain through the jungle to an appointed spot on the far side of the lake overlooked by the Fatahgarh Fort. At a given hour, well past midnight, Wazir and a few trusted companions like Shahzad Masih and Bakhshi Bahadur would slip stealthily through the rear gates of the fort and swim across the lake with their empty mushuks. These mushuks would be filled with grain and on return, rationed out to the starving population. Another source of food was the Hindu corn-merchants who had been commissioned to supply the besieging Marhatta army. Exorbitant sums were paid to the merchants in surreptitious deals that led to a minimal supply of wheat into the besieged fort. The corn-merchants sold wheat to the Marhatta army at one rupee for five seers. They black-marketed the wheat to the Bhopalis at ten rupees a seer.

Faced as they were with extreme danger and even annihilation, the Siege of Bhopal brought out the best and the worst in the people. While there were numerous examples of heroism and sacrifice, Bhopal also saw acts of treachery, for instance when guards were bribed to open the Budhwara gate. By the sixth month of the siege there was nothing left to eat, lack of water and of sanitation and pestilence all around. The enemy attacked every night. Ammunition was almost exhausted and morale was reaching dangerous depths of despair.

Led by the brave Zeenat Begum, the women of Bhopal, both Muslim and Hindu, played a vital role in the siege. They threw off their veils and became an effective defensive rearguard in support of the beleaguered Bhopal army. They supplied food and water to the men who guarded the ramparts. They learnt to fill cannons with gunpowder and sometimes, dressed as men, would load and fire the cannons themselves. They quickly acquired the technique of musketry and even evolved their own method of crisis defence by filling stoves with dynamite and throwing these home-made explosive devices at intruding enemy columns.

The siege was also a great leveller between the nobility and the ordinary folk, the rich and the poor. In this burning cauldron of suffering, the women of Bhopal were a great source of strength. They were led by Ghous's sterling wife, Zeenat Begum who chose to stay behind in the fort with her 14-year-old daughter Qudsia, while her decadent husband decided to move out into comfortable house arrest. Zeenat rallied the women by her example. Rich and poor sat shoulder to shoulder at her open table. One day, her cleaning woman was late, explaining that her children had not eaten for two days and she had boiled some *imli* (tamarind) leaves to sustain them. Zeenat immediately asked her daughter to bring out the two chapatis that had been kept for her son Faujdar and hand them over to the cleaner. Qudsia gave the cleaner one chapati, hiding the other under her clothes for her little brother. As the cleaning woman was leaving, Zeenat stopped her and counted the chapatis. She then turned angrily to her daughter and said, 'I knew you would cheat and keep one for your brother. I told you to give both chapatis to the cleaner woman.'

On another occasion, Zeenat's eldest son Moiz, who had earlier been returned to Bhopal by Raghoji Bhonsle, was manning a cannon on the ramparts of the fort when he was wounded by enemy musket-fire and fell unconscious. Zeenat rushed to the rampart, dressed her son's wound with her *dopatta* (long scarf worn across the body) and took over the loading and firing of the cannon herself for several hours until Moiz revived.

Eventually, after nine months of deprivation, when resistance was at an end, a council of war was held by Wazir. He announced that he would ask for safe passage for the women and children and the remaining 300 able-bodied men would mount a final, suicide attack on the besieging Marhatta army. Accordingly, Qazi Mohammad Yusuf and Maulvi Nizamuddin were sent out as emissaries to the enemy to negotiate free passage for the women and children. Legend has it that when the last rites had been completed, Wazir went to the resident Pir called Pir Mustan Shah (the Dancing Pir) and laying his sword and turban at the Pir's feet asked to be given his final blessing. The Pir went into a trance of devotion and suddenly putting his ear to the ground began chanting 'Fatah, fatah, nacho, nacho' ('Victory, victory, celebrate, dance'). He then pointed to a spot in the fort and asked Wazir to dig. There, in a shallow depression, the Bhopalis found a hidden arsenal of dynamite.[1] Filling their cannons with gunpowder, they decided to postpone their surrender for a day. The next morning, the parapets of the fort were lined with women dressed up as men to show the Marhattas that the Bhopalis had a significant force available. They then prepared themselves for the final assault on the besieging army. At this point, Qazi Mohammad Yusuf and Maulvi Nizamuddin resigned in disgust, rightly feeling that they had been used and their word undermined.

Unknown to the besieged Bhopalis, Jagua Bapu's army had suffered from a grievous attack of cholera which had devastated its strength. Moreover, Sadiq Ali, who commanded the Nagpur army, had fallen out with Jagua. Legend has it that he was visited in a dream by a saint who admonished him for the sacking of fellow Muslims in the fort of Fatahgarh. The following day, Sadiq Ali decided to withdraw. Thus, miraculously, on the fateful morning, Sadiq Ali and Jagua's forces were in disarray and had decided to withdraw from the siege. When the gates were opened for the final assault, only a weakened part of Jagua Bapu's force was besieging the fort.

With cannons, fired by women, booming from the Fatahgarh ramparts, Wazir with his loyal men mounted a ferocious attack on Jagua's forces and put them to flight. Sardar Bakhshi Bahadur Khan was again wounded in battle with a gashed stomach but, strapping up his protruding entrails with his turban, continued the battle until Wazir's forces achieved a heroic victory. Jagua Bapu died of cholera and Kachua committed suicide by swallowing diamond dust as he saw his force

---

[1] Another version is that an old servant of Nawab Yar Mohammad Khan recalled that the late Nawab had stocked dynamite in a secret chamber of the fort. 500 bags of dynamite were found in the chamber indicated by the old man.

retreat. Incredibly, Bhopal was saved. Wazir had turned the tide in the most historic battle recorded in Bhopal's annals.

The heroic defence of Fatahgarh Fort saw Wazir recognized as the saviour of Bhopal and for the first time since Dost, Bhopal was ruled by a charismatic leader under whom the family, the nobles and the people of Bhopal united in total obeisance. True to his noble tradition, Wazir declined to formally claim the title. He pensioned off the treacherous, decadent Ghous to Islamnagar, still treating him as the titular Nawab even though he was now a spent force.

Wazir Mohammad Khan – An assessment

By 1813, Wazir's epic triumph in resisting the Siege of Bhopal left him the undisputed hero, saviour and de facto ruler of the state. Triumphant and resurgent, Bhopal emerged from its major crisis, the second most important Muslim state in India after Hyderabad. It was now firmly on the map, having weathered the onslaught of the Marhattas. Like his great-grandfather Dost, Wazir was a brilliant military strategist and charismatic leader. His fearsome reputation, especially after the Siege of Bhopal, spread like wildfire across the region with the result that Wazir, despite continuing hostility from Gwalior, Nagpur and the Pindaras, recovered most of the lost territory.

Wazir was a man of extraordinary qualities. He was immensely brave, gifted in physique, noble and dedicated to the family's honour. Some of his exploits illustrate his unique character. Before the siege, Wazir was persuaded by a relative, Kuli Khan, to join him in a campaign against a Nagpur incursion. The two forces joined together after a long march and Wazir pleaded with his colleague to postpone battle till the following day as the Bhopal forces were tired. Kuli declined and engaged immediately in battle. Predictably, the Nagpur contingent had the better of the skirmish and looking back, Wazir saw Kuli deciding to withdraw his force. Kuli called on Wazir to join him in retreat, but Wazir replied that once he went into battle, he would either die or win. Wazir fought on with a few brave stalwarts who eventually put the Nagpuris to flight.

On another occasion, Wazir was touring the villages, riding his tail-less horse, Pankhraj, when he was ambushed by a contingent of Marhattas. Wazir galloped away with the assassins in pursuit and came to a river 12 yards wide. He approached it at full gallop and saw Pankhraj jump the entire breadth of the river, taking his master to safety while his pursuers stood by and watched.

Wazir was also a diplomat. When Ghous treacherously invited the Gwalior Marhattas to occupy the Islamnagar Fort, the Marhatta force was headed by a Muslim General, Hakim Asad Ali. Wazir did not resist the superior force and allowed Asad to occupy the fort peacefully. Wazir knew that Asad's brother had been mistreated by Ghous in the past. In a few months, Asad recognized Wazir's sterling qualities and the esteem in which the people of Bhopal held him for his just and fair governance. He also realized that Ghous was a degenerate and treacherous man.

Accordingly, after six months, Hakim Asad Ali voluntarily withdrew his force from Islamnagar and announced that Wazir was the rightful leader of the Muslim state and its people.

Soon after the Siege of Bhopal came another defining moment of Bhopal's history that has so far been passed over in virtual silence. Stung by the failure of the siege, Daulat Rao Scindia began preparing another force to punish and subjugate Bhopal. Gwalior again claimed Bhopal as a tributary state and demanded subjugation. At this point, the British Resident,[1] Sir Barry Close, stepped in and conveyed a clear warning to Gwalior that the British would not countenance the subjugation of Bhopal and would support its territorial integrity which the British proceeded to define. For several years, Gwalior insisted with the British that, according to a treaty with the Marhattas signed in 1805, Bhopal was a tributary of Gwalior, but the British steadfastly refused to accept Gwalior's contention. Eventually, in 1819, the Governor-General wrote to the Maharajah of Gwalior and also to Nagpur, Indore and Hyderabad informing them that the British did not accept Gwalior's suzerainty over Bhopal – a state that was considered independent and under British protection.[2] Gwalior heeded the Governor-General's warning, returning five districts to Bhopal's territory and the forts of Islamnagar and Raisen, which approximated to Dost's initial conquest. The East India Company's warning to Gwalior and its support for Bhopal symbolized the predominant influence of the British in Malwa as also the pattern of alignments that the Company had decided to pursue in the region.

Wazir established regular contact with the East India Company sending emissaries to General Sir John Ochterlony in Delhi with a copy of General Goddard's testimonial. Later, he entered into correspondence with the Governor-General Lord Wellesley and other officials of the Company. British support for Bhopal's territorial integrity was the logical progression of events that began with General Goddard and continued throughout Bhopal's history. Sir Barry Close's support for Wazir against the gathering onslaught by Gwalior was another milestone in Bhopal's history.

Wazir then raised armed contingents and finances to support the East India Company's campaign to suppress the resurgent Pindaras. This support strengthened further the evolving relationship between Bhopal and the East India Company. Surprisingly, Lord Minto, the Governor-General, declined attempts by Wazir to sign a treaty – an event that took place only after Minto had been replaced by Lord Hastings and Wazir succeeded by his son Nazar. British documents indicate that several factors combined to oppose the signature of a treaty with Bhopal. First, a policy decision was taken by the Governor-General (Lord Minto) not to sign formal treaties with the princely states – a decision that was reversed soon afterwards by Lord Hastings. Secondly, the British were

---

[1] Resident is a synonym for Agent to the Governor-General (AGG). The Resident supervised the work of Political Agents appointed to princely states.
[2] Federal Department Political Consultation (FDPC) Records No. 60 dated 18 May 1815, Indian National Archives, New Delhi.

not absolutely sure of Wazir's reliability as an ally because they had intercepted messages between Wazir and Jean Baptiste Filoze, the French commander of the Gwalior army. Wazir had also formed secret alliances with the Pindaras chiefs Chitu and Karim Khan who were being mercilessly hounded by the British. A third possible reason for British hesitation could have been their doubts about the principal Bhopal negotiators, Inayat and Shahzad Masih, who were Frenchmen. Thus, negotiations were engaged, but no treaty signed with the British during Wazir's lifetime.

Wazir's rule lasted until 1816. It was an enlightened reign during which the army was strengthened, the administration tightened up, taxes collected and peace and amity restored between feuding nobles and different segments of the Bhopali ethnic mix. The town flourished and technicians, craftsmen, administrators and literary figures were encouraged to make their homes in Bhopal. Peace and security pervaded the realm under Wazir's enlightened, just and progressive administration.

By 1816, Wazir was the most powerful ruler Bhopal had known since Dost. He had, however, become addicted to alcohol, an addiction that gradually undermined his health. Wazir died on 16 March 1816 at the age of 50. He was buried at Bara Bagh. Sir John Malcolm's appraisal of Wazir provides an apposite epitaph for the saviour of Bhopal:

> Wazir Mohammad died in February [sic] 1816, A.D., aged fifty-one, after having governed Bhopal little more than nine years; but of this short period he had not passed one day in repose. This principality, from the hours he assumed the Government until that of his death, was threatened with destruction. Such a man could alone have saved it. Though as remarkable for prowess and valour as the most desperate of the Afghan race, he was, in his manners, mild and pleasing; but his look and stature were alike commanding, and there was in his disposition a sternness that inspired awe.[1]

The Bhopal Bourbons

In the early years of Bhopal's foundation, the influence of two famous families of Bhopal left a deep imprint on its history. The first was a branch of the French Bourbon family which had wandered into Bhopal in 1783 and eventually decided to settle there. The second was the Mishti-khel Pathans of Tirah who had joined Dost in his adventure when he settled in Bhopal.

The history of the Bhopal Bourbons is so romantic that it is almost unbelievable. Pieced together from family annals and chroniclers of the Bhopal Bourbons, the extraordinary story begins around 1560 with Jean-Philippe de Bourbon de Navarre, a close relative of Henri IV. A high-born aristocrat and son of the Constable of Pau in southern France, Jean-Philippe had the misfortune of killing a Gascon aristocrat in a duel. Fleeing to Portugal, he set sail from a Mediterranean port, was captured

---

[1] *A Memoir of Central India.*

by Turkish pirates and sold for 2000 ducats as a slave to the Ottoman Emperor Sultan Soliman the Magnificent, who occupied Egypt at the time. In Cairo, the Sultan recognized Jean-Philippe's qualities as a military strategist and a man of culture, employing him in a high-ranking position. When Soliman died in 1566 and the Ottoman rule in Egypt collapsed, his successor placed Jean-Philippe in prison from where, with the help of some Abyssinian Christians, he made his escape, landing in Abyssinia. From there, Jean-Philippe, accompanied by a small group of Indian Christians, set sail for India. He sailed round the eastern coast of south India to the mouth of the Hoogli River near Calcutta. Thence he travelled by boat, mooring every night, up the Rivers Ganges and Jumna to Delhi, where the Moghul Emperor Akbar the Great was at the height of his imperial power. Letters of introduction obtained him an audience with the greatest of Moghuls, on whom he made an immediate favourable impression. Tall and of gallant bearing, he coloured the tale of his own achievements and high family connection in true Gascon style and so impressed the Emperor that he was given charge of reorganizing the Moghul army's artillery and a grant of land with the title of Nawab.

The family annals of the Bhopal Bourbon family provide an even more romantic version of Jean-Philippe's escape from Egypt to Abyssinia. This account describes Jean-Philippe's Egyptian imprisonment in a large compound in which thousands of slaves and prisoners were kept. In this prison, the Bourbon aristocrat met an old woman, also a prisoner, who was called 'Maryam the Sorceress of Ethiopia'. In fact she was the dowager queen of Ethiopia whose son had been deposed and killed by a usurper in a palace coup. The King's mother had been sold as a slave in Egypt. Jean-Philippe, and Maryam the Sorceress, accompanied by her granddaughter Madelena, made a courageous escape from prison and returned to Abyssinia to lead a cabal against the usurper. Thanks to Jean-Philippe's brilliant strategy, the usurper was defeated at the Battle of Debrador and Madelena restored to her father's throne. By now, Jean-Philippe and Madelena had fallen deeply in love and decided to get married. Fearing the wrath of her grandmother for marrying a 'foreigner', the young couple decided to elope to India, Madelena giving up the throne and riches that were hers by right. By the time Jean-Philippe reached Bengal, his beautiful Abyssinian wife Madelena appears either to have died or turned back to her homeland.

The extraordinary adventure of the handsome and brave Bourbon aristocrat in India continued at the court of the Moghul Emperor Akbar with the arrival in Delhi of two beautiful, young Portuguese sisters, Maria and Juliana Mascrenhas. These girls were of noble birth and had set sail from Portugal to be betrothed to Portuguese military and civilian officers who had reached the zenith of their power on the west coast of India, notably Goa. However, as often happened in these turbulent times, a Dutch privateer got wind of the boatload of attractive cargo and waylaid the ship before it could reach port. The Portuguese girls were then taken to the port of Surat and sold as slaves to the highest bidder, a fate worse than death for girls of sheltered backgrounds. However, some of the lovely Portuguese girls found happiness – one of them was crowned Queen of the Maldives – while the two sisters Maria and Juliana Mascrenhas were taken by a slave trader to the Emperor's court in Delhi. Allured by their beauty and grace, the Emperor Akbar made Maria his Christian wife in his large harem. Maria soon became a favourite among Akbar's many wives, to the extent that one of the murals in the Emperor's palace at Fatehpur Sikri is adorned by her fresco.

The extraordinary romantic history of the Bourbons of Bhopal relates to the fate of Maria's sister, Juliana, who was appointed 'doctor' to the imperial *zenana* (women's quarters). Juliana was not a qualified doctor, but had probably acquired a rudimentary knowledge of nursing. Since Jean-Philippe de Bourbon was already a notable figure at Akbar's court, the Emperor decided that Jean-Philippe and Juliana Mascrenhas would make an ideal match and should get married. Neither party complained. Jean-Philippe found a beautiful Christian wife who already enjoyed the benevolence of the Emperor through her sister, while Juliana accepted as her bridegroom the debonair Bourbon aristocrat who had been made responsible for reorganizing the artillery of the Moghul army and who was already a favourite of the Emperor. On their marriage, the couple were granted a large estate in Shergarh south of Delhi where Jean-Philippe established himself as governor in splendour and luxury. The couple had children and grandchildren on the vast seraglio and built a Catholic church and cemetery for the Bourbon family in Agra.

After Jean-Philippe's death his son Alexandre became a favourite of Akbar's son, the Emperor Jahangir. The Bourbon family continued to live in Shergarh through prosperous times until the fall of the Moghul Empire. Then in 1740, when Nadir Shah sacked Delhi, the Bourbons abandoned their estate in Shergarh and moved to Gwalior where Salvador de Bourbon, the senior member of the Bourbons from Shergarh, was appointed by the Moghul Emperor as killedar of the famous and impregnable fort of Gwalior. By then, Moghul rule was crumbling fast, leading to widespread plunder and chaos. The Marhatta Confederacy had mounted the major assault against Moghul bastions and Gwalior, along with its fort, had fallen to the Marhatta chieftain, Mahadji Scindia who imprisoned Salvador and his family in the fort's dungeon. Then, in 1780, Colonel Popham, in his famous and daring capture of the Gwalior Fort, rescued the Bourbon family, but Salvador decided to move on and rode away from Gwalior to neighbouring Bhopal, which had the reputation of being a tolerant and peaceful state. In Bhopal, Salvador was welcomed by Mamola Bai and allowed to settle with a grant of land, an hospitable act that was repaid to the Bhopal family over and over again in the following years.

Salvador de Bourbon – known in Bhopal as Inayat Masih – reached Bhopal around 1783, probably liked the beauty of Bhopal's landscape and its tolerant atmosphere, and decided to drop anchor in the state. With the passage of time, Salvador's family took a fancy to their new environment and obviously to their compatriots to whom they gave their total loyalty. In 1786, Inayat Masih, who married a Miss Thome, had a son Balthazar – known as Shahzad Masih – and they soon became leading figures in the Bhopal court. Inayat was not only a brilliant tactician, but as an educated man of breeding, his advice on martial, administrative and even personal matters was regarded as invaluable. Inayat Masih became a trusted friend of Wazir Mohammad Khan who appointed him to high military posts. He died around 1817, leaving his young son, Shahzad, to carry on the Bourbon tradition in Bhopal.

Over a period of time, these fair-skinned, handsome, talented *farangis* (foreigners) became part of the scene in Bhopal. They were loyal and trusted and showed no inclination to return to their homeland. Like his father, Shahzad Masih was a man of outstanding qualities. A scholar, military strategist and brilliant organizer, his hobby was to dismantle and re-assemble clocks. In due course, Shahzad Masih decided to live permanently in Bhopal and integrated himself totally in the life of Bhopal. He learnt Urdu and Farsi to the extent that he wrote poetry under the *nom de plume* of Fitrat.

Wazir, his younger son Nazar, Inayat Masih and Shahzad Masih fought many a battle together, side-by-side. This trial in blood and adversity set the seal on their friendship and probably on Shahzad's decision to stay on in Bhopal. From being roaming adventurers, a kind of refined hired gun, Inayat and Shahzad Masih gave up their entire family and European upbringing to become loyal supporters of the house of Bhopal. From the role of military tactician, Shahzad Masih graduated to a position of political counsellor and trusted family friend of Bhopal's royal household. He was one of Bhopal's pillars of strength during the siege, organizing defences, bravely warding off the Marhatta onslaughts and swimming across the lake with Wazir to fetch rations from the loyal Rajput thakurs.

Clearly, the Siege of Bhopal consecrated the loyalty and friendship that the Bourbon family developed towards the Wazir-khel branch of the Bhopal dynasty. The siege had shown up the loyal from the intriguers, the brave from the cowardly, the stalwarts from the idle and pleasure-loving. Inayat and Shahzad had thus made common cause with Wazir, Nazar, the Mishti-khels and their brave womenfolk who had discarded their veils and their effete way of life to help defend Bhopal's citadel. Theirs was a bond formed in extreme adversity and forged in steel, in which they jointly opposed the Marhattas who had earlier persecuted many of the Bourbon family and turned them out of Gwalior.

During the siege, Inayat and Shahzad Masih distinguished themselves in bravery and loyalty to the Bhopal ruling family. They admired the courage, resilience and moral strength of Zeenat and her 15-year-old daughter Qudsia who was to marry Wazir's son Nazar. Later, Shahzad Masih's personal devotion to Qudsia saw him pass through numerous sacrifices and always remain at her side as the family's most trusted supporter.

One of the most bizarre and romantic images was the confrontation, after the siege had been broken, between Inayat Masih leading the Bhopal forces and his Bourbon cousin, Jean Baptiste Filoze, who was providing similar expertise to Scindia of Gwalior. They met on the battleground at Sehore, leading opposing armies. They are said to have recognized each other, embraced and decided that it was futile continuing the battle after the siege had been broken. The Gwalior Bourbon then withdrew his forces from Bhopal and prevented further bloodshed.

When Wazir died in 1816, Shahzad Masih transferred his total loyalty and friendship to Nazar, the younger son who succeeded Wazir by consensus. In fact, it is virtually certain that it was Shahzad Masih who persuaded Wazir to nominate Nazar as his successor in preference to his elder son Amir. Shahzad Masih was also prominent in moving Bhopal to sign a treaty of friendship with the British and it was he who represented the Bhopal nawabs in negotiating the treaty which was signed in 1819 between Bhopal and the East India Company.

After Nazar's death, Shahzad Masih gave his full support to Nazar's young widow, Qudsia to rule Bhopal as Regent. It is certain, that without the support of the powerful and influential Bourbon, Qudsia's regency would not have been accepted, especially as male contenders with legitimate claims to succession were available.

Shahzad Masih married and brought home from Delhi a young English girl called Isabella Stone – the daughter of an English nobleman – who was given the title of 'Sarkar Dulhan'. Isabella established a close friendship with Qudsia and became an influential member of Bhopal's ruling circle. Shahzad Masih was poisoned by jealous Afghan courtiers and died in 1829 at the age of 43. He is buried in the Catholic cemetery at Agra. His young widow continued to live in Bhopal with her two children. Qudsia and her daughter Sikandar Begum continued to shower Sarkar Dulhan and her children with affection and favours which meant that the Bourbons of Bhopal prospered and became leading members of Bhopal's gentry. Sarkar Dulhan built a Catholic church and a cemetery and became a prominent social worker in Bhopal. Her son Sebastian was, briefly, Prime Minister to Sikandar Begum. So deep was the Bourbon influence on Bhopal that the Begums adopted the Bourbon *fleur de lys* as the state's ceremonial emblem. Sarkar Dulhan lived to a ripe old age of 80 and died in 1882, a year after Qudsia Begum.

The Bhopal Bourbon family's fortunes began to decline in the reign of Bhopal's third Begum, Shahjehan, when she came under the influence of her second husband, the bigoted Siddiq Hassan. Their jagirs were cancelled and the Bourbon family properties recovered by the state. Gradually, the Bhopal Bourbons lost influence, became poor and faded from the scene, but they remained in Bhopal, faithful to their family roots and to their Christian ideals. Their fortunes did not revive under Bhopal's fourth and last Begum, Sultan Jahan. Though Sultan Jahan was a deeply committed Muslim, she was tolerant, liberal and a reformer. Yet she continued the ostracization of the Bourbon family in Bhopal who had, by then, inculcated middle-class professional values in their children so that they became doctors, priests, nurses and teachers living in Bhopal's Christian enclave.

The Bhopal Begums, even Shahjehan, were generally tolerant of non-Muslims and encouraged them to build their temples and churches and to freely engage in their religious functions. Rather than religious bigotry, the reason for the Begums' ostracization of the Bhopal Bourbons probably lies in their indignation over the allusions that the Bourbon family annals have perpetuated regarding Shahzad Masih's romantic liaison with Qudsia Begum. The Begums, particularly Sultan Jahan, considered these allusions to be a slanderous vilification of the chaste and puritanical Qudsia whose entire life-style negated any such 'scurrilous' aspersion.

Thus, to this day, the Bourbons survive in Bhopal, proud of their heritage, faith and tradition. Princess Abida Sultaan, Sultan Jahan's granddaughter and the author's mother recalls her Bourbon schoolfriends whose fair complexions and blue eyes set them apart from other schoolgirls. She recalls that their Christianity was never a negative factor, but that Sarkar Amman (Sultan Jahan Begum) never warmed to the Bourbon family, probably for family reasons.[1]

The Mishti-khel of Bhopal

The second family that made a deep impact on Bhopal was that of Bakhshi Bahadur Mohammad Khan, the brave Commander-in-Chief of the Bhopal army during the siege. Bakhshi Bahadur was the descendent of Kilig Khan, son of Bayazid Khan, who belonged to the Mishti-khel[2] clan of the Orakzai tribe and came to Bhopal from Tirah with Dost's family. After Dost's death, Kilig's son, Umar Khan, loyally served Bhopal's second Nawab, Yar Mohammad Khan, and Umar's son Alif continued the family tradition and became Nawab Faiz Mohammad Khan's force commander. Alif passed on the banner to his son, Mohammad Khan, who served Hayat during Chottey Khan's administration. Mohammad Khan's son, Bahadur, continued the long family tradition and became the outstanding military figure of the time. During Wazir's rule, Bahadur Mohammad Khan earned his spurs for extreme bravery and became known as a legendary fighter and military strategist. Bahadur was given the title of Bakhshi – Commander-in-Chief of the Bhopal forces – and remained totally loyal to Qudsia Begum during her regency. Along with Shahzad Masih, he helped to scotch the revolts that were hatched by Qudsia's male relatives. Eventually, having to choose between serving Nawab Jahangir Mohammad Khan and the Begums, ousted by the British, he escorted the Begum's palanquin to Islamnagar with his two teenage sons, Sadar and Baqi, walking with swords unsheathed on each side.

On Bakhshi Bahadur's death in 1849, his elder son Sadar took over the command of the Bhopal forces. His younger brother Baqi was made Deputy. Sadar died relatively young in 1851 and was succeeded by his younger brother Bakhshi Baqi Mohammad Khan, who served Sikandar Begum as loyally as his father had Qudsia. Eventually, Sikandar rewarded generations of unstinting loyalty by the Mishti-khel Pathans by

---

[1] See Bourbon family tree in Appendix 5.
[2] See family tree of the Orakzai settlers of Bhopal (Mirazi-khel, Mishti-khel and Jalal-khel) on p 262.

ordering Baqi to marry her only daughter, Shahjehan, giving him the title of Umrao Doulah.

Bakhshi Bahadur's family were brave, fearless fighters who gave their total loyalty to their leader. Typical of Bakhshi Bahadur's legendary bravery and loyalty was an incident during the siege when Wazir decided to hold a council of war and seek amnesty. Bakhshi Bahadur turned to his ruler and said, 'Young man, you can offer amnesty if you like, but every drop of my blood is dedicated to defending these barren rocks of Bhopal. You go. I will stay.' They all stayed.

This form of total devotion seems a speciality of the Sub-Continent and of the princely states of India where loyal followers made the greatest personal sacrifices without demur, sometimes to the most capricious whims of their masters. Umrao Doulah died in 1867. His only surviving daughter from Shahjehan (he had several children from earlier marriages) was Bhopal's last Begum, Sultan Jahan. The Mishti-khel or Baqi-khel remained the most loyal and most prominent members of the Bhopal gentry.

Wazir died almost 100 years after Dost had planted Bhopal's ensign on Fatahgarh Fort. During this century, the wheel of Bhopal's fortune had turned full circle as Wazir recovered territory that had initially been conquered by his great-grandfather, but had been mostly lost by succeeding generations of weak rulers. Both men were incredibly brave, totally dedicated to the salvation of Bhopal and gifted with extraordinary powers of leadership. Dost had won territory after the abrupt decline of the Moghul Empire which saw a vacuum of power develop in Malwa. Wazir won back lost territory from powerful neighbours and successfully threw off the tutelage of the Nizam and the Marhattas to regain Bhopal's independence. During this period, the nawabs after Dost had mostly been abject failures, frittering away territory won through blood and sacrifice. Only Mamola Bai had managed to preserve the core of the state on which Wazir built a new foundation. Bhopal would certainly have subsided were it not for the extraordinary courage and leadership of the Nawab with the tail-less horse.

Shrewdly, Mamola Bai had read the first signs of Britain's capacity to help Bhopal and welcomed General Goddard. Subsequent rulers had sought to consolidate this bond in order to resist pressure from neighbouring Marhattas. With the British increasingly dominant throughout India in the first half of the nineteenth century, the die was cast for a relationship of mutual support between Bhopal and the British East India Company.

Nazar Mohammad Khan, 1816–19

Wazir married two Hindu wives. The first, Rani-jee, was the daughter of a *pandit* (Hindu religious scholar). The second was a Rajput lady who bore him two sons, Amir Mohammad Khan and Nazar Mohammad Khan. Amir was spoilt and pleasure-loving, while Nazar Mohammad Khan was a young man who had inherited his father's qualities of leadership, dignity, charisma and nobility. He had fought alongside his father in many of the battles with the Marhattas. He had also taken part in the heroic resistance during the Siege of Bhopal. Like Wazir, Nazar had earned the respect of the people of Bhopal. The crown was officially worn by Ghous who languished contentedly in a palace knowing that Wazir, through his innate decency, would not allow any harm to come to him. Nevertheless, for all practical purposes and to the people of Bhopal, Wazir Mohammad Khan was the Nawab of Bhopal.

On Wazir's death in 1816, the nobles and people of Bhopal who had suffered grievously under two weak rulers, quickly closed ranks behind Nazar Mohammad Khan as the chosen (elected) de facto ruler, conveniently bypassing the older Amir Mohammad Khan on the grounds that the discarded Nawab, Ghous, was still alive. This manoeuvre was carried out efficiently by the two stalwart power-brokers of Bhopal, Bakhshi Bahadur Mohammad Khan and Shahzad Masih, both of whom considered Nazar the ideal successor to Wazir. They both gave their full support to Nazar so that the succession went through smoothly. A legalistic solution to the problem of succession to Wazir's de facto rule had already been found in the betrothal of Nazar Mohammad Khan to one of Ghous Mohammad Khan's 65 children, Qudsia Begum. Thus, after Wazir's death, even though Ghous was alive, there was no question of the real succession passing to anyone other than the capable son of the heroic saviour of Bhopal. Wazir had announced Nazar's engagement to Qudsia a few months before he died. Nazar married Qudsia in 1817, a year after he became de facto ruler.

In terms of legal and customary law of succession, Nazar being accepted as Nawab had profound repercussions, particularly 100 years later during the 1925 succession case (Chapter 8). The special points of interest were, first, that Nazar was the younger of Wazir's two sons. Secondly, the titular ruler Ghous himself and his legitimate sons, Moiz and Faujdar, were alive and were claimants to the gaddi. Nazar's succession was, therefore, based on: i) the fact that he was a lineal descendant of Dost (and of Wazir); ii) that the Bhopal *ulema* (clerics) and family caucus considered him the most worthy; iii) that he was betrothed to the titular ruler's daughter and their offspring would be expected to combine the two contesting streams; and iv) that the East India Company – the new sanad-holder – raised no objection to Nazar becoming the Nawab. Nazar's de facto succession in 1816 was, therefore, unanimous and smooth. Within a year, he improved on the excellent administration of his father and fully earned the respect of the people of Bhopal. Nazar was seen as an even more accomplished personality than his father since, allied to his courage and statesmanship, Nazar was educated, urbane and sophisticated. He was particularly clean in his personal life, doing away with courtesans, lackeys and an expensive life-style. He married once, Qudsia, and did not keep a harem.

Nazar continued to nourish the friendship between Bhopal and the East India Company that had first been recognized by Mamola Bai and subsequently confirmed by his father, Wazir. Nazar supported General Adams, the British commander who set out to defeat the Pindaras, by raising 51 lakhs of rupees in financial support and helping General Adams with arms and soldiers. In recognition, the British formally handed back to Bhopal the five parganas ceded to the Marhattas and also the Hoshangabad and Islamnagar Forts which had been occupied by Scindia. The main difference between Wazir and Nazar was that, as de facto ruler, Nazar increasingly assumed all powers of the Nawab of Bhopal though he did not actually depose Ghous. The Bhopal public, the neighbouring states and the East India Company referred to Nazar Mohammad Khan as the Nawab of Bhopal without questioning the legality of the epithet because Ghous was still alive.

The treaty between Bhopal and the East India Company

In 1818, encouraged by Shahzad Masih and Bakhshi Bahadur, Nazar Mohammad Khan signed Bhopal's first treaty with the British East India Company who were convinced of Nazar's loyalty after he had supported the British campaign against the Pindaras.

The treaty was negotiated at Fort Raisen between Captain Stewart representing the East India Company and Sardar Bakhshi Bahadur Mohammad Khan, assisted by Shahzad Masih, acting on behalf of Nawab Nazar Mohammad Khan.[1] The treaty was signed on 8 March 1818 and ratified within two days by Lord Hastings and Nawab Nazar Mohammad Khan, thereby granting the seal of authority on Nazar as Nawab of Bhopal.

The 1818 treaty between Bhopal and the East India Company was a defining event in Bhopal's history, securing the independence and territory of the Muslim state surrounded, as it was, by powerful Marhatta and Rajput neighbours. The British East India Company saw Bhopal as an ally against their most dangerous adversaries in the region, the Marhatta kingdoms of Scindia and Holkar. The treaty formed the bedrock of Bhopal's sovereignty. It also provided the British with a means to maintain stability in central India and to oversee internal developments in the state.

In essence, the treaty guaranteed Bhopal's security and territorial integrity in return for acceptance of the East India Company's overall sovereignty. 'The friends and enemies of one would be the friends and enemies of both.' The Nawab and his heirs were to act in 'subordinate cooperation' with the British government and would not enter into negotiations with any neighbour or state except with the British government's prior approval. In return, the Nawab and his successors would remain 'absolute rulers of their country and British jurisdiction would not be introduced in any manner into the principality'. The British were given a garrison to which Bhopal agreed to provide 400 troops and 600 horses. Immediately after the signature of the treaty, a British garrison was located in the cantonment at Sehore which also became the resi-

---

[1] The treaty is reproduced in Appendix 6.

dence of the Political Agent who reported to the Agent to the Governor-General in Indore.

Then, on 10 November 1819, tragedy struck the Bhopal firmament. While Nazar had taken his infant daughter, Sikandar, to relax at the Islamnagar Fort, his eight-year-old cousin, Faujdar Mohammad Khan (Qudsia's younger brother), playing with a loaded pistol, 'accidentally' pulled the trigger and fatally shot Nazar in the temple. Nazar died immediately, leaving the Bhopal royal family, its nobles and its public in a state of shock, turmoil and acute distress.

Another version of the tragic incident is that Nazar was assassinated by Faujdar who was coached by rival members of Nazar's family to pull the trigger on him while he slept. Pathan boys learn to handle weapons at a young age and it is conceivable that Faujdar deliberately shot and killed Nazar Mohammad Khan. In this way, Ghous Mohammad Khan's family aimed to regain the title and power from the 'saviour' of Bhopal, Wazir and his son Nazar. While Wazir had ruled Bhopal through a de facto exercise of power and had not challenged Ghous's legal title, Nazar had lost no time in having himself recognized as the legal and de facto ruler of Bhopal. Ghous and his sons had everything to gain by Nazar's death as they reasoned that the title and power would revert to Ghous and his direct descendants. Politically, therefore, the assassination theory makes sense.

Major Henley, the Political Agent sent a report of Nazar's death to the Secretary of State[1] in which he stated that the pistol shot that killed Nazar had been fired from such close range that the Nawab's hair had been singed and his facial skin burnt. Henley had no doubt that Faujdar had fired the pistol, probably accidentally.

Major Hough describes Nazar Mohammad Khan's qualities in the following terms:

> Nazar Mohammad Khan, when he died, was only 28 years of age; he had governed Bhopal, Malcolm says, three years and five months; but he has left a name that has been attained by few during the longest life. Schooled in adversity, he early attained a remarkable maturity of judgement. His appearance was noble, and his manners those of a prince who knew the value of possessing the hearts of his subjects. His mind was so superior, and his courage so elevated him above suspicion, that the whole family of the rulers of Bhopal whom he had supplanted, as well as his elder brother who had resigned his birthright to him, lived not only without restriction, but on the most intimate footing of familiarity with him, coming and going through every apartment of his palace at their pleasure. Nazar Mohammad held in just detestation the vices and indulgences to which some Mahomedans are addicted. His Haram contained but one princess, and no slaves. He was a good Mahomedan, but so far removed from bigotry, that his favourite companion and minister, was a *Christian*, by name Shahzad Masih or Belthazar Bourbon, with whom Sir John Malcolm was well acquainted.[2]

---

[1] Major Henley's report is reproduced in Appendix 7.
[2] A *Brief History of the Bhopal Principality of Central India*.

4

Qudsia Begum, 1819–37

Qudsia's regency, 1819–37

Stunned by the news from Islamnagar, Bhopal was plunged into a state of despair and uncertainty. The stability that Wazir and Nazar had brought to Bhopal through strong leadership and fair governance was again at risk as there was no obvious successor to Nazar. The light that had been provided by father and son to the people of Bhopal after the siege had gone out. Suddenly, they were looking down a dark tunnel. As a pall of gloom settled over Bhopal, the main contenders to mount the *masnad*[1] girded their loins and prepared themselves for a protracted battle of succession.

Amir Mohammad Khan, Nazar's elder brother, was the leading contender. He had been passed over in favour of his younger brother but, as Wazir's elder son, was the first claimant. He was supported by his wife, Munawwar Jahan, and her brother, Asad Ali Khan of Basoda, who became Amir's principal adviser and schemer. The second aspirant was Moiz Mohammad Khan, Ghous's eldest son and Qudsia's real brother. Though Ghous was still alive,[2] he was too feeble and discredited to reclaim the gaddi for himself. Moiz thus considered himself heir apparent to the title of Nawab. In the third group of aspirants were other direct descendants of Dost Mohammad Khan and also the remainder of Ghous's brood of 60 children who fancied their chances to fill the power vacuum. Of course, the British Political Agent, Major Henley, was expected to have a strong, perhaps determining, influence on the issue of succession.

In this atmosphere of gloom and foreboding, the family gathered for the *soyem* (mourning ceremony) at Nazar's palace on 13 November 1819, with all the contending rivals for the succession present in the durbar hall. Nazar's supporters, Mian Karam Mohammad Khan (a loyal, Mirazikhel cousin), Hakim Shahzad Masih, Bakhshi Bahadur Mohammad Khan and Raja Khushwakt Rai (a wise, Hindu administrator) – the Loyal Quartet – were also present, as were senior state officials including the state's religious functionaries, the Qazi and the Mufti.

---
[1] A ceremonial carpet usually signifying ascension of the throne; alternatively, seats of honour.
[2] Ghous died in 1826; his wife, Zeenat, in 1827.

In this room stood Qudsia, veiled in a burqa, the tall, willowy, 19-year-old widow of Nazar Mohammad Khan with her 15-month-old daughter, Sikandar, clutching her tightly by the hand. Qudsia was several months pregnant with her second child.

As soon as the eldest family member had completed his funeral oration, tension bristling among the various family heads, the congregation was shocked to see Qudsia take off her veil, move to the centre of the room and, in a calm and dignified address, hold the gathered congregation in awe by her passion, her impeccable reasoning and her extraordinary oratory. Qudsia stated that Bhopal could only survive through unity, surrounded as it was by enemies. The sacrifices of Dost, Wazir and the family would be dissipated if there were rival factions seeking power. The competing strains of the family had come together in her marriage with Nazar and to reverse this unifying bond would be catastrophic for the family and for Bhopal. The only way forward was for all branches of the family to recognize her daughter, Sikandar, as the rightful ruler. Until Sikandar reached the age of maturity and married, she, Qudsia Begum, would govern the state as Regent. Qudsia then produced Nazar's will in which he had ordained that, in the event of his premature death, Sikandar should be declared the ruler and Qudsia act as Regent until Sikandar's marriage to 'a close family member' who would then become the Nawab. Qudsia added that this succession was also the wish of the people of Bhopal and sanctioned by the religious authorities. She then challenged anyone who objected to her proposal to speak out. Everyone kept silent, partly because by raising an objection, they would have attracted the accusing finger of suspicion over Nazar's death.

Qudsia's address to the family is one of the most poignant moments in Bhopal's history. A girl not yet 20, brought up traditionally in purdah, had dared to take the congregation of elders, rival family contenders and senior state officials by the scruff of their necks. Qudsia had taken full charge of the meeting and through a brilliant and passionate address won the day. The Loyal Quartet, who had rallied to Qudsia's side after Nazar's death, were the first to announce their allegiance. The remaining members of the congregation followed suit and soon the town was rejoicing with the news that Sikandar was to be ruler and Qudsia Begum the Regent. Thus, in 1819, began the first period of women's rule in Bhopal which lasted almost uninterrupted for 107 years.

To contain their opposition, Qudsia shrewdly struck deals with her rivals for power. She bought off her elder brother, Moiz, by giving him a jagir knowing that he would dissipate himself in the pursuit of carnal pleasures, shikar and a life of ease. Her younger brother, Faujdar, who had pulled the trigger on Nazar, was still too young to pose a threat and was taken under Qudsia's wing. Turning to her principal rival, Amir, Qudsia agreed to betroth her daughter Sikandar to Amir's elder son, Munir, so that on marriage, he would take over as the Nawab of Bhopal. As Sikandar was only 15 months old, Qudsia could count on at least 16 years of regency before Sikandar reached marriageable age.

Armed with these deals, Qudsia approached the British Political Agent, Major Henley, for approval. To strengthen her case, she referred to Nazar's will. There is no doubt that the British, equally shocked at Nazar's death, had reservations about a woman taking control of a state in which the East India Company had obviously made a political investment by opposing Marhatta dominance of the region. Evidently, the British saw greater chances of continuing stability in Bhopal if the reins of control were held in the hands of a man rather than a woman. Faced, however, with a virtual fait accompli that had family consensus, the general public's support and the backing of Britain's staunch Bhopali friends – the Loyal Quartet – the British acquiesced in the arrangement and gave their seal of approval to Qudsia's regency, pending her daughter's marriage to Amir's son when power would be transferred to the male consort.[1] It was a fairy-tale arrangement which had little relevance to the earthy power-play that later degenerated into a vortex of intrigue, division and attempted murder.

Thus, on 13 November 1819, three days after her husband's death, Qudsia Begum boldly announced herself as Regent on behalf of her infant daughter. To counteract the *Shariat* (Islamic law) being quoted as an impediment to women's rule, Qudsia had a document attested by the highest religious authorities, the state Qazi and the state Mufti, acknowledging a woman's right to govern. She then had the document countersigned by her nobles, jagirdars, officials and kinsmen, no doubt under the benign and supportive gaze of Sardar Bakhshi Bahadur Khan and Shahzad Masih. All this tension and the malicious rumours implicating Qudsia in her husband's violent death took a heavy toll on Qudsia who miscarried on 18 November, thereby ending the possibility of a male heir who would unite the Wazir and Ghous branches of Dost's family.

After Qudsia's miscarriage, Major Henley the British Political Agent sought advice from Colonel Maddocks, the Resident in Indore, regarding the Bhopal succession. The British officers agreed that Sikandar's betrothal to Munir, which had the family's blessing, should be confirmed and that according to Nazar's will and Qudsia's specific commitment, Munir should be declared Nawab. Accordingly, on 9 December 1819, the British formally seated Munir on the masnad and in a public durbar announced him as the Nawab of Bhopal. Qudsia was to act as Regent until Sikandar was old enough to have *rukhsati* (conjugal relations) with her consort. Meanwhile, Munir would be brought up in Qudsia's household and groomed to take over responsibilities as Nawab of Bhopal.

Having overcome the immediate crisis of her husband's death, Qudsia realized that in the lawless jungle of post-Moghul India, it was a question of survival of the fittest. She took riding lessons, attended military exercises, learnt the art of war, camped in the outlying villages to meet the ordinary country-folk and actually led her troops in military skirmishes. Herself a devout Muslim, Qudsia Begum refused to accept that Islam had precluded women from governing their own states. She

---

[1] Political Agent Major Henley's report dated 26 November 1819, India Office Library, L/RIS/10/1114.

quoted references in the Quran and Hadith to the Queen of Sheba and to the Jang-e-Jamal in which the Prophet's wife, Hazrat Ayesha, had led the Muslim force. Qudsia Begum maintained that any prohibition against women assuming political power had been introduced by vested interests and that Islam had never forbidden women from exercising such power. Otherwise, she argued, the Prophet's Companions would never have followed Hazrat Ayesha in her campaigns or accepted her leadership.

Qudsia Begum thus became the first protagonist in favour of recognizing a Muslim woman's legal right to rule a state. Earlier, the women of Bhopal, Fatah Bibi (1709–25), Mamola Bai (1730–94) and even Bahu Begum (1755–77) had exercised de facto authority. None had claimed the legal right to rule. Qudsia Begum broke fresh ground by asserting a Muslim woman's right to legally assume the title of ruler against the claims of valid male heirs. At least in south Asia, she was the first Muslim woman to assert this right successfully. It is a remarkable feat that Qudsia, who lived to the age of 80, saw three succeeding generations of women rulers of Bhopal; two of them, her daughter Sikandar (1847–68) and granddaughter Shahjehan (1868–1901), actually assumed the title of ruler of Bhopal in her lifetime. The third, Sultan Jahan Begum (1901–26), knew her great-grandmother as a child and was proclaimed heir apparent before Qudsia Begum died in 1881.

So with Qudsia Begum's regency began the extraordinary saga of the Begums of Bhopal. Qudsia proved herself to be a woman of unique accomplishment, verve and wisdom. Only 19 years old, she was courageous, wise and decisive as was apparent when she declaimed herself Regent after Nazar's death. She was also extremely shrewd as was evident by her obtaining, in advance, the support of the state's religious functionaries for the concept that woman's rule was sanctioned by Islam. She was astute and diplomatic in gaining time for herself by offering the title of Nawab to a family suitor who would marry her daughter. In this stratagem, Qudsia showed Machiavellian propensities by playing off one rival for power against the other while also keeping British interference at bay. Even Nazar's will, which Qudsia produced, must be viewed with some doubt as it seemed to fit too perfectly into an unexpected event. Above all, Qudsia Begum was fearless in breaking with dogma and tradition in assuming the reins of real power by quickly acquiring the craft of governance.

Though barely 19 years old when she assumed the regency, Qudsia had immense strength of character, drawing from a deep well of Islamic belief. She had seen the best and worst of princely conduct during the Siege of Bhopal when, as a girl, she had helped her mother Zeenat galvanize the women of Bhopal in a heroic defence of their state. On the other hand, her father was a treacherous, lascivious hedonist who, halfway through the siege, preferred the comfort of a palace and the company of his eunuchs and courtesans. Qudsia had not led a protected or pampered life. Nor was she unaware of the decadence of the nobles and the deprivations of the poor. For Qudsia, her mother Zeenat had been a role model – religious, caring, ascetic, fair and egalitarian. Qudsia believed in these virtues and implemented them in her daily life.

Young Qudsia's early years as Regent saw her focus on two main fronts. She had to prove to the British and to her own people that, as a woman, she was a worthy ruler and successor to Wazir and Nazar. Secondly, she had to keep a close watch on Amir and his brood who were impatient for Munir to marry Sikandar and take over the reins of power. Though superficially cordial, the two households watched each other like hawks, always ready for a swift manoeuvre to gain advantage.

Qudsia's administration

In the first decade of her regency, Qudsia Begum consolidated her hold on power. She introduced administrative reforms that helped effective governance of the state. She led her armies by example, riding out into the field to counter skirmishes and consolidate her power in the state's territory. She built the Moti Masjid (Pearl Mosque) and a number of solid buildings in the city. She broke new ground by employing a British engineer, David Cook, to construct a water pipeline that provided free drinking water to the people of Bhopal through a trust that she created. Later in life, she negotiated a railway through Bhopal and provided funds from her personal account as distinct from state funds for the construction of part of the railway. She also bought *rubats* (lodging houses for pilgrims) in Makkah and Medina[1] to provide Bhopali Hajj pilgrims with free lodging. Above all, Qudsia Begum's rule initiated Bhopal into the tradition of simple living, close contact between ruler and subject, Hindu–Muslim harmony and a deliberate avoidance of the opulence, pomp and decadence normally associated with Indian princely states.

The image of Qudsia's administration was calculatedly Spartan, almost puritanical. Qudsia Begum was known to tour the town in disguise listening to the plaints and comments of the townsfolk. She would regularly ask her sentries if people living in their suburbs had any complaints. She would visit the needy herself and provide relief. She would hold *kucheris* (open-house meetings) in her garden and dispense justice on the spot. She was meticulous in separating state funds from private expenses, insisting that her daily household expenses be met from a small cottage industry that she started from her palace. Within a short time, Qudsia had earned the respect and affection of the people of Bhopal through just governance and personal example.

During this difficult period, Qudsia was supported by the Loyal Quartet who were almost a reflection of Alexandre Dumas' four musketeers. Shahzad Masih had known Qudsia as a brave young girl during the Siege of Bhopal. He had become her late husband's closest friend and trusted adviser. He obviously transferred this deep bond of friendship, perhaps of affection, to this courageous, principled widow of his erst-

---

[1] The Holy Cities of Makkah Mukarrama and Medina Munawwara are referred to simply as Makkah and Medina for brevity.

while friend. Shahzad Masih's devotion saw him by her side throughout the trials and sacrifices that Qudsia and her daughter were to suffer. Bakhshi Bahadur was the wizened, gnarled hero of the Siege of Bhopal. His sons, Sadar and Baqi Mohammad Khan, were worthy and equally loyal sons of a family that was devoted to Wazir's memory and to his family. Mian Karam Mohammad Khan was an urbane, educated and highly respected adviser, of Mirazi-khel stock and a direct descendant of Dost Mohammad Khan.[1] Raja Khushwakt Rai was in the line of Hindu elders who had distinguished themselves in the service of the state and helped consolidate Hindu–Muslim harmony in the realm.

The struggle for power

As an insurance against foul play, Qudsia decided to take her future son-in-law, Munir, under her wing, ostensibly to train him as the future Nawab but, in fact, to keep him as a kind of hostage against Amir and his brother-in-law Asad's machinations. Munir was given tutorials at the palace by learned men and taught the rudiments of administration. Munir, however, showed greater filial loyalty than could be suborned by any inducements that his future mother-in-law could offer and soon joined his father in agitating for a formal ceremonial wedding to Sikandar, even though she was still only a child. Clearly he was egged on by his father whose impatience and ambition were reaching the point of exasperation. Amir pressed his son's claim with the British, based on the pledge made by Qudsia and endorsed by the Resident. He also kept agitating that woman's rule was un-Islamic and pressed Qudsia to perform the *nikah* (marriage contract) immediately, while *rukhsat* (consummation ceremony) could follow when Sikandar reached maturity.

Qudsia played for time. She had already obtained a written undertaking from Amir that in lieu of Munir's betrothal to Sikandar and his eventual takeover of the gaddi, Amir would cease to interfere in her regency. She now pleaded that Sikandar was too young for marriage and that Amir should be patient. 'Are you so dissatisfied with my governance that you are insisting on immediate marriage between two young people who are barely adolescent and who cannot effectively assume the reins of power? Surely you should wait a short while longer,' Qudsia innocently asked of her brother-in-law.

Amir was not convinced and wanted power immediately. Accordingly, he and his brother-in-law, Asad, hatched a plot to overthrow Qudsia. They lured some disenchanted family members, gathered some Rohilla mercenaries and were ready to strike when Qudsia's intelligence network informed her and the Loyal Quartet of the plot. Shahzad Masih decided to counter-attack and immediately took a posse of loyal supporters to Munir's hide-out from where he was to lead the revolt. Fighting erupted in Bhopal and there was some bloodshed. After a four-day skirmish, Shahzad Masih and the loyalists won the day and brought a whinging,

---

[1] Mian Karam Mohammad Khan was the great-grandson of Dost's elder brother, Aqil Mohammad Khan.

contrite Munir to fall at Qudsia's feet, begging forgiveness. Amir and Asad were banished while Qudsia forgave the errant Munir. The British had been alarmed by this encounter and Thomas Henry Maddocks, the Resident in Indore, promised to support Qudsia by sending a British contingent headed by Captain Johnstone from Sehore to Bhopal. The Resident also requested Qudsia not to renege on her initial pledge of Sikandar's betrothal to Munir. Once the dust of battle had settled, the British welcomed Qudsia's forgiveness of Munir and reverted to pressurizing Qudsia for an early marriage.

Realizing that she was being pushed into a corner, Qudsia Begum played another temporizing trump card. In 1827, she declared Munir, the acknowledged suitor-consort, to be impotent! This was an extraordinarily brazen gambit by a religious, ascetic woman in whose household Munir had been brought up. Young men of noble birth were often encouraged by their parents to learn the art of sexual *savoir-faire* from courtesans before they were married. Qudsia now virtually acknowledged that Munir had failed the test. The fact that Qudsia's manoeuvre was a device was proved later by Munir producing several children from a subsequent marriage. Amir then matched Qudsia's stratagem by gaining his younger son Jahangir's betrothal to Sikandar instead of the 'impotent' Munir. This arrangement was supported by the Political Agent and the British hierarchy but gained for Qudsia a few extra years as Jahangir, three years younger than Munir, needed to be groomed for office and was still too young to be married and given full powers of Nawab.

British chroniclers have referred to Jahangir as Amir's illegitimate son. In fact, Jahangir was the son of Amir's second wife, a Muslim from a neighbouring state. He was legitimate since his mother was legally wedded to Amir. The tag of an illegitimate child was attached to children born out of legal wedlock or from courtesans, housemaids or village girls with whom some form of quasi-legal marriage may have taken place. Children of non-Muslim wives who had not converted to Islam were also regarded as illegitimate. Clearly Jahangir did not fall into the category of an illegitimate child.

Lancelot Wilkinson – Political Agent in Bhopal

Twelve years after Qudsia became Regent, an important player entered the stage in Bhopal. He was Lancelot Wilkinson who, in 1830, was appointed the British Political Agent in Bhopal. During his 11-year tenure, Wilkinson played a highly controversial role in opposing Qudsia's regency and promoting the early transfer of power to Sikandar's young consort. Wilkinson's critics state that he was corrupt and won over by Amir's family through expensive gifts, alluring women, pleasurable shikar outings and male camaraderie. He was also seen as a typical pre-Victorian misogynist. Wilkinson disliked the ascetic Qudsia and her woman's rule that, he felt, was unlikely to provide meaningful support to the British against the Marhattas. The other, more charitable, view of Wilkinson's character is that by supporting Amir, he was only implementing a solemn pledge that Qudsia had made to the British government and which she appeared to be reneging on. Secondly, he may have come to the honest conclusion that British interests would be better served by a male ruler than a woman and that the earlier the transition was made the better.[1]

The Political Agent combined the role of today's ambassador with that of civilian administrator. Apart from a small secretariat, the Political Agent could call on the garrison of British troops that were usually billeted in the same town – in the case of Bhopal in Sehore. The Political Agent's principal task was to ensure that British interests were safeguarded, treaty commitments fulfilled and the state's administration carried out in conformity with broad parameters set forth by the Viceroy. Political Agents were initially East India Company employees but with the passage of time, British official hierarchy comprised members of the elite Indian Civil Service which became a crucial pillar of the British Raj in India. The Political Agent exercised a significant influence on British policy towards the state and its rulers, as the Resident's, and ultimately the Viceroy's, decisions were based on the Political Agent's reports and assessments.

On 1 July 1829, Shahzad Masih died at the age of 43. His family annals contend that he was poisoned by Afghan nobles, jealous of his power. Shahzad Masih was buried in Agra at the Catholic cemetery that his Bourbon ancestors had built in the reign of Akbar the Great (1556–1601). His widow Sarkar Dulhan remained in Bhopal and built a Catholic enclave comprising a cemetery and a church which survives to the present day. Shahzad Masih had been a devoted pillar of strength for Qudsia who felt more vulnerable as a result of his passing. Shortly afterwards, in 1830, Lancelot Wilkinson was appointed Political Agent in Bhopal. His tenure, which lasted until his death in 1841, was to have a far-reaching effect on Bhopal. On assuming office, Wilkinson began inquiring from Qudsia when she intended to marry Sikandar to the 15-year-old Jahangir, to which he was given the tart reply, 'Not until he is 19 or 20'. The British continued, however, to insist on an early handover of power to Jahangir on his marriage to Sikandar.

Around 1832, Qudsia Begum decided to emerge from purdah.[2] She had already reigned as Regent for 13 years and the decision to cast purdah aside was obviously profoundly agonizing for a woman who held deep religious convictions. Qudsia reasoned that purdah was more a traditional rather than a religious obligation. Knowing the translation of the Quran by heart, Qudsia must have recognized that while Islam prescribes modesty of appearance and dress for women, it does not prescribe the rigidity of purdah. Moreover, the Prophet's (Pbuh) wives

---

[1] Incidentally, Wilkinson's salary as Political Agent was 2000 rupees per month.
[2] Purdah literally means (behind) a curtain. It is the most extreme interpretation of the Islamic concept of Hejab (modesty in appearance). In its more liberal interpretation, Hejab requires women to wear a scarf over their heads and to cover arms and legs, but in South Asia purdah meant covering the entire body from head to foot (burqa) and the seclusion of women from men so that only husbands and close male relatives were permitted to set eyes on women in purdah.

had not adopted the veil and had attended to state and executive functions without covering their faces. Nevertheless, breaking with long tradition required immense courage on Qudsia's part. Probably political expediency rather than religious rationalization tipped the scales in favour of breaking purdah.

Qudsia had groomed her only daughter, Sikandar, to assume full executive power and realized that Sikandar would be handicapped against her male adversaries if she were to rule from purdah. Secondly, by emerging from purdah, Qudsia may have attempted to impress the British that there were no religious inhibitions to women exercising full executive authority in the state. From 1832, the Begums of Bhopal cast purdah aside with Sikandar and her daughter following Qudsia's example until Shahjehan's second marriage to a religious zealot who drove her back into purdah.

In January 1833, the Governor-General, Lord Bentinck, passed through the neighbouring city of Sagar. Qudsia Begum decided to send Jahangir Mohammad Khan to call on him, accompanied by her loyal advisers now reduced by Shahzad Masih's death to the Loyal Trio. In Sagar, the young 17-year-old consort waited upon the Governor-General. Qudsia's message to the Governor-General was that while she would remain faithful to her pledge of marrying Sikandar to Jahangir, she requested an extension of her regency for a period of ten years, so that Jahangir would become more experienced in the affairs of state. Unknown to Qudsia, Wilkinson had probably briefed Lord Bentinck in advance about Qudsia's attempt to prolong her rule. Jahangir had also been coached by his father and uncle and, in a separate meeting with Lord Bentinck, complained of Qudsia's machinations and affirmed that he was ready to marry Sikandar and assume full powers as Nawab. Lord Bentinck advised Jahangir to be patient but his reply to Qudsia's message was clear. Not agreeing to the extension of her regency, he insisted on an early marriage and handover of power. As a sop, the Governor-General praised Qudsia's rule as Regent and promised her a substantial jagir. He also guaranteed her security. The Governor-General's letter clearly indicated that it was time an interfering mother-in-law allowed free rein to her grown-up children.

Qudsia was furious with the Governor-General's reply. She blamed her advisers for not representing her credentials accurately and questioned Wilkinson's impartiality in his capacity as Political Agent of Bhopal. In 1834, soon after this setback, Mian Karam Mohammad Khan died, leaving Qudsia weakened further, particularly as Bakhshi Bahadur was too old to offer effective support. Only Raja Khushwakt Rai remained of the Loyal Quartet, now joined by Bakhshi Bahadur's sons Sadar and Baqi Mohammad Khan who were every bit as devoted to Qudsia as their father.

During the grooming period, both rival houses for the title had prepared their respective offspring for the role of ruler. Sikandar Begum had been brought up so that she should not feel inferior to any male rival. From a young age, Qudsia impressed on her daughter the virtues of learning the skills of combat, riding, leadership, administration and the arts. She was taught Farsi and the Quran. From her mother, she learnt the craft of diplomacy and how to deal with her subjects ranging from the affluent jagirdars down to the humblest peasant. By the age of 18, Sikandar was exceptionally strong in physique, an outstandingly brave rider, a peerless swordswoman, a crack shot, an able administrator and a charismatic personality. Like Annie, she could boast to any of her male cousins, 'Anything you can do I can do better.' She was not a beautiful woman but handsome and, through her unique accomplishments that were rarely found in women, arrestingly attractive. Qudsia had given her daughter an upbringing that would equip her to resist male domination through her own strength and capabilities. In every sense, Sikandar had fulfilled her mother's highest expectations. At the age of 18, Sikandar presented a picture of an accomplished, attractive and fearsome wife for a prospective husband.

Unlike Munir, his younger brother Jahangir had been brought up in Amir's household. Jahangir was a remarkably handsome and accomplished young man. He was physically powerful, it being said that he could split an ox with one stroke of the sword! He was a splendid horseman, a poet, a shikari and lover of the arts. Being exceptionally good-looking, he enjoyed the good life and the company of courtesans. Jahangir was thus a worthy groom for Sikandar who willingly accepted him as a consort.

However, personal relationships, even union through marriage, had to be subordinated to family loyalty. Both Qudsia and Amir's families saw the impending union between the families and Jahangir's assumption of the title of Nawab as a murderous square-dance of scorpions locked in mortal combat. Each side was not only bent on politically outmanoeuvring the other, they were out to destroy the other. What added extraordinary piquancy to this murderous contest was that Sikandar was in love with Jahangir!

Jahangir's marriage to Sikandar

As months passed and Qudsia continued to temporize, pressures again built up into an armed confrontation between the two households. Amir and Asad, with Wilkinson's support, saw the tide turning in their favour and pressed for an early marriage. Jahangir was nearly 20, ready for marriage and to assume his 'rightful' place as Nawab. Qudsia continued to make excuses to delay the marriage until Amir concluded that Qudsia would not willingly release power and began another round of armed confrontation with Qudsia's forces which erupted around the town of Bhopal. As battle raged, Qudsia touchingly ordered her force to ensure that no harm should come to Jahangir, the prospective consort with whom her daughter was in love. Eventually, the loyal forces gained the upper hand, but this time the British force came from Sehore and stayed. Wilkinson insisted that they would not leave until Qudsia redeemed her pledge 'and the kettle-drums announce the marriage date'. Unable to temporize any further and goaded constantly by Lancelot

Wilkinson, Qudsia decided to celebrate Sikandar's marriage to Jahangir on 18 April 1835.

The union promised to Amir Mohammad Khan 16 years earlier at Nazar's funeral had at last been realized. The wedding was celebrated with great pomp and rejoicing among the people of Bhopal who hoped it signified a reconciliation between the two rival branches of the family. Neither side had any illusions, however, that this union would heal the breach. Amir knew that Qudsia would aim to retain power by manoeuvring to circumscribe her son-in-law's activities. Nor did Qudsia doubt that Amir and Jahangir would attempt to arrogate full power and assume the traditional role of male rulership after a brief 'observation' of Qudsia's regency. In fact, rather than dissipate the tension and latent animosity between the two families, the marriage served to bring the murderous confrontation into the open.

Immediately after the wedding, Wilkinson insisted on the handover of power to Jahangir, but Qudsia stubbornly maintained that he was still not ready to assume the full powers of Nawab. As tension between Qudsia and Amir built up beneath a wafer-thin pretence at cordiality, Jahangir and Sikandar began living together as man and wife. Soon afterwards, Sikandar became pregnant. At this point in time, Sikandar's love for her handsome husband overcame filial loyalty and she too became insistent that her mother hand over the reins of governance to the young couple. Some tension, therefore, developed between mother and daughter.

Hostilities between the two households took a new turn as Amir was totally convinced that Qudsia had no intention of handing over power to Jahangir. He began his campaign to claim the title, warning his son not to be deceived by Qudsia's machinations. In this remarkably hostile, intrigue-filled atmosphere the two young cousins played the role of a honeymoon couple. Sikandar, hopelessly in love with her debonair, flippant husband assumed at night the role of a caring wife – a role that she shed in the morning as she left his bed to ride out and take charge of her state duties as ruler, beside her mother, the Regent.

After the marriage, with Qudsia still clinging on to power, tension between the two families was at breaking point. While Amir and Asad clamoured with the British for the promised transfer of power to Jahangir, Qudsia pleaded for an extension of her regency because Jahangir was still not ready to take on the reins of governance. Staunchly opposed by Wilkinson, Qudsia appeared to be losing ground by the day with only the prop of public support to sustain her regency. As a last resort, she sent a letter to Lord Auckland, the Governor-General who was in Simla for the summer. The letter was carried personally by two loyal emissaries who were charged with the responsibility of persuading the Governor-General to prolong Qudsia's regency by drawing a bleak picture of Jahangir's character and the likely degeneration that would follow after a transfer of power. Lord Auckland received the Begum's emissaries cordially but, in a brutally uncompromising reply to Qudsia Begum, asked her to route all correspondence through the Political Agent whose advice the Governor-General believed was sound and in the Begum's interest. He urged the Begum to redeem her pledge of transferring power to Jahangir. Auckland ended his letter by stating, 'I have nothing more to say to you.' Qudsia was again furious with her emissaries for diluting and soft pedalling her message. Despite the Governor-General's reply, she dug her heels in and refused to hand over power.

Unable to contain themselves any longer, Amir and Asad planned a coup on the occasion of a religious festival in commemoration of Pir Abdul Qadir Gailani. Once again, Qudsia's intelligence network forewarned the Begum of the conspiracy and her loyal force under Bakhshi Bahadur Mohammad Khan managed to pre-empt the putsch and place Jahangir under house arrest. Meanwhile, Amir and Asad gathered in Sehore, obviously at the instance of Wilkinson, and began recruiting a fighting force. In Bhopal, after several days of incarceration, Jahangir made a dramatic escape from custody by disguising himself as a woman, walking barefoot to the outskirts of the town where Amir's emissary, Ghaffur Khan, met him with a horse on which Jahangir sped away to Sehore to rejoin his father and uncle. Throwing all pretence at impartiality aside, Wilkinson gave Jahangir a welcoming salute of 11 guns. Shortly afterwards, Jahangir began running a parallel administration from Sehore by annexing adjoining districts and thereby mounting an open rebellion against Qudsia's regime. Skirmishes between the armed contingents of each side began to take place with Sikandar leading Qudsia's force on horseback, frequently routing Jahangir's men and taunting them for their cowardice.

The final showdown between the opposing family houses took place near Ashta. Qudsia sent Raja Khushwakt Rai to lead the loyal army and, after four days of fighting that left hundreds of casualties, Jahangir's poorly trained army faced defeat. At this point, Wilkinson arrived in Bhopal heading a strong British contingent which again occupied the town. Wilkinson then delivered a letter addressed to Qudsia by Charles McNaughten, the British Secretary of State, insisting that she hand over power to Jahangir as promised. Wilkinson, on whose counsel McNaughten's letter had obviously been written, added his own piece of advice to Qudsia by stating that even though she had won the battle at Ashta, she had to fulfil her pledge of handing over the reins of the state to Jahangir. He also urged Qudsia to send Sikandar back to her husband.

Qudsia hands over power – Jahangir's reign, 1837–44

McNaughten's letter and the British show of force were the last straw for Qudsia. Seeing herself cornered, like a stag at bay, Qudsia decided to hand over power. She quietly and with great dignity obeyed the British edict and withdrew to Islamnagar. Relieved by their successful intervention, the British gave Qudsia a vast jagir comprising 816 villages with an income of 5 lakhs of rupees, and honoured her with an 11-gun salute for life.

Thus, on 29 November 1837, at a special durbar held by the Resident and in the presence of Lancelot Wilkinson, Jahangir was crowned the sixth Nawab of Bhopal to less than enthusiastic acclaim from the public that had come to respect and love the brave, just and puritanical woman who had so successfully ruled the state for 18 years. Amir savoured this moment of triumph that he had dreamed of since the death of his brother. Wilkinson, too, felt vindicated that he had succeeded in replacing the two Begums by a male ruler. On Jahangir's formal installation on the gaddi, his first act was to nominate his uncle Asad as Dewan in place of Raja Khushwakt Rai. He next offered Bakhshi Bahadur Mohammad Khan the command of the Bhopal army and vast jagirs, provided he forsook loyalty to Qudsia. Bakhshi's famous reply to Jahangir was 'I prefer to share half a loaf of dry bread with my benefactors in adversity rather than prosper in the service of a coward'. Bakhshi Bahadur along with his two sons, Sadar and Baqi, with swords unsheathed, then escorted the palanquin which took the Begums from Bhopal to their jagir in Islamnagar. The roles of husband and wife had been reversed. Jahangir was now the Nawab and Sikandar the consort. Suddenly, a sea change had overcome the state of Bhopal.

On becoming Nawab Jahangir, the poet-philanderer, immediately changed the atmosphere of the palace. The stern, Spartan, ascetic regime of Qudsia Begum gave way to decadent high-life with courtesans, dancing girls, wine and merriment. Jahangir occupied himself with tiger hunts, womanizing and abundant drinking. He built a new suburb, called Jahangirabad, a cantonment for the Bhopal army, and also a palace for himself. Almost overnight, the Spartan, simple atmosphere of Bhopal was transformed into a mirror image of the decadent Moghul Court of Delhi.

Qudsia retired to her vast jagir which the British had given her in gratitude for handing over power. Sikandar was a regular visitor to her mother, but willingly returned to her marital bed at night to fulfil her conjugal obligations. Tensions between the families continued to simmer beneath the surface and typical of the contempt in which Sikandar held Wilkinson was an incident when, at a state function, Wilkinson walked up to Sikandar and cheekily touched her diamond earring saying, 'Begum Saheb, what beautiful jewellery you are wearing.' Sikandar, in full public view, proceeded to give him a tight slap across the face, angrily replying, 'Wilkinson Saheb, don't you know that it is an insult to touch a Muslim woman?'

The assassination attempt

All along, Amir kept warning his son to be vigilant against the machinations of his wife and her family which included the powerful Bakhshi Bahadur and his two sons, Sadar and Baqi Mohammad Khan. In fact, as soon as Jahangir was firmly in the saddle, Amir hatched a plot to assassinate Sikandar and to remove this thorn permanently from his flesh. Jahangir was himself charged to perform the evil deed by slaying his wife in the middle of the night while giving, as his alibi, his presence in the distant village of Samardha. Jahangir was reluctant. Perhaps he lacked the courage to go through with such a dastardly act. Though his primary loyalty was to his own family, Sikandar was his cousin and a loving wife, and was now carrying his child. Jahangir's pleadings fell on deaf ears and the murder was planned with great precision.

On 2 May 1838 the attempted assassination of Sikandar began with Jahangir, primed with drugs and alcohol, almost being shamed into performing the evil deed. On that hot, airless night, Sikandar, whose devotion to her husband had not been diminished by family tension, waited for her husband to come to her bedroom. She knew that he would spend most nights of the week with courtesans and village girls claimed as *droit du seigneur*, but she still yearned for him. As she lay awake around midnight, Sikandar heard the sound of hooves in the courtyard and felt a surge of pleasure as she anticipated a visit from her handsome husband.

But something was wrong. Sikandar could make out that the lamps burning in the alcoves were being snipped off by a sword as her husband silently mounted the staircase. Instinctively, Sikandar knew she was in grave danger as there was no exit from her bedroom. One by one the lamps leading up to the landing were extinguished and then, in the doorway, silhouetted against the darkness, stood the swaying, murderous figure of her treacherous husband. Sikandar had no time to think; she silently covered herself with a *gao-takya* (large pillow) and a sheet. In a swift frenzied assault, Jahangir attacked what he saw was his wife's sleeping figure. His sword struck the reclining figure and there was a gush of blood which covered the weapon; having performed the dastardly act, Jahangir dashed out, jumped on his horse and rode out to his alibi *shikargah* (hunting preserve) in Samardha.

By a miracle, Sikandar and her six-month enceinte child were saved. Jahangir's blow had cut through the pillow and had wounded Sikandar on her side and arms, but she had not been seriously injured. Immediately, the guards were roused and news of the attempted assassination travelled in a flash through the town and to the villages.

Qudsia and Sikandar's just and humane rule had won them the deep affection of the Bhopali people. Both were held in the highest esteem while the debauched, decadent Jahangir was unpopular. By the following morning, the news of the assassination attempt brought a wave of sympathy for the two Begums. All pretence at cordiality between the two families was now at an end. The die of open enmity was cast between the two families as Sikandar was reconciled with her mother and withdrew to Islamnagar, escorted by Raja Khushwakt Rai, Bakhshi Bahadur Mohammad Khan and their loyal supporters.

On 20 July 1838, Sikandar Begum gave birth to a bonny daughter that she named Shahjehan. There was no reconciliation between the two families, however, with Qudsia and Sikandar living in Islamnagar while Jahangir ruled from Bhopal. From Islamnagar, Qudsia sent messages and letters to the British Governor-General championing the legitimacy of her daughter's right to rule. At the same time, she campaigned against

Jahangir's profligacy, his debauchery and his mismanagement that were bringing Bhopal's finances and administration into swift decline. Despite the attempted assassination, Wilkinson continued to support Jahangir so that Qudsia's entreaties to the Viceroy fell on deaf ears. As time passed, however, Jahangir's misrule and decadence began to leave their mark on the public and even Wilkinson wrote a letter to Jahangir warning him of his mistakes. Wilkinson died in 1841 and Henry Trevelyan, his successor, as Political Agent took a more balanced view of the situation. It was apparent that there had been a serious lapse of judgement by Wilkinson in supporting Jahangir, and the British gradually realized that in doing so they had backed the wrong horse. The Political Agent began issuing frequent warnings to Jahangir about his misrule, urging him to mend his ways.

Jahangir's death – The Begums return to Bhopal

In 1844, Jahangir's wayward, decadent existence led to a serious illness, probably cirrhosis of the liver, brought on by excessive drinking. As Jahangir, the poet Nawab, lay dying in his palace, he sent a moving letter to Sikandar in which he expressed his abiding affection for her. Blaming the older generation for their separation, he stated that had Sikandar been at his side, caring for him, he would never have been in his present state and that he would have ruled Bhopal under her guidance. Fate had decided otherwise and he was now dying of an incurable illness. On receiving this sad, touching letter, Sikandar, who had always loved her errant husband, forgave everything, including the assassination attempt and set off from Islamnagar with her little six-year-old daughter Shahjehan, to be at his side. Sikandar spent a week caring for her dying husband whom she had loved but with whom she had fought a mortal battle for power. Jahangir showed great affection towards his little daughter, but a final reconciliation was prevented by Jahangir's father and uncle so that, after a week in Bhopal, Sikandar and Shahjehan bid a tearful farewell to Jahangir and set off for Islamnagar. They had reached half-way when Jahangir died at the young age of 27, having reigned for seven years.

Jahangir's father and uncle now attempted to preserve the succession in the family. Amir wrote to the Governor-General claiming the gaddi as his right while Asad, who was Dewan, announced the succession of Dastgir Mohammad Khan, Jahangir's illegitimate son from a courtesan, as Nawab. The British were, however, wise to Amir's machinations. Wilkinson was long dead and these pleadings fell on deaf ears. R.C. Hamilton, the British Resident in Indore, rejected Amir and Dastgir's claims and announced that the Political Agent, Major J.D. Cunningham, who had replaced Henry Trevelyan, would supervise the administration until the Governor-General agreed to a successor.

In considering the various options for a successor, British documents indicate a clear prejudice against women's rule and a preference for male governance in Bhopal. After Jahangir's death, the British hierarchy decided to hand over the reins of power to one of Qudsia's brothers, Moiz or Faujdar, eventually discarding Moiz. Their rationale for passing over Qudsia and Sikandar's claims was that the two Begums had engaged in armed resistance against Nawab Jahangir whom the British had recognized. The Begums had, therefore, forfeited their right to govern! After due deliberation and consultation between the Political Agent, the Resident and the Governor-General's advisers, a decision was taken and a proclamation issued on 15 April 1845 that the seven-year-old infanta, Shahjehan, would be the next titular ruler and that her uncle, Faujdar Mohammad Khan (Qudsia's younger brother who as an eight-year-old boy had 'accidentally' shot Nazar), act as Regent. Sikandar Begum would be her guardian and 'would be consulted on all important issues'.

This decision by the Governor-General meant that the claims of Jahangir's father and uncle had been peremptorily dismissed. Qudsia, the former regent and only 46 years old, had also been passed over and not given a formal role in the running of the state. The 27-year-old Sikandar was to be guardian but the regency was given to Qudsia's younger brother, Faujdar, with Sikandar being assured that the Political Agent would 'consult her on all important issues'. Obviously, the British decision smacked of compromise and opened the way for Qudsia and Sikandar's return to the seat of power. In fact, Amir and Asad made one last attempt to wrest power by force but were easily defeated by the British contingent led by the Political Agent, Major Cunningham. Amir was put in prison where he died in 1854 and Asad was banished to Benares for life.

Qudsia and Sikandar returned to Bhopal on 11 April 1845 when three generations of women rulers drove back to Bhopal in a triumphant procession to universal public acclaim. The coach carried grandmother, Qudsia, who had so brilliantly lit the flame of woman's rule in Bhopal through a remarkably just and successful governance of the state; her daughter, Sikandar, who had been the titular ruler for 18 years and was now to act as guardian to her six-year-old daughter Shahjehan; and Shahjehan herself. Events had fully vindicated the Begums as they returned to Bhopal to a tumultuous welcome from the people.

Bhopal was united again after a seven-year interregnum of male rule that had led to strife and the dissipation of Bhopal's strength and fortunes. Jahangir had involved himself in the hedonistic pleasures of drink, women and shikar. His main contribution was to build new suburbs in Bhopal but in doing so he had squandered the hard-earned finances that Qudsia had built up during her frugal and effective regime. History has judged him as a profligate, degenerate ruler who dissipated, in seven years, what Dost and his successors had built up over generations. The decision by the British to support Jahangir, spearheaded by Colonel Wilkinson, but supported all the way up to the Viceroy, must also be viewed as a major error of judgement in assessing the qualities of the two contending camps.

The dual-control arrangement set in place by the British was obviously fraught with problems and pitfalls as Bhopal's public and most of the jagirdars were able to compare the enlightened reign of Qudsia with the degenerate waste of Jahangir. They were wholeheartedly in favour of the two Begums, Qudsia and Sikandar, alone, ruling on behalf of Shahjehan.

Supporting this groundswell of public opinion in favour of Qudsia and Sikandar were the loyal stalwarts Bahadur Mohammad Khan[1] and Raja Khushwakt Rai. Within a year, the British realized the damage that a dual-control regency would cause in a state that the British had clearly decided to support and sustain. Sikandar wrote to the Governor-General explaining the problems of dual control. She stated that the public came to her to seek justice, but that she had no power to decide. She also berated the British for giving her the responsibility of bringing up her little daughter as the ruler, but not appreciating that she had no male member in the family, no father, no husband nor brother who could help her in the task. To be denied the power and authority that was rightfully hers was, she claimed, a manifest injustice perpetrated against her. The British recognized the strength of Sikandar's argument and, aware of her extraordinary qualities, sent a reply acknowledging her claim. Accordingly, in 1846, Faujdar Mohammad Khan resigned his regency and Sikandar became sole Regent and guardian for her daughter, Shahjehan. On assuming full charge, Sikandar's first act was to reappoint the loyal Khushwakt Rai as Dewan.

Qudsia – An assessment

Qudsia was 47 years old when Sikandar became sole Regent. While Qudsia continued to guide and counsel Sikandar as the senior Begum of the family who had navigated Bhopal through one of its stormiest periods, she now allowed her dynamic, talented and charismatic daughter to take on all executive powers. In fact, Sikandar soon assumed a powerful presence as Regent with a dominating, Amazon-like personality that made all the nobles shiver in their boots in her presence. None of her advisers or officials dared look her in the eye as her commands had a withering resonance in her court.

Sikandar gave Qudsia her complete obeisance, in the true oriental tradition. She never took a seat in her mother's presence and was deeply reverential towards her. Despite their earlier difference, Qudsia and Sikandar had, together, lived through great vicissitudes and were obviously devoted to each other and remained partners in governance. In fact, Qudsia survived Sikandar and saw her granddaughter Shahjehan crowned Begum of Bhopal.

An assessment of Qudsia Begum must begin with her personality. Though brought up in a palace, Qudsia's childhood had not been a bed of roses. Her father was a weak, pleasure-loving debauchee surrounded

---

[1] Initially, when Bahadur Mohammad Khan refused to serve under Nawab Jahangir Mohammad Khan and accompanied Qudsia to Islamnagar, the Nawab ordered the confiscation of his jagirs and stopped payment of his salary. Qudsia compensated Bahadur by giving him part of her jagir in Islamnagar. After a few years, Bahadur accepted restoration to his former position of Chief of Army and the return of his former jagir (see *Tazkirat-e-Baqi* by Sultan Jahan).

by a decadent circle of flatterers, charlatans and glorified pimps. Under his treacherous rule, Bhopal was in a state of disarray and the deep sense of insecurity and foreboding must have affected even those who lived relatively protected lives in the palace. In contrast to her father, her mother Zeenat was a woman of sterling qualities that blossomed during the siege. Qudsia took after her mother. She was disciplined, deeply religious, generous and highly principled. Her character was etched in steel as was apparent when she took charge of the crisis situation on the death of her husband. Widowed at the young age of 19, she dedicated herself to the welfare of her people and to running an effective government.

As Regent, Qudsia set out to demonstrate that a Muslim woman could rule as effectively as any man. She abandoned the veil, acquired the craft of administration, learnt to ride and led her forces in combat. Above all, she set the highest standards of probity by personal example. She lived frugally, almost ascetically, with her personal household expenses being separated from state expenditure. She set up a small cottage industry in the palace whose simple products were sold in the market, providing the financing for her daily household necessities. She regularly performed her prayers, including the *tahajjud* (midnight prayer), an optional prayer that only the most devout performed. She was a Hafiz-e-Quran, knowing the Holy Book and its translation by heart.

Qudsia was also a consummate politician, as was apparent in her handling of her ambitious and dangerous brother-in-law, Amir. She was dedicated to bringing progress to her people by administering justice personally to the aggrieved, regularly touring the outlying villages and listening to the grievances of the townsfolk. Qudsia took care in selecting upright and loyal advisers, notably the Loyal Quartet, who helped her to rule the state during particularly turbulent times.

During her 18-year regency, Qudsia introduced reforms that transformed Bhopal into one of the better-run princely states of India. She built mosques and bought pilgrimage homes in Makkah and Medina for Hajj pilgrims from Bhopal. These rubats are being used by Bhopali Hajis even today. She built a dispensary and rest-house for pilgrims in Ajmer. She also built similar places of worship and succour for the Hindu population. Qudsia transformed the administration, introducing a regular system of justice and fair methods of revenue collection. She hired David Cook, a British engineer, to install a waterworks, providing tax-free drinking water for the citizens of Bhopal. Later in life, long after her daughter Sikandar had taken full charge as ruler, Qudsia financed, from her personal funds, the extension of the railway to Bhopal which led to significant economic benefit for the state. The atmosphere of Hindu–Muslim harmony in Bhopal was such that all the shops around the Jamia Mosque were owned by Hindus.

Qudsia endured a difficult relationship with the British. She recognized the importance of maintaining equable relations with the East India Company, as the British were the guarantors of Bhopal's integrity. Nevertheless, relations were soured by Wilkinson's 11-year tenure during which he openly ranged himself against Qudsia's rule by supporting her opponents. In the end, history proved Wilkinson to have misjudged Qudsia's qualities and his advice to the Governor-General placed British–Bhopali relations under an unnecessary strain. Wilkinson's successors recognized his folly and were able to recover the damage and restore relations on an even keel. However, the mutual hostility between Qudsia and Wilkinson left its imprint as the British passed over Qudsia as Regent after Jahangir's death and, later during the Mutiny, requested her daughter not to allow Qudsia to interfere in state affairs. For her part, Qudsia was not sympathetic to the British, an attitude that was apparent during the Mutiny.

Some incidents in her life illustrate Qudsia's remarkable character. After she had built the Jamia Mosque, Qudsia went to the ceremonial opening, but never lifted her eyes and continuously sat under a tree in the courtyard, gazing downwards. Later, when asked why she had not lifted her eyes to see the beautiful building, she replied, 'I was afraid I would be imbued with too much pride.' Qudsia was a great walker. She would walk through the town and pay impromptu visits to the houses of the poor from whom she learnt of their problems. She also installed a large bell in her garden so that anyone could come and ring the bell and plead their case. Qudsia would often listen to the plaints herself. Qudsia's integrity was legendary. Food left over from state functions would be invariably distributed to the poor. She issued a standing order that two *maunds* of grain should be kept in her courtyard to be distributed daily, before dawn, to the needy. Yet, despite being devout and a woman of searing integrity, Qudsia had a joyous streak to her character. For instance, she would join her old maids in the household for singing sessions, often entertaining her foreign guests to a sing-song after dinner in which she sang and played the *dholak* (cylindrical drum).

Qudsia's portraits, made late in life, depict her as a tall, thin woman wearing spectacles and with a benign countenance. Even in her youth, she was always simply dressed and never wore jewellery. Like her mother, she hated pomp and show, preferring to spend her time with the poor and the underprivileged. Qudsia lived to the ripe old age of 80. All along her devout, simple, ascetic, principled way of life left a deep imprint on her successors and on the people of Bhopal who saw in Qudsia the epitome of selfless dedication to the well-being of her people.

The only breath of scandal relating to Qudsia was the suggestion, in the memoirs of a Bhopal Bourbon, that she and Shahzad Masih were lovers. Certainly, Shahzad Masih was Qudsia's most loyal supporter and constant companion. He had been a true friend to Nazar, Qudsia's husband, as was his father Inayat Masih to Wazir Mohammad Khan. These friendships had been forged in extreme adversity – as during the siege – and became life-long chains in iron that were cherished by both the Mirazi-khel and Bourbon families. It would, therefore, be perfectly natural for Shahzad Masih to transfer this total loyalty to the widow of his erstwhile friend and to support her through the most difficult of times. To suggest an illicit basis to this relationship seems unlikely considering the characters of both Shahzad Masih and Qudsia Begum.[1]

Though sketched in autumnal hues, Qudsia's character and manner of governance had a lasting impact on succeeding generations of Bhopal rulers. Hers was the model that they would all aspire to follow, especially the frugal simplicity, the inter-communal harmony, the fair and sensitive governance, the welfare of the poor and the commitment to reform.

Qudsia was the first Begum of Bhopal. She lived through the most tortuous trials, hounded by her male relatives and the British representative, Lancelot Wilkinson. She carried out a withering struggle against these daunting forces, temporarily ceding her right to rule, but eventually returning in triumph to reclaim the state for her daughter. Qudsia was a role model for three succeeding generations of women rulers of Bhopal and for the Muslim women of India in general. Only her tenacity and steely strength of character could have achieved this extraordinary success. Qudsia was remarkable in that she actually wrested power from male contenders. The remaining Begums ruled through hereditary right as there were no male heirs in the line of succession.

---

[1] The matter is discussed further in Appendix 8.

5

Sikandar Begum, 1847–68
The Golden Reign

Sikandar Begum assumes sole regency

On 27 July 1847, at a specially convened durbar in Bhopal, Captain J.D. Cunningham, the Political Agent, read out a proclamation on behalf of the Governor-General announcing that Sikandar Begum would be the sole Regent and exercise full executive powers in the state of Bhopal on behalf of the minor ruler, Shahjehan, her nine-year-old daughter. In an extraordinary repetition of history within a generation, Sikandar who had herself been titular ruler for 18 years while her mother, Qudsia, exercised full executive authority as Regent, was now to perform exactly the same role for her only daughter! So began Sikandar's reign of 21 years as the Begum of Bhopal, the first 13 as Regent and the last eight as ruler in her own right.

Of all Bhopal's women rulers, Sikandar Begum was the most aggressive, dynamic and charismatic. From childhood, Sikandar had been brought up to understand that, in a man's world, she had to be better, stronger and more accomplished than all the men around her. Steeled in adversity, her early upbringing had been littered with extraordinary trials and upheavals. As a child, she was recognized as heir to the masnad, a title that was fiercely coveted by male contenders in her own family and was eventually wrested away from her, on marriage, with the help of the British Political Agent. The transfer of power had ended with a murderous assault on Sikandar by her own husband, followed by seven years of self-exile in Islamnagar.

During her exile, Sikandar had matured into a remarkably complete person. She was 27 years old, a mother, tough as nails, physically strong and hardened by the hostility of her husband's family and the deprivations of exile. When she returned to Bhopal, the public saw the charismatic, outgoing Sikandar rather than the ascetic, low-key Qudsia, as their saviour and rising star. In fact, initially there was some tension between Qudsia and Sikandar as Qudsia expected to be made Regent and sulked at the British government's bypassing of her. Later, reconciled to Sikandar's capacity to govern, Qudsia gave her daughter her full support. With the reins of governance firmly in her hands, Sikandar quickly asserted her dominance over Bhopal while Qudsia gradually withdrew from the public arena to concentrate on charity, prayer and the social uplift of the women of Bhopal.

With a strong wind of public support billowing in her sails, Sikandar launched herself with a vengeance to prove to the British and to her own people that a woman ruler was not just equal but better than any male ruler of a princely state. Square-jawed, muscular, handsome and with those piercing eyes, Sikandar's personality was overpowering. She rode, played polo, went tiger hunting and was an expert swordswoman, a crack shot, archer and lancer. She rode out to distant villages to take personal stock of her agrarian reform and the welfare of the village folk. She commanded the army and personally inspected the courts, the district offices, the mint and the treasury to ensure that all the wheels of state were functioning smoothly. Like her mother, Sikandar was a devout Muslim but did not take to the veil. She believed that purdah was voluntary and had not been prescribed in Islam as obligatory. Like Qudsia, she believed that for a woman to govern effectively, the veil had to be cast aside. In her personal habits, again like Qudsia, she lived simply but less frugally, shunning the pomp and show normally associated with the princely states.

To her courtiers and staff, Sikandar presented an awesome personality. No one dared look her in the eye because of the ferocious glare with which she fixed them. Soon, the whole of Bhopal – the court, the administration, the gentry and the populace – was in awe of this amazing woman who led by example, whose reforms were leading to a remarkable renaissance among the people of Bhopal and whose abilities were being recognized far beyond the frontiers of the state.

Sikandar's reforms

Sikandar's reforms had an immediate impact on her subjects. She first reorganized the Bhopal army into a disciplined, well-trained force. She began the process by ending the system of contingents being supported by jagirdars and replaced it with regular salaries for her army. Separate cavalry and *top-khana* (artillery) regiments were formed with proper cantonment arrangements and also a proper arsenal. Sikandar took special interest in the welfare of the army, taking parades herself and inquiring personally from the *jawans* (soldiers) about their problems.

She then turned to the administration of her territory by first conducting a chain survey of the state and dividing it into three parganas with 21 *zillas* (sub-districts). She constructed boundary pillars and demarcated Bhopal's frontiers for the first time. Each district was headed by a *nazim* (revenue officer) and sub-district by an *amil* (administrator). These officers were also paid by the state. She appointed 50 revenue officers 'with horse' and 50 on foot, to collect taxes. Within a year of taking over, Sikandar paid off Bhopal's debt of 30 lakhs, most of it accumulated by her late husband but partially increased during

Faujdar's regency. A separate police force was formed and posted out into the villages. Sikandar also started her own permanent secretariat, an intelligence network and customs posts. She introduced a modern, judicial system which had a Court of Appeal, encouraging jurists and lawyers from all over India to seek employment as judges and magistrates in Bhopal. Sikandar took great care to ensure that her courts dispensed justice according to both Muslim and Hindu family laws. She constructed a treasury and a mint so that Bhopal produced its own coins and currency. Sikandar started a postal service which served the outlying towns of Bhopal and connected the state with the rest of India. She appointed an Accountant General to check waste and corruption.

Sikandar's most innovative and advanced reforms related to the fields of politics, education and government. She introduced a *Majlis-e-Shoora*, a nominated parliament, comprising professionals, nobles and intellectuals representing different regions, religious groups and professions. The Majlis-e-Shoora recommended laws and freely discussed major issues, representing at that time a daring step in the direction of democratic reform. The Majlis-e-Shoora was permitted freedom of speech and passed laws by a majority. In fact, the Shoora passed 134 laws between 1847 and 1864, Bhopal becoming the leading state in enacting laws through a parliamentary process.

Sikandar was equally forward-looking in introducing schools for girls and encouraged men of learning to take up residence in Bhopal. She invited scholars from Yemen and Arabia who were given homes, jagirs and stipends so that their families dropped anchor in Bhopal and taught Arabic, Quran and Hadith to the royal household.[1] Sikandar also replaced Farsi with Urdu as Bhopal's official court language. This radical change in Bhopal took place in 1862, 20 years ahead of Hyderabad – the largest Muslim state – and was aimed at bringing the court and government closer to the people of Bhopal.

Above all, Sikandar brought immense progress and relief to the common people. She built roads across the land, connecting villages and markets to towns. She widened the streets of Bhopal so that alleys became streets in which carriages could pass comfortably. She lit the main streets with gas lamps placed at 50-yard intervals, reducing crime and insecurity. She built mosques and serais for Muslims and Hindus. She constructed a hospital and dispensaries, inviting hakeems from all over India to settle in Bhopal. A Health Act was passed and chemist shops instructed to provide medicines for Muslims and Hindus, separately. In fact, every effort was made to reassure the majority Hindu population that they would be treated with dignity and sensitivity.

Within three years of taking over as Regent, Sikandar had personally toured every village in her domain on horseback, listening to the prob-

---

[1] Generation after generation of Arab scholars continued this teaching tradition in Bhopal. In recent times, Allama Khalil Arab – a noted Arabic scholar – acted as interpreter between the Nawab of Bhopal and King Farouk immediately after the Second World War. Both his daughters, Ruqaiya and Atiya Bint Khalil Arab, were Pakistan's leading Arabic scholars and are from the same Yemeni family, having migrated from Bhopal to Pakistan on Partition. Atiya is currently Professor of Arabic at Karachi University.

lems of her subjects. She arranged for agricultural loans to peasant farmers and started a forestry department to preserve Bhopal's environment. Tightening up the decadent ambience of the gentry, Sikandar put an end to the drinking, gambling and promiscuity that her husband had encouraged during his seven-year rule. She cleaned up this atmosphere of revelry by Spartan personal example in court, a strict compliance with law and order through a disciplined police force, an effective network of intelligence and support for a judiciary that brought the decadent gentry to heel.

Sikandar's last gift to the people of Bhopal was to conceive the building of a railway line that linked Bhopal with the national grid. Sikandar and Qudsia recognized the importance of a railway connection and spent private sums of money to help build the railway. This was another far-sighted move, strongly supported by the Resident, Sir Henry Daly, that brought prosperity and importance to Bhopal as a railway junction that was virtually a cross-road between north and south, east and west. Sikandar's dream of opening a railway line in Bhopal was realized several years after her death and even Qudsia, the lean old dowager died two years before the first locomotive steamed into Bhopal on 18 November 1882.

Sikandar was a complete hands-on ruler who scanned every file with meticulous care, built up every institution that she created and ensured that justice and fair play were provided to her subjects. Within ten years, Sikandar had not only brought Bhopal to par with the best administration found in India but, in several fields, she had placed Bhopal ahead of any other state as a model, reform-oriented haven of good governance. More than ever before, Bhopal became a magnet for the Muslim elite of India. The beautiful scenery, the mild climate, Hindu–Muslim harmony, good governance, justice and employment facilities saw craftsmen, scholars, men of religion and the professional classes settle in Bhopal.

Sikandar's dedicated and enlightened rule led to a rapid advancement and prosperity for the people of Bhopal. Sikandar Begum was fortunate that Raja Khushwakt Rai was at her side in 1847 to resume his post of Dewan. Raja Khushwakt Rai was the only survivor of the Loyal Quartet that had suffered banishment with Qudsia and Sikandar Begum, as Bakhshi Bahadur Mohammad had died soon after Sikandar Begum became regent. After Khushwakt Rai's death in 1852, Sikandar Begum installed Maulvi Jamaluddin – a noted scholar and theologian from Delhi – as her Dewan. Maulvi Jamaluddin proved to be an efficient and loyal administrator and soon gained the Begum's full confidence. Maulvi Saheb's loyalty to Sikandar Begum was gauged by his frequent journeys to Indore to deliver the Begum's messages to the British Resident. Twice a week, Maulvi Jamaluddin would set forth after evening prayer on camel-back and ride eight hours, non-stop, to Indore. On completing his business, he would ride back the same afternoon, reach home well past midnight and report for duty to the Begum the following morning.

By the 1850s, British control over India was complete. The French had been defeated, the Dutch and Portuguese dispersed and the indigenous contenders for power routed and subjugated. British Raj was totally dominant in India with no real contestants. Bhopal had established a relationship of trust with the British, dating back to General Goddard's march through Bhopal in 1778 and the treaty signed by Sikandar's father, Nazar Mohammad Khan, with the East India Company in 1818. The foundation of this relationship was based on mutual political advantage. Bhopal was provided security and ensured territorial integrity while the British could count on the support of Bhopal against their common opponents in Malwa, the Marhatta states. In fact, only through alignment with the East India Company could Bhopal have withstood the repeated assaults on its sovereignty by its powerful Marhatta neighbours. Over the years, this relationship between the East India Company and Bhopal was consolidated, as the British assumed full control over the Sub-Continent.

Apart from strategic considerations, Sikandar's progressive, just and dynamic governance earned the East India Company's genuine admiration. Repeatedly, Governors-General began to acclaim Sikandar's reforms and effective governance in glowing terms. Letters of appreciation were followed by statements by Governors-General that went beyond the pale of courtesy, indicating real admiration for Sikandar's rule.

Shahjehan's suitors

By 1854, Sikandar's only daughter, Shahjehan, was 16 years old and marriageable. She was petite, attractive and, unlike her mother, entirely feminine. Shahjehan had been educated by a succession of professors and scholars, not least Maulvi Jamaluddin himself who became her tutor and virtual father figure. Shahjehan was like a fairy-tale princess whose numerous suitors vie for her hand to win a kingdom. Except with Shahjehan, it was no fairy tale but the reality. As Shahjehan neared maturity, Sikandar was troubled by the memory of her own marriage to Jahangir and the subsequent tragic handover of the state to him at the insistence of the British. The pledge made by Sikandar to the British was exactly the same as the one Qudsia had made after Nazar's death – that Shahjehan's husband would become the Nawab of Bhopal. The time had come for a consort to be chosen and to see if history was to repeat itself.

There were, however, three major points of difference between Qudsia and Sikandar's dilemma. First, Qudsia, and especially Sikandar, had conclusively demonstrated that a Muslim woman's rule was in no way inferior to a man's. In fact, Bhopal under Sikandar had been recognized by successive Governors-General as a model state. Secondly, in 1837, Queen Victoria had ascended the British throne and now Britain itself had a woman ruling monarch. If Britain could have a ruling queen, why not Bhopal? Thirdly, there was no Lancelot Wilkinson around to queer the pitch for the Begums. Sikandar felt she had a chance to persuade the British Governor-General that Shahjehan should, even after marriage, rule in her own right and not hand over the reins of power to her consort.

Taking courage in her hands, Sikandar Begum began a long correspondence with the British Governor-General and his Resident in Indore in which through legal, political and at times highly convoluted arguments she made the following claims:

1 By insisting that the infantas whom the British had formally recognized as titular rulers should hand over executive power to their husbands on marriage, the British had acted illegally, unfairly and against the terms of the 1818 treaty with Bhopal. Sikandar demanded that this condition be expunged in the case of Shahjehan whose husband should not be given executive powers but act as a non-executive consort, like Prince Albert!
2 That the decision on Shahjehan's husband would be taken by Sikandar, in consultation with the family and the British government, and
3 That she, Sikandar Begum, should be made Regent for life, Shahjehan succeeding as ruler on her death.

All along Sikandar, artfully, underlined her allegiance to Queen Victoria, implying that what was sauce for the English goose was sauce for the Bhopali gander!

As regards finding a husband for Shahjehan, Sikandar appeared to be reasonable. She informed the Governor-General that she had gathered in Bhopal the sons of 16 distinguished Muslim Pathan families from all over India so that Shahjehan could meet them and make her own choice of consort. Sikandar had, in fact, invited several noble Pathan families to Bhopal with some of whom Shahjehan enjoyed brief, flirtatious, letter-exchanging romances. Moreover, a number of princes and scions of jagirdars from far and wide who had heard that by winning the hand of the rich Muslim princess a state could be gained, came uninvited to Bhopal to chance their luck. Among them Shahjehan even mentions the descendants of Taimur (Tamerlane). Sikandar gave them all short shrift and eventually reduced the list to six. She then wrote to the Governor-General informing him that, given Bhopal's tortuous history of power-hungry consorts, none of the six suitors were found to be suitable.[1] This was evidently a ruse by Sikandar to keep British pressure for marriage within the family at bay.

Then, dramatically, in 1854, the 36-year-old Sikandar, obviously after consulting her mother, summoned the loyal, grizzly 32-year-old Commander-in-Chief of the Bhopal Army, Sardar Baqi Mohammad Khan, son of the legendary Bakhshi Bahadur Mohammad Khan, and ordered him to marry her 16-year-old daughter Shahjehan! Baqi begged Sikandar not to insist because, as the Begum's most loyal subject, he could never think of sharing her daughter's bed. Secondly, he was already twice married and had children Shahjehan's age. The same day, General Baqi, unable to face the Begum, sent a silver tray to Sikandar

---

[1] The main branches of Dost's descendants vying for Shahjehan's hand were the families of Moiz Mohammad Khan (Qudsia's eldest brother), Amir Mohammad Khan (Nazar's brother) and Dastgir Mohammad Khan (Jahangir's illegitimate son).

carrying his bottle of hair-dye, false teeth and spectacles,[1] pleading again that Sikandar should not insist on the marriage. Unimpressed, Sikandar had made up her mind and, fixing General Baqi with her famous piercing glare, told him that she would not hear any feeble excuses and that the royal wedding would take place as soon as blessings from the Governor-General were received.

Evidently, Sikandar and Qudsia had decided that they could not risk a repetition of the tragedy that had overtaken Bhopal when Jahangir claimed the gaddi after his marriage to Sikandar. Neither outsider nor family member could be trusted. The only way to preserve Shahjehan's right to rule was to marry her to the person whose loyalty to the Bhopal royal family was total and unquestionable. The finger pointed immediately to General Baqi Mohammad Khan and though it would be cruel to marry the vivacious, youthful Shahjehan to a twice-married, middle-aged man, statecraft required that this sacrifice be made to preserve power and the dynasty.

Meanwhile, the British hierarchy, obviously impressed by Sikandar's superb track record and recalling the injustice towards Qudsia, reviewed the condition requiring Shahjehan to hand over power to her consort. After seeking instructions from London, the Governor-General conveyed on 7 November 1854 the British government's approval of Shahjehan becoming ruler in her own right and for her husband to act as a non-executive consort. As regards Sikandar's demand to be made Regent for life, the British replied that they could not renege on a commitment made publicly to Shahjehan. As a sop to Sikandar, the British indicated that the handover of authority to Shahjehan would be delayed to when she reached the age of 21 and not when she was married.

Once this decision had been formally conveyed, Sikandar sought the British government's blessing for Shahjehan's marriage to Sardar Baqi Mohammad Khan explaining that, after careful deliberation, she felt the marriage would be in the best interests of the family and of the state. The Governor-General duly gave his approval on 4 July 1855. Thus, in stark contrast with Qudsia's unsuccessful entreaties to the Governor-General, Sikandar had managed to persuade the British hierarchy into changing two official and public decisions. First, Sikandar ousted her uncle Faujdar and obtained Britain's assent to assuming the sole regency on behalf of Shahjehan. Secondly, the condition that, on marriage, the titular ruler would hand over power to the consort was expunged and Shahjehan given the right to succeed to full executive power on reaching the age of 21, with her husband playing the role of a non-executive consort!

The wedding between the gamine Shahjehan and Sardar Baqi Mohammad Khan, the crusty son of Bakhshi Bahadur Mohammad Khan, Commander-in-Chief of the Bhopal army, took place on 18 July 1855 with unusual pomp and celebration in Bhopal. General Baqi was given the title of Umrao Doulah, a gun salute within the state and allotted a

---

[1] This account may be an exaggeration as Baqi Mohammad Khan was only 32 years old at the time.

vast jagir, a palanquin and an elephant. The elfin, attractive, 17-year-old Shahjehan became the unenthusiastic bride of the 33-year-old General Baqi whose two daughters from earlier marriages assumed the role of bridesmaids. In this way, Qudsia and Sikandar ensured that no threat would develop against Shahjehan's rule. Perhaps mother and grandmother recognized that, unlike Sikandar, Shahjehan was not a dominant, forceful personality but feminine, vulnerable and partial to the pleasures and comforts normally associated with royalty. Deep down, Shahjehan resented being forced into a loveless marriage with Umrao Doulah, a resentment that was later to embitter her relations with her grandmother and her mother.

Sardar Baqi Mohammad Khan, Umrao Doulah, was the younger son of the legendary Bakhshi Bahadur Mohammad Khan who belonged to the Mishti-khel clan of the Orakzais. The Mishti-khel had proven their unstinting loyalty to Bhopal and particularly to the Wazir-khel branch of the dynasty. As a young boy, Baqi had lived through the supreme challenge and deprivations of the siege and had been rewarded with the highest military office and, unexpectedly, the hand of the heir apparent in marriage. Umrao Doulah was a man of phenomenal physical strength. He exercised for three hours before breakfast with dumb-bells weighing 20 kilos each. He then consumed an enormous breakfast consisting of six seers (a seer is two kilograms) of condensed milk. He could singlehandedly turn a water-wheel which required two bullocks and was known to have lifted a sambar that four men could not raise off the ground. He was also reported to be able to hold his breath under water for an hour.

Bhopal and the Indian Mutiny, 1857

While Sikandar consolidated her rule and chose a safe and reliable groom for her daughter, a huge political crisis billowed across the land in the form of the Indian Mutiny or the Sepoys' Revolt[1] of 1857. This bushfire began with both Hindu and Muslim soldiers mutinying against their British officers because the bullets rationed to them were rumoured to be covered in jelly made of pig and cow fat. This spark lit the fire that soon engulfed the entire Sub-Continent in a spontaneous revolt against the British. Historians view the Indian Mutiny as the first stirring of the Indian people against colonial rule which culminated in independence 90 years later. For a brief period, Hindus and Muslim joined in a people's uprising against the British overlords and it was touch and go whether the British would be able to suppress the rebellion. The British mounted a massive effort to combat the crisis, using brute force, guile, persuasion and corruption as the situation demanded.

The Mutiny spread like wildfire across the Sub-Continent and soon an insurrection had erupted against the British in the neighbouring states of Malwa, especially Indore.

---

[1] A sepoy is an infantryman or soldier.

The growing rebellion was the supreme test for the calm, mature and far-sighted governance of Sikandar Begum. At the first signs of trouble, Sikandar banned the circulation of seditious pamphlets, introduced strict security in the state and threw a sop to the army by improving their accommodation, food allowance and pay. She even wrote personal letters to selected soldiers, asking them not to heed seditious rumours against the British. She then tightened up her intelligence network and ordered patrols and guards at markets in order to control the sale of arms. She sent emissaries to the strongholds of the rebel leaders and managed to win over the Gond soldiers who had joined their ranks by offering them better monetary benefits.

However, Sikandar's measures only partially succeeded in stemming the rebellion and in August 1857, a major eruption took place when Bhopali mutineers under the banner of the *Sepoy Bahadur* (brave soldier) revolt attacked the British garrison in Sehore and Berasia.

Three focal points developed in Bhopal which stirred the cauldron of revolt against the British and indirectly against the ruler, Sikandar Begum. The first was Fazil Mohammad Khan, the influential jagirdar and great-grandson of Dost Mohammad Khan. Fazil raised the banner of revolt against the British, seeking to align Bhopal's gentry to his cause. Next, by August 1857, came the rebellion of the sepoys and non-commissioned officers in the Bhopal army who began to mutiny in increasingly large numbers. They were led by non-commissioned officers (NCOs) Wali Shah and Mahavir and their number comprised both Muslim and Hindu soldiers who linked up with other army mutineers across India and also with Fazil. Their bastions were Sehore, where the mutineers attacked British officers in their garrison; and Berasia, where they killed some officers. The third focal point were the ulema, operating from Bhopal and Sehore who joined the anti-British rebellion by giving *fatwas* (religious rulings or edicts) in favour of *jehad* (holy war) against the British, urging the people to respond to Moghul Emperor Bahadur Shah Zafar's call to free India from British Raj.

It was evident that the rebellion in Bhopal was well coordinated and prepared. It was not a spur of the moment revolt as Bhopal mutineers were later found to have established links with leaders of the rebellion all over India. The rebel forces in Bhopal gained sufficient strength to declare an alternative government in Sehore which called itself the Sepoy Bahadur government.

They captured cannons from the Bhopal army, took control of Sehore and the western districts and even set up a military court. The crisis in the confrontation between the palace and Sepoy Bahadur government came to a head in December 1857 when the rebels encircled the royal palace and demanded that Sikandar Begum be handed over to them. It was touch and go whether the Sepoy Bahadur government would succeed in bringing down the Begum's rule, as she was seen as a staunch supporter of the British. Certainly this period saw the greatest crisis in Sikandar Begum's reign which she handled coolly and with immense composure. Sikandar called in her son-in-law, Umrao Doulah, and faced off with the encircling rebels by a promise to negotiate their demands. The following day, she met their demands for increased pay and the immediate crisis was averted.

During these tense months, the Bhopal rebels were initially encouraged by Qudsia who provided them with finance and moral support from her vast jagir in Islamnagar. Qudsia even declined to send her personal force to support the beleaguered Bhopal army until Sikandar wrote a stiff, admonitory letter to her mother explaining the dire consequences to the Bhopal royal family if the rebels succeeded. Qudsia quickly fell in line and was the cause of no further dissent to her daughter.

The far-sighted Sikandar realized that if the Sepoys' Revolt succeeded in Bhopal, it would mean the end of the state. Neither Fazil, nor the alternative government nor certainly the ulema would be able to rule over a state that would either be carved up between powerful Marhatta neighbours or descend into anarchy. Sikandar's support for the British was in safeguard the sovereignty of the state which her forefathers had carved out through blood and sacrifice.

Between September and December 1857, Bhopal's loyal forces under the command of her son-in-law Umrao Doulah, Bakhshi Baqi Mohammad Khan, gradually gained the upper hand over the rebels in Sehore. This led to the backbone of the Sepoys' Revolt being broken. Once the rebellious sepoys had been neutralized and the Sepoy Bahadur alternative government snuffed out, the remaining outposts of the revolt, Fazil's jagirdars and the ulema posed a lesser threat to Sikandar's rule.

Sikandar's method of dealing with the growing insurrection in the state was the proverbial stick and carrot. To bolster her authority she called Umrao Doulah out of retirement and sent him out heading the most loyal regiments of her force, drawn from recently recruited Pathans from the North-West Frontier. The carrot came in the form of increased pay and bonuses for sepoys who had joined the rebels in the Mutiny. Gradually, this policy, along with the Begum's awesome personality that made the most rebellious sepoy wither under her gaze, began to take effect and the revolt was brought under control with the help of the British contingent, headed by Sir Hugh Rose. After the successful resistance against the palace besiegers and the gradual buying off of rebel support, the state forces began to gain strength as the sepoy rebellion waned. Berasia was recaptured and with the British regaining control in Delhi, the Bhopal Mutiny began to lose heart. The last bastion of rebel strength, Sehore, was recaptured and many rebels hanged. The rebels now took refuge at Rahatgarh Fort which was Fazil's stronghold. The Bhopal forces, supported by a British contingent, attacked and captured the fort on 28 January 1858. Fazil, Mahavir and Wali Shah escaped, but Fazil was caught hiding in the jungle three days later and hanged. Mahavir and Wali Shah were also caught, tried and hanged within a week. The state records state that 149 rebels lost their lives. Supporters of the rebellion claim that 356 'martyrs' were hanged or shot.

During the Mutiny a piquant exchange took place between the famous Jhansi-ki-rani, a legendary woman leader who had taken up arms against the British, and Sikandar Begum who was leading her forces in favour of the East India Company. The Jhansi-ki-rani sent a message to

Sikandar during the Mutiny which threatened, 'As soon as I have my hands free, I shall deal with you at the point of a sword.' Sikandar replied defiantly to the message, 'I have firearms in readiness for you. Come when you will.' The Jhansi-ki-rani died fighting, dressed as a man. Sikandar on the other hand, had backed the winning horse!

Sikandar's far-sighted approach saw her ostensibly 'protect' the British contingent in Sehore by surrounding their garrison with loyal Bhopal forces. She also made sure that British civilians who were being murdered in neighbouring states were given protection and succour in Bhopal. Sikandar played for time, suggesting to the Bhopal populace that the Bhopal army had sequestered the British garrison while she made it clear to the British Political Agent and the commander of the British garrison that her troops had been sent to protect them against a violent backlash led by firebrands. Shrewdly, Sikandar had attempted to protect both her flanks.

Nevertheless, compared to the neighbouring states, Bhopal seemed a haven of security. While the Bhopal army surrounded the British garrison in Sehore, Sikandar ensured safe passage for important British civilians, including Colonel Durand, the British Resident in Indore, to the safety of Hoshangabad Fort which was protected by a loyal Pathan contingent. The following account by a British lady who sought refuge in Bhopal from rebellious forces in Indore, describes the hazardous journey that the British group took before reaching the safety of Hoshangabad Fort:

> The troops of the Indore cantonment were the first to revolt in Central India. They murdered several Europeans, and this obliged Colonel Durand, Agent to the Governor-General, Mr Shakespeare, Mr Stockley, and Colonel Trevor to go to Sehore, via Ashta, along with their wives and children. But the Bhopal contingent at Sehore contained a large number of purbiahs, or natives of eastern Hindustan; and as these men had been induced to join the rebellion, all the officers above-mentioned took refuge in Bhopal. Nawab Sikandar Begum treated them with great kindness, and sent them (with the exception of Colonel Trevor who remained with the Sehore troops) in safety to Hoshangabad. The state provided them with provisions and clothing, as well as twelve elephants for the journey. These acts of kindness greatly pleased them. They questioned the Muhammadan messenger who told them that her Highness the Begum had herself undertaken the responsibility of preserving order at Sehore.
>
> They accordingly set out, and reached Ichawar at 2 o'clock at night, and the gate of the Fort was at once opened to them. The next day, they went on to Larkui. Here they were met by a man named Kanadan Singh, who told them, with many threats, that he was a spy in the service of the Maharajas Sindhia and Holkar, and that he had had strict orders not to allow any Feringhi to pass that way alive. 'Behind yonder hillock,' he said, 'are stationed five hundred men under my command. Three days ago the Resident of Indore passed this way, and he had to give me five hundred rupees, besides a large number of swords and guns, before he was allowed to proceed on his way.' The European party, on hearing this, were greatly astonished. They possessed neither money, arms, nor, what they regretted much more, any means of punishing the man for his treachery. It afterwards transpired that Kanadan Singh was a brother of Dulip Singh and Narpat Singh, Jagirdars of Larkui. The object of

these men was merely to plunder. But the fear of having their jagir confiscated, and of even heavier punishment to follow, caused them to abandon their evil designs, and the party journeyed on unmolested till they reached Budhni, where they crossed the Narbadda, and arrived safely at Hoshangabad.

Here they met Major Rikardes, Captain Tod, Colonel Holland, and, to their great joy, Captain Harrison also. All thought that the latter had been murdered, and the greatest compassion had been felt for Mrs Harrison, who was of their party, and who had given birth to a child twelve days before their arrival at Hoshangabad. Soon after these events, the Indore troops induced the Sehore contingent to break out into open revolt. Nawab Sikandar Begum at once sent a force to Sehore, which took possession of the Government treasury, and kept the mutineers in check until the arrival of British troops. The men of the contingent were then made prisoners, and the ringleaders hanged. At Bairasia, Babu Shab Rao Sahib, Superintendent of Police, was murdered at the instigation of Sarfaraz Khan, a Resident of Rahatgarh, and Namdar Khan Pindara. The Bhopal troops captured these men along with Fazil Muhammad Khan, Jagirdar of Ambapani, in a small village near Rahatgarh. They were handed over to the British General, and were hanged at the Fort gate. Their jagirs were confiscated. Nawab Sikandar Begum, besides doing her utmost to preserve order within the boundaries of her territories, sent provisions to a number of Europeans who had taken refuge at Kalpi, and dispatched her soldiers to Sagar, Chandheri, Jhansi, and other parts of Bandalkand, to help in the restoration of order. On November 29th, 1858, the Agent to the Governor-General expressed, through the Political Agent, his great appreciation of the valuable work they had done. It was acknowledged in all dispatches and Government reports that, during the Mutiny, no ruler had remained a firmer friend to the English than Nawab Sikandar Begum, and that the state had done signal service to British rule.[1]

As the British recovered control, Sikandar appeared to have been vindicated in providing succour and help to them. This support, given at a time of extreme tension, was seen as ultimate proof of Bhopal's loyalty to the British government and earned for Sikandar – and for the state – Her Majesty's lasting gratitude. Throughout the Mutiny, the wily, far-sighted Sikandar remained calm and is reputed to have told a confidant who asked her what she would have done if the British had lost the battle. 'In that event, the Bhopal army had made sure that the British garrison was neutralized,' she replied with a smile. Through her canny statecraft, Sikandar had ensured that by surrounding the British garrison in Sehore, she would win in either eventuality. Clearly, Dost's direct descendant had inherited not only his fearsome bravery but a bit of his devilish statesmanship!

Once the British had suppressed the Mutiny and regained control of India, the Governor-General sent a message of profound gratitude to Sikandar through the Resident, Sir Robert Hamilton. The message also had a sting in its tail because there was criticism of Qudsia and her brother Moiz's role during the Mutiny, even a warning for them, couched in the following admonitory language:

---

[1] India Office Library Records.

> Be pleased to instil into the minds of your relations, this fact, that a sure foundation for the state is to be found in its dependence on a single resolute authority; the separate authority of your uncle Nawab Moiz Mohammad Khan had nearly plunged the state into discord and rebellion.
>
> You must not pay any regard to the pain which may be given to your relations in affairs which nearly concern the state, and these remarks especially apply to the affairs of your respected mother, the Qudsia Begum; the management of her estate ought to be given to such a person that no stain should attach to her good name.[1]

As events turned out, Sikandar's 'support' to the British Crown placed her on the highest pedestal of reverence and admiration by the British government. Accolades, tributes, decorations and messages, even from Queen Victoria, were showered on the Begum who now became a leading jewel in the British Crown.

Shahjehan's abdication

On 9 July 1858, almost three years after her marriage to Baqi Mohammad Khan, the 20-year-old Shahjehan gave birth to a daughter whom she named Sultan Jahan.[2] For ten years until Sikandar's death in 1868, the ruling family of Bhopal witnessed the extraordinary historical scene of four consecutive women rulers being alive at the same time. When Sultan Jahan was born, her great-grandmother Qudsia was 58 years old, her grandmother Sikandar, the Regent, was 40 and her mother Shahjehan, who held the title of ruler, 20. Three years after Sultan Jahan, another girl, Suleiman Jahan, was born to Shahjehan so that for three generations after Nazar Mohammad Khan, the ruling family of Bhopal had produced four children – all of them girls! Suleiman Jahan died of smallpox at the age of five leaving a third generation of Bhopal women rulers with only a solitary girl-child.

Having demonstrated her loyalty to the British Crown and riding on the crest of a British wave, Sikandar saw an opening to revive her claim to be made Regent for life. The date of Shahjehan's 21st birthday, 20 July 1859, was fast approaching when she would be ready to assume full powers according to the public commitment made by the British Resident in 1855. In March 1859, Sikandar wrote a letter to the Governor-General and stated her claim in the following terms:

> That at the time of the transfer [of India] to the Crown, I found two infringements in the executed treaty with this state; one that the husband of the Chief was being made Ruler of the State, the other that after the death of my father which occurred when I was fifteen months old, I was indeed made Ruler of the state according to the treaty, but that when I became fit to govern the state and to have my powers put to the test, then the control of the affairs of the state, which was my inalienable inheritance for life, without any trial

---

[1] India Office Library Records.
[2] Although the spelling and root in Urdu for Shahjehan and Sultan Jahan is the same, in English the spelling preferred by the Begums themselves has been retained. Hence, throughout the book, Shahjehan is spelt as one word and Sultan Jahan as two.

and contrary to the faith of the contracting parties, and contrary also to the letter of the treaty was given to my husband, and after his death was not even restored to me, but notwithstanding its being mine, was given away to my daughter, a child of seven years old; and this Kharita[1] was sent to me.

'That the British Government agree to sanction the raising to the throne of the Shahjehan Begum, the daughter of the late Nawab and yourself, in the same manner as your title was sanctioned after the demise of Nawab Nazar Mohammad Khan, with the consent of the nobles of the state, and the approval of the British government; and afterwards, on the occasion of her marriage, arrangements for the conduct of affairs will be made agreeably to the wishes of yourself, the chiefs of Bhopal, and of the British government, and her husband will be considered the Ruler.'

On fully comprehending the purport of this document, immediately on my accession to power, and previous to the marriage of the Nawab Shahjehan Begum, I proffered a request to this effect: That the chief power of the state should not be conferred on any youth selected to be my daughter's husband, and this prayer which was in accordance with the treaty, was granted by the Supreme government, and this infringement of my rights by consigning the inheritance of the chief to a son-in-law was removed. Now there has been a recurrence of a similar state of circumstances. Her Majesty's Court is not bound for the purpose of giving effect to the terms of the treaty to consult the nobles, nor to defer to the opinions of persons who may or may not be connected with the ruling family; the chief power in the state cannot be inherited by the children of the chief, while the chief himself is still alive. If the words heirs and successors, which repeatedly occur in the treaty, are to be allowed their full weight in Her Majesty's Court, then that order which declared me to be the chief on the death of my father, according to the stipulation of the treaty ought to be upheld for my lifetime.[2]

Sikandar's action placed the British government in an awkward dilemma. On the one hand, Sikandar had been an outstandingly successful ruler and, at the age of 41, was in her prime. She had demonstrated her loyalty to the British during the Mutiny and had made valid legal points in support of her claim. On the other hand, the British had given a formal public commitment that Shahjehan would become the ruler on reaching maturity. To renege on a public commitment would undermine the British government's credibility. The British reply to Sikandar was delayed by several months as the British government agonized over an awkward decision.

The British Governor-General had already indicated that Shahjehan would assume full powers at the age of 21 and Sikandar had groomed her for this role. Accordingly, the Resident, Sir Richmond Shakespear, was sent to Bhopal from Indore to negotiate a resolution to the issue of Sikandar Begum's repeated requests to the British to be declared Regent for life. He arrived in Bhopal, accompanied by the Political Agent, Major Hutchinson. Sikandar told the Resident that she had demonstrated her loyalty to the British Crown and had been acknowledged as an outstanding ruler of the state. She argued that by accepting Shahjehan as the titular ruler, the British had accepted a woman's right to rule. Why

---

[1] An official letter addressed to or from the ruler carried in a pouch lined in silver.
[2] *Taj-ul-Iqbal*.

then did the British deny her the same right to which she claimed to be legally entitled according to the 1818 treaty? Shakespear replied that Sikandar had not earlier questioned the arrangement under which Shahjehan was declared the titular ruler and that the British government was committed to the agreement. Shakespear was prepared to accept giving Sikandar the authority to rule as Regent for life but not as the titular ruler. Sikandar insisted, however, that if she could be given the authority, there were no grounds to deny her the title.

Sikandar's reasoning was impeccable and placed Sir Richmond Shakespear in a deep dilemma. Then, in one of the most poignant moments in Bhopal's history, Sir Richmond Shakespear sought permission to speak privately to Shahjehan. He called on Shahjehan, had the room cleared and met her accompanied only by Major Hutchinson. At this meeting, Shahjehan Begum informed the Resident that, of her own free will, she had decided to abdicate in favour of her mother. Shakespear sought confirmation that Shahjehan's decision was free from any pressure and having been so assured, reported his conversation and Shahjehan's decision to the Governor-General.[1] Shahjehan's decision resolved an agonizing problem for the British and on 31 December 1859, Sir Richmond Shakespear, who was acting for Sir Robert Hamilton as Resident, wrote a letter to Sikandar informing her that, in view of Shahjehan's abdication, Her Majesty's government would recognize Sikandar as the ruler and Shahjehan as heir apparent with Umrao Doulah her non-executive consort. This decision was formally announced at a special durbar held in Bhopal on 1 May 1860. At last, two years after Queen Victoria became Empress of India, the British government had formally recognized a Muslim woman's right to rule.

Sikandar Begum thus became, for the second time, the recognized ruler of Bhopal, a title she had held as a child but saw wrested away from her by her husband. Shahjehan's noble sacrifice in favour of her mother is unique in history. While abdications of ageing monarchs in favour of their grown-up children are known, seldom, if ever, had a young ruler voluntarily abdicated in favour of a middle-aged parent. Sikandar resumed her governance of Bhopal as fully fledged ruler, a status that she retained until her death, eight years later in 1868, at the age of 50.

Sikandar's fame as a woman ruler with one of the finest administrations of all the Indian princely states, reached all corners of India and beyond. She was now the star of all durbars of which there were several. Although she had abandoned the veil in Bhopal, Sikandar covered herself when travelling abroad and at official functions so that she sat among ruling princes, the only woman ruler, wearing a white silk burqa with dazzling jewellery worn on the outside.

---

[1] Shakespear's report is reproduced in Appendix 9.

Sikandar attends durbars and travels

The first Imperial Durbar that Sikandar attended was held at Jabalpore on 15 January 1861, when India's first Viceroy, Lord Canning, convened a special durbar of Central Indian princes to honour the Begum of Bhopal. There, the Viceroy congratulated Sikandar Begum for her courage, ability and success and announced that the district of Berasia would be handed over by the British and annexed to the state of Bhopal. Berasia was the pargana that Dost Mohammad Khan had leased, way back in 1709, as the first piece of territory that he could call his own. From Berasia, Dost had expanded his domain to found the state of Bhopal. The district had later been lost to the neighbouring state of Dhar which, in turn, had ceded it to the British. The wheel had now turned full circle with Dost's great-great-great-granddaughter winning back the district not by force of arms but through shrewd and far-sighted statecraft!

At Jabalpore, Sikandar Begum's reception by the Viceroy is described by her daughter Shahjehan as follows:

> The reception was held at 11 o'clock on Tuesday, the 15th January 1861; all the nobles of Bhopal in their best attire, mounted on elephants, proceeded towards the Governor-General's tent; when near the appointed place, the cavalry and infantry halted, and the elephants waited at the edge of the encampment. The agent to the Governor-General for Central India, and the Foreign Secretary to the government of India, then came forward on elephants to the edge of the Governor-General's camp to meet them. In front of the durbar-tent was pitched a shamiana,[1] before which the Secretary took the hand of my sainted mother in his, and the agent to the Governor-General took the Qudsia Begum's hand and assisted them down from their howdahs, while the Political Agent of Bhopal approached the elephants ridden by Nawab Moizz Mohammad Khan and Nawab Umrao Doulah and the others, who all dismounted from their elephants. When we entered the shamiana, arms were presented to the party by a guard of honour of British soldiers, and then we all passed on to the durbar tent and took the chairs labelled with our names, as the Secretary pointed them out to us. Afterwards the other chiefs, whose reception had been appointed for that day, took their seats without any confusion or talking; and when all had assembled, the Governor-General, accompanied by four aides-de-camp, made his appearance, the company of British soldiers presented arms, and all rose from their chairs as a mark of respect. Then the Governor-General took his seat, and the four aides-de-camp sat on his right, while on his left were all the Hindustani chiefs.[2]

After Jabalpore, the next durbar was held at Allahabad on 1 November 1861. Sikandar set forth on her journey on 1 October 1861 with a retinue of over a thousand men, elephants, horses, sepoys, a travelling kitchen, cooks, footmen, drummers, servants and maids. Qudsia and Shahjehan, along with Umrao Doulah and Faujdar, accompanied Sikandar to Allahabad. The 200-mile journey took four weeks and several stops en route.

---

[1] A shamiana is a large ceremonial tent.
[2] *Taj-ul-Iqbal.*

At Allahabad, Sikandar Begum was awarded the Grand Cross of the Star of India (GCSI). She was one of only two princely rulers out of 86 – the Maharaja of Gwalior being the other – to be awarded this rare honour. In an elaborate and impressive ceremony the Viceroy, Lord Canning, pinned the star on the Begum's silk burqa and read a speech full of praise for the Begum. Sikandar was obviously a star, being the only woman and a ruler that had been singled out for praise by the Viceroy. Not only was she invested with the GCSI, but the Viceroy also announced that the Begum of Bhopal would be given a 19-gun salute. The following were the gun salutes announced at Allahabad:

Gwalior	19 guns[1]
Bhopal	19 guns
Patiala	17 guns
Rampur	13 guns

Immediately after the Allahabad durbar, Sikandar Begum decided to make a tour of the historic cities of India. The tour took her to Benares, Faizabad, Delhi, Jaunpur, Lucknow, Kanpur, Mutra, Ajmer and Jaipur. Sikandar learnt and absorbed a great deal from her tour. She saw the good and bad points of every city's administration. She met with princes and governors and discussed policies and administration with them. She visited the mosques, temples, palaces and shrines in these famous cities and recorded her impressions in a diary. She loved the gardens of Delhi and the architecture of Lucknow, but felt Benares was 'unhealthy'. Perhaps the most colourful welcome given to the Begum was by the Maharajah of Jaipur, one of the leading Rajput chieftains of Rajputana. Shahjehan describes the scene as follows:

> On the 27th Rajab, we commenced our march from Delhi to Jaipur, which we reached in safety on the 11th Shaaban. The Maharaja of Jaipur arranged the ceremony of our reception in the following fashion: As soon as the elephants of our procession, with the Political Agent of Bhopal, reached the city gateway, there appeared a band of about 200 horsemen and footmen, with coloured wands of office in their hands, calling out 'make way, make way' in a respectful manner; behind them about 30 gentlemen, relatives of the Maharaja, were mounted on horseback, drawn up in a line parallel with the gate; outside the gate the artillerymen fired a salute. Then the Raja himself, accompanied by the Political Agent of Jaipur, appeared mounted on an elephant, whose howdah was of the Hindustani pattern, and made of gold, while the Political Agent's howdah was of the English pattern, and made of silver. The Raja wore a white coat and a red turban, he had on an emerald necklace, a dagger in his waist-band, and a scimitar suspended from a shoulder-strap, while a second jewelled sword was placed in front of him in the howdah.
>
> On our side my revered mother and the Political Agent urged on their elephants and shook hands with the Maharaja. After the usual greetings on both sides, the party advanced together. The Maharaja led us into a summerhouse, where, under a canopy supported by silver poles, were placed two

---

[1] The 561 princely states of British India were divided into several categories according to their status. Hyderabad was given a 21-gun salute and was in a category of its own. The 16 states recognized in the first category and given 19-gun salutes were Mysore, Kashmir, Gwalior, Baroda, Travancore, Cochin, Udaipur, Jaipur, Jodhpur, Bikaner, Indore, Bhopal, Rewa, Kolhapur, Patiala and Bahawalpur.

chairs, on one of which the Raja took his seat, and my revered mother on the other to his right. Minstrels came and sang and then withdrew, then twenty-five nautch girls, in beautiful dresses, began to dance to an accompaniment of a drum and two guitars: after a short time the Maharaja offered with his own hands attar, pan, and garlands of flowers to my revered mother, the two Political Agents, to Mian Faujdar Mohammad Khan, Nawab Umrao Doulah, and the Minister [Madar-ul-maham], while the Jaipur Minister distributed attar and pan to the rest of the assembly, after which we took leave and went to our camp.

On Thursday, the 13th Shaban, the Raja sent uncooked provisions for the whole camp and invited us to dinner to be given in his own palace; In the building in which dinner was served was a large reservoir full to the brim with water, and in the reservoir was a raised platform containing a fountain. All round the tank were arcades, in which nautch girls were dancing, but after a short time the dancing ceased, and the dinner was served, of which all partook. One hundred and twenty dishes of different kinds were put on the table, all dainty and appetising.

In front of this building was a very large tank, in which some 40 or 50 fountains were playing. Here trays of presents were set out and fireworks let off; after which we and the two Political Agents visited the Maharaja. Some two hundred gentlemen were present at this durbar, and nautch girls danced in gold-spangled dresses; after the usual formal salutations on both sides and sitting a short time, we took leave, on which the Maharaja presented each guest with a necklace of gold lace, a garland of flowers.[1]

During her tour, the most important symbolic act performed by Sikandar Begum was to have Delhi's famous Juma Masjid reopened after it had been closed by the British during the Mutiny. The Juma Masjid, built by Emperor Shahjehan, was closed by the British during the Mutiny because they felt it provided a sanctuary for Muslim resistance. Not content to simply shut the gates, the British heaped insult on to injury by using the famous mosque as a stable. Sikandar Begum persuaded the British to reopen the Juma Masjid, washed the courtyard with her own hands and was the first person to pray in it since the Mutiny. Through this symbolic act, Muslims throughout India recognized Sikandar Begum's contribution to Islam and to reviving the spirit of the Muslims — a role that was continued by succeeding generations of Begums of Bhopal. By this symbolic act, Sikandar was able to expiate some of the criticism that she faced in her lifetime and afterwards for supporting the British in the Indian Mutiny.

After Allahabad, another durbar was held in Agra in February 1863 to commemorate Queen Victoria becoming Empress of India. This time, Sikandar set forth from Bhopal with a retinue of 2470 persons. On her way to Agra, Sikandar Begum's caravan stopped at Gwalior, the Marhatta state with which Bhopal had the longest memory of enmity. A sign of a change of the times, the Maharajah of Gwalior greeted the Begum of Bhopal with a colourful welcome described by Sikandar Begum in her own words as follows:

---

[1] *Taj-ul-Iqbal.*

On the 5th Shaban, Monday, at 8 a.m., accompanied by eighteen principal officers of state and the Political Agent of Sehore, we went to the Maharaja's palace, and were received with a salute of nineteen guns, and Satulia Sahib met us at our carriage. There was a guard of honour of two companies of soldiers. On entering the palace we were shown into a room most beautifully furnished, in front of which was a canopy of cloth supported on silver poles. The Maharaja advanced ten steps and shook us by the hand, begging us to be seated. In this audience there were nearly fifty persons of distinction. After the usual conversation on such occasions, the Maharaja first presented attar to me, next to the Political Agent, Mian Faujdar Mohammad Khan, Nawab Moizz Mohammad Khan, and Nawab Amrau Dula, but with the packets of betel he only honoured me and the Political Agent; the rest of the party were served by his Minister, and in the same way the garlands of flowers were presented. Then two white handkerchiefs steeped in rose-water were brought in and presented by the Maharaja, one to me, and the other to the Political Agent, after which we took leave, the Maharaja escorting us to the edge of the carpet.

Next day, Tuesday, the 6th Shaban 1279, corresponding with the 27th January 1863 A.D., the Maharaja returned the visit at my tents, and the same ceremonies were observed by us, and both at his arrival and departure a salute of 21 guns was fired, and arms were presented by a guard of honour of cavalry and infantry. The arrangement of the Maharaja's escort was as follows: First of all was an advanced guard of cavalry, then columns of Mewatti infantry, then a troop of carbineers, then a number of elephants with gold embroidered trappings and howdahs of great beauty; next came led-horses caparisoned in gold and silver, then a body of mace-bearers with lion-headed maces, behind them messengers. Then archers, then spearmen, next three troops of lancers, next four principal Sirdars of the state, and then the Maharaja himself mounted on a grey horse, and behind him the officers of his army and his cavalry in red.

From Gwalior, Sikandar Begum proceeded to Agra where the Viceroy, Lord Elgin, welcomed the gathered Maharajahs, Nawabs and the solitary Begum.[1]

Sikandar returned to Bhopal having spent by far the heaviest sum so far on her travels, amounting to 41,636 rupees, 3 annas and 6 paisas.

Sikandar Begum's pilgrimage to Makkah[2]

In November 1863, Sikandar Begum embarked on a momentous journey to perform the pilgrimage to Makkah. The event was unique in that no previous Muslim ruler, from the most powerful emperor down to the smallest chieftain, had ever performed the pilgrimage from the Indian Sub-Continent. Thus, Sikandar was not simply the first Indian Muslim woman ruler but the first ruling head of state – male or female – to perform Hajj. The journey was momentous because the Begum took a retinue of 1500 with her, travelling by road, rail and then by sea in three ships chartered specially by her.

The journey began on 5 November 1863 after months of preparation. Sikandar Begum first prayed at the graveside of all her ancestors before

---

[1] Shahjehan, *Taj-ul-Iqbal*.
[2] The account of Sikandar Begum's Hajj is drawn from her book *A Pilgrimage to Makkah*, translated into English by Mrs Willoughby Osborne, the Political Agent's wife.

embarking on her momentous journey. The Begum was accompanied on the journey by her 64-year-old mother Qudsia, her uncles Moiz and Faujdar, her Dewan, Maulvi Jamaluddin, the Commander-in-Chief of the army, several ministers, officials, religious leaders, jagirdars, doctors, nurses, companions, guards, cooks, cleaners, soldiers, footmen, barbers, maids, washer-women, *syces* (grooms) and assorted servants. In all a retinue of 1500 of both sexes set forth by road in a caravan from Bhopal for Mahargam. There, a special train took the Begum's caravan to Bombay from where they set sail on 6 January 1864 in three ships – one steamer and two sailing boats – for Jeddah. They arrived in Jeddah on 23 January 1864. On arrival, the Begum was received with a gun salute and a ceremonial welcome by the Turkish Governor and Sherif of Makkah, Sheikh Abdullah Ibn Muhammad Ibn Aun. Sikandar described the scene in her diary as follows:

> Jeddah is situated on the sea shore, and the houses rise to the height of seven storeys, which gives the town a striking appearance from a distance. The walls and foundations are brick and mortar, but the roofs are of mud. Masonry bathrooms and kitchens form part of the houses themselves. The town contains a mixed population of Arabs, Turks, Abyssinians, and a few Hindustanis principally engaged in trade. The Arab costume is adopted, and Arabic is the language in common use. The better classes are well fed and well clothed. The water in the town is brackish, which necessitates the storage of rain water in huge reservoirs outside the town, whence the drinking water of the whole population is drawn throughout the year.

Sikandar Begum's sojourn in Jeddah and Makkah was not all plain sailing and ceremonial. Problems of protocol, lack of communication between hosts and guests and a failure by the Begum's retinue to adjust to local customs led to a series of misunderstandings and grating incidents.

First, on arrival, reports were conveyed to the Begum that her sea-chests had been broken into and Bedouin thieves were helping themselves to the contents. Customs officials had also taken a fancy to the embroidered shawls carried in the Begum's luggage and were demanding huge duties or appropriate gifts. Next, the Begum proceeded to the house that the Sherif had placed at her disposal only to be informed, on arrival, that as an Egyptian princess was expected, the Begum would have to make alternative arrangements. Sikandar and Qudsia rented another house, obviously disgruntled at the shoddy treatment shown to them. It transpired later that the Egyptian princess never arrived!

The journey by caravan from Jeddah to Makkah was full of incident and could have ended in tragedy. The caravan was escorted by the Ottoman Emperor's emissary, Suleiman Beg, and by the Sherif of Makkah's brother who headed a posse of Turkish and Arab guards assigned to protect the Begums. Sikandar had also taken her own Bhopali guards as part of her retinue. Of course, the Begum's reputation as a rich, generous ruler had spread across the sands of Arabia, especially after Qudsia's regrettable habit of showering currency notes from her carriage which led to the Begums being constantly hounded by a swarm of beggars every time they set out from their homes. Sikandar tried, unsuccessfully, to stop her mother from this ludicrous demonstration of charity that never reached the genuinely poor but was avariciously lapped up by professional mendicants. Clearly, the news of rich Indian Begums, carrying bagfuls of jewels, gold and currency had spread from the beggars of Jeddah to the desert Bedouin who lay in wait for their quarry as it took to the road to Makkah. Initially, there were some sniping incidents which were repulsed by the Ottoman escorts, but the most serious incident occurred in the dead of night when some Bedouins surreptitiously approached Qudsia Begum's camel and began leading it away from the rest of the caravan. The Bedouins had almost succeeded in their villainous hijacking of the royal camel when Qudsia realized that mischief was afoot and began shouting at the top of her voice, 'Help, help, my camel is being led away by strange people.' On hearing the Begum's cries, members of the Bhopali guard chased the Bedouins and after a brief skirmish in which rifle butts were used, the Bedouins were driven off and Qudsia Begum's camel returned to the main caravan.

On arrival at Makkah, a serious protocol incident took place when the Sherif's offerings of 50 royal dishes of Arabic food three times a day were left untasted by the Begums. This was seen as an affront to the Sherif whose staff remonstrated with the Begum's entourage, stating that they would 'chop off the heads' of anyone who declined the Sherif's generous offer of hospitality. Probably the Begum's staff, unfamiliar with the protocol and traditional hospitality of the hosts, fuelled this hostility with loose talk and unnecessary bravado of their own to the extent that their insolent remarks reached the ears of the Ottoman Governor. One morning, about 20 Turkish soldiers burst into the Begum's kitchen, manhandled the Begum's servants, flung the kitchen utensils to the floor, broke up the crockery with their swords and began tearing up the carpets in the Begum's house. They then beat up the venerable Maulvi Jamaluddin, remarking aloud that they were punishing those that had spoken ill of the Sherif and the Turkish Governor.

The commotion led to a crisis in the relationship between the Begum and her hosts. The Begum wrote a letter of protest to the Sherif stating that, as the ruler of a Muslim state who had come solely to perform Hajj, she had not expected such ill treatment at the hands of her hosts. The letter evoked a defensive reply from the Sherif, reassuring the Begum that she was a revered visitor and that 'the minor incidents' were due to misunderstandings over protocol. The Sherif sent a peace offering in the form of another set of 50 Arab dishes which the Begum reluctantly ate out of politeness, remarking at the same time that the food tasted awful as the dishes were 'cold, without flavour and congealed in icy dew'.

The enforced consumption of the Sherif's food led to the simmering down of the stand-off between the Begums and their hosts. Sikandar Begum paid a courtesy visit to the Sherif and noted that he had four wives, two beautiful Georgian Sherifas, an Arab and an Abyssinian. Later, she made peace with and called on the Ottoman Governor (Pasha) who had a Georgian and a Turkish wife. Sikandar Begum described her call on the Sherif of Makkah and on his (Georgian) wives as follows:

On the 16th Ramadhan 1280 A.H., I visited the Sherif at his house, and after the 'istikbal' reached the palace, three eunuchs conducted us to the first floor, and then withdrew to be succeeded by Georgian slave girls in clean dresses, who, in like manner, escorted us to the second floor and made way for the Egyptian women, who were drawn up in a row to receive us. They took us by the arm and carefully led us up the stairs to the third storey, where we were received by two wives of the Sherif, and conducted into the hall of audience. The Sherif's mother rose on seeing me, and advanced to the edge of the carpet to meet us; then his two wives shook hands with us, and kissed us on both sides of the neck, on both cheeks and on our lips and chin, and, with the greatest politeness, led us to the seat in the room. The whole house was furnished with glass lamps and beautiful carpets. The Sherif's wives were young and very beautiful, and from their heads to their waists were quite smothered in diamonds. They had silk kerchiefs, called in Arabic 'asabah', tied on their heads; and on their kerchiefs were set circlets of diamonds in clusters like a coronet; their elegance and beauty was beyond description. The sprays of diamonds shook with the least motion when they spoke or moved. After an hour had elapsed, the Sherif asked leave to be introduced; so he came and conversed with the greatest courtesy. Coffee, pomegranate sherbet, rosewater, and incense burning in a censer were set before us, and, according to Arab custom, I drank coffee and sherbet, and after fumigating my skirts and sleeves with the fragrant censer, took leave, the wives accompanying us to the door.

Mohammad Hussain, our interpreter, told us that gentlemen visiting the Sherif had to kiss the back of his hand before taking their seats, and that Bedouins and common people kiss the skirts of his coat, and attendants and slaves kiss the corner of his Divan, although this custom is not sanctioned by the divine law, but is disapproved and even condemned.

Sikandar then described the Hajj ceremonial in the following words:

On the 8th, 10th, and 14th Zilhij, a state procession is made by the Sherif. In front are led twenty-two Arab horses with trappings and housings of gold and silver, studded with gems; then swift she-camels with gold embroidered coverings, two of which are for the Sherif Sahib's special use, and have their necks adorned with strings of pearls, the value of which cannot be less than four lakhs of rupees (400,000); behind them come 200 or 300 horsemen in Turkish costume; next a regiment of Turkish infantry; next 400 slaves of the Sherifs all well-armed and well-dressed, then the Sherif's sons and kinsmen mounted on horses with saddles of gold, followed by Elders, Arab Shaikhs, Turkish officers, and Abyssinian and Georgian slaves; next come the various Arab clans and hermits, all on camels, to the number of nearly a thousand; and finally the Sherif Sahib himself, mounted on a horse, with jewelled furniture. The procession is accompanied by music. After the Hajj, for three days the table of the Sherif is kept ready spread, and all visitors are entertained with food.

Sikandar Begum was not impressed by what she saw in Arabia. She was appalled at the fact that women would have eight to ten husbands in a lifetime and seemed to marry more frequently than men. A woman who became tired of her husband would obtain a divorce by appealing to the Governor on the most whimsical grounds. The Governor would then pass orders for a *khula* (divorce).[1] The woman would then marry a younger and perhaps richer man until she moved on to the next husband! Sikandar also found the cities dirty and full of beggars and unsavoury characters. She remarked that, seemingly, all the bad characters of India had gathered in Arabia. Of local customs and culture, Sikandar Begum was even more critical, describing the singing and dancing of Arab women in the following words:

> In Makkah, people can neither sing nor dance but most of the women whistle, clapping their hands and snapping their fingers. On weddings, ladies dance and sing comic songs but they do both so badly that there is no pleasure in hearing or seeing them, but one is rather disgusted.

Sikandar noted that the jungles around Mina were full of wild beasts and that Hajj was performed amidst much lying and cheating by the local population. Towards the end of her Hajj, Sikandar made a speech in which she remarked that if she was given 30 lakhs of rupees, she would clean up the whole city so that it became a worthy place for the performance of the pilgrimage. This parting kick by the Begum led to an angry response from the Pasha who caustically responded that 'some people come to perform the Hajj with humility'.

Thus ended, in some acrimony, the momentous pilgrimage of Sikandar Begum and her mother Qudsia. They returned to Bombay on 10 October 1864 in the same three ships in which they had set sail, 11 months earlier.

Sikandar's return to Bhopal on 15 October, almost a year after her departure, was received with tumultuous joy and celebrations by the people of Bhopal. The Begum had demonstrated her profound commitment to Islam by being the first Muslim ruler from India ever to have performed Hajj. During Sikandar Begum's absence, Shahjehan the heir apparent had performed the formal duties of ruler, under the guidance of the Chief Minister, grooming her for the responsibilities that lay ahead. Sikandar had had reservations, however, about Shahjehan's capacity to rule in her absence and had made sure through precise orders given before her departure that executive authority would be exercised, in her absence, by her ministers and that Shahjehan's role of caretaker would be solely titular. Thus, the first signs of tension between mother and daughter were becoming apparent.

For Sikandar, the birth of a granddaughter, Sultan Jahan, had added a new, softening, dimension to her life. According to custom among Muslim families, the grandmother took over the upbringing and education of the first-born grandchild. The momentous journey to Makkah provided an insight into the loving and caring side of Sikandar's character. Her exterior had always appeared harsh, masculine and domineering but her letters to her six-year-old granddaughter are full of the tenderness of an affectionate and doting grandmother, as the following letters illustrate:

---

[1] Khula is a divorce exercised at the wife's initiative, usually specifically provided for in the marriage contract.

From Aden, 12 Shawwal 1280

I have bought for you, on board the ship, a box with a small space to hold an inkpot, and another to keep your letters in; also a small tooth-powder casket, a tea-kettle, a cup, a sweetmeat basket, and a bouquet of real sea flowers that grow in the sea; and I am sending them, together with similar presents for Sulaiman Jahan Begum, with this letter. Give your sister's share to her, and keep your own. The coloured ruler which I am sending is for you only, and not for Sulaiman Jahan Begum.

From Aden, 14 Shawwal 1280

I have received your two letters of the 2nd Ramazan, and I heartily thank God to hear that you are quite well. But the letters are not signed by you. I understand that Nawab Shahjehan Begum Sahiba has asked Kanwal Sen to write answers to my letters addressed to you; but he has neglected to make you sign them. In future, whenever you receive a letter from me, you should go to Raja Sahib Bahadur, and dictate an answer to it with your own lips. Your seal that was with Injir Nana[1] I am now sending you through Haji Husein, the Agent of Haji Ismail, and, God willing, you will soon receive it. I learn from the letter of Munshi Husein Khan that you still cry whilst reading the Koran, and that you have to be punished.

You must remember that you are almost grown up, and that it is, therefore, a great shame for you to cry while you are reading, and to have to be punished. It is quite time that you gave up this bad habit. Whenever you are tired of reading, and you want to do something else, you should tell your teacher so, but do not cry. When you have finished reading you can go to Alik-ullah and practise handwriting. Always tell me about Sulaiman Jahan Begum in your letters.

From Makkah, 20 Shawwal 1280

To the fruit of the tree of my heart, the star of my prosperity and good luck, Sultan Jahan Begum. May God enhance her happiness and prolong her life.

I learn from the letter of Munshi Husein Khan that you very often think of me, and grieve very much over our separation. Now, therefore, I write to tell you that when children are parted from their parents they should pray to God for reunion, and He will grant their prayer, and bring back their parents to them. I told you before I left Bhopal that, God willing, I should return after a year. Now there are 12 months in a year, and 30 days in a month; and if you go to the Raja Sahib he will help you to find out how many days there are in a year, and then you will know when I am coming back. I should like to know what words you are learning to write now; so send me some of your copy-books. When you dictate your letters to me, say everything that comes into your mind: but, dear child, do not grieve for me at all. God willing, I will return as soon as I have performed my Hajj. Your Injir Nana performs the Tawaf oftener than anyone else. He prays continually for your health, prosperity, and long life. He hopes you will finish the Koran before we return, and that you no longer cry whilst reading it, for it is our Sacred Book, and it is our duty to study it cheerfully.

These tender and caring letters written by Sikandar to her granddaughter also epitomize, better than any graphic description, the simplicity

---

[1] Injir Nana – literally Grandpa Fig – was Sultan Jahan's affectionate pet name for Maulvi Jamaluddin, who was her tutor for the Holy Quran.

and temperance of Bhopal's royal court. The all-powerful, rich and resplendent Begum of Bhopal, received in Arabia by princes and governors with ceremonial gun salutes was sending her granddaughter no gift of pearls or golden ornaments or brocade or silk, but a tea-kettle, a sweetmeat basket, a small box to hold an inkpot, a tooth-powder casket and a coloured ruler!

After almost a year of separation, the meeting between grandmother and granddaughter was full of yearning tenderness. Sultan Jahan describes it in the following words:

> These letters I read with the most eager joy; but how much greater was my pleasure when, after the expiration of a year, came the news of my grandmother's approaching return! On the day of her arrival, my father, Nawab Umrao Doulah, together with all the nobles and chief officials of the state, assembled at Sikandarabad, three miles outside Bhopal, to bid her welcome; and, to my great joy, I was taken with them. As soon as her cavalcade came in sight, she saw me, though she was yet a long way off, for we were both mounted on elephants. Instinctively she stretched her arms towards me, and I remember how I wished that I had wings that I might fly to her.
>
> In a short time our elephants were side-by-side, and the next moment I was in her lap. Until the appointed halting-place was reached she continued to shower blessings and caresses upon me, while tears of joy and thankfulness fell from her eyes.[1]

Sikandar Begum returned to Bhopal to find her daughter's marriage predictably on the rocks. Shahjehan was not only much younger than her husband but was vibrant, headstrong and coquettish. The proud and loyal Umrao Doulah was beginning to wear the mantle of a cuckold as his attractive wife received the adulation of courtiers from Bhopal and also of princes and nobles from afar. An account is told of how Nawab Umrao Doulah, visiting his wife's chamber – an event that was deliberately announced with much noise and notice so that Shahjehan could clear the decks and receive him without embarrassment – found a young man of his own household sheepishly emerging from Shahjehan's private quarters. Umrao Doulah stopped him and said, 'Young fellow, why don't you go for a deer hunt in my shikargah today and bring me back a nice black buck as a trophy.' Overjoyed, the young man accepted. Umrao Doulah then turned to his subordinate commander and ordered, 'That boy will not return alive. Make sure there is a hunting accident.'

No amount of pressure, however, could make Shahjehan assume the role of a dutiful, eastern wife. She had been the titular ruler and was now the heir apparent. Her husband, despite his age and venerable standing, dared not question her conduct and had to assume a subordinate role. There was tension between mother and daughter, and even a touch of defiance in Shahjehan's attitude towards Sikandar. There was talk of a separation which was not accepted by Sikandar. Eventually, Umrao Doulah could not take it any longer and asked Sikandar Begum to allow him to go on pilgrimage. Permission having been granted, Umrao Doulah took his time over Hajj, stopping in Egypt on his way

---

[1] *An Account of My Life.*

back where he fell gravely ill. In June 1867, Umrao Doulah died soon after his return, leaving Shahjehan, at the age of 29, a distinctly merry widow.

The Jalalabad connection

Concerned at her daughter's mismatch and her expansive love life and with images of her own turbulent marriage rolling through her mind, Sikandar began to fret about her little granddaughter's future. Her own Mirazi-khel Pathan nephews were dangerous and covetous. Outsiders, even though they might be of high birth or Pathans from other tribes like the Yusufzais or Feroze-khel, could also not be trusted. Accordingly, Sikandar began a search for the ideal consort by sending loyal emissaries to Orakzai strongholds in India. Ironically, Sikandar's quest led to Sardar Jalal Khan's family in Lohari where Dost had found shelter among Mirazi-khel relatives when he first arrived in India.

Sikandar Begum sent her Minister to Jalalabad who reported back that a number of young, well-bred Orakzai boys were available for selection as future grooms for Sultan Jahan. Accordingly, Sikandar decided to interview them personally during her stay in Agra where she was to attend the Grand Durbar in 1866.

On arrival in Agra, Sikandar Begum invited the families of her long-lost relatives to her tent. Among them came the recently widowed Mohammadi Begum with her 12-year-old son, Ahmad Ali Khan. For the occasion, Ahmad Ali Khan wore a brocade *sherwani* (formal frock-coat), a beautifully tied turban and a *talwar* (scimitar) encased in a golden scabbard.

Sikandar found Ahmad Ali Khan not only strikingly handsome, but also his manners and upbringing showed him to be a thoroughbred aristocrat. Sikandar took an immediate liking to the boy and saw in little Ahmad Ali Khan the ideal consort for her eight-year-old granddaughter. Ahmad Ali Khan had no brothers, only an elder sister, Chanda Bi. His father was dead and Mohammadi Begum was a simple, homely 'purdah-lady' from the north, quite unlike the precocious, domineering, aggressive women of Bhopal. Sikandar immediately asked Mohammadi Begum to settle in Bhopal with her family, promising them a home and an allowance.

When Mohammadi Begum arrived with her family in Bhopal, little Ahmad Ali Khan was virtually taken over by Sikandar and became the regular companion of Sultan Jahan, along with other children of the family of both sexes. He was soon being given lessons in religious studies, literature, poetry, riding and hunting, earmarking him for the role of consort when the time came for Sultan Jahan to marry. For a highly religious, conservative and traditional household, the introduction of a young boy into the family's inner sanctum was a remarkably bold and liberal step for Sikandar to take. For the Bhopal and Jalalabad wings of the Mirazi-khel clan, the wheel of fortune had turned full circle from the time when Dost Mohammad Khan had sought shelter with

Sardar Jalal Khan, 150 years earlier, and had run for his life after killing his young son. Now the families were reunited in Bhopal with Ahmad Ali Khan Sikandar Begum's chosen suitor for her little granddaughter.

As expected, Mohammadi Begum proved to be innocuous and immensely grateful to Sikandar for having given her a home in Bhopal. Her daughter Chanda Bi married another Jalalabadi noble, Mian Wilayat Ali Khan, with whom she had seven daughters and three sons. The seven daughters grew up into beautiful women, four of them being exceptionally alluring. Perhaps with the exception of Rani Kamlapati, Bhopal society had never known such beauty. The Jalalabadi girls were tall and extremely fair, with large doe-like eyes, aquiline noses, upright figures, elegant gaits, graceful manners and the most dulcet diction. In due course, these seven girls became the rage of Bhopal with royal scions, jagirdars and noblemen falling over themselves to gain the hand of these delectable maidens.

Sikandar Begum had chosen wisely in bringing the homely Mohammadi Begum from Jalalabad to Bhopal with her little son and daughter. There were no men in her family to pose a threat or cast acquisitive glances towards the state and finances controlled by the Begums. What Sikandar Begum had not bargained for, however, was that Chanda Bi would produce seven devastatingly beautiful girls whose influence on Bhopal would be deeply felt during the reign of Sultan Jahan Begum, the fourth and last Begum of Bhopal.

Sikandar attended her final Grand Durbar in Agra in November 1866, convened by the new Viceroy, Lord Lawrence. Shortly after returning from Agra, Sikandar Begum fell ill. She died of a kidney ailment on 30 November 1868 at the age of 50, a year before the death of the famous poet, Mirza Asadullah Khan Ghalib. Amidst scenes of deep grief, she was buried in the Bara Bagh park.

Sikandar Begum – An assessment

In terms of progressive reform and advancement, Sikandar's 21-year reign was unquestionably the golden period in Bhopal's history. By force of her personality, by sheer diligent good governance and by her wise statecraft, Sikandar had seen Bhopal emerge as one of the best governed, enlightened and stable princely states. Sikandar, protected by the British, was at peace with her Marhatta and Rajput neighbours and no threat developed from outside. Nor was she threatened by family intrigues from within. Sikandar took effective control of all the levers of power, snuffing out all possible dissent. Hers was a towering presence that was recognized as a colossus by her own public and by her protectors, the British.

In the administrative sector, Sikandar presided over a dynamic, reform-oriented regime that placed Bhopal at the pinnacle of well-administered princely states. In the field of foreign affairs, Sikandar had the wisdom, against enormous internal pressures, to back the winning horse in the 1857 Mutiny and gained the reward for her steadfast

Dost Mohammad Khan.
Founder of the State.

Dost's Tomb.
Headstone in English, installed around 200 years after his death.

3. ABOVE. The author praying at the derelict tomb of Yar Mohammad Khan at Islamnagar (December 1998).

4. BELOW. Ginnor Fort, 1998.

5. Shahzad Masih (Balthazar de Bourbon).

6. Dulhan Saheba smoking a hookah with her "slave" Sheeda.

7. ABOVE. Raisen Fort with one of the water reservoirs (non-perennial).

8. LEFT. Qudsia Begum.

support. Subsequently, Sikandar Begum became the star of several British durbars held for Indian rulers. She had earned the accolades by her wisdom, enlightened governance and high moral character. She was a good judge of human beings and collected upright men around her as advisers and officials.

A practising Muslim, Sikandar reasoned that Islam did not prevent woman's rule nor did the Quran prescribe purdah. Her commitment to Islam was not only through her personal example of praying five times a day, but especially by her setting the unique precedent of being the first Muslim ruler, male or female, to perform the pilgrimage to Makkah from India. In confirmation of her Islamic credentials, Sikandar had the famous Juma Masjid in Delhi reopened after the British had closed it during the Mutiny. Despite providing loyal support to the British during the Revolt, Sikandar earned her credentials as a committed Muslim and as a dedicated standard-bearer of Islam. Sikandar had an awesome charismatic personality. Athletic, physically strong and masculine, she led by example from the front. As ruler, she mostly inhabited a man's world and relished outshining her male relatives. Strangely, Sikandar's main love of her life was for Jahangir, the man who set out to usurp her throne and eventually to murder her. Sikandar saw these attempts as family machinations aimed to gain control over the state and forgave her husband as he lay on his deathbed. Later, Sikandar was too involved in governance, too committed to building a modern stable state to find time for personal relationships. She loved and respected her mother and to her granddaughter she gave all her tender affection. Shahjehan was an only daughter whom Sikandar also loved but was possibly a little disappointed in because of her feminine, hedonistic character. Nevertheless, to the best of her ability, she groomed Shahjehan to succeed her as ruler.

An indication of Sikandar's character and sense of justice is given by the following two incidents. Sikandar, like her mother, was in the habit of touring the town incognito to ascertain the temper of the common people towards her governance. One night she returned from a nocturnal visit to be halted by the palace sentries, who were under strict orders not to allow entry into the palace without the given password. Sikandar had forgotten the password and the sentry on duty refused to allow the Begum into the palace even after she had shed her disguise. Next morning, the sentry was summoned to the royal presence, shivering with trepidation at not having recognized his ruler. Sikandar fixed him with her famous glare and then ordered her Minister to give him a bonus for faithfully carrying out his duties.

On another occasion, Sikandar wanted to build a new palace – the Hawa Mahal – for herself, but was informed that a poor Hindu family declined to give up their small hut which was located in the compound where the palace was to be constructed. Sikandar's Minister advised a requisitioning of the hut with adequate financial compensation and alternative accommodation for the Hindu family, but the poor man of the household insisted on staying put. Sikandar decided that the man should be allowed to keep his hut and the palace was built with the hut remaining in the precincts.

If there had been any doubts about a Muslim woman's capacity to rule a state, they had first been set at rest by Qudsia's regency and emphatically answered in the affirmative by Sikandar's golden reign. The two Begums had paved the way for succeeding Begums to govern without hindrance or stigma attached to women's rule.

Sikandar Begum's golden rule saw Bhopal prominently placed on the map of India. It was well administered with reforms in agriculture, the police, the army, civil administration and finance. New currency, a postal service and greatly improved road connections saw the revival of economic activity in the state. Law and order were also maintained through an intelligence network and streetlights. Above all, Bhopal exuded an aura of fair governance, communal harmony, simplicity and encouragement for the skilled and learned to settle in this beautiful city. Bhopal became a model state and Sikandar Begum was acclaimed by the British not only for her loyalty but for her fair and progressive administration. Urdu replaced Persian as the court language and a 19-gun salute boomed a welcome to the Begum every time she stepped out of her domain. Sikandar had ably and comprehensively demonstrated that, in every sense, she was superior to men.

6

Shahjehan Begum 1868–1901

Shahjehan becomes ruler

On 16 November 1868, at a durbar held 17 days after Sikandar's death, Shahjehan was crowned Begum of Bhopal for the second time in her life. The Agent to the Governor-General, Colonel Meade, read out the Viceroy's proclamation and, surprisingly, also announced that ten-year-old Sultan Jahan would be heir apparent. The little princess made a plucky speech at the durbar, thanking God and the British government for the honour. Shahjehan Begum's succession as ruler was the first in Bhopal's history that was non-controversial, legal and free from competing family claims. Bhopal was stable, well governed and secure after Sikandar's golden reign and, with Queen Victoria resplendently presiding over the British Empire, a discreet veil was placed over previous British doubts on accepting women's rule in India. The recently widowed Shahjehan who had held the title of ruler until she abdicated in favour of her mother, now eased into the role like a hand fitting comfortably into a glove.

The surprising element of the announcement of Sultan Jahan as heir apparent was that Shahjehan was still only 30. She was fertile, having produced two daughters, and could have more children from a second husband. According to Islamic and British laws, a son born to Shahjehan would take precedence over an elder daughter. It, therefore, seemed premature for the British government to nominate Sultan Jahan as heir apparent.

The probable reason for the announcement was that Sikandar Begum had, before her death, sought and obtained from the British government an assurance that her beloved granddaughter's rights would be protected.

Moreover, both Sikandar and the British preferred that the succession in Bhopal be kept within the Orakzai Pathan lineage that had ruled Bhopal since Dost Mohammad Khan – the very reason that had prompted Sikandar Begum to select an Orakzai Pathan from Jalalabad as Sultan Jahan's future consort. The British had probably noted that

Shahjehan was emotionally vulnerable and could marry a second time outside her Pathan clan. Their announcement aimed at closing off any such rivals from the succession.

From its earliest days, Bhopal's court ambience had been simple, egalitarian and austere. Some nawabs, notably Hayat and Ghous, had shown signs of princely decadence, but this trend had been more than reversed by the reigns of the two succeeding Begums – Qudsia and Sikandar – who were dedicated, ascetic and pious. Shahjehan's rule, however, saw the emergence of a new, feisty atmosphere in Bhopal. The Begum became a patron of the arts, drawing poets, musicians and literati to Bhopal. Like her Moghul namesake, Shahjehan began building magnificent palaces, mosques and monuments. She encouraged the arts and paid particular attention to humanitarian issues like housing, health and education. The most discernible change from the past was the relaxed atmosphere in the court where renowned classical singers like Ustad Mohammad Khan, kathak dancers like the famous Kalka Binda and instrumentalists like the great tabla player, Kishan Maharaj, would perform regularly at the Begum's court. A number of these artists stayed on to make their homes in Bhopal, encouraged by the beneficence and patronage of the Begum. The jagirdars, nobles and court officials, taking their cue from the royal palace, also began to enjoy the good life with shikar, *mujras* (performances by dancing girls) and a general atmosphere of freewheeling decadence becoming the order of the day. Shahjehan was also fond of festivity, celebrating every possible event like the opening of a new palace with great pomp and eclat. The town would be lit with dazzling illuminations, followed by firework displays, banquets and mujras that would be held for months on end. Drummers, dancing girls and qawwals would be summoned at the capricious drop of a hat.

Shahjehan was also in a different character mould to her mother and grandmother. She had aspirations to being a poetess, loved the sound of music and was coquettishly feminine. She was no polo player, tiger hunter or *tahajjud-guzar* (one who performs voluntary late-night prayers). Widowed at the young age of 29 – a year before she ascended the masnad – Shahjehan was not averse to being courted by ambitious young men. However, she soon became besotted by one man who spun a web of charm and allurement around the Begum and who became the love of her life. He was Syed Siddiq Hassan.

Syed Siddiq Hassan, 1832–90

Syed Siddiq Hassan was born on 14 October 1832 in Bareilly. He was from a distinguished family of theologians who, as Syeds, traced their ancestry back to the Prophet. Descendants of Hazrat Ali, Siddiq Hassan's Shiite ancestors first settled in Bokhara and then migrated to Multan. There they became guardians of mosques and holy places until the family moved again, nearer to the centre of power in the United Provinces, where they spread themselves in the well-known bastions of Shiite culture, Bareilly and Kannauj. Siddiq Hassan's grandfather was an acclaimed scholar and theologian. He was employed in a high post in Hyderabad and was comfortably off, owning lands and property. The family prided itself on its erudition and scholarship, engaging itself in the doctrinal debate between various Muslim schools of thought.

Siddiq Hassan's father, Syed Awlad Hassan, was also steeped in Islamic scholarship and became an ardent disciple of the Muslim reformers, Syed Waliullah and Syed Ahmad Shahid. These scholars belonged to the school of thought that believed in the puritan values of Islam, drawn directly from the Quran and Sunnah. They opposed the sanctification of pirs and the Sufic rituals that had spread across the Sub-Continent. They also believed that the Door of Ijtehad[1] should not be regarded as closed and were consequently ranged against the four main schools of Islamic jurisprudence of which the Hanafi was predominant in south Asia. This doctrine was called Wahabism, named after the Arab evangelist Abdul Wahab. Syed Awlad Hassan became so immersed in propagating the preachings of his mentors that he shunned all material values and assumed the role of a zealous missionary, showing scant concern for the welfare of his family.

Syed Awlad Hassan's first somewhat bizarre act was to publicly announce that he had converted from Shiism to become a Sunni. This action led to ostracization from his family and from the Shiite fold. His next, equally bizarre, step was to renounce all interest in material benefits, notably the land and property that his family owned and which Syed Awlad could have inherited but spurned. Syed Awlad Hassan explained to his mentor, Syed Ahmad Shahid, that as a Sunni convert, he could not justifiably claim an inheritance from Shiite family estates. Thus, Syed Awlad Hassan's missionary evangelism led his family into self-imposed penury. He and his family suddenly found themselves ostracized and impecunious – a state that was all the more embarrassing because they belonged to a class of respected and educated citizens who had to maintain appearances. Syed Awlad Hassan died in 1837 when Siddiq was only five years old. Siddiq was thus brought up by his mother in hard times – often saved by friends and associates of his late father who ensured that Siddiq received a proper education in Arabic, Persian, Quranic studies and Hadith. Siddiq was a worthy student, but unlike his father, recognized the importance of material benefits. As soon as he was 17 years old, still poor as a church mouse, he began looking for work and in 1854 landed in Bhopal, which was a haven for Muslim scholars and theologians. Siddiq arrived in Bhopal selling perfume, but soon found a job as a schoolteacher, augmenting his meagre income by preaching at mosques where he gave vent to the Wahabi views held by his father, opposing the Hanafi school of jurisprudence and propagating a return to Islam's pristine values. In 1857, Siddiq was banished from Bhopal. His supporters claim he fell foul of a leading Hanafi Maulvi in Bhopal, Abbas Chiryakoti, who had him shunted out of the state.

---

[1] The closing of the Door of Ijtehad signified a consensus between the four Sunni schools of theological and legal interpretation of the Quran and Sunnah, the Hanafi, Hambali, Maliki and Shafi – that no further interpretation was warranted.

Siddiq's detractors maintain that Sikandar Begum recognized his ambitious and seditious nature and expelled him.[1]

Siddiq then went to the neighbouring state of Tonk, but when the Mutiny swept across India, returned to Kannauj to protect his family. During these difficult days, Siddiq suffered from extreme poverty and anguish at not being able to support his family. He had only one change of clothes and his family frequently spent days without a proper meal.

Eventually, Prime Minister Maulvi Jamaluddin, who had taken a liking to the scholarly, intelligent Siddiq, persuaded Sikandar to relent and allow Siddiq's return to Bhopal. Sikandar, this time, was favourably inclined towards Siddiq and commissioned him to write a history of Bhopal, paying him a substantial salary. For the first time in his life, Siddiq was secure and brought his sister and mother to Bhopal. He was soon employed by Maulvi Jamaluddin as a clerk in his office and in 1860, Siddiq married Maulvi Jamaluddin's widowed eldest daughter, Zakia. Clearly, this marriage was one of convenience for both sides. Siddiq sought security by marrying the boss's daughter who was 11 years older than him, while Maulvi Jamaluddin wanted his widowed daughter to have an educated husband. Zakia was 39 years old and already had children from her first husband, but she and Siddiq had three more, Nurul Hassan in 1862, Safia in 1863 and Ali Hassan in 1868.

By the mid-1860s, Siddiq Hassan, enthusiastically sponsored by his father-in-law, began climbing the administrative ladder until he was given the responsibility of acting as tutor to the vivacious, feisty heir apparent, Shahjehan. In 1865, Siddiq was 33 years old and Shahjehan 27. It was not long before rumours were circulating that Siddiq and Shahjehan were emotionally entangled, being closeted alone for hours, ostensibly studying Arabic, Persian and Hadith!

After Shahjehan became Begum, she promoted Siddiq Hassan to be her Chief Secretary and, as a result, the private meetings grew longer and the scandal more intense. Shahjehan also began referring to Siddiq as Siddiq Hassan Khan, the subtle addition of the name Khan suggesting, falsely, that Siddiq Hassan was from Pathan stock. It was apparent that Shahjehan was deeply in love with Siddiq Hassan who developed a complete intellectual and emotional hold over the Begum. She became Trilby to his Svengali.

Shahjehan's early years

In the first four years after she became ruler, Shahjehan addressed her responsibilities with rare enthusiasm and commitment. She had been thoroughly groomed in administration and statecraft by her mother and had practical experience of running the state. Shahjehan toured the

---

[1] Some reports indicate that Siddiq Hassan and Maulvi Chiryakoti fell out when Siddiq criticized the Maulvi for smoking a hookah. Sikandar Begum was reported to have suspected Siddiq over the theft of a *khillat* (expensive robe) that was stolen from an office supervised by him.

provinces, improved the revenue system, increased tax collection, raised the pay of her cavalrymen and modernized the police and postal service. To make up the financial deficit in the treasury, Shahjehan commissioned the cultivation of opium. She re-surveyed the land, held another census which showed Bhopal's population as being 744,000, a decline due to two famines and the plague. Shahjehan also enjoyed visits to Viceregal durbars, the first of which was held in 1869 in Calcutta to honour the Duke of Edinburgh. She seemed to have enjoyed herself in Calcutta and took the opportunity to visit the theatre, Fort William, the Calcutta Citadel, the museum and the mint.

On her return from Calcutta, she built a dam behind the Eidgah Hill which led to another artificial lake, enhancing Bhopal's scenic beauty. She also constructed a proper arsenal for the Bhopal artillery and built a new jail. This dedicated round of effective governance drew appropriate applause from the British government and by 1872, a kharita arrived from the Resident informing the Begum that she would be made a Grand Commander of the Star of India. Shahjehan had thus made a worthy start as the Begum of Bhopal.

At home, after Sikandar's death, the ten-year-old Sultan Jahan moved to her mother's palace where she found the atmosphere quite different. There were musical soirees, poetry-reading sessions, dancing and intrigue and everyone seemed to be enjoying the good life. Siddiq Hassan was always around and constantly at her mother's side. In her autobiography,[1] Sultan Jahan describes her daily routine at her grandmother's house as follows:

From 5 o'clock to 6	Open-air exercise
From 6 o'clock to 7	Morning meal
From 8 o'clock to 10	Reading of the Quran
From 10 o'clock to 11	Breakfast with Nawab Sikandar Begum
From 11 o'clock to 12	Recreation
From 12 o'clock to 1	Handwriting lesson
From 1 o'clock to 3	English lesson
From 3 o'clock to 4	Persian lesson
From 4 o'clock to 5	Arithmetic
From 5 o'clock to 5.30	Pashtu lessons and fencing practice alternately
From 5.30 o'clock to 6	Riding lesson
From 6 o'clock to 7	Evening meal
8 o'clock	Bed

Sultan Jahan laments that when she moved to her mother's household, her lessons were cut by half. For a serious, pious child, Sultan Jahan's life with her mother was a little disconcerting, particularly as she could sense Siddiq Hassan's baneful influence on her mother that was creating friction within the family. This led to a certain distance between mother and daughter which is best illustrated by a comparison between Sikandar Begum's tender letters to her granddaughter from Hajj and the

---

[1] *An Account of My Life.*

following, rather cold and unfeeling instructions that Shahjehan handed over to Sultan Jahan:

> It has been brought to my notice that at the present time your studies are not being pursued with regularity, and it is not clear in what manner you employ your time from morning till evening. These are the hours which you should devote to study. You are, therefore, to draw up a timetable of the work that you are doing. On receiving this, I will myself send you a revised timetable for your daily guidance.
>
> You are to study the Holy Quran, with translation, from 7 a.m. till 9 a.m. with the Madar-ul-muham Sahib. You may then take your morning meal and rest. Between 2 and 4 p.m., you are to read the official papers which I shall send to you, and write on them any orders that you consider necessary. After 4 o'clock, your time is at your own disposal. You may go for a walk, or attend to household matters, or employ yourself in any way that you like.[1]

Nevertheless, in February 1871 relations between mother and daughter were still warm and loving as Shahjehan held a huge celebration for her 13-year-old daughter's *nashra* (completion of the Quran). As usual, Shahjehan never hesitated to announce extended celebrations and for her daughter's nashra, special festivities were commissioned for 40 days with firework displays, special illuminations all over town, singing, dancing and banquets. In the tradition of Bhopal Begums, the inculcation of Islamic values was a major requirement for a ruler. The momentous celebration of Sultan Jahan's nashra was an indicator of her capability to assume the reins of power when her time came.

Shahjehan marries Siddiq Hassan

Siddiq Hassan's attempt to reach the levers of power began immediately after Shahjehan became ruler. Having ousted his venerable father-in-law, Maulvi Jamaluddin, from the corridors of power, Siddiq Hassan increased the emotional and intellectual grip that he already exercised over the besotted Shahjehan. He made her promote him *madar-ul-maham* (Chief Minister) and began influencing her in state as well as in family matters. Surprisingly, in furthering this manoeuvre Siddiq received the support of his first wife, Zakia, who probably saw in her husband's new conquest an opening for the advancement of her own children. By 1871, Zakia was already 50 years old and had probably given up any thought of holding her virile, 39-year-old husband against the attraction of his 33-year-old paramour. Bizarrely, far from reacting as a jilted wife, Zakia encouraged Siddiq to consummate his liaison with Shahjehan.

Siddiq moved quickly. He allowed word to get through to Major Edward Thompson, Political Agent in Bhopal, that Shahjehan was pregnant with his child. In a report sent by the Resident, Sir Lepel Griffin, to the Secretary of State for India, Sir Henry Durand, Griffin states that Siddiq Hassan convinced Major Thompson, that honour could only be saved

---

[1] *An Account of My Life.*

through immediate marriage.¹ Faced with the awkward and embarrassing dilemma of a ruling Begum carrying an illegitimate child, the British agreed to Thompson's advice that marriage was the best way out and would scotch the ugly rumours that were circulating in Bhopal. In an example of the most devious chicanery, the British Resident and Political Agent who accompanied Shahjehan on a visit to Agra in 1871, artfully suggested to the Begum that she should re-marry, as Islam encouraged widows to marry again. They added that it would be helpful for the Begum to have a non-executive consort by her side to guide and assist her in her onerous duties.

In her memoirs, Shahjehan makes out, with apparent innocence, that she accepted the Resident's advice and then looked around for a suitable, cultured, educated, man and conveniently found that the 'noble and learned' Siddiq Hassan would fit the bill perfectly. Contradicting herself in the next sentence, Shahjehan adds that the marriage would also scotch ugly court rumours because the two were obliged to spend much time alone together. Shahjehan then omits to mention that Siddiq Hassan was already married to the daughter of her devoted father-figure, Maulvi Jamaluddin. For an attempt at pulling the wool over people's eyes, the following extract from Shahjehan's *Taj-ul-Iqbal* takes a lot of beating:

> I thought it proper to openly ask for the sanction of the Governor-General to this fitting act [marriage]. On the 8th of May 1871 A.D., or 7th Safar 1288 A.H., I received an English letter from Colonel John William Willoughby Osborne, C.B., Political Agent, in which he said that he had great pleasure in sending to me a letter from the Foreign Secretary, regarding my proposed marriage, and that he should be much pleased to see me married again. This gentleman [Siddiq Hassan] had been for seventeen years in the service of this State, and was for a long time Munshi to my sainted mother, the Nawab Sikandar Begum, who, appreciating his learning and good qualities, which were second to no other Munshi in Bhopal, appointed him superintendent of the Annals of Bhopal. Suffice it to say that I followed the mandates of the holy Quran and the counsels of English officers, and put an end to evil report, because it was considered improper in the eyes of the world for me to be alone with a stranger and he not my husband, and it often happened that, in the conduct of State affairs, it was absolutely necessary for my secretary and myself to be alone together.

Once the suggestion had been made by the British, it did not take Shahjehan much time or persuasion to announce her marriage to Siddiq Hassan, which took place on 8 May 1871. The wedding ceremonies were low-key, but a public function was held at which the British formally gave their seal of approval, underlining the fact that Siddiq Hassan, like his predecessor Umrao Doulah, was to play a non-executive role as consort. The Resident, Colonel Meade, then took Siddiq Hassan to Qudsia Begum's palace to receive an icily cold benediction from the 70-year-old dowager. Qudsia had openly resented Shahjehan's relationship and subsequent marriage to Siddiq and acquiesced in the fait accompli

---

¹ Enclosure to Bhopal Memorandum sent by AGG, Sir Lepel Griffin to Secretary of State, Henry Durand, 18 August 1885, India Office Records.

only because there was no other option. Siddiq Hassan never forgave the old lady for her contemptuous attitude towards him and gradually created a wall of mistrust between the two households.

Having married the Begum of Bhopal, Siddiq Hassan set about gaining control of the state. He first persuaded his wife that it was beneath his and her dignity for him to be Chief Minister and that the British government should give him exactly the same status as her first husband, Umrao Doulah. On Shahjehan's insistence, the British were obliged to agree and on 15 October 1872, at a special durbar, Siddiq Hassan was formally given the title of Nawab Wala-Jah, Amir-ul-Mulk and, like Umrao Doulah, accorded a 17-gun salute at home. Overjoyed at the British government's decision, the love-lorn Shahjehan, dressed up her husband in a brocade sherwani, covered him with jewellery, mounted him on an elephant and, with the 17-gun royal salute booming over the ramparts of Fatahgarh Fort, made him lead a ceremonial procession through the city, having ordered her subjects to rejoice at the happy event. Unfortunately, all segments of Bhopal's society, except some paid lackeys and Siddiq Hassan's Wahabi colleagues, resented and disliked the new Nawab so that his ceremonial procession around the city was greeted with a deafening silence from the people of Bhopal. An angry and humiliated Siddiq Hassan returned home and complained to his wife of the conspiracy against him by the Begum's family and the Barru-kat Pathans of Bhopal. Incidentally, during the first year of marriage no child was born to Siddiq and Shahjehan. Either the foetus was aborted or Siddiq had faked news of the pregnancy and successfully taken the British for a ride with an empty shotgun!

Siddiq's next manoeuvre was to insist that Wahabi tenets required Shahjehan to adopt purdah. Shahjehan dutifully obeyed and virtually handed over running of the state to her husband. Ironically, Shahjehan had reversed the practice that two older generations of women rulers had adopted. Both Qudsia and Sikandar had insisted that Bhopal's Begums should rule in their own right and that their consorts should not hold executive power. They had both abandoned purdah and had ruled effectively by interacting open-faced with the opposite sex. Now, Shahjehan who had, so far, ruled with face unveiled, moved in the opposite direction by going into purdah at the age of 34, virtually handing over the reins of government to her husband.

Predictably, Shahjehan's marriage led to a number of complications in the Begum's personal life. Strain increased between Shahjehan and her grandmother Qudsia. They were opposites in character and Qudsia did not hide her contempt for Shahjehan's lavish and undisciplined conduct of her personal life and especially her choice of husband. Shahjehan's marriage strained her relations with Qudsia to the extent that, in her final years, the dignified and popular dowager was formally ostracized by the Begum's court. Qudsia was not invited to attend state or family functions and not even permitted to present a gift to her great-granddaughter on her wedding. Typical of Shahjehan's churlish and disrespectful attitude towards Qudsia was the following note issued when Qudsia sought the ruler's permission to bring a traditional gift at the *Juma* (Friday) ceremony of Sultan Jahan's wedding: 'I have on several occasions informed you that there is no necessity for you to put yourself to this trouble. God, in His bounty, has satisfied all the wants of Sultan Jahan Begum, and she stands in need of nothing more.'

The second complication related to the status of the venerable and trusted Maulvi Jamaluddin, Siddiq Hassan's father-in-law. The poor Maulvi found himself ousted from court circles by an increasingly arrogant Siddiq Hassan, whose latest conquest had landed a much bigger prize than even the Maulvi's daughter could offer. Furthermore, as Shahjehan showered ceremonial honours on Siddiq Hassan and gave him increasingly important appointments at court, Bhopal's jagirdars and Barru-kat elite resented the arrogation of power by Siddiq Hassan; he was seen as an ambitious schemer bent on using his emotional domination over Shahjehan to wrest control over the state. The fact that he was not a Pathan and had arrived in Bhopal selling perfume made Siddiq Hassan the target of jealousy and condescension on the part of Bhopal's gentry.

Thus, Shahjehan's 33-year reign was dominated by a single factor, the influence of her second husband, Siddiq Hassan. This relationship affected Shahjehan's capacity to govern, it influenced her relations with her grandmother and only daughter, it undermined her standing with the British and tarnished her image in the eyes of Bhopal's gentry and public. In short, Shahjehan's devotion and loyalty to her husband grew in inverse proportion to the criticism and hostility that she increasingly faced from her family, Bhopal's public and the British hierarchy. It became a heavy cross to bear.

Sultan Jahan's marriage

At the age of 13, Sultan Jahan saw her mother, descendant of the proud Orakzai conquerors of Bhopal, marry an impecunious, non-Pathan clerk. Sultan Jahan sensed Shahjehan's aloofness towards her – even though she was by then an only child – and noted her blind devotion to Siddiq Hassan who had already turned Shahjehan against her grandmother. Despite the fact she had been brought up as an obedient child, a certain distance crept into the relationship between daughter and mother.

Sultan Jahan writes in her memoirs that Siddiq Hassan next attempted a devilish stratagem to consolidate his hold on power. He attempted to break the betrothal between Sultan Jahan and Ahmad Ali Khan and to substitute his elder son, Nurul Hassan – though he was already married – as Sultan Jahan's consort. Shahjehan did not object, but Sultan Jahan adamantly refused to contemplate such a union. Sensing her mother's coldness, Sultan Jahan could not wait for the day when she would be old enough to marry her beau and chosen consort. Theirs was a union blessed in heaven since they were brought up together as children, grew up into adolescence knowing that they were expected to marry and, at least in the case of Sultan Jahan, promptly fell in love. Eventually, in 1874 Shahjehan called in the family elders and nobles of the state and sought their advice on Sultan Jahan's marriage. They were unanimous that Shahjehan should marry Ahmad Ali Khan and hence the die that was set by Sikandar six years earlier was finally cast by Shahjehan. The Viceroy was duly informed of the proposed marriage and eventually the acting Resident, Colonel Watson, was sent to Bhopal to seek Sultan Jahan's voluntary consent. Colonel Watson requested the ruler's permission for a separate meeting with Sultan Jahan and asked her if she would take Ahmad Ali Khan as her husband. Feigning oriental shyness, but with her heart jumping for joy, Sultan Jahan replied in her broken English that she would. The Viceroy soon gave his approval and the engagement was announced, with the wedding to be held a year later.

This one-year waiting period saw the latent friction between the households of the ruler and the heir apparent emerge into the open. Quoting strict Wahabi tenets, Siddiq insisted on the separation of the young couple and virtually made Ahmad Ali Khan a prisoner for the entire year, hoping to evoke from him an intemperate response that would provide an excuse for the engagement to be broken off. Sultan Jahan describes the mental torture in the following words:

> Although my mother's intentions were perfectly good, this delay proved unfortunate, for it afforded Siddiq Hassan Khan abundant opportunities for harassing Ahmad Ali Khan, whose life from that time began to resemble that of a state prisoner. Sentries were posted outside his sleeping-apartment, and no one was permitted to have access to him, while he himself could not go forth without permission. To such an extent was his freedom curtailed that he was not allowed to hunt, ride, walk, or to enjoy any form of recreation whatever. But he bore all these trials with such exemplary patience, that even his worst enemies could find no blot in his behaviour. Everything possible was done to enrage and irritate him, but he never lost his self-control, and displayed all through this period of probation, tact and wisdom far beyond his years. Fate willed that Ahmad Ali Khan should be my husband, and all the machinations of Siddiq Hassan Khan and his friends could not alter Fate's decree.[1]

Eventually, the long agonizing months of waiting passed and the celebration of the heir apparent's wedding took place on 1 February 1875. Ahmad Ali Khan was given the title of Ihtisham-ul-Mulk, Sultan Doulah and awarded a jagir. There was the usual festivity and rejoicing, but Shahjehan introduced an acrimonious note into the proceedings by not inviting Qudsia to the ceremony despite British entreaties. Siddiq also drew up a marriage contract for Sultan Jahan and Ahmad Ali that was at the same time humiliating for the groom but also revolutionary in giving the most liberal rights to a Muslim wife.

For the bridegroom, the humiliating part of the marriage contract saw him sign an agreement that would lead to the marriage being annulled if he should change his religion (which in real terms meant convert from Sunni to Shia). He was to obey his wife and not interfere in the state, jagir or financial affairs. Failure to do so would give his wife the right to bring about a separation. The bridegroom agreed not to take a second

---

[1] *An Account of My Life.*

wife (permissible under Muslim law) and not to interfere in the upbringing of his children who would be brought up under the direction of his wife and mother-in-law. Finally, the bridegroom agreed that he would not allow his relatives or friends to interfere in the affairs of state, authorizing his mother-in-law (the ruler) to decree a separation in the event of a disagreement between his wife and himself – a separation that would be binding and not questionable in a court of law. For the wife, the marriage contract contained conditions which would enable her (or the ruler) to end the marriage in case of disagreement, interference or sheer incompatibility.

Thus, within a span of three years, Bhopal witnessed the weddings of both mother and daughter – Shahjehan for the second time. The ruler and heir apparent set up separate household in palaces next to each other and with every passing month the friction between the two houses began to grow. Shahjehan made it known that she wanted a son from Siddiq, increasing Sultan Jahan's sense of insecurity and distance from her mother. During this period, Shahjehan embarked on a succession of visits to Viceregal durbars in Calcutta and Delhi and attempted to pitchfork her consort into the forefront by various stratagems. For instance, at the Duke of Edinburgh's arrival ceremony in Bombay, Shahjehan proposed that Siddiq represent her because of her daughter's confinement. Later, she stated that since she had adopted purdah, her husband should receive the award of the GCSI on her behalf at the investiture ceremony. The British, who had become wise to Siddiq's machinations, steadfastly declined to accept Siddiq Hassan as a surrogate ruler so that Shahjehan backtracked and attended the durbars in person, dressed in a burqa!

Rift between ruler and heir apparent

Nine months after her wedding, Sultan Jahan gave birth to her first child, Bilqis Jahan, on 25 October 1875. Three other children followed in rapid succession. Next came Mohammad Nasrullah Khan, born on 4 December 1876, the first male child in four generations of women rulers, followed by another son, Mohammad Obaidullah Khan, on 3 November 1878 and another daughter, Asif Jahan, on 5 August 1880. Then there was a gap of 14 years before a fifth child – Mohammad Hamidullah Khan – was born on 9 September 1894.

While Sultan Jahan was in a constant state of pregnancy after her wedding, there was acute disappointment and frustration in Shahjehan's household as she was unable to conceive Siddiq's child. Shahjehan had been counting on producing a male heir from Siddiq especially as Zakia had given Siddiq three children when she was well into middle age, the last when she was 47 years old. Shahjehan had also given birth to two children from Umrao Doulah, so there was every reason to expect that Shahjehan would bear Siddiq's children. In a feverish effort to conceive, the couple tried doctors, hakeems, saints and rustic witch doctors – both Muslim and Hindu – to cast a spell of fertility. Nothing worked. In her frustration and envy towards Sultan Jahan, Shahjehan would go into intemperate rages against her husband for interfering in state affairs, using colourful and base language to heap contempt and derision on Siddiq Hassan. Strangely, these tantrums were usually calmed and a loving relationship restored through the healing efforts of Zakia, Siddiq's first wife.

After Sultan Jahan's marriage in 1875, tension between the two royal households increased with every passing week. Bhopal's society was divided into two camps with court intriguers having a field day, fuelling the suspicions that mother and daughter harboured against each other. On Shahjehan and Siddiq's side were the establishment Wahabi sympathizers and jagirdars who sought to benefit from the power that flowed from the ruler's control of the state. Coalescing around the heir apparent and her husband were the Baqi-khel – Umrao Doulah's powerful family from his first wives – and the Jalalabadi clan that had arrived in Bhopal with Ahmad Ali Khan. The strongest moral support for Sultan Jahan came from her great-grandmother, the venerable and respected Qudsia Begum, tilting the Bhopali public's backing in favour of the serious and devout heir apparent.

A barometer reading of the growing friction between mother and daughter could be taken from Shahjehan's attitude towards her four grandchildren. For the eldest child, Bilqis, widespread celebrations were ordered by the ruler who adopted the first-born into her own household. For Nasrullah, the festivity was rudely interrupted by Siddiq as being un-Islamic. For the third, Obaidullah, and fourth, Asif Jahan, there were practically no celebrations, with Shahjehan paying only brief visits of felicitation to her daughter. Later, when Nasrullah and Asif Jahan fell seriously ill, Shahjehan chose not to visit. Nor did she pay a courtesy call when the fifth child, Hamidullah, was born. Shahjehan never set eyes on her fifth grandchild until he visited her on her deathbed a week before she died.

As friction increased between the two households, Bilqis Jahan – a loving, sensitive child – became the only link between mother and daughter. The gradual closing of the door between the two households was as much physical as metaphorical as the two palaces were adjacent and connected by a door through which Bilqis was allowed to pass once a day, for an hour, to bid 'Salaam' to her mother before returning to her doting grandmother's palace.

Siddiq Hassan's growing control

After a cautious, low-profile start as Nawab and consort, Siddiq Hassan accelerated his attempt to gain control over the state. By 1875, he had placed his own appointees in key positions like *Madar-ul-Maham, Mir-Munshi* (Chief Clerk) and Chief of Police. Shahjehan was in purdah, rarely going out to meet her subjects – a task that she increasingly left to her consort. Despite an undertow of tension during these years, mother and daughter maintained a superficial cordiality, with Sultan Jahan attending state functions and accompanying her mother to durbars in Delhi and Calcutta.

In 1877, however, the smouldering tension between the two houses burst into flames. The occasion was a durbar that Siddiq Hassan specially summoned and addressed in the name of his wife, the ruler. Siddiq Hassan made a vicious attack on Sikandar Begum's reign, describing it as despotic, tyrannical and barbaric. He then made a frontal attack on Sultan Doulah and members of Umrao Doulah's family, calling them conspirators who would be punished if they did not mend their ways. The virulent attack on Sikandar's reign, on the person of Sultan Doulah and the entire Bhopal Barru-kat hierarchy shocked and stunned the Bhopal gentry gathered at the durbar. Sultan Jahan described it in the following words:

> The occasion selected by Siddiq Hassan Khan for the promulgation of this slander was a large durbar held, apparently, with no other object but his own glorification. It was attended by all the leading nobles and officials of the State, and the proceedings opened with a proclamation, in the course of which the administration of the late Begum was subjected to the most offensive criticism, her reign being described as a period of barbarism and oppression. With the exception of his own adherents, all who were present were disgusted at the tone of the proclamation, and took no pains to conceal their contempt for its originator. It was followed by a speech from the Nawab Sahib himself, of such prodigious length that to give even a summary of it would tax a far better memory than mine. But there were some passages in it which, by reason of their very malignancy, I can never forget. In attempting to draw a comparison between the present reign and the past, he stigmatised the Sikandar Begum as a despot, and described the whole State as groaning under the tyranny and injustice of her rule. My mother he praised in the most extravagant terms. She was the most enlightened, generous, and capable administrator of her day, and her reign was the reign of peace, justice, and mercy. Then, as though he were a magistrate addressing an unlawful assembly, he warned his audience not to mistake clemency for weakness. He was well aware, he said, that a number of evilly disposed persons were attempting to make mischief and to stir up sedition in the State. Amongst others he mentioned Latif Muhammad Khan and Majid Muhammad Khan, the two sons of Nawab Umrao Dula, who, he stated, were well known to be in the habit of paying secret visits to Nawab Ihtisham-ul-mulk, and, by working on his inexperience with evil advice, were endeavouring to form a party hostile to the Begum and to the State. But by the Grace of God – and his own prowess – their base designs would soon be frustrated. Much more followed in the same strain, and he eventually brought his harangue to an end with an outburst of self-glorification, and a fulsome expression of his gratitude and devotion to the Begum and the British Raj.
>
> Although the charges brought against my husband and the sons of Nawab Umrao Dula were without a particle of foundation, it may well be imagined that such words, spoken as they were at a public durbar, and by one who was to all intents and purposes a stranger to the State, inflicted on me, and many others, wounds which time will not easily heal. Out of regard for Nawab Shahjehan Begum, we refrained from giving expression to our feelings, and heard both the proclamation and speech in silence.[1]

---

[1] *An Account of My Life.*

The British viewed the ruler–heir apparent tension in clear black and white terms in which Sultan Jahan and her husband were the innocent victims of Siddiq Hassan's ambitious and unscrupulous attempts to gain full authority in Bhopal. As reports of corruption, mismanagement and tyranny grew with Siddiq's lackeys being placed in key posts, the British rued the day that they encouraged the Begum to marry her paramour. British concern was even greater when it became apparent that Siddiq was using his power to disseminate anti-British Wahabi literature from Bhopal.

In 1881, all the royal princes of India were invited to another durbar in Calcutta. Though barely on speaking terms with them, Sultan Jahan was ordered to accompany her mother and Siddiq Hassan to the durbar. On arrival at Calcutta's railway station, the ruler and her consort drove off in a specially arranged carriage leaving the heir apparent and Ahmad Ali Khan standing haplessly at the station. No arrangements for their transport had been made and Sultan Jahan had to hire a buggy to reach her residence! The following day, another protocol incident took place during the audience at the Viceroy's Lodge. Forewarned of the wrangling over precedence, the British drew up a detailed seating plan for the Begum and her entourage, according to which Sultan Jahan as heir apparent took precedence over the consort. While Sultan Jahan was engaged in greeting the Viceroy, Siddiq Hassan surreptitiously took her place in the seating order. Immediately, a British equerry approached him and requested him to vacate the chair and to sit in his appointed place. Glumly, Siddiq obeyed but the humiliation struck deep into the heart of Shahjehan, who made it known to her daughter through emissaries that she was enraged at her husband's humiliation. Sultan Jahan, though generally humble and deferential to her mother, stuck to her rights and sent the following note to her mother:

> Three days ago I sent Your Highness a letter in regard to the seat assigned to me at the durbar on the occasion of the return visit of His Excellency the Viceroy of India. Having received no reply, I venture to call Your Highness's attention to the matter a second time. On former occasions my seat has always been above that of Nawab Siddiq Hassan Khan. This was so at the durbar in Bombay when Your Highness was decorated with the Star of India, as well as at the Calcutta durbar held during the visit of His Royal Highness the Prince of Wales. Indeed, for many years it has been customary in the State for the eir apparent to take precedence of the Nawab Consort. Your Highness has given me to understand that my letter has been forwarded through the State Vakil to the Political Agent, and that his reply will be communicated to me. As this reply has not reached me, I feel that my position is seriously compromised. I had intended not to be present at the last durbar, and it was only the advice of the Political Agent and my respect for the Government of India that induced me to change my mind. I now beg that you will be good enough to forward this letter also to the Political Agent, and that the communication may be marked urgent; for I am determined not to leave Calcutta until a regular and formal decision has been come to. It is within the power of the

Government of India to increase or decrease the rank of any person; and I ask for nothing more than an explanation of the change that has been made.[1]

The 1877 durbar in Bhopal and the Calcutta visit saw the tension between mother and daughter turn into an unbridgeable chasm. From Calcutta onwards, Shahjehan declined basic courtesies towards Sultan Jahan as all contact ceased between ruler and heir apparent. Shahjehan refused to invite Sultan Jahan to official ceremonies or to receive her on festive occasions such as Eid. The only link that remained between mother and daughter were the visits of the bright and intelligent Bilqis who now came to her mother's house with a chaperone.

The next few years were difficult times for Sultan Jahan and her family. Shahjehan refused to release the income from Sultan Jahan's jagir and formally objected to her being referred to as 'princess'. Though living in a palace with a jagir, servants and the outer paraphernalia of abundance, Ahmad Ali and Sultan Jahan's daily lives passed through humiliation and hostile pressure from Shahjehan and Siddiq Hassan. Sultan Jahan would recount to Abida Sultaan, her granddaughter, that weeks would pass without a square meal for the family and, taking pity, old servants would steal gram intended for the royal stables to feed the heir apparent's family.

After the initial burst of enthusiasm, Shahjehan allowed governance to continue on auto-pilot. Shahjehan continued her mother's reforms, but with less personal commitment and dedication than earlier. Essentially, it was the British Political Agent and Resident who were the guiding force behind these reforms. She improved the land revenue and tax system, introduced new coinage and currency, ordered a fresh survey of state lands, reformed the postal services and expanded the judicial system. Typically, Shahjehan released young courtesans from the iron hold of their *madames* and encouraged their marriages.

In 1881, Qudsia Begum died at the age of 82, an event which cast a deep shadow of grief over the people of Bhopal who had deeply revered the old Begum. A superficial reconciliation between Qudsia and Shahjehan had taken place so that Shahjehan attended her grandmother's funeral. Qudsia had committed her life to the welfare of the state and its people. Her death was a special blow for Sultan Jahan, as more than any of her ancestors, Sultan Jahan had modelled herself on the ascetic Qudsia. Shortly afterwards, the loyal Maulvi Jamaluddin also died so that Bhopal was left without two venerated figures who had contributed with heart and soul to the stability and progress of the state. Sarkar Dulhan, the wife of the Bourbon Shahzad Masih and loyal friend of the Bhopal ruling family, died in 1882.

---

[1] *An Account of My Life.*

British concern at Siddiq's activities[1]

During this period when Siddiq Hassan virtually ruled the roost in Bhopal, the British began casting an anxious eye at his political and religious activity against the British. To them, his articles, books and pronouncements bordered on sedition and soon state funds were being used to promote the more politically active ulema into creating a groundswell of opposition against the British, based on religious grounds. Siddiq's emissaries established contact with counterparts abroad, notably in Sudan where the Mahdi was active against the British, and also in Arabia, Turkey and Burma.

The British were also alarmed at the arrogation of power by Siddiq Hassan, the dissipation of state funds and the promotion of his family members in the state hierarchy. Furthermore, resentment towards Siddiq Hassan and therefore against Shahjehan had built up among Bhopal's principal families, with the result that the achievements of Sikandar Begum were being visibly dissipated by Siddiq Hassan's political adventures and Shahjehan's profligacy. Warning signals were, therefore, conveyed to Shahjehan to control her 'wayward' husband and she was reminded that her consort was not expected to interfere in state matters.

Shahjehan Begum paid scant attention to these warnings and invariably replied that Siddiq Hassan was a dutiful consort who did not interfere in state matters and that occasionally she sought his advice on particular issues. The British did not believe her and considered her to be a puppet in Siddiq's control. Eventually, in 1881, Sir Lepel Griffin, the Resident, wrote a formal letter cataloguing Siddiq's misdemeanours and requesting the Begum to rein in her errant consort. Shahjehan gave the warning short shrift and continued merrily on the path chosen for her by Siddiq.

By 1885, Siddiq Hassan's activities had, as far as the British government was concerned, exceeded all limits. Sir Lepel Griffin was particularly critical of Siddiq Hassan's activities and wanted the British government to take action against him. However, Lord Dufferin, the Viceroy, held his hand in deference to the Bhopal royal family's longstanding relationship of trust and proven loyalty. They saw Shahjehan as being totally dominated by Siddiq Hassan who was not only agitating against British rule but was also destroying the harmony and loyal relationships between the ruler and the main families of Bhopal. Correspondence quickened between Sir Lepel Griffin and Sir Henry Durand, Secretary of State for India, in which Griffin pressed for the withdrawing of Siddiq Hassan's titles and for his arrest on charges of sedition and corruption. It was even suggested that, if found guilty, he should be banished to the Andoman Islands. Durand counselled restraint in order to preserve Shahjehan's dignity. Durand was convinced that the charge of sedition was justified, but felt that there was insufficient proof for

---

[1] Telegrams, notings and memoranda on Siddiq Hassan's activities are contained in documents at R/1/1/33 dated October to December 1885, India Office Records.

charges of corruption and mismanagement. Eventually, in August 1885, weighing up all relevant factors, Durand instructed Griffin to read out a charge sheet to the Begum and Siddiq Hassan and to inform them that the British government's action would be taken after receiving their response.

Sir Lepel Griffin arrived in Bhopal on 27 August 1885 and called a restricted meeting to which ministers and leading officials were summoned. Griffin then catalogued the charges against Siddiq Hassan while praising the Begum for her administration and loyalty to the British Crown. Siddiq was not present, but Shahjehan sat, stone-faced, listening to Griffin's indictment that covered Siddiq's seditious literature, his interference in state matters and the misgovernance at the hands of his henchmen. At the end of the meeting, Shahjehan was clearly shaken, but resolutely denied Griffin's charges.

The following day, Griffin called a smaller gathering at which he insisted that the Begum and Siddiq be present. At this meeting, he read out passages from Siddiq's books which were considered seditious if not treasonable. He also put forward evidence of misgovernance and corruption, accusing Siddiq of taking all the decisions while Shahjehan was denied access to information behind purdah.

Siddiq's explanations were unconvincing while Shahjehan adamantly denied that Siddiq was interfering in state affairs. Siddiq acknowledged that some of his articles were anti-British and in mitigation explained that some of the offending articles had been included in a compendium of sermons due to an error. Showing contrition, both Shahjehan and Siddiq informed Sir Lepel Griffin that, in future, Siddiq would not publish anti-British articles. As he departed, Griffin repeated that the action that would be taken against Siddiq and the Begum would be decided in the near future by the British government. After Sir Lepel Griffin left, Shahjehan issued a *yaddasht* (memorandum) in which she publicly proclaimed that Siddiq would not interfere in state affairs. This was obviously an attempt to pacify the British and to pre-empt punitive action.

By 1885, the British government had put in place a reliable network of informants who reported to the British government that Shahjehan continued to be blindly supportive of her husband. Intelligence reports also confirmed that Siddiq was unrepentant with regard to his anti-British Wahhabi campaign, which he now pursued clandestinely. Accordingly, six weeks after his visit, Sir Lepel returned to Bhopal, announcing in advance that he was carrying an important decision by the British government.

In an atmosphere charged with drama, Sir Lepel Griffin arrived in Bhopal on 24 October 1885 and summoned a durbar, at which he insisted that Siddiq Hassan be present. In his report, Sir Lepel Griffin stated that, on arrival at Bhopal railway station, he was warmly greeted by an unusually large crowd. Clearly, word had filtered down to the public that the British Resident was arriving in Bhopal to take action against Siddiq Hassan. Griffin felt that the presence of the large crowd and its enthusiastic welcome indicated Siddiq's unpopularity in Bhopal.

Griffin proceeded to the durbar and, in front of the gathered nobles and gentry, entered the hall accompanied by a posse of armed British soldiers in uniform. Tension bristled among the nobles because they had advance notice that Griffin would be taking action against the Begum and her consort. Despite their resentment of Siddiq Hassan's conduct, the Pathan nobles of Bhopal were not prepared to see their ruler humiliated in public and had assured Shahjehan Begum that if Sir Lepel Griffin were to deliberately humiliate the Begum, he would not leave the durbar alive, whatever the consequences. Shahjehan had also sent a written warning to the British government stating that she would not be responsible for Sir Lepel Griffin's safety if he decided to publicly humiliate her husband.

Sir Lepel noticed the tension in the durbar hall. He walked slowly to the dais and immediately began his speech in which he praised the reforms introduced by the Begum. This reference was well received and eased tension in the hall. At the end of his speech, Sir Lepel levelled charges of sedition against Siddiq Hassan and announced that all his titles were being withdrawn but that he would be allowed to stay in Bhopal. Sir Lepel made a special point of stating that he would not be allowed to interfere in state affairs. To drive his point home, he announced the arrest of two notoriously corrupt officers and clamped handcuffs on Siddiq's chosen henchmen himself, in full view of the nobles gathered at the durbar. Sir Lepel had judged the mood perfectly. He had praised the Begum, deposed Siddiq Hassan and arrested his hated henchmen.

Two contradictory versions of the conclusion of the durbar are recorded. Griffin reported to the Viceroy that the Begum, though shocked, took the decision silently and with dignity. Siddiq Hassan had sat glum and silent, breathing heavily from nervousness.[1] The second account, recorded by Bhopali chroniclers, states that Shahjehan stormed out of the durbar, hand in hand with Siddiq, stating aloud that 'Griffin is worth less than the dirt off my shoes!'

A further announcement from the British Resident followed. In view of Siddiq Hassan's mismanagement of state affairs, it had been decided that the British government would appoint a minister who would take over the administration of the state. Shahjehan Begum would remain the ruler and preside over all ceremonial functions. But governance of the state would pass to the Chief Minister who would, of course, be guided by the Resident and Political Agent.

As expected, Shahjehan bucked against this decision as an insult and a humiliation, but in the face of the Viceroy's firm orders she had no alternative but to accept. She did, however, insist that the appointed Chief Minister should have her approval and, when the Viceroy agreed, Shahjehan proceeded to undermine the upright Indian Muslim Minister, Abdul Latif Khan, who after only a four-month tenure decided to resign rather than suffer the implacable hostility of the Begum. Shahjehan then

---

[1] Sir Lepel Griffin's report to Henry Durand dated 29 October 1885, India Office Records.

insisted on the appointment of a British minister as it was humiliating for her to take orders from an 'Indian Civil Servant'.

The British, and especially Sir Lepel Griffin, were upset at the Begum's uncooperative attitude and, in a curt telegram addressed to the Begum, Griffin made it clear to her that the decision on whom to appoint as Chief Minister was entirely in the hands of the British and not the Begum. Eventually, as a sop to the Begum, it was decided that an Englishman rather than an Indian Muslim should be appointed. The Begum quickly proposed Colonel Brook, a nominee of British legal sharks operating in Calcutta with whom Siddiq had established contact and who saw an opportunity to make a fast buck. Griffin vetoed this stratagem immediately, sensing Siddiq's malevolent influence behind the Calcutta-based proposal.

Eventually, the British nominated an upright administrator, Colonel C.H.E. Ward, as Chief Minister. Ward was in Simla when he received the Viceroy's orders; close on the heels of this message arrived an emissary from the Begum offering a thinly camouflaged bribe to Colonel Ward who immediately refused. Undaunted, the emissary inquired if Mrs Ward would accept a gift of jewellery![1]

Ward's appointment, therefore, got off on the wrong foot as far as Siddiq and the Begum were concerned. It was not surprising that Ward was sympathetic to Sultan Jahan and not particularly popular with the Begum. However, having insisted on a British minister, Shahjehan was obliged to accept him, and Ward's tenure saw Bhopal recover from the laxity and corruption that the state had seen during Siddiq's control. Ward immediately set about implementing the sort of reforms in Bhopal that had, during Sikandar's reign, made it into a model state. Hospitals, schools, roads, municipal works and the sewerage were developed, and police and administrative reforms were implemented, with Shahjehan Begum presiding over the ceremonies and festivities, but taking no part in executive decisions.

For Shahjehan, the deposing of her husband and his public humiliation in a durbar was a shattering experience. Divested of executive authority, she found herself powerless and the object of sniggering ridicule from her own public. She was convinced that the British action was due to successful intrigue against her by her daughter and son-in-law. She was equally convinced that Sir Lepel Griffin bore a personal grudge against Siddiq Hassan and herself and that other British officers were well disposed towards her. In her mind, it followed that, once her case could be pleaded in a higher court than Griffin's, matters would be reversed. Little did Shahjehan realize that the British decision to depose Siddiq had been taken after long debate on her dossier which had been seen by the Secretary of State for India, Sir Henry Durand, and also by the Viceroy, Lord Dufferin. The decision had, eventually, been a compromise because Griffin had sought a harsher penalty against Siddiq, while Durand had counselled restraint to save the Begum's honour. The final decision by the Viceroy stopped short of arresting Siddiq and

---

[1] C.H.E. Ward's letter to Henry Durand dated 17 October 1886, India Office Records.

expelling him to the Andoman Islands or Rangoon. He was divested of all titles and honours but allowed to stay in Bhopal, albeit in a separate palace to the Begum's.

The death of Bilqis

Bilqis Jahan had been taken over by her grandmother from the age of four. This was in keeping with the tradition in most Muslim families in which the first-born grandchild was brought up by the grandmother. Bilqis was a frail and sensitive child who increasingly became the object of Shahjehan's motherly affection as she failed to produce another child of her own. As tension between the ruler and the heir apparent's household increased, Bilqis became the only link between her mother and grandmother.

When Bilqis was around 12 years old, Sultan Jahan was alarmed at reports of Siddiq's younger son, the 19-year-old Ali Hassan, who was already married, being groomed to marry Bilqis. He was made her constant companion at lessons and during free time, and rumours were soon circulating that Shahjehan would shortly announce Bilqis's engagement to Ali Hassan. Shahjehan had built herself a new palace, suitably named the Taj Mahal, and the two households were no longer adjacent. In 1887, Bilqis fell ill of a mysterious illness causing even greater concern to her parents. She was treated by doctors and hakeems and managed to make a partial recovery. After months of high anxiety, when Bilqis came to visit Sultan Jahan, she was a pale image of her usual self with dark rings around her eyes. Desperately agitated by Bilqis's condition, Sultan Jahan and her husband decided not to send her back to Shahjehan.

This decision struck deep into Shahjehan's heart. She was incensed and raged about the palace decrying her daughter's insensitive treachery. She then asked Colonel Ward to mount an attack on the heir apparent's palace to forcibly restore Bilqis to her. Of course, Ward was too wise and mature a man to act on such whims. He called on Sultan Jahan and when given the background, took no further action except seeking a reconciliation and a negotiated settlement on the subject of the custody of Bilqis Jahan. The felicitous link that Bilqis had provided between the households now became an acrimonious tug-of-war.

Initially, Bilqis was upset at being taken away from her doting grandmother. Sultan Jahan writes that, after a while, Bilqis came to appreciate the circumstances and decided voluntarily to stay with her mother and father. The little child again started her shuttle between the two palaces, constantly attempting to reconcile her grandmother with her mother but to no avail. Soon, Bilqis's illness reappeared and this time took a more serious turn. As she began to sink, Sultan Jahan decided to make an attempt to seek her mother's forgiveness. Out of sheer desperation for her daughter, Sultan Jahan went unannounced to her mother's palace. Surprisingly, it was the first time Sultan Jahan had set foot in the Taj Mahal. On arrival, the heir apparent did not know where to find her mother. Sultan Jahan describes the scene in the following words:

> Knowing the dangerous nature of the disease my daughter had contracted, and that in less than twenty-one days the crisis must come, I determined to make a final effort to overcome my mother's anger. Choosing a time in the afternoon when I knew that she would have risen from her siesta, I went to the Taj Mahal, and, alighting from my carriage, made my way towards her bedroom, where I found her seated on her prayer-seat. Salaaming to her with deep respect, I begged her to forgive whatever fault I had committed, and to return with me to the bedside of my daughter, and help me with her advice in my hour of need. Without vouchsafing any reply, but apparently in great anger, my mother rose from her seat, and withdrew to the apartment of Siddiq Hassan Khan; and though I remained for three hours waiting for her, she did not come to me again.[1]

Shahjehan's description of the event was different. In her subsequent appeal to the Viceroy, she described Sultan Jahan's sudden arrival as follows:

> Bilqis then fell sick, and when she was on the point of death my daughter suddenly, and without giving any previous intimation, came to my palace and with clasped hands, asked me to forgive her and accompany her. I also with clasped hands told her in reply to excuse me. Her attempt was mere sham: her real object was to have a reconciliation brought about independent of the agreement, in order to prevent me from instructing and admonishing her, and to leave her free to act according to her own whims and wishes. She never went down to me on her knees, as falsely represented to you. She might be asked to take her oath on this. Even had she gone on her knees, what good could I do by going to see Bilqis, who was then on the extreme verge of death: and moreover I really feared I might be accused of poisoning the child in the same way in which my husband was unjustly accused of sorcery towards her. She kept Bilqis separated from me for a year and three months. Bilqis was allowed to associate with everybody and to resort to the gardens and other places, while I was never allowed access to her even for a second.[2]

Whichever version is true, Sultan Jahan's attempt at seeking her mother's forgiveness ended in tragic failure. Bilqis died a few weeks later and with her death were buried the last vestiges of Shahjehan's capacity to forgive her daughter. The second time Sultan Jahan set foot in the Taj Mahal was 14 years later, eight days before Shahjehan died.

No doubt Shahjehan felt that Bilqis's separation from her had contributed to her untimely death. The tug of war between mother and grandmother for the dying Bilqis is a profoundly tragic episode in their lives with the young and sensitive Bilqis trying desperately to reconcile her mother and grandmother if only to gain her own peace of mind. The following crumpled note written in Bilqis's hand that Sultan Jahan found in Shahjehan's drawer after her death amply describes the pathos and agony of the little child, torn between her mother and grandmother:

> My dear Grandmother, do you not love me still? She [Sultan Jahan] is thinking about you just as much as you think about me. Please forgive her for my

---

[1] *An Account of My Life.*
[2] *Appeal and Correspondence.*

sake. Tell me when you are going to call her to you. If you do not call her, I shall know that you do not love me.

Shahjehan's attempts to reverse the British decision on deposing Siddiq[1]

Between 1885 and 1890, Shahjehan spent her energies attempting to reverse the decision against her husband. Colonel Ward described her mood as full of wrath and anger. Every time there was a change of Viceroy or of Secretary of State, she would take the train to Calcutta, Delhi or Simla to plead her case before the new incumbent. Shahjehan would argue that her husband was innocent and the object of vicious intrigue by her daughter and son-in-law. She would then give solemn assurances that even if Siddiq had unwittingly erred by implying anti-British views in his writings, he would desist from doing so in future and would restrict himself to purely religious matters on which he was an accepted authority. She further undertook that Siddiq would not interfere in matters of state. Finally, Shahjehan would refer to Sir Lepel's personal prejudice against her, citing his insistence on her discarding purdah as proof of his animus (see Appendix 10).

Each new Viceroy would give Shahjehan a patient hearing, recognizing Bhopal's and its ruling family's loyalty to the British Crown. Privately, they would appreciate the Begum's fighting spirit, but the decision to depose Siddiq remained unchanged. In a typically British gesture to the Begum, after declining to restore Siddiq's titles, Lady Durand, the Secretary of State's wife, spent an entire day with little Bilqis Jahan taking her to Calcutta's botanical gardens, a flower show and for a boat ride! The British government's intransigence over Siddiq Hassan was due to Sir Lepel Griffin's reports that Siddiq continued to cast a hypnotic spell over his wife and that there was no dilution in his interference in state matters as Shahjehan secretly sent every file to him and sought his views on every important issue. Sir Lepel also blamed Siddiq Hassan's influence on his wife for the clashes with the two ministers appointed by the British. Griffin, recalling his earlier advice, felt it would have been better if Siddiq had been banished from Bhopal and that, if he did not mend his ways, it would still be advisable for the British government to take the more drastic course. The succeeding Viceroy, Lord Lansdowne, did not accept Griffin's advice and in fact censured him for using intemperate language when addressing the Begum. The Viceroy remarked that Griffin's actions appeared to be motivated by a personal vendetta.

By this time, the British administration was thoroughly organized and streamlined. It was several steps ahead of Shahjehan. Through their censors and intelligence reports, the British had intercepted Siddiq's

---

[1] The description of British interaction with Bhopal is based on documents available in the India Office Library. These include letters, telegrams, memoranda and reports by British officials with notes about life in India.

instruction to his emissaries in Sudan, Turkey, Arabia, Yemen and Burma. His books and pamphlets which he denied publishing were located at booksellers in Cairo and Lahore. Thus, in 1887, Sir Lepel Griffin was ordered to undertake another urgent mission to the Begum to place before her proof of Siddiq's continued sedition and interference, even after he had been deposed. Griffin asked the Begum if she would see him alone or with her husband. Shahjehan opted for Siddiq being present and in a long meeting, Griffin again read out seditious passages from the books 'written by Siddiq'. He also referred to the messages sent to Siddiq's envoys and gave instances of Siddiq's continued interference in state affairs. The Begum remained adamant and refused to admit her husband's guilt.

Several harsh exchanges took place between Griffin and the Begum in which accusations and counter-accusations were fired by each side. Shahjehan loyally stood by her husband and refused to bend to Griffin's threatening onslaughts. Twice, Griffin refused to convey the Begum's kharitas addressed to the Viceroy, stifling her appeals and protests at inception. Eventually, a few months before he was transferred, Griffin came to Bhopal for a final showdown with the Begum. Griffin accused Siddiq of killing Bilqis Jahan through 'black magic' – an amazingly wild charge by so senior an official – and of using Shahjehan to further his dastardly aims. The Begum was adamant and totally unbending. She gave Griffin as good as she got as the minute of their final meeting (Appendix 10) demonstrates.

In 1888, Sir Lepel Griffin was replaced by Francis Henvey as Resident and Shahjehan lost no time in lobbying him to restore Siddiq's titles. Henvey's assessment of the Bhopal situation was less critical of the Begum and her husband. He was even prepared to give Siddiq the benefit of the doubt regarding his seditious propagations, suggesting that his writings were essentially theological and not necessarily agitational. The Viceroy and Secretary of State were sympathetic towards the Begum, but were still not prepared to reverse their earlier decision, mainly because it would show that the government's initial action had been ill conceived. They were prepared, however, to review the case on the grounds that Siddiq had served an adequate period of punishment.[1]

While this debate was being held in the corridors of Viceregal power, Siddiq Hassan fell gravely ill of a liver complaint. By 1890, it was evident that he was dying. The Resident despatched his own medical superintendent, Colonel Dane, to Bhopal who reported that Siddiq's liver was so enlarged that it had spread across his abdomen. Dane diagnosed that Siddiq would die in a few days. He added in his report that Siddiq was attended by '10 Hakeems and a Hindu Joshi' and that he had not administered any medicine as the British would be accused of murdering Siddiq. Within a few days of this report having been sent, on 26 May 1890, Siddiq Hassan died, and was buried in a simple grave at Bara Bagh.

---

[1] Viceroy, Marquess of Lansdowne's letter to AGG Francis Henvey dated 28 January 1890, India Office Records.

Siddiq's death made no difference to Shahjehan's determination to have his name cleared, even posthumously. Nor did she relent in her condemnation of Sultan Jahan and, despite several attempts at reconciliation sponsored by the British, Shahjehan remained unrelenting in her hostility towards her daughter and son-in-law. The deep and underlying reason for Shahjehan's uncompromising attitude was almost certainly the death of Bilqis. For Shahjehan, a hedonistic, spoilt and stubborn woman, the only real love in her life had been her granddaughter. Bilqis had been brought up in her grandmother's household and had grown up to adore her. Suddenly, at the age of 12, her mother wrested her away from Shahjehan's home on the grounds – true or false – that Siddiq Hassan wanted his younger son Ali Hassan betrothed to Bilqis. This impression may have been true or simply concocted by intriguing palace busybodies whose closed lives led to exaggerated sexual motives being ascribed to the most mundane events. The image of her dying granddaughter pining for her grandmother left a deep scar on Shahjehan that closed down all efforts at reconciliation with her daughter.

Shortly after Siddiq Hassan died, the Viceroy agreed to Siddiq Hassan posthumously resuming the title of Nawab. Shahjehan was overjoyed and felt vindicated in her belief that she had all along been the subject of her daughter's intrigue and Sir Lepel's personal wrath. There was now a fresh spring in her step and a renewed enthusiasm for fulfilling her mission as Begum. Shahjehan commissioned the building of two famous mosques. The first was in Woking, Surrey,[1] and was one of the only mosques in Europe where Muslims could worship until after the Second World War. The second – Tajul Masajid – was to be the largest mosque in India and was conceived on a grand scale with marble ordered from Belgium. Regrettably, the mosque remained uncompleted because funds ran out.[2] Siddiq Hassan's children were given jagirs and riches, as were favoured members of her own family that had been part of her cabal. Conversely, Sultan Jahan, her Jalabadi in-laws and her Baqi-khel stepbrothers and sisters felt the increasing wrath of the Begum's temper. Fortunately for Sultan Jahan, executive authority was still in the hands of the British who protected the heir apparent's rights but Colonel Ward found it increasingly difficult to work with the Begum and resigned.

By 1891, Shahjehan had charmed the new Viceroy, Lord Lansdowne, into believing that a basic injustice had been done to her. That year, full executive authority was restored to Shahjehan who surrounded herself with Siddiq's family and sympathizers. Colonel Ward was replaced as Chief Minister by Munshi Imtiaz Ali who soon reverted to the old ways of corruption and nepotism that had marked Siddiq Hassan's heyday. Nevertheless, the Resident and Political Agent kept a close watch on Bhopal to ensure that Sultan Jahan and her sympathizers were not

---

[1] The first mosque built in Great Britain was in South Shields. Woking was probably the second.
[2] The Tajul Masajid was completed in 1952, several years after Bhopal State had been merged into the Indian Union. The final works were financed by donations from prominent Bhopal philanthropists, notably Maulana Mohammad Imran Khan.

victimized. By now, the Jalabadi clan had spread its wings and influence in Bhopal and had joined the Baqi-khel in a powerful cabal supporting the heir apparent.

The remaining years of Shahjehan's reign were spent presiding over a reasonably well-run state. She contemplated going on Hajj, but decided against it because of frail health and a pathological fear of shipwrecks. Shahjehan received the first Viceregal visit to Bhopal by Lord Lansdowne in November 1891. She seemed buoyant, almost her old flirtatious self, when welcoming Lord and Lady Lansdowne in Bhopal amidst great pomp and ceremony. The Viceroy wrote a letter to his mother in England in which he described his meeting with Shahjehan Begum in the following words:

> We arrived here on the 20th. The Begum received me at the station completely enveloped in a pale 'greenery-yallery' kind of domino, and moreover concealed from the public gaze by a sort of hoarding covered with brilliant tinctures. When she paid her respects she slipped off to her carriage, in which she followed mine as far as this house. Arrived there, she took leave of me through her carriage window, in which glass was replaced by the thinnest gauze, and oh! rapture! behind this was the royal countenance, uncovered and plainly visible. She is a determined-looking lady, not disagreeable to look at, and young for her age (52). She is in great good humour, as this is the first time a Viceroy has been to Bhopal in her reign.
>
> In the afternoon (6:30) I drove to the Palace to return H.H's visit. The city was brilliantly illuminated and the Cour d'Honneur at the palace was really a fine sight. At the foot of the steps was my hostess, more like a green chrysalis than ever. We toiled up the staircase and through long corridors, hand in hand, to the Durbar room, which was bright and pretty. Gorgeous gold-embroidered carpets, the finest I have seen yet. We had a very friendly conversation, and then came the usual anointment with nauseous attar of roses, followed by garlands, very splendid. Then she and I walked downstairs again, I holding tight to her tiny little hand, lest she should trip up over her draperies and roll down to the bottom in a bunch. The little hand in question was encased in a green silk glove, with the fingers much too long.
>
> In the evening we had the State banquet here in the big tent, 60 Europeans in all. At dessert in came the Begum, her face still invisible, stood up boldly at the head of the table, and, quite unabashed, proposed the Queen's health and then mine in a very loyal little speech, which was translated by the Resident. It was really a very courageous performance on the little lady's part, and there was, in spite of the grotesqueness of the costume, a certain pathos and dignity about the whole proceeding. The worst thing about her is her voice, which is shrill and unpleasing. I forgot to tell you that she paid Maud a private visit after hers to me in the morning. I also did not say that I began the day (like an idiot) by getting up at 6:30 to shoot snipe. There were no snipe to shoot and I should have been better in bed.[1]

Shahjehan received two further visits from British Viceroys, Lord Elgin on 4 November 1895 and Lord Curzon on 25 November 1899. Sultan Jahan was not invited to any of the functions held for the Viceroy, but

---

[1] Viceroy, Marquess of Lansdowne's letter to his mother dated 22 November 1891, India Office Records.

the protocol adopted by the British was for the Viceroy's wife to call on the heir apparent.

In 1894, Sultan Jahan suffered another tragedy in the death of her second daughter, Asif Jahan. Again the malady was not properly diagnosed and the 12-year-old child died after a painful illness. Shahjehan did not visit her dying granddaughter nor did she congratulate Sultan Jahan a few months later when she gave birth to a third son – Hamidullah Khan – after a gap of 14 years. 'Little Hamid's' arrival tempered the loss of a second grown-up daughter for the 36-year-old heir apparent.

Between 1894 and 1899, Bhopal suffered from two famines that saw death and destruction spread across most of India. The famines were followed by the plague. The British Political Agent estimated that Bhopal's population had been reduced by a third due to death and migration. The first famine struck in 1894, creating havoc in the state. For the second, in 1899, Bhopal was better prepared then most other states with sufficient stocks of wheat and maize that were carefully rationed out to a starving population. In 1899, there was an influx of people from neighbouring states escaping the ravages of famine.

The Bhopal railway

By far the most important project in Shahjehan's reign was the building of a railway line that connected Bhopal to the national railway network – Bhopal being virtually the central crossing-point between east and west, north and south. Initially, the project of connecting Bhopal to the national network of railways had been conceived by Qudsia Begum and Sikandar Begum. Both had contributed from their personal – as opposed to state – funds towards the survey and the construction of the railway. As late as 1876, when funds were short for the construction of the railway, Qudsia provided financing from her private fund. Regrettably, she did not live to see the first steam engine chugging into Bhopal's new railway station on 18 November 1884.

The railway gave a special importance to Bhopal as an economic cross-road for India. The town was expanded and the railway station itself became a hub of activity with its engineers, maintenance crew, station masters and linesmen, many of them Indian Christians, forming a colony of expatriates and adding colour and variety to Bhopal's ethnic and cultural kaleidoscope.

Then in 1901, after a 33-year reign, Shahjehan developed cancer in the mouth. As the cancer spread, Shahjehan refused to have herself operated on by the civil surgeon who had arrived from Indore. In the most tragic and haunting scene in Bhopal's history, Sultan Jahan decided to seek her mother's forgiveness by visiting her on her deathbed. Mother and daughter had not spoken to each other for over 13 years and Sultan Jahan's decision was taken after agonizing for long hours. Eventually, Sultan Jahan, accompanied by her seven-year-old son Hamid who had never set eyes on his grandmother, went to the Taj

Mahal. Again, Sultan Jahan had to ask the way to her mother's bedroom. It was a hot May afternoon as Sultan Jahan stood trembling with sorrow and anguish at the bedroom door. She then plucked up enough courage to enter a dark room where her mother lay alone, motionless, except for an old maid-servant. A rancid smell of impending death filtered across the room as Sultan Jahan tiptoed towards her mother's bed. The entire visit is best described in Sultan Jahan's own words, as follows:

Days passed, and my mother's condition grew steadily worse. A few days before her death, she caused the following pathetic notice to be published:

'If there are any among my subjects who, during the thirty-three years of my reign, have received unmerited punishment at my hands, I ask them, in the name of God, to forgive me.'

The people of Bhopal received this last message from their dying ruler with sorrow and sympathy, and there was not one amongst them who did not pray to God that the burden of her afflictions might be lightened. My own emotion as I read the words I will not attempt to describe. I longed for only one sentence more, 'I too forgive the faults of others,' and I read and re-read the message in the vain hope that I had overlooked it. With such words to support me I could have gone to my mother, and, having won the forgiveness which she could no longer have withheld, I could have cheered the last moments of her life with the pent-up love of twenty-seven long years. I prayed for her recovery night and day, and the thought of her sufferings filled my mind. At last, as every day brought worse tidings, my anxiety became more than I could bear, and I determined to go to the Taj Mahal, let my enemies put what construction they would upon my visit. I set out with my heart full of misgivings. My husband was even more uneasy, and, fearing that his presence might stir my mother to anger, and that her sickness might thereby be aggravated, he did not accompany me.

I took with me only Hamidullah Khan, my youngest son. He was then seven years old, and I know not what were the thoughts that filled his childish mind as he passed, for the first time in his life, beneath the gateway of his grandmother's palace. I myself had been there but once, when my daughter Bilqis Jahan was sick, and since that time thirteen years had elapsed. It was 2 o'clock in the afternoon when we arrived, and the day was intensely hot. Few people were about, and, for all the notice that was taken of us, we might have been utter strangers. I inquired the way of one person after another, and we at length entered the chamber where my mother lay, with a female attendant seated by her side. My first impulse was to throw myself weeping at her feet, but the fear of her displeasure, and the remembrance of the last occasion when I had ventured into her presence, restrained me. I approached a few steps and waited, and Hamidullah, in fear and wonder, stood by my side. Her Highness turned her face towards me, but thirteen years of grief and trouble had made some change in my appearance, and in the subdued light of the sick room she did not at first recognise me. She asked me who I was, but my fear of her displeasure, and of being sent away from her presence, was so great that I gave no answer. Again she put the same question, and asked me why I did not speak. Still I made no reply, and it was not until the question had been asked a third time, and the attendant had spoken my name, that I found my voice, and with clasped hands begged her forgiveness. The fears which kept me silent had not been groundless. In a voice in which sorrow and anger were mingled she said, 'Leave me; after my death you may come here.'[1] Seeing that I still stood there, she repeated the words even more sternly. This time I did not venture to disobey. It was plain that my presence troubled her, and I returned weeping and with a heavy weight at my heart to the Sadar Manzil.[2]

Shahjehan died on 6 June 1901, four months after Queen Victoria. Despite her capricious, wayward nature she had given Bhopal much that its public was grateful for, particularly festivity, *joie de vivre* and beautiful mosques, gardens and buildings. There was genuine grief at her passing and Bhopal saw a vast turnout for her funeral. She was buried at the Nishat Afzah Garden.

In another unusually lyrical passage of her autobiography, Sultan Jahan described her feelings as she prepared for the funeral in the following words:

> The melancholy news was conveyed to me by the Minister. From early morning I had been unusually depressed, and the news came to me as the fulfilment of the gloomy forebodings which had taken possession of my mind. Weeping bitterly, I set out for the Taj Mahal. As I drove along, I seemed to be in a trance. I saw the days of my childhood as in a beautiful picture. My mother was smiling down upon me, and there was no cloud in the sky. Then the picture faded, and another took its place; but it was dark, and there was no sky: and I seemed to see all the trials and sorrows of the succeeding years of my life moving to and fro in it like gloomy spectres. Then it, too, faded, like the circles on a pool of water; and, almost before it had gone, I seemed to be gazing on the World itself; and whilst I looked, a mighty whirlwind, with a sound like the roaring of oceans, swept over it, and the earth and sky were shattered, and out of the darkness which followed came a voice. [She then quoted a verse from the Quran.][3]

Siddiq Hassan – An assessment

Shahjehan's 33-year reign was dominated by the single-dimensional enigma of Siddiq Hassan's character. Like a light seen through different sides of a prism, it reflected contrasting colours from different angles. Or, like the story of Roshomon, different players witnessing the same event came away with contradictory accounts.

To the British, Siddiq Hassan was a scheming, immoral scoundrel who had climbed the political ladder by first marrying the daughter of the Chief Minister and subsequently seducing the Begum herself. Having achieved total emotional domination over the Begum, Siddiq attempted to control all levers of state governance by pushing the Begum into purdah and using the state's finances and machinery to propagate his anti-British Wahabi campaign and to promote the financial welfare of his family and supporters. The British blamed Siddiq for the corruption and

---

[1] Hamidullah in a letter to his daughter recalls even harsher language used by Shahjehan. He recalls her saying, 'Why do you want to hover over my body like vultures? I will die soon and the state will be yours. Let me die in peace.'
[2] *An Account of My Life.*
[3] *Ibid.*

misgovernance, and for the friction within the family. Above all, he was seen as an unscrupulous man who sought power through the propagation of anti-British Wahabi extremism that called for jehad against the ruling infidels. They saw him as a charlatan suffering from *folies de grandeur*, especially when he wrote letters to the kings of Egypt and Turkey, signing himself grandiosely and falsely as 'Amir-ul-Momineen' (Head of all Believers). At the time, British domination of the Middle East and Asia was opposed by an undercurrent of Islamic revivalism that had emerged in Sudan under the leadership of the Mahdi and in Turkey under the Turkish Sultanate. The British were, therefore, particularly sensitive to Islamic nationalism rearing its head in India.

On the other hand, modern Muslim historians see Siddiq Hassan in heroic proportions. He is regarded as one of the earliest anti-colonial stalwarts who used the power of the pen to assert Muslim nationalism. These historians consider Siddiq Hassan's writings neither extremist nor seditious. They accuse the British of deliberately misinterpreting Siddiq's works in order to strike down any political or religious movement that smacked of a nationalist revival. These historians regard Siddiq Hassan's political views as a courageous expression of anti-colonial sentiment, representing the first stirrings of Islamic nationhood. His religious beliefs are considered to be based on genuine conviction aimed at channelling Islamic values towards its pristine roots. Siddiq's supporters either deny that he arrogated power to himself or simply accept that it was part of a necessary evil in achieving the laudable objectives that he had set himself. The humiliation and persecution that he suffered at the hands of the British is seen as a badge of honour.

For Sultan Jahan, Siddiq Hassan was the evil spirit that caused the deep schism in the royal family. Sultan Jahan held Siddiq entirely responsible for Shahjehan turning against her grandmother and eventually against herself. She considers Siddiq's emotional hold over Shahjehan as the moving force that blinded her mother to reality and led to her accepting every piece of advice that Siddiq whispered in her ear. Sultan Jahan was certain that Siddiq wanted his elder son, Nurul Hassan, to replace Ahmad Ali Khan as her suitor-consort. She was equally alarmed at rumours of Siddiq Hassan grooming his younger son, Ali Hassan, to be engaged to Bilqis. Sultan Jahan absolved her mother from all responsibility in promoting these stratagems which she laid entirely at the doorstep of her scheming stepfather. Sultan Jahan points to Siddiq's performance at the 1877 durbar as proof of his malevolence. She quotes her dying daughter, Bilqis, when Sultan Jahan tried desperately to seek a reconciliation with her mother, as saying, 'Don't even try, Siddiq Hassan will never allow it.' For Sultan Jahan, her steadfast refusal to bend to Siddiq's will was the only hope for Dost Mohammad Khan's family to preserve their birthright to rule. In her implacable hostility towards Siddiq, Sultan Jahan was supported by the British. It led to more than two decades of tension, deprivation and humiliation for her and for close members of her family, but she remained steadfast and resolute in preventing Siddiq Hassan taking over Bhopal lock, stock and barrel.

Shahjehan's relationship with Siddiq Hassan was probably fashioned by her experience as a child. She was made the titular ruler of Bhopal at the age of nine, but her mother, Sikandar, a towering, overbearing personality, totally dominated the scene as Regent. Shahjehan, a feminine, headstrong, pleasure-loving girl probably resented being married off to a much older man. She then voluntarily and graciously abdicated in her mother's favour, but was not considered sufficiently reliable or capable of being given charge of state affairs when her mother went for pilgrimage and was absent for nearly a year. Sikandar left her Hindu Minister, Kishen Ram, in charge. Shahjehan's final resentment against Sikandar was probably that she did not give Shahjehan a private jagir and, instead, provided one for Umrao Doulah which he quickly converted to the benefit of the children from his first two wives. Shahjehan, in her history of Bhopal, refers reverentially to Sikandar as 'my sainted mother' but, deep down, an undertow of resentment against her can be sensed in some of Shahjehan's remarks.

Against this background of resentment, Shahjehan rebelled against conformity and fell deeply in love with Siddiq Hassan. The more he was criticized for being a non-Afghan and an impoverished perfume-selling clerk who had made his way up the ladder, the more adamant Shahjehan became about not only marrying Siddiq Hassan but also about giving him every possible support as her consort. Family opposition, British warnings and the scorn of Bhopal's gentry only strengthened Shahjehan's stubborn commitment to Siddiq Hassan.

She argued that even though he was not Afghan, Siddiq came from good stock. The fact that he was educated and learned was admitted even by his enemies. Siddiq Hassan's religious convictions were borne of a sincere desire to rid Islamic society of the ills of pirs and saints. Siddiq wanted Muslims to return to the simple, pristine values which he considered to be the true spirit of Islam. Shahjehan argued that, in propagating these values, Siddiq had been labelled a Wahabi extremist, bent on adopting an anti-British, nationalistic stance. She considered Siddiq a reformer and not an anti-British political campaigner.

Another factor that sharpened Shahjehan's hostility towards Sultan Jahan was the fact that while Sultan Jahan gave birth to five children, including the first male heir in four generations of Bhopal rulers, Shahjehan did not conceive an heir that could have replaced Sultan Jahan as heir apparent. Shahjehan's barrenness accentuated her chagrin and envy towards her daughter.

As regards interfering, or taking over, state responsibilities, Shahjehan denied any such attempt by Siddiq. She claimed that all decisions were taken by her, sometimes after consulting Siddiq, but that no powers were transferred to him. She took full responsibility for all acts of state. Shahjehan firmly believed that opprobrium towards Siddiq was the result of her daughter and son-in-law's intrigues and of over-reaction from Sir Lepel Griffin. In her appeals to the Viceroy, she called Sultan Jahan a wayward, ambitious and frustrated schemer.

Shahjehan justified going into purdah as respect for a normal Islamic tenet and disagreed with Sir Lepel Griffin that it was almost impossible

9. ABOVE. Sikandar Begum flanked by her Minister, Maulvi Jamaluddin (left) and Army Chief, Mattu Khan.

10. RIGHT. Shahjehan Begum.

11. LEFT. Siddiq Hassan

12. BELOW. The derelict Taj Mahal.

13. RIGHT. Portrait photograph of Sultan Jahan, London 1926.

14. BELOW. Sultan Jahan Begum (far right) with the Viceroy, Lord Minto, Lady Minto and grandchildren. Bhopal, 1911.

15. Sultan Jahan Begum with eldest grand-daughter, Abida Sultaan, London 1926 (during succession case).

16. Hamidullah Khan, last Nawab.

to govern from behind purdah. Finally, Shahjehan believed that for some unexplained reasons, Sir Lepel built up a personal animus against Siddiq Hassan and herself. She believed that Sir Lepel, alone, was responsible for her downfall and that other British officers were well disposed towards her. She deeply resented Sir Lepel's private calls on the heir apparent, stating that no such calls were made on her by British officials when she was heir apparent!

Given these contrasting assessments, can a rational judgement of Siddiq Hassan's character be made a hundred years after his death? What was his real persona? Was he a seditious fanatic or genuine reformer? Anti-British agitator or nationalist hero? Unscrupulous power-grabber or loyal supporter of the Begum? Jekyll or Hyde? Can the contradictory views of Siddiq's critics and supporters be reconciled? An objective evaluation of all the elements reflecting on Siddiq's personality does build up a plausible pen picture of the man. Clearly, he belonged to an upright, educated family, though not Pathan, that deserved to be respected. Siddiq's wayward father had plunged his family into a state of penury which probably made Siddiq determined never to be poor again. To his credit, Siddiq withstood poverty and hardship to continue his family tradition of seeking erudition and enlightenment. Siddiq's writings, when closely examined, appear to be reformist and not fanatical in their theological content. He was not a barnstorming fanatic and there were no explicit exhortations for Muslims to rise against the British. Nevertheless, at a time when the British were acutely sensitive towards Islamic revivalism, Siddiq's writings were seized upon as seditious.

Had he been frank and truthful, Siddiq might have escaped censure. He was rather naive in denying the publication of certain books (that were located at a publisher in Lahore), contact with extremist mullahs (which British intelligence intercepted) and the publication of a sermon calling for jehad against the British (which, when he was confronted, Siddiq claimed had been included in his anthology of sermons in error). The discovery of these falsehoods condemned Siddiq in the eyes of British as a liar who was up to sinister mischief.

There can be little doubt, however, that Siddiq nurtured *folies de grandeur*. Having achieved a complete hypnotic hold over the Begum, Siddiq sought to translate this power into gaining administrative and financial control of the state. In the pursuit of this objective, Siddiq was unscrupulous, devious and hugely ambitious. He saw Sultan Jahan as the only hurdle standing in the way of attaining his objective and focused all his energies on attempting to undermine her status. Much of the corruption, chicanery and financial degeneration of the state must, therefore, be laid at Siddiq's doorstep, as must the deep schisms that were created between Shahjehan and her family.

The charge that Sir Lepel Griffin bore a personal grudge against Siddiq needs also to examined. Francis Henvey, Griffin's successor, more than hints that Sir Lepel had over-reacted to Siddiq.[1] The Viceroy later

---

[1] AGG Francis Henvey's letter to Viceroy, Marquess of Lansdowne dated 2 February 1890, India Office Records.

censored Griffin for his intemperate language towards the Begums, recording that Griffin may have been influenced by personal factors.[1] The record of Griffin's last meeting with the Begum, during which he accused Siddiq Hassan of killing Bilqis by black magic, is an extraordinarily bizarre statement which confirms the view that Griffin may well have pursued a personal vendetta against the Begum. Overall, however, too many British officers were involved in deciding the ultimate fate of Siddiq Hassan and the prejudiced view of one man cannot be regarded as outweighing the general opinion of the British hierarchy. Sir Lepel may have overstated his criticism but, in general, British assessment of Siddiq's character as opposed to his writings appears to be accurate. In fact, Henry Daly had expressed similar fears about Siddiq Hassan and had recommended severe measures to curb his 'pernicious' activities. Other British officers, like Colonel Kincaid, the Political Agent in Bhopal, shared Sir Lepel Griffin's views on Siddiq. As Resident for six years, Sir Lepel had to bear the brunt of warning and finally deposing Siddiq which led to an element of personal jousting between Sir Lepel and the stubborn Begum. However, the decision to depose Siddiq and to withdraw his titles was taken by consensus and was not the work of one man.

The family tension between Shahjehan and her daughter that built up into an unbridgeable chasm also cannot be laid at the door of a single person. Both Shahjehan and Sultan Jahan were stubborn, even cussed personalities. Both had spouses that coveted greater responsibility and control than was ascribed to them. Each male consort egged on his wife to adopt uncompromising attitudes towards the other. In fact, Sultan Doulah emerged as a stern, ruthless and covetous character. He had a foul temper, frequently beating up his wife and imposing a tyrannical regime on his sons. Left to themselves, mother and daughter may have been reconciled, but with the Jalabadis and Baqi-khels supporting Sultan Jahan and Siddiq's relatives urging Shahjehan towards confrontation, reconciliation became impossible in an atmosphere laden with intrigue. Sultan Jahan's character and subsequent conduct as an enlightened, humane and caring personality indicates that the hardness towards reconciliation came more from the hedonistic, spoilt Shahjehan, whose heart was full of 'wrath and anger' and who showed no compassion for her daughter. On the other hand, Sultan Jahan constantly sought her mother's forgiveness and in her biography always absolved her from blame. Probably, the wrenching away of Bilqis and her subsequent death left a wound in Shahjehan's heart for which she never forgave her daughter.

On the issue of corruption and mismanagement in the state, it is evident that, after her second marriage, Shahjehan handed over the running of the state to her husband. Siddiq proceeded to appoint loyalists who were mostly corrupt and frequently terrorized the population. Siddiq cannot escape censure for this downturn in the state's administration. Nor can there be any doubt that his children and their

---

[1] Letter from Secretary of State Henry Durand to AGG Sir Lepel Griffin dated 8 June 1886, India Office Records.

relatives were granted bountiful jagirs and had access to finances that they transferred out of Bhopal. Sultan Jahan claimed that cartloads of silver and ornaments were carried out of Bhopal, with Shahjehan's connivance, by Siddiq Hassan's family after his death. This was probably an exaggeration, given Sultan Jahan's antipathy towards Siddiq Hassan, but there can be little doubt that Siddiq, who had arrived impecunious in Bhopal, died a rich man leaving a fortune for his family.

Neither Siddiq Hassan's lineage nor his poverty deserve to be sneered at. Moreover, if in the pursuit of his normal functions he found the Begum of Bhopal to be enamoured of him, he should not be blamed for converting this emotional liaison into an acceptable second marriage for both parties.

Shahjehan's reign – An assessment

During her 33-year tenure, Shahjehan Begum presided over a settled reign. This was mainly due to the momentum of Sikandar's trail-blazing reforms and to the guidance and support provided by the British who were now more focused, organized, experienced and discerning in their governance of India. A Victorian ethos pervaded British India in which the British, the Indian princes, the gentry, the bourgeoisie and the peasantry lived, relatively peacefully, in an ordered class structure. Thus, after Shahjehan became ruler, the court scandals, Siddiq Hassan's dominance over her and the ensuing family tensions caused minor tremors but did not shake the overall firmament of Bhopal's social and political structure. Reforms continued at a reasonable pace, the court's atmosphere was less austere and no threat to Shahjehan's title was conceivable, so that she could enjoy herself with musical soirees, endless festivity and generally basking in the pleasure of building palaces, monuments and mosques.

The main crisis in her reign came when her beloved husband overstepped the limits of British tolerance and was unceremoniously deposed and humiliated. Even this event, followed by the reins of governance being taken away from Shahjehan, did not lead to a crisis of governance as, apart from the royal court, life in Bhopal continued normally with its upward graph of economic and social advancement, spiced with shikar, polo, gaiety and romance.

Shahjehan was a committed supporter of the arts and education. She was a poetess herself and encouraged scholars, writers, poets and musicians to settle in Bhopal. She built beautiful palaces, mosques and state buildings. She supported education for girls and built dispensaries and serais for visitors. She even liberated courtesans, bringing them into the mainstream of a dignified existence. Above all, Shahjehan brought to Bhopal, a more liberal and relaxed ambience leading to a *joie de vivre* that had been singularly absent during the ascetic rule of preceding Begums.

Apart from being a builder of mosques, palaces, momuments and even a tramway that connected the Taj Mahal to Nawab Siddiq Hassan's residence, Shahjehan was a sponsor of the liberal arts and began the long association of Bhopal rulers with Aligarh University when she received Sayyed Ahmad Khan and gave a donation to his foundation for a Muslim university. She was herself an authoress who published prose and poetry in Urdu and Persian. She adopted the *nom de plume* of 'Tajwar' for her Urdu works and 'Shirin' for her Persian poetry. Shahjehan's published works include the Urdu *Mathnawi Siddiq-ul-Bayan*, *Taj-ul-Kalam* and *Tehzib-un-Nissa* while her poetry in Persian was published under the title of *Dewan-e-Shirin*. None of the other Begums of Bhopal aspired, as Shahjehan did, to literary accomplishment.

An incident that provides insight into Shahjehan's personality was told by Kishan Maharaj, the tabla maestro at Shahjehan's court, who made his home in Bhopal. A famous classical singer from Bombay arrived in Bhopal announcing that she had heard of Bhopal's growing reputation as a cultural centre and that she wanted to purvey her art before appreciative audiences. The singer waited for a few weeks, but as her fees were too high, none of the local gentry could afford her recitals; so after a period of waiting, the diva began announcing contemptuously that Bhopal's reputation had been over-rated, that it was full of boorish uncivilized gentry and that Shahjehan's court was obviously not up to the mark. When the diva's derisive remarks reached Shahjehan – as they were intended to – the Begum sent the singer a message, inviting her to a recital at the royal court. Obviously, the diva's stratagem of taunting the Begum had worked and she appeared for the recital in a dazzling sari and wearing her most sparkling jewellery. On the Begum's entrance, the singer made a deep salaam and settled down to begin her recital in front of the gathered audience that included the Begum's court and Bhopal's gentry. Hardly had the diva started the *alap* (opening stanza) of her favourite raga, than Shahjehan put her hands to her ears and in a loud voice announced, 'I have never heard such a *be-sura* [out of tune] voice – please spare me this torture.' Then, turning to her treasurer she announced, 'Pay this woman double her fees but I cannot spoil my evening with the murder of these beautiful ragas and would prefer to listen to my instrumentalists.' The diva withdrew, humiliated by the Begum, who had paid her back for her arrogant and contemptuous remarks about Bhopal's culture.

At a personal level, Shahjehan was cast in a different mould from the other Begums of Bhopal. She was vivacious and enjoyed the good life and was totally feminine in her outlook and habits. She was petite, attractive and exuberant. She enjoyed being courted by princes and nobles with some of whom she mischievously began a clandestine correspondence. Old servants recounted that Sikandar once caught her daughter exchanging romantic messages with an admirer, locked her in a room and gave Shahjehan a good spanking. Her marriage to Umrao Doulah was obviously a loveless one and, after bearing him two children, it was evident that Shahjehan had become bored with him and preferred younger company. Her second marriage dominated her life as Begum.

The greatest contribution to the development of Bhopal during Shahjehan's reign was the opening of the railway. The real credit for this far-sighted project must go to Qudsia and to Sikandar, who with Sir Henry Daly's support conceived and financed this link. The opening of the railway line in Bhopal took place during Shahjehan's reign with the consequent economic and political benefits to the people.

Shahjehan left behind a stable, settled and well-governed state. She had not been a trail-blazing reformer nor a puritan like her immediate predecessors, but had given Bhopal a new, liberal dimension adding colour, gaiety and panache to the somewhat austere landscape that the earlier rulers had painted in Bhopal. Shahjehan built glorious palaces and the largest mosque in India; there was always the sound of music in the palaces, endless festivity and more than a whiff of decadence.

7
Sultan Jahan Begum 1901–26

Sultan Jahan becomes Begum

On 4 July 1901, Sultan Jahan assumed the title of ruler at the mature age of 43 after serving 33 arduous, harrowing years as heir apparent. All three preceding Begums had mounted the masnad at a young age – Qudsia was 19 when she became Regent, Sikandar was Regent at 26, while Shahjehan was titular ruler at the age of seven and fully fledged Begum of Bhopal at 30. As she was proclaimed ruler, Sultan Jahan looked older than her 43 years. Rather plain even when young, she saw the freshness of youth evaporate as she delivered four children in the five years immediately after marriage. Most of Sultan Jahan's term as heir apparent was spent under harsh and acrimonious pressure from her mother who refused even to receive her during the last 14 years of her reign. This bitter rift between the two royal palaces had led to constant humiliation and even penury for Sultan Jahan. The sorrow of losing two grown-up daughters had aged Sultan Jahan further so that she appeared matronly, dumpy and careworn as she took on the responsibilities of ruling her state. Only her deep faith in Allah, her cussed determination and the support of the British had kept Sultan Jahan going during these difficult years.

Immediately after Shahjehan's death, the British, who had all along supported Sultan Jahan, moved quickly to announce her succession as ruler. Although there was no doubt about the legal successor, Bhopal's gentry was divided into two camps – Shahjehan's and the heir apparent's – and there was always a possibility of intrigue and mischief exacerbating tensions. Sultan Jahan's formal recognition saw the Shahjehan/Siddiq lobby melt away, many of them – servants, officials, jagirdars – now feigning allegiance to Sultan Jahan. The Investiture Durbar was held at Saddar Manzil, at which Lord Curzon, the Viceroy and Governor-General of India, was represented by Mr Wyndham, the first Assistant to the Resident, while Colonel Malcolm Meade, the Resident, and Mr Lang, the Political Agent, attended in their official capacities.

Sultan Jahan was a devout, stoic and mature woman. She was in the Qudsia mould, being deeply religious, homely, frugal and ascetic. Having lived through long periods of deprivation, she craved the simple life and disliked pomp, show and signs of decadence. She was not outgoing and masculine like Sikandar and was, in many ways, the opposite of her mother, shunning extravagance, caprice and *la dolce vita.*

As Sultan Jahan took over the state's administration, she found, like Mother Hubbard, that the cupboard was bare. The finances had been dissipated by Shahjehan and Siddiq's henchmen to the extent that the state was heavily in debt and only 40,000 rupees were left in the treasury. Corruption had become so entrenched that no one seemed prepared for or even capable of an honest day's work. Sultan Jahan describes the disarray that she faced in the following words:

> Unhappily, the generation that succeeded to this rich inheritance paid little attention to the opportunities for progress and improvement which it offered. By nature prone to indolence and pleasure-seeking, the people of Bhopal came to regard the indulgence of these habits as the goal of their existence. Not only were they incapable of work, but they showed no desire to overcome their incapacity; and the result has been that in every branch of the State service, and in the military department in particular, practically all important posts have had to be filled with strangers from without. Since the day I assumed charge of the administration, nothing has caused me deeper anxiety and distress than this innate apathy of my subjects, which makes it impossible for me to employ them in any important duties, civil or military.[1]

A fighter by nature, Sultan Jahan resolved to put matters right, rolled up her sleeves and began the uphill task of rehabilitation and revival. She diverted funds from her personal account to the state treasury so that salaries could be paid. She took Sir Malcolm Meade, the British Resident,[2] and Mr J. Lang, the Political Agent, into her confidence and with the support of her consort, Sultan Doulah (Ahmad Ali Khan's title), she strode out with evangelical zeal to recapture the spirit of Sikandar's reign. She first selected upright and worthy advisers and placed them in important positions. She came down heavily on the corrupt and indolent jagirdars. She then suppressed the degenerate revelry and decadence that had pervaded Bhopal's society and replaced it with her own example of simple, pious living.

Sultan Jahan was a caring, meticulous and conscientious ruler. She was fully hands-on and did not believe in delegation of authority. Soon, she was personally examining every file, inspecting the treasury, looking through the registers and appointing every state employee herself. Sultan Jahan took disciplinary action against erring officials and word soon got around that the Begum was scrutinous, tight-fisted and highly disciplined.

Inevitably the Chief Minister, Abdul Jabbar Khan, who was used to authority being vested in him, could not accept a change of status and resigned. For over a year, Sultan Jahan assumed the responsibilities of

---

[1] *An Account of My Life.*
[2] Sir Malcolm Meade's grandfather had been present at the installation ceremony of Sikandar Begum in 1847.

the Chief Minister herself and built up her own team of upright and conscientious officials who helped her put the ship of state back on an even keel. She then decided that the pressure of work required the appointment of two ministers whom she selected with care and after seeking the Resident's advice.

Finding Sultan Jahan an unusually dedicated ruler, the British gave their full support to the determined, just and thrifty Begum. In her autobiography, Sultan Jahan recalled the advice that her grandmother drummed into her ears as a child in the following words:

> The cultivators of the soil are our wealth; that we are able to rule, and to live in state and luxury, is owing to the labour and industry of these poor people. When you become Ruler of the state look upon the fostering of this humble but useful class as your first and highest duty.[1]

Accordingly, Sultan Jahan saw her first task to be gaining the confidence of her rural subjects and helping Bhopal recover from Shahjehan's lax and divisive rule. Sultan Jahan's visits to the outlying villages were not simply representational tours, but serious attempts at seeking solutions to agrarian problems. The atmosphere was all work and austerity, with long hours spent listening to the plaints of the village folk. There was no shikar, polo-playing or midnight revelry as in Shahjehan's days, but an ambience of rigorous hard work for herself and her staff. She inducted her grown-up sons, Nasrullah and Obaidullah, into the process of governance and administration and even 'Little Hamid', her eight-year-old third son, accompanied his mother to be given a taste of royal responsibility.

Sultan Jahan describes a typical day's work on tour in the following words:

> When I am on tour, it is always my practice to hold friendly and informal intercourse with the wives and daughters of *mustajirs* and ryots; for in this way I not only give a great deal of pleasure, but I often glean much useful information. As soon as the people of a village become aware of my approach, the women come out in crowds to meet me, with their little ones in their arms, and carrying tiny bowls of water, the sprinkling of which, as they firmly believe, is to bring good fortune to their Chief and protector. As my carriage draws near, they all join together in a song of welcome, which I acknowledge by dropping bakshish into their little water vessels. I have always considered that to give pleasure to these people, and to sympathise with them in their griefs and difficulties, are among my most important duties. To entertain them in my own tents, and to watch their enjoyments, is to me a very real pleasure, and I usually spend the hour of the midday siesta in their company. At such times, they talk to me freely of their families and their circumstances, and their chatter throws many interesting side-lights on the general condition of the district.

---

[1] *An Account of My Life.*

The rise of the Jalalabadis

As soon as Sultan Jahan had taken effective control of the state, her husband began insisting on the wedding ceremonies of their grown-up sons, Nasrullah and Obaidullah. In fact, before Shahjehan died, Sultan Jahan and her husband had decided that their two older sons needed to find brides. By then, Chanda Bi's seven little cygnets had grown into the most elegant swans and were prized by every young, high-born Bhopali. As part of Sultan Doulah's Jalalabadi clan, they were aligned with the heir apparent's party as were Umrao Doulah's Baqi-khel. Both clans were now poised to reap the benefits of loyalty shown to Sultan Jahan throughout the most difficult times.

Sultan Doulah was anxious that his two older sons should marry Chanda Bi's daughters. Sultan Jahan was not so keen because of her deep-seated dislike of her Jalalabadi in-laws. She may even have sensed that the Jalalabadi girls were seeking power alignments for the future. So when Sultan Jahan sought permission from her mother for her sons' betrothal, she silently hoped that Shahjehan would refuse permission for her grandsons marrying into the Jalalabad family. Instead, Sultan Jahan received a curt, dismissive reply from her mother through the Court Minister stating that Sultan Jahan was free to select any brides she wanted for her sons provided they were not from Umrao Doulah's family. Shahjehan also stated that Sultan Jahan should not bother her with invitations to the ceremonies for the nuptials.

Egged on by Sultan Doulah, the two royal princes had first choice of the lovely Jalalabadi girls. The elegant Qaisar Dulhan was chosen as Nasrullah's bride and the imperious and dazzlingly beautiful Shaharyar Dulhan as Obaidullah's. The engagement ceremony was, as usual, celebrated in a subdued manner, but shortly afterwards Shahjehan Begum died and the marriage of the two royal princes had to be postponed because of mourning.

Six months after Sultan Jahan became Begum, she suffered another personal tragedy. In December 1901, during the holy month of Ramadhan, the Begum had left her husband well past midnight writing out personal invitations to the wedding ceremonies. At *sehri*,[1] Sultan Jahan sent a servant to the Nawab's chambers for a wake-up call. The servant returned stating that the Nawab was slumped in his chair and could not be roused. Sultan Jahan rushed to her husband and found him dead, evidently from a massive heart attack. Shocked and distraught, Sultan Jahan sent for her family and by morning the entire population of Bhopal had learnt of the news of Sultan Doulah's death. Sultan Jahan had been relying on her husband's support to help her through the difficult early years. His sudden death was a severe blow to the Begum, especially as, despite his harsh conduct towards her, she had loved him ever since they were childhood companions and had steadfastly withstood the difficult years of oppression by Siddiq and Shahjehan.

---

[1] Sehri is the pre-dawn meal before beginning the fast.

The loss would have demoralized a lesser woman, but Sultan Jahan was resilient and a fighter who believed that Allah had destined for her the role of reigning over her people. Helped by the strength of three strapping sons, Sultan Jahan resolved to overcome this personal tragedy and to guide the ship of state, alone, through the turbulent waters that lay ahead. The immediate result of Sultan Doulah's death was to postpone, once again, the wedding ceremony of Sultan Jahan's two older sons. However, as soon as the period of mourning was over, on 17 January 1902, the Begum celebrated the double marriage of Nasrullah and Obaidullah who brought home their brides to subdued rejoicings across the state. Nasrullah and Obaidullah moved to their own palaces on Eidgah and Shamla Hills, leaving Sultan Jahan to bring up her eight-year-old favourite son, Hamidullah, in her own palace. The Bhopal gentry quickly lapped up the remaining Jalalabadi girls, Umrao Doulah's grandson Sadda Mian marrying two sisters – the younger after the death of the elder, as required by Islamic law. Within a few years, all seven Jalalabadi daughters were married, to the royal princes, to Umrao Doulah's grandson and to Jalabadi jagirdars, spreading their influence right across Bhopal's political landscape.

The Coronation Durbar

After a year's intensive crisis management of a corrupt and totally flawed administration, Sultan Jahan was able to plug the holes in her ship and look to the more pleasant representational responsibilities that she was expected to undertake as Begum of Bhopal. The first of these ceremonies was the Coronation Durbar in Delhi. The durbar was to be held on 1 January 1903 and the Viceroy sent formal invitations to the ruling princes of India in March 1902, giving them nine months' notice of the function! Sultan Jahan had planned to proceed on Hajj in 1902, but agreed to Lord Curzon's special request to postpone her pilgrimage until after the Coronation Durbar. Sultan Jahan described preparations for her visit to Delhi as follows:

> Mr Cook, the State Engineer, was sent to Delhi to superintend the pitching of the Bhopal camp, a plan of which had been made beforehand, and tents, *shamianas*, and furniture were dispatched by rail. The military contingent proceeded to Delhi by road; it included the Imperial Service Troops, half of the Ihtishamia Horse, detachments of the State cavalry and infantry, the band of the State troops, and a number of riding elephants. As soon as the camp equipment had arrived and the tents had been pitched, Muhammad Kudrat Ali, Assistant Revenue Minister, Syad Muhammad Mansab Ali, my Secretary, Munshi Inayat Ali, *kamdar* [manager] of my sons' *deorhi* [estate], and Munshi Imam Khan, treasurer of the same *deorhi*, proceeded to Delhi to superintend the decoration and furnishing of the camp. When this had been done, and the above mentioned officers had returned to Bhopal, I dispatched Munshi Israr Hasan Khan to make the many other arrangements necessary for the accommodation and provisioning of so large a party – a task which he accomplished in a most able manner. I left Bhopal by special train on December the 24th,

and 142 persons accompanied me. My whole retinue consisted of 568 people, but of these, 426 had been sent in advance.[1]

It is interesting to compare the visits to ceremonial durbars by each of the three Begums of Bhopal. Sikandar Begum's visit to Agra in 1863 saw her accompanied by 2460 men, with horses, elephants and camels forming part of her retinue. She travelled on horseback and in a horse-driven coach, taking two months to reach Agra. Sikandar was not in purdah but attended the Viceroy's durbar in a burqa. Eight years later, in 1871, Shahjehan Begum attended her first durbar in Calcutta accompanied by a much smaller retinue of 550 persons. She travelled most of the distance by train, enabling her to reach Calcutta within a week of departure from Bhopal. Initially, Shahjehan pleaded that, being in purdah, she should be allowed to be represented by her husband. This was a device intended to push her ambitious husband to the fore but the British saw through the stratagem and disallowed Siddiq from replacing her. Shahjehan then agreed to attend the durbar in a burqa. A further 32 years later, in 1902, Sultan Jahan's first durbar saw her reach Delhi by train in less than 24 hours. She took a retinue of 568, of which 142 travelled with her; the other 426 were sent ahead as an advance party to set up camp at Delhi under the leadership of the long-serving British engineer, David Cook, who had built Bhopal's waterworks from Qudsia Begum's private funds and was entering his 40th year of service. Cook set up a comfortable camp for the Begum in a designated enclosure provided by the British. As she was in purdah, Sultan Jahan also attended the durbar in a burqa.

A measure of Sultan Jahan's insistence on deciding even minor issues herself and not delegating authority can be gauged from the meticulous instructions to her Chief Minister's Council that she issued before leaving for Delhi. In these orders, she prescribed that all important decisions required her express approval and were to be referred to her, by telegram, in Delhi. Also, that all other decisions by the council would be temporary, to be confirmed by her on return. Not a sepoy, servant or sweeper could be employed or dismissed during her absence. In fact, the Council had virtually no powers and the Chief Minister was a glorified clerk, implementing instructions issued by the ruler.

The Delhi durbar saw nine days of ceremonial, pageantry and spectacle. There were magnificent parades in which Bhopal's Victoria Lancers were led by General Obaidullah Khan, banquets, exhibitions, balls and ceremonials. Lord Connaught represented King Edward VII and was accompanied by Lord Curzon at all the functions.

Not since the heyday of the Moghul Empire, 250 years earlier, had India witnessed such a display of power, pageantry and colonial hauteur. The Delhi durbar reflected the zenith of the British Raj in all its magnificence. For the durbar week, there were polo matches between the British and teams from Jaipur, Kashmir, Bhopal and Mysore. There were early morning duck and partridge shoots, colourful parades and military march-pasts in resplendent uniforms, banquets, garden parties and

---

[1] *An Account of My Life.*

white-tie dancing soirees at which bejewelled memsahebs danced the night away to military bands. Glamorous rajahs and ranis, bedecked in brocade costumes and shimmering jewellery, mingled with British officers dressed in their starched uniforms. Amidst this ceremonial and glittering display of richesse, stood the simple, pious Sultan Jahan – dressed in cotton – proudly wearing her Grand Cross, conversing in broken English with British officers, but already the subject of immense respect and admiration at the Viceroy's court. She was unique, not only because she was the only woman ruler at the durbar but because of her serious commitment to the progress of her people and the enlightened administration of her state. Unlike her mother, she was not an *enfante terrible* that the British had to humour but an upright and just ruler of a state that the British had always considered the most loyal jewel in its crown. Sultan Jahan enjoyed the pageantry and social intercourse with fellow ruling princes and with British leaders. Delhi was a pleasant break from the rigorous labour of running the administration in Bhopal, surrounded as it was by disease, poverty, corruption and misgovernance.

Within a short period of time, Sultan Jahan had broken the back of these problems. Her governance had proved to be fair and enlightened. The Bhopal public recognized in Sultan Jahan a woman of rectitude and compassion, driven by a desire to lead her subjects from poverty and decay to progress, tolerance and enlightenment. The torture, corruption, nepotism and bigotry which had prevailed during Siddiq Hassan's governance gave way to a fair and humane governance of the state. Within three years of becoming ruler, Sultan Jahan's control over Bhopal was supreme, with a grateful, supportive public looking to her not only as ruler but as their adopted mother.

The education of Sultan Jahan's sons

The education and upbringing of Sultan Jahan's older sons had been traditional and feudal, strongly influenced by their father. Both sons learnt the traditional martial arts of hunting, fencing, and riding. This was an essential part of developing a feudal machismo. For their academic development, personal tutors had been employed to teach them the Quran, Hadith, Urdu, Farsi and a smattering of English.

Nasrullah was the first male heir in four generations. Much was expected of him as the successor to Wazir. Nasrullah was short of stature and grew up into a rather mild, stolid and obedient character. He was extremely deferential towards his parents and never appeared before them bare-headed, donning his enormous turban every time he was called to their presence. His real love was shikar. He became an expert marksman, spending long weeks on his estate hunting the tigers and big game for which Bhopal was famous. Nasrullah's second love was for automobiles, which had only recently been seen in Bhopal. He drove around in a T-model Ford which he converted into a 'shikar-mobile' equipped with searchlights, rifle racks and various hunting aids.[1] The reserved, quiet Nasrullah found solace by living in the country, close to nature with the simple village folk and the animals of the jungle. In short, he was a thoroughly decent, reliable, simple man who showed no signs of charisma.

The second son, Obaidullah, was tall, debonair and mercurial. He revealed an early inclination towards military affairs and was encouraged by his mother to study the art of warfare and to enter Bhopal's military service. He also showed promise in learning the Quran and, to his mother's delight, became a Hafiz-e-Quran at the age of 12. Clearly, out of the two older boys, Sultan Jahan's preference was for Obaidullah, but her real favourite by a long chalk was 'Little Hamid'. Sixteen years younger than Obaidullah, Hamidullah was born when his two older brothers were almost ready to get married!

The race to produce Sultan Jahan's first grandchild was won by the younger Obaidullah or, more accurately, by Shaharyar Dulhan, who gave birth to a daughter – Birjis Jahan. Later, Nasrullah, by now formally proclaimed heir apparent, had a son, Habibullah, both princely houses following up with more children. Meanwhile, Sadda Mian and Bhopal's gentry were also busy producing children from their Jalabadi wives so that Bhopal's powerful and influential families had a flush of beautiful Jalalabadi children from Chanda Bi's delectable daughters.

Sultan Jahan's pilgrimage[2]

Once Sultan Jahan had achieved reasonable control over the administration, she set herself on performing the pilgrimage to Makkah. She was delayed a few months by the Coronation Durbar of King Edward VII, but by autumn 1903, arrangements were taken in hand for the pilgrimage whose preparation and strategy took the form of a vast, minutely planned military campaign.

Given her meticulous attention to detail, Sultan Jahan first sent a volley of letters and telegrams to the British government, seeking their help in chartering a ship and arranging accommodation, protocol, quarantine, stores and medical attendants. She wrote to the Ottoman Emperor, Sultan Abdul Hamid of Turkey, informing him of her impending pilgrimage and received a most courteous reply. The Begum also sent emissaries in advance to His Highness Aun-ur-Rafiq Ibn Abdullah Ibn Aun, the Sherif of Makkah, and to the Governor of Jeddah who had earlier been Shahjehan's state guest in Bhopal. Unfortunately, the *nazrana* (ritual gift) and gifts sent to the Sherif were deemed to be insufficient and set the relationship between the Begum and Sherif off on the wrong foot. The Bhopali emissaries were not well treated and were

---

[1] Nasrullah achieved the rare distinction of becoming a 'Nausher wan' - a hunter who bags nine tigers in a 24-hour period. Many years later, his equally sharp-shooting younger brother Hamidullah could only manage eight.
[2] This account is largely based on Sultan Jahan Begum's book, *The Story of a Pilgrimage to Hijaz*.

curtly informed that the Begum's cash offering would be given to the Hejaz Railway Fund! This affront to the Sherif of Makkah was later to have discomforting consequences for the Begum during Hajj.

In the palace, there was a flurry of activity with relatives, ministers, officials, gentry and household staff engaged in feverish preparations for the momentous journey. Everyone wanted to be part of the Begum's Hajj caravan, ostensibly to achieve permanent salvation, but partly for the adventure and also for the shopping. Sikandar Begum had performed her pioneering Hajj only 37 years earlier and there were still a fair number of people who could give first-hand accounts of the momentous journey, appropriately adorned by colourful exaggerations, whetting the enthusiasm of aspirants hoping to be selected. It was finally decided that Nasrullah, the reliable, stolid heir apparent, would stay behind and hold the fort. Obaidullah, the military strategist, Hafiz-e-Quran and more dashing, stalwart son, would accompany Her Highness along with his wife and nine-year-old brother Hamidullah. Among those finally selected for the journey were ministers, close relatives, jargirdars, an armed guard, civil servants, footmen, personal servants, cooks, petty cooks, syces, clerks, *booas* (senior maidservants), story-tellers,[1] general hangers-on, chickens and goats. Altogether a retinue of 300 persons was to be the Begum's escort for Hajj, one-fifth the number that Sikandar Begum had taken with her in 1866.

Apart from her personal entourage, Sultan Jahan had offered to take selected citizens of Bhopal, free of charge, on board her ship chartered for the pilgrimage. Not a single application was received as the Bhopali citizens rejected the offer of free passage, stating that Hajj was required to be earned and not performed on charity.

While the Begum's retinue was being selected, fervid preparations were being made in the palace for the journey. Currency, gold coins, special dresses and gifts of every kind had been gathered together, foodstocks like rice, atta, spices and millet had been sewn into jute bags for the pilgrims, and jars of Sultan Jahan's favourite pickles had been prepared and sealed. Eventually, in October 1903, the British government informed the Begum that a ship – the SS *Akbar* – had been chartered for her and that Colonel MacWatt had been nominated as her accompanying medical attendant. On 25 October the Begum's Hajj caravan moved to a special quarantine area on the outskirts of Bhopal. The Begum was 'excused' the more rigorous isolation, spending her quarantine living in a tent in her own garden! Meanwhile, Sahibzada General, Hafiz-e-Quran, Obaidullah Khan was sent to Bombay to inspect the SS *Akbar* and reported it to be satisfactory. The caravan then set off by rail to Bombay and Her Highness's special saloon was shunted adjacent to SS *Akbar* where, on 30 October, she alighted in a burqa, took a guard of honour and with a gun salute booming over the sea, entered the ship on a palanquin. There her retinue greeted her with the pilgrims'

---

[1] Professional story-tellers were an important part of a royal household. They would recount epics of past history, Hindu, Muslim, Christian or Buddhist, usually with an enlightened message to be absorbed by the royal princes.

chant of Allah-o-Akbar and Allah-huma-Lubbaik. Colonel and Mrs MacWatt were also waiting on board to greet her.

The SS *Akbar* set sail the same afternoon and arrived in Jeddah on 11 November. During the passage to Jeddah, the Begum struck up a warm friendship with Mrs MacWatt who introduced Sultan Jahan to painting in water-colours. The Begum found that painting gave her solace and she developed her skills to become a fairly gifted water-colour artist later in life.

As part of Sultan Jahan's carefully planned pilgrimage, she had decided not to disembark at Jeddah, as was customary for Hajj pilgrims proceeding to Makkah, but to continue northwards to the port of Yembu, and from there proceed overland to Medina where she intended to spend the month of Ramadhan before arriving in Makkah. The reason for this decision was that her grandmother had not been able to make the journey from Makkah to Medina because the Bedouins had learnt of the rich quarry from India and had threatened that they would hold her to ransom. Accordingly, the Turkish governor, had advised Sikandar against the overland journey. Sultan Jahan was determined to visit Medina and decided to go there first; after spending Ramadhan in Medina she would return to Yembu, sail to Jeddah and complete the pilgrimage to Makkah.

On arrival at Jeddah, where the ship was placed in quarantine, the first clash took place with the disgruntled Sherif of Makkah. While anchored in Jeddah harbour, the British Vice Consul – an Indian Muslim – and a group of the Sherif's representatives rowed across in a boat to the SS *Akbar* and, on being received by the Begum, informed her that the Sherif desired that she should disembark and first proceed to Makkah where all preparation to receive and accommodate her had been made. The Begum consulted her kitchen cabinet and politely but firmly announced her decision to continue her journey to Yembu according to her initial programme. The Begum's decision led to consternation among the Sherif's emissaries and the Vice Consul who made it clear that the Sherif would be greatly annoyed by the Begum's decision. Sultan Jahan refused to budge, but, as a compromise, agreed to take four of the Sherif's emissaries as her guests to Yembu and all the way to Medina. The ship was also visited by a representative of the Turkish Governor, Ali Yamani Beg, who informed the Begum that the Sultan of Turkey had ordered that a contingent of 700 Turkish troops should form part of the Begum's escort accompanying her caravan. Ali Yamani Beg proposed to send 200 Turkish troops from Jeddah to be joined by the remaining contingent of 500 at Yembu. The Begum gratefully accepted the Sultan's gesture and took on board 200 Turkish troops led by the *bimbashis* (officers) Ahmed Effendi, Suleiman Effendi and Omar Effendi.

After a five-day quarantine, the SS *Akbar* set sail for Yembu with the additional load of the Turkish guard and the Sherif's emissaries. They passed through a storm in the Red Sea which led to nearly everyone being sea-sick and arrived in Yembu on the first day of Ramadhan. Seemingly no one had been informed of the Begum's arrival as the Begum's advance party had not been able to rustle up an appropriate welcome. However, the accompanying Turkish contingent came to the Begum's rescue. They disembarked and made contact with the local Turkish officials, and by the following morning an honour-guard had been arranged and a house rented for the Begum. A special purdah palanquin was prepared and the Begum, accompanied by Shaharyar Dulhan, landed at Yembu in a purdah rowing-boat. She was welcomed by a gun salute and took the guard of honour of a smart Turkish contingent from the window of her house which overlooked the city square. Thereafter, Colonel MacWatt made a stirring speech on behalf of the Begum in reply to the welcome address by the Turkish governor and everyone repaired to their quarters to recuperate after three rough weeks at sea.

As nearly everyone had been laid low by the sea voyage, a few days' rest in Yembu was ordered before setting forth on the arduous trek to Medina. The Sherif's emissaries now came out in their true colours and began creating difficulties for the Begum. For instance, the Bhopal caravan needed to hire around 100 camels and suddenly the market price of camels found itself almost doubled. It was evident that the Sherif's emissaries had bargained with local Arab camel-owners to hike the camel-rent and were going to receive a rake-off to be shared between the emissaries and the owners!

Eventually, preparations were finalized, expensive camels hired, a special purdah palanquin prepared for the Begum, guard duties organized, arms inspected, travelling kitchen, rations and water collected and jars of pickle sealed. The caravan then set off from Yembu with the Bhopal guard surrounding the Begum's palanquin as the inner protective cordon, and the Turkish guard forming the outer ring. Every five minutes, the Turkish buglers at the front of the caravan would sound the bugles announcing the progress of the Begum's caravan. Thus the Begum's caravan entered ceremonially the rocky, parched terrain inhabited by the marauding Bedouin to the sound of Turkish buglers and the jangle of camel bells.

The first day, the caravan proceeded without incident under the military command of Hilmi Effendi. At sundown, the caravan halted in the open at Bir Said and a tent was pitched for the Begum and Shaharyar Dulhan. The night passed in reasonable comfort under a starry sky. The next day, the caravan proceeded towards Medina with an excited Obaidullah careering about the perimeter of the caravan on his horse. He found the terrain flat and hard, ideal as he said for polo, and told his mother that he wished he had brought his polo sticks with him. So excited was Obaidullah that he rode out alone some distance away from the caravan and suddenly found himself surrounded by four leering Bedouins who appeared from nowhere. They obliged Obaidullah to accompany them some distance and then, seating him on a large rock, malevolently quoted a verse from the Quran which referred to the rich helping the poor, but which the Bedouins clearly intended as a ransom demand. Fortunately, Obaidullah, being a Hafiz-e-Quran, was able to recite the entire chapter of the Quran, starting from the verse that the Bedouins had quoted. This recitation completely stupefied and disarmed the menacing Bedouins. Though buzzards and land pirates of the desert, a Bedouin will invariably succumb to the glory of the Quran, especially when recited as lyrically as Obaidullah had done. The Bedouins saluted the young prince and escorted him back to his caravan without even asking for a small *baksheesh* (gratuity). On his return, Obaidullah found his mother and the Turkish guards exceedingly distraught at his long absence. In fact, Hilmi Effendi asked the Begum to warn her errant son not to engage in such escapades again as the Bedouins were ready to pounce on the smallest quarry for ransom.

The second night, the caravan reached Ain Hamra, an oasis with a few date trees and a mud fort occupied by a Turkish company. This was Bedouin territory and they were already astir at the arrival of the Begum's caravan. The Turkish commander at Ain Hamra advised against camping inside the fort as the Bedouins could easily mount a siege. Accordingly, the camp was pitched in the open with a double guard placed around the Begum's tent. That night, the Bedouins circled menacingly around the camp, firing in the air and generally assuming a threatening attitude. In the morning a ransom note duly appeared, stating that the local Bedouin sheikh had been promised a large sum of money by an Indian merchant when he passed through the year before. The sum had remained unpaid and, unless the Begum settled the account, the Bedouins would stop her caravan proceeding further! This threat led to a council of war. The Sherif of Makkah's emissaries strongly advised payment, otherwise dire consequences could follow. They said that the Bedouins had, the previous year, killed members of a similar passing caravan. The Begum was also inclined to pay, but the doughty, swashbuckling Obaidullah would have none of it. He was supported by the Turks who were under orders to protect the Begum and not to preside over a negotiated passage. After much discussion, it was decided to reject the ransom and to take the Bedouins on.

The next morning, the caravan proceeded on its journey through Bir Abbas to Medina and soon there was sniper fire from the rocky hilltops. The Turks returned the fire and charged up the hillsides to take on the Bedouins. Skirmishes took place every mile or so with bullets whizzing past the caravans. One landed close to Sultan Jahan's palanquin, while another missed Obaidullah by a whisker. The only casualty, however, was a camel. The Turks had shown themselves to be brave fighters and by evening they had chased away the marauding Bedouins. By the fourth evening, the caravan reached Bir Darwesh, a village near Medina. There Hilmi Pasha, the Turkish commander, at a gathering of welcoming Arab sheikhs loudly informed them that the Begum was the Ottoman Sultan's guest and that he had been commissioned to protect her. Every Turkish soldier was prepared to lay down his life to implement the orders of the Sultan. This little speech was intended to put the fear of God into the hearts of the Bedouins and to demonstrate Turkish resolve to protect the Begum. It obviously had the desired effect and for the rest of the journey the Begum's caravan proceeded without trouble. Eventually, the Begum's caravan reached Bir-i-Ali from where Medina could be seen in the distance. Everyone was overwhelmed with joy at the first ever visit to

Medina of a Bhopal ruler, but Sahabzada Obaidullah could not contain his fervour and charged away at a fast gallop into the Holy City, leaving his mother to sedately make her way into Medina at the head of her caravan.

In Medina, a further skirmish awaited the Begum. The Sherif sent a message that the house rented by the Begum in Medina belonged to a political opponent of the Sherif and that it would be 'unsuitable' for her to stay in it. Accordingly, he had arranged for another house for the Begum. By now, the stand-off between the Begum and the Sherif had become fairly acrimonious. The Begum reluctantly agreed to take the Sherif's residence, but only for four days: it was at a considerable distance from the Haram-Shareef and the Begum preferred to live in a house closer to the Holy Mosque so that she could spend most of her time in prayer. In fact, it took Sultan Jahan three days to install herself in the Sherif's house and to arrive at the mosque for the first time.

Despite it being Ramadhan when the mosque was open for prayer 24 hours a day, the Imam of the mosque and the Governor of Medina made special arrangements for the Begum. Half of the mosque was partitioned off for her and closed to men. Eunuchs were specially provided to care for the Begum. After four days, she moved to her original rented house and spent most of her time in prayer and visiting religious sites.

At this stage, Obaidullah reminded his mother that his brother, Nasrullah, had requested her to bring some thoroughbred Arab horses back for him. Accordingly, Sultan Jahan despatched her trusted grooms with sufficient funds to purchase the horses from the famous stables of Najd. A couple of weeks later, the grooms returned with 12 measly looking horses which everyone recognized as being far from thoroughbred. It was evident that the Begum had been swindled by the grooms who, in turn, passed the blame on to the Arab sheikhs who supplied the horses.

After Ramadhan, as the Hajj season approached, the Begum was advised not to return to Yembu because the Bedouins would be ready to mount another assault. Instead, she was advised to accompany the Syrian caravan that carried the traditional black *Ghilaf-e-kaaba*[1] every year from Damascus to Makkah via Medina. After much deliberation and vacillation, it was decided that the Bhopal caravan would accompany the Syrian cortege. This meant cancelling ship charters and other arrangements previously made from Yembu. There was much haggling over cancellation charges, another round of camel hiring and problems of the Begum's accommodation in Makkah, as the Sherif had once again put a spanner in the works by insisting on certain conditions for the Begum.

Eventually, the caravan started from Medina with the Syrian cortege and soon entered dangerous Bedouin territory. The accompanying Turks were prepared for trouble and had worked out a plan of action in which a dummy purdah palanquin was placed in a prominent position while the Begum travelled incognito in a camouflaged carriage. As the caravan

---

[1] The black, ornamental covering of the Holy Kaaba – the holiest place of worship in Islam at Makkah – is traditionally prepared in Damascus and then carried, annually, in a caravan to Medina and Makkah.

entered hilly terrain, it was met with a barrage of bullets, fired from hilltops, that struck the dummy palanquin. The Turks immediately mounted a counter-offensive and were soon scampering up the hills to clear them of brigands. A small-scale battle took place in which one Turkish soldier was killed and several wounded. Some Bedouins were also killed but the Turkish counter-attack was successful, having effectively chased the Bedouins away. Thereafter, the Turkish advance guard first took charge of high vantage points before waving the caravan onwards, which meant that progress was slow but without further incident.

On arrival in Makkah, the Begum's caravan was given a warm reception by the Arabs, Turks and British. Sultan Jahan repaired to her rented house and refused to call on the Sherif of Makkah, stating she was too exhausted from the arduous and dangerous journey. She sent her two sons to call on the Sherif who designated his deputy to receive them!

For the next two weeks, Sultan Jahan immersed herself in the religious rites of Hajj. She also inspected the Bhopal rubats that her great-grandmother, Qudsia Begum, had built for Bhopali pilgrims as a *waqf* (gift for religious purposes). Eventually, before she set off for her return journey, the Sherif of Makkah delivered a final kick in the Begum's face by insisting that she stay as his guest for the final days of her stay in Makkah. He then presented her with an exorbitant bill for the rent of the house! The Begum, who had been swindled by stud-owners, camel-drivers, ship-charterers and landlords throughout her journey, had no funds left to pay for the rent demanded by the Sherif. In desperation, she delayed her departure and turned to the British Consul-General for help. She also sent a telegram to the Viceroy in India explaining her predicament and seeking his assistance. Fortunately for the Begum, the telegram was intercepted by the Turkish censor who informed the Governor of its content. The Turkish Governor was incensed at the Sherif's attempt to extort money from the Begum. He saw it as a mark of dishonour and a failure by the Turkish Governor to protect the Sultan's guest. The Governor disallowed the onward despatch of the telegram and then made the following remarks about the Sherif to Sultan Jahan's emissary:

> The Vali expressed to me his deep regret at such conduct on the part of the Sherif, and, by way of apology and reassurance, added that the house was not worth so much rent, the sum asked being exorbitant; that, as your Highness is the guest of H.M. the Sultan, no rent could be lawfully taken from you, and lastly that, even supposing that it had been permissible to charge rent, the demand ought to have come from him as it was he and not the Sherif who had provided the house in which your Highness is staying. The Sherif, as a matter of fact, had nothing to do with it.
>
> Then referring to the Amir [Sherif] he said that the man seemed to be in his dotage, that his ideas were those of a Bedouin and that no importance ought

to be attached to his words and acts as he was very fickle, changing his mind frequently.[1]

The Governor then forbade the Begum to pay a single dirham in rent to the Sherif, adding that it was out of the question for a guest of the Sultan to pay rent for the pilgrimage. The Governor's intervention saved Sultan Jahan from acute financial embarrassment and she was able to embark on her return journey without further ado. She arrived in Bombay on 26 March 1904, exactly five months after her departure, and was greeted by Nasrullah Khan, the heir apparent, the British Governor and a large number of dignitaries.

Sultan Jahan's return to Bhopal from Hajj was extremely high profile. For a woman who hated pomp, festivity and expenditure on herself, no holds were barred when it came to revering a religious rite. Huge preparations were authorized with fireworks, illuminations, buntings and ceremonial arches, and the whole population of Bhopal was encouraged to come out and welcome the returning pilgrims. The celebrations were not for the Begum and her accompanying caravan, but for the religious relics that she had brought from Makkah and Medina. These relics were paraded through the town on the backs of elephants, gilded in gold. The procession passed through cheering crowds and the relics were ceremonially displayed at the Moti Masjid so that the public could reverentially offer their homage. Though Sikandar's pioneering Hajj had been more historic, there is no doubt that Sultan Jahan's return from the pilgrimage was celebrated with far greater ceremony.

Maimoona Sultan

Soon after Sultan Jahan returned from Hajj, it was apparent to the Begum that a qualitative change in her family relationship had been brought about by the birth of Nasrullah and Obaidullah's children from their Jalalabadi wives. They were now engrossed in their own families and, though loyal and obedient to their mother, it was clear that their family priorities were now to their own households. Umrao Doulah's grandson had also married from among Chanda Bi's daughters. It did not take long for the shrewd and far-sighted Sultan Jahan to realize that the Jalalabadis were assuming a dominant influence in Bhopal through marriages to the most important scions of Bhopal's gentry.

Sultan Jahan had tolerated the Jalalabadis during her beloved husband's life as necessary allies against the Siddiq–Shahjehan cabal. But deep down she resented their influence and was perhaps also envious of their extraordinary beauty. Sultan Jahan was now virtually alone in her palace with 'Little Hamid', her favourite son. The Jalalabadis were already preparing an engagement between Hamid and the youngest of Chanda Bi's daughters when Sultan Jahan read the danger signals of a complete Jalalabadi takeover of her family and decided that Hamid must break out of the traditional, conservative, Bhopal-bound gridlock.

---

[1] Sultan Jahan Begum, *The Story of a Pilgrimage to Hijaz.*

Sultan Jahan realized that Hamid would not succeed her because both Nasrullah and Obaidullah were not only older, but also healthy and capable. She decided that security and renown should come to Hamid not through jagirs and financial stipends, but through education, political acumen and the nurturing of academic ability. During her long tenure as heir apparent, Sultan Jahan had met outstanding Muslim administrators, educators and politicians. She had also seen the rise of educated Indian women – both Muslim and Hindu – who could hold their own in intellect, poise and language with the British elite. Sultan Jahan felt that, given the opportunity, Hamid could rise to their standards of education and sophistication, perhaps even become part of the wave of indigenous political thinkers who were emerging on the scene in India after the birth of the Congress Party and Muslim League. Sultan Jahan realized that the feudal upbringing that her older boys had received did not equip them to meet modern, twentieth-century challenges. They had received a traditional upbringing and were surrounded by flatterers, courtesans, personal tutors, shikar, polo and the wildlife on their estates. For Hamid, Sultan Jahan conceived an entirely different game-plan with a boarding school education, a tough apprenticeship in politics and insulation from feudal influences. But the first priority was to stop 11-year-old Hamid's marriage to any local families, especially the Jalalabadis, and to find him a suitable bride elsewhere. In this search, Sultan Jahan looked beyond Bhopal.

Nor did Sultan Jahan wish to find a bride among the neighbouring Muslim states who were of Afghan extraction. She set her sights on going back to Tirah and the Pathan families from Afghanistan. Sultan Jahan recalled her own betrothal to Ahmad Ali Khan that her grandmother had arranged by seeking out the Jalal Khan family in Lohari. She sought similar roots in the North-West Frontier Province, and sent a trusted emissary, Qandhari Khan, to forage about in Pathan territory in search of the ideal bride.

Qandhari Khan made a thorough investigation of the leading Pathan families in Peshawar, Mardan, Bannu and Kohat. It is said that while visiting one of the noble Afghan families in Peshawar, Qandhari Khan saw a beautiful little child taking an impromptu shower under a tap. The five-year-old girl was extremely fair, had light-brown hair and the most winsome features. Qandhari Khan was enchanted with this little girl and on making inquiries was informed that she came from the royal family of Afghanistan. She was Maimoona Sultan and her great-grandfather, Shah Shuja, had been deposed as King of Afghanistan in 1812. His family had subsequently taken up residence in Peshawar and were the Shahzada-khel from the Durrani tribe of Pathans who traced their lineage directly to Ahmad Shah Abdali, the victor over the Marhattas in the famous Battle of Panipat in 1761.

After receiving Qandhari Khan's enthusiastic reports, Sultan Jahan lost no time in completing arrangements for the betrothal and subsequent wedding of 'Little Hamid' to Maimoona Sultan. An impressive wedding party, headed by Obaidullah Khan and including Shaharyar Dulhan, ministers, notables, jagirdars and an army contingent from

Bhopal's Victoria Lancers, was despatched to Peshawar where they announced themselves with great pomp and gusto, firing cannons and muskets in the air and bringing on the drummers, elephants, horses and camels. The nikah was celebrated in Peshawar on 5 September 1905 and the wedding party returned to Bhopal by train to be greeted with even greater festivity and éclat. The whole town was out to greet the five-year-old child bride and her 11-year-old consort, Hamidullah.

As with Ahmad Ali Khan, Maimoona Sultan's family members came with her to be given accommodation, stipends and jobs in Bhopal. Thus the Shahzada-khel injected a new, pristine, Pathan flavour into Bhopal's social and cultural milieu. They were fair, even lighter skinned than the Jalalabadis, with high-cheekboned features. They spoke Pashto and Farsi at home, and Urdu with a strong Pathan accent. In contrast to the fawning obsequiousness and flowery manner of the Muslim gentry of India, they were direct and egalitarian.

For Maimoona, the child bride, Sultan Jahan had sketched out a completely different character cast. As her favourite son's wife, she was to be the epitome of the perfect Muslim woman. Maimoona Sultan would be educated in the traditional Muslim manner of learning the Quran and Hadith, Urdu and Persian. She would observe purdah, but also learn to ride and shoot as was expected of women from the Bhopal royal family. She would be taught needlework, cooking and silk embroidery. However, the critical difference in Maimoona Sultan's upbringing was that she was to be educated to hold her own in a sophisticated western milieu. Maimoona was, therefore, taught English by a British governess, Miss Oliver. She learnt to play the piano and the violin. She studied French, chess and mah-jong. She was thoroughly groomed in western etiquette, but also carried herself gracefully in a sari and in Muslim dresses. Maimoona Sultan proved to be an excellent student. She was the Eliza Doolittle to Sultan Jahan's Henry Higgins. Sultan Jahan attempted and succeeded in creating a woman who could easily and gracefully straddle both cultures – oriental and western. By the time she reached adolescence, Maimoona Sultan was beautiful, graceful and highly sophisticated – a truly crafted jewel.

Sultan Jahan was extremely proud of Maimoona Sultan whom she took completely under her wing. She was proud of her, not only because in beauty and grace she matched the Jalalabadi women, but because in mastering both eastern and western cultures she became infinitely more accomplished than the oriental, feudal Jalalabadi women whose education was limited and whose mores were steeped in Bhopal's traditional culture. For the first time in Bhopal's history, a member of the ruling family could converse easily and graciously with the Viceroy's wife and with all the foreign women who called at the palace or lived in Bhopal.

While Sultan Jahan presided over the culturing of her little pearl from Peshawar, she ensured that Little Hamid embarked on the course that she had outlined for him. He was given the best tutors[1] in English, civics, politics and administration. He accompanied his mother at all

---

[1] One of these was Mr C.H. Payne who was later appointed Principal of the Alexandra School.

official functions and was encouraged to develop his considerable sporting skills and became an outstanding polo player, a fearless shikari and expert marksman. Sultan Jahan visited all the leading boarding schools and colleges (private boarding schools) herself, but eventually decided that Hamid should go to school at Bhopal's own Alexandra School that she had founded. The young prince's involvement would serve as an example for children of other jagirdars to follow and it would also provide Hamid with an opportunity to rub shoulders and interact with young boys from Bhopal, inculcating in him a democratic and egalitarian spirit. He studied at Alexandra School until he was enrolled at the Aligarh Muslim College and became the first boarder in an educational institute from the Bhopal royal family. He was subsequently selected as one of the Viceroy's honorary ADCs. Although formally married, Hamid and Maimoona lived in separate apartments under the scrutinous gaze of the Begum who would decide, at the appropriate time, when conjugal relations were to be permitted.

Sultan Jahan's reforms

In the first ten years of her governance, Sultan Jahan stamped her personality on Bhopal's administration and its society. Sultan Jahan was fair, enlightened, frugal and devout. She was totally in control and a hands-on ruler. Within a few years, Bhopal's finances were healthy and state income rising to record levels. The only temporary setback was a brilliantly conceived heist of the state treasury by robbers who approached the lake-side building in boats, bored holes in the treasury wall from the water side and stole over 1½ lakhs of rupees in cash. A huge police operation to catch the thieves was mounted. Eventually, they were caught and most of the booty recovered.

Completely loyal to the British, she instituted, with British advice, reforms in agriculture, taxation, armed forces, police, the jails, irrigation, the judiciary and public works. Sultan Jahan toured the villages, patiently listening to the problems brought to her by the womenfolk. The following extract from her autobiography[1] illustrates Sultan Jahan's total commitment to improving the conditions in her state:

> The hot weather was fast approaching, and I had determined to complete the inspection of eighteen mahals before my return to headquarters. Even after lengthening the ordinary office hours, it was impossible to get through the work of a single mahal in less than eight days. My own work occupied me eighteen hours daily. From seven o'clock in the morning till ten o'clock, I received in durbar the officers of the local tahsil [district] and thana [compound], and received visits from jagirdars, mustajirs, and muafidars [freeholders], with whom I discussed all the affairs of the surrounding mahals. At ten o'clock, I took my morning meal, after which I disposed of the petitions that had been presented to me at the previous durbar. This done, the Revenue Minister came to submit papers dealing with rents and assessments. These papers were endorsed with his own suggestions and opinions, and it

[1] *An Account of My Life.*

remained for me to settle finally the amounts to be demanded, in accordance with which leases were then granted. At two o'clock Dewan Thakur Parshad, whose experience of settlement work dated from the fifteen years' settlement established in the reign of my grandmother, brought me the leases which he had drafted, and in my presence they were delivered to the mustajirs concerned. This occupied me till six o'clock; and then Sheikh Muhammad Hasan and Munshi Israr Hasan Khan came with papers and accounts connected with the collection of arrears. I have spoken in a previous chapter of the state of confusion which these accounts presented when I took charge of the administration. I had now ordered statements to be prepared showing the amounts for which the mustajirs themselves acknowledged their liability, and I spent two hours every evening, from six till eight o'clock, in examining these statements. At eight o'clock I took my evening meal, after which, until eleven o'clock, and sometimes until past midnight, I was occupied with correspondence on various state matters, and in devising and directing measures for the suppression of plague, which had, at that time, begun to make its appearance in Bhopal.

Sultan Jahan revived the Majlis-e-Mashwara, an advisory body that served as a legislative parliament. She decided to have elections for municipalities, thereby providing the first democratic impetus to the people of Bhopal. She paid special attention to health, propagating inoculation and vaccination after central India had been ravaged for several years by bubonic plague. The municipalities of Bhopal's main towns were geared up to improve sanitation, hygiene and communication, and to supply tax-free water. Above all, Sultan Jahan recognized the need for the uplift, education and enlightenment of women. She built schools and insisted on high standards by appointing qualified teachers drawn from far and wide. Young girls from middle-class families were urged to become girl guides and married women encouraged to join the Bhopal Ladies Club. Technical institutes were opened in which embroidery, handicraft and needlework were taught. Bhopal's handicrafts became famous and even the jails began producing carpets that Sultan Jahan presented to a visiting Viceroy, remarking that ten years earlier, the prisoners could not even produce a blanket!

In her quiet, frugal way, Sultan Jahan galvanized Bhopal's society to become productive, serious and modern. Shikar and mujras had their place, but the real challenges were in increasing agricultural produce, harnessing water resources, building up the administration, helping law and order and, above all, in becoming better educated and enlightened members of society.

For most of her life, Sultan Jahan had lived under the shadow of personalities whom tradition required her to obey. The first was her mother, with whom Sultan Jahan lived under the severest tension. The second was her husband, whom Sultan Jahan adored but who knew only the feudal, traditional life-style of the Muslim gentry. Sultan Jahan, for all her enlightened ideas, could not break out of the cage into which these dominant personalities had locked her. It was only after her first years of governance as ruler that it dawned on Sultan Jahan that she was as free as a bird in the sky and capable of not only expressing her own thoughts and ideas, but also holding the power to implement them.

Of course, it was too late for Sultan Jahan to change her own personality which was cast in the traditional, conservative mould. She wore the veil and was extremely conservative, insisting, for instance, that visiting wives of British officials should cover their arms when calling on her. She was devout and virtually epitomized the preachings of her archenemy, Siddiq Hassan, in promoting an orthodox form of Islam known as the Deoband school of thought.[1] Behind this conservative, traditional appearance was Sultan Jahan's deep desire to bring education, enlightenment, liberalism and modernization to Bhopal, especially to its women.

Quietly, serenely, determinedly, this extraordinarily far-sighted woman set herself to bring about a silent revolution in Bhopal's mores, its society, its sense of values. The longer she reigned the more she was convinced that she had adopted the right path and that enlightenment could best be achieved through education in which the women would have to play a leading role.

During these ten years, Sultan Jahan attended and enjoyed the ceremonials at which her presence had been denied by Shahjehan in the last years of her reign. Apart from attending the Coronation Durbar (of Edward VII) in 1901, Sultan Jahan received the Viceroy Lord Curzon who visited Bhopal a second time in 1902 and renewed her friendship with Lady Curzon from her earlier visit. Other distinguished visitors to Bhopal included Lord Kitchener, Commander-in-Chief of the British forces in India, who found the Bhopal army to be efficient and well trained. His Highness the Landgraf of Hesse also visited Bhopal. Sultan Jahan received the German prince warmly, but found his recourse to using a monocle somewhat disconcerting. She also attended durbars in Delhi, being awarded the Grand Cross of the Indian Empire in 1907, and meeting at a durbar in Agra the Amir of Afghanistan, with whom she spoke in Pushto and Farsi. By the end of this period, Sultan Jahan had built herself a new palace away from the city centre which she named Ahmedabad Palace after her late husband. Not an inveterate builder like her mother, Sultan Jahan explained that, since her older sons had built themselves palaces at Eidgah Hill and Shimla, she needed a palace for herself and her 'Little Hamid'. Moreover, she wanted the palace to be built on Hamid's jagir and not on state land because she feared a takeover by the Jalalabadis after her death.

In 1906, the Prince of Wales (later George V) toured India. A durbar was held at Indore at which the prince invested Sultan Jahan with the GCIE. Several meetings took place with the Their Royal Highnesses and it appears that the Begum struck up a specially warm relationship with Princess Mary to whom she presented some of her water-colours and proudly exhibited the embroidery and handiwork of the girl students of Sultania School. During their four-day stay in Indore, Colonel Obaidullah proudly led a march past of the Bhopal forces. Unfortunately, due to the extreme heat, Their Royal Highnesses could not visit the neighbour-

---

[1] The Deoband school signified an orthodox pristine interpretation of Sunni Islam in South Asia as distinct from the more liberal attitude of the Sufic schools.

ing princely states of central India and their projected visit to Bhopal was cancelled. In anticipation of the Prince of Wales's visit to Bhopal, a State Council and a Legislative Assembly, with elected and nominated members, had been established as a step towards a representative government.

Sultan Jahan's visit to Europe

By 1911, Edward VII had died and George V was to be crowned. Sultan Jahan was invited to attend the Coronation in London and decided to accept, making it clear that she would attend the ceremonies dressed in a burqa. Sultan Jahan's decision to attend the Coronation was the result of a confluence of several considerations. First, as a loyal supporter of the British Crown which had stood by her during the difficult period of tension with Shahjehan, Sultan Jahan felt obliged to attend. She had met the future King and Queen in Indore during their visit as Prince and Princess of Wales and she had established a personal relationship with them. She knew also that the British valued Bhopal's loyalty.

Secondly, a visit to Europe would be a voyage of discovery for Sultan Jahan. She would absorb, at first hand, the organization, the technological progress, the achievements and the history of this great continent whose people had conquered the world and led it in education and scientific advancement. Sultan Jahan was eager to see all these achievements herself. Thirdly, her second son, Obaidullah, had not been keeping well and a heart ailment was suspected. Sultan Jahan wanted to have him treated in Europe. Finally, Sultan Jahan felt the magnetic pull of the Islamic Middle East, particularly from the great cauldrons of Islamic civilization of Egypt, Palestine and Turkey which she proposed to visit on her homeward journey.

Sultan Jahan again left heir apparent Nasrullah in Bhopal to hold the fort while she took Obaidullah, his wife Shaharyar Dulhan, Hamid and his child bride Maimoona Sultan with her on her journey to Europe. By the time the royal family boarded the SS *Caledonia*, Maimoona was 11 years old. Her English was good enough for her to write and later publish a sensitive and lucid diary of the Begum's voyage to Europe.[1] If it was a voyage of discovery for Sultan Jahan, it was also a journey of learning for Maimoona Sultan.

Maimoona Sultan describes the tour with a wide-eyed fascination at the different civilizations that she encountered on their passage across Europe.

First came the stops at Aden, the Suez Canal, where the King and Queen of Belgium boarded the ship, the Mediterranean Islands, the coast of Italy and finally the port of Marseilles where the ship dropped anchor.

The Begum's arrival in Marseilles led to the first protocol crisis. The port was thronged with press reporters and a large crowd had gathered

---

[1] *A Trip to Europe.*

to catch a glimpse of the Begum. Indian princes carried with them a huge aura of mystique and glamour for Europeans, but a woman ruler was a complete rarity that drew a large inquisitive crowd to the quayside. The Begum refused to disembark, claiming privacy on religious grounds. There was much consternation at the docks and eventually the reporters and crowds were dispersed by the French police to enable the Begum to enter a purdah carriage and drive to the railway station where she boarded a special train that had been commissioned for her by the French government. The Begum's party were soon on their way to Paris, Maimoona Sultan recording in her diary a fascination for the French countryside scene. As the train sped past the historic towns of the south and central provinces, Maimoona marvelled at the neatness of the French villages, the clean dresses worn by the village womenfolk and the beauty of the countryside. Maimoona also admired the furniture and upholstery of the saloon.

In Paris, the Begum stayed at the Hotel Majestic. Maimoona Sultan noticed that the bathrooms had two taps, one for hot and one for cold water. Again a flurry was caused by the Begum insisting on eating *hallal* meat (Islamic Kosher) prepared by her Muslim cook, but the hotel management were specially deferential and allowed half of the hotel kitchen to be partitioned so that the Begum's chef could prepare her food according to Islamic tenets. Maimoona Sultan noted that a room cost a guinea a day and that the Begum's fortnight's stay at the hotel, for her entire party, cost 10,000 rupees. This fortnight was spent sightseeing at Versailles, Fontainebleau, the Elysée Palace, the Bois de Boulogne, the famous galleries and the historic sites of Paris.

After a week in Paris, Obaidullah proceeded to Bad Nauheim in Germany to take a course in the spas, while the Begum headed for England to attend the ceremonies related to the Coronation. In an interesting comment reflecting Sultan Jahan's preference for the (British) system of monarchy over the (French) one of a republic, Maimoona remarks in her diary that in a republic, the people have no one to centre their affection on because a head of state is in power for only a few years, while in a monarchy the loyalty of the people to a single family is virtually permanent!

After crossing the Channel, the Begum and her party installed themselves in a large rented house – Pattison Court – in Redhill, a town 18 miles south of London. The Begum, who had never set foot in Britain, remarked that France, despite its excellence, seemed a foreign country and on reaching England she felt 'at home'! As in Marseilles and Paris, local people and press correspondents were curious about the Begum and her large retinue, but the elders of Redhill had obviously been briefed about her and soon established a relationship based on discretion and cordiality with the Begum's household. Gifts were exchanged and later, when the Begum left Redhill, the citizens of the town gave her a warm send-off.

Pre-Coronation garden parties, levees, dinners and lunches now began to build up which meant the Begum had to visit London frequently, all her travel and accommodation being arranged by the travel agents

Thos Cook and Son. The famous sights of London were taken in, including Madame Tussaud's, Kew Gardens, the famous galleries, in which the Begum was specially interested, and the Coronation exhibition at Crystal Palace where the exhibits from Bhopal included the world record sambar (with antlers measuring 51 feet) that had been bagged by Ahmad Ali Khan and the record tiger (10 feet 7 inches, nose to tail) that the heir apparent, Nasrullah Khan, had shot a few years earlier. The Begum was particularly interested in visiting schools for girls and women's clubs and institutes. She also received a large number of British women whom she had known in Bhopal and also former Residents and Political Agents who held the Begum in special affection.

As 22 June – the day of the Coronation – approached, Sultan Jahan installed herself in St Ermine's Hotel near Buckingham Palace. She took her two sons and ministers as part of her Coronation Party, but, rather surprisingly, left her two daughters-in-law behind in Redhill. At the Coronation itself, the Begum caused a stir and mild amusement by appearing in a burqa with her awards worn on the outside. The ceremony was magnificent and there were several occasions, such as investitures and garden parties, when the Begum was received by King George V and Queen Mary. Sultan Jahan was also received by other members of the royal family and seemed to strike a particularly warm chord with the King's mother, the recently widowed Queen Alexandra, with whom she talked long into the night. Queen Alexandra seemed to find solace in the dignified Begum who recounted that she too had recently lost three loved ones, a husband and two grown-up daughters. Clearly, the British royal family felt a special sympathy for Sultan Jahan who was the ruler of a state with a proven record of loyalty to the British Crown. This ruler was a woman who had set a course of social advancement in her state and was doing everything possible for their uplift to bring education to her people and especially to the women. Sultan Jahan with her burqa thus became a figure of fascination, admiration and even affection for the British people. She seemed unique among Indian ruling princes not only because she was the fourth woman ruler of Bhopal in nearly a hundred years but because she held high the lamp of enlightenment for her people. Thirteen years later, Sultan Jahan was to draw on this vast reservoir of goodwill that she and her ancestors had built up with the British royal family.

Of course, the common folk and the ill-informed press also saw the Begum as a bit of an oddity, a woman of extraordinary mystique who insisted on visiting Buckingham Palace in what appeared to be a dressing gown! The press began publishing titillating accounts of the Begum using her own water because British water was considered impure and the Begum's party eating live chickens for dinner! In fact, the Begum had brought some *Aab-e-zam zam* (water from a Makkah spring) as a gift for Muslim heads of state that she intended to visit on the return journey. The live chickens were brought to Pattison Court and St Ermine's Hotel for Kosher preparation according to Islamic tenets!

Once the Coronation ceremonies were over, Sultan Jahan departed on her return journey. She went to Bad Nauheim where the spa treatment did not agree with her. She then stayed a week in Geneva which, with its lake and hilly contours, reminded her of Bhopal. In Geneva, Sultan Jahan learnt of an earthquake disaster in Turkey and immediately sent a donation of £3000 to the Ottoman Sultan. Proceeding eastwards, she travelled by the Orient Express to Istanbul via Vienna.

As the Orient Express sped across the Balkans, Maimoona Sultan noted the gradual lowering in the standard of living, the unkempt farm houses, the fallow lands, the poorly maintained railway stations and raggedly dressed station guards. She found the Turkish terrain almost as backward as the Indian landscape which disappointed her because the Indian Muslim has had a long and historic love affair with the Turkish people. The 11-year-old Maimoona Sultan described the scene in the following lucid paragraphs of her diary:

> Green fields of jowari and maize could be seen, even buffaloes and camels were to be seen, as well as bullock-carts. The fields were ploughed by oxen. The scenery just before entering Stamboul looked like that of Bhopal, and at times like Gwalior, Indore, or the Punjab territory and sometimes like the hillside of Simla and Mussoorie, but it was almost Rajputana when we entered the Ottoman Empire.

> In the Turkish territory, good scenery, flowers, human beings or habitations were not to be seen for a long time. Our train whirled through a wilderness of waste, relieved here and there by the sight of the red fez, which now took the place of the rose and the lilac. There were customs posts almost in ruins in some places, with one or two customs officers in charge. And with these rare exceptions there was nothing to be seen but an expanse of wild grass. The condition of the railway stations was no better. They were lit with dim and dingy lamps and our Indian stations are far superior to these. A few streams were seen trickling past the railway line and it was altogether a weird sight. The flash of the weapon of a nomad Turk or a shepherd grazing his sheep and goats occasionally caught the eye. After a long and weary journey, Constantinople came into view, presenting a most beautiful sight with its golden pinnacles over the domes of numerous mosques. It was a pleasant sight to see an Islamic country after five months.

Istanbul was wondrous. The Begum was ceremonially received by the Sultan's Minister, Raghib Bey, and driven in style to her hotel the Pera Palace. From there, the Begum visited the beautiful mosques, the great Ottoman palaces and the Topkapi Museum where the greatest treasures of Islamic civilization are lovingly kept.

Modern Turkish women called on the Begum, shocking her slightly because of their liberal dress and western mores. But the Begum also found much to admire in Turkish society, especially the emancipation and education of Turkish women.

Sultan Jahan called on the British Ambassador at his holiday residence in Therapia. She then had an audience with Sultan Mehmet Reshad at which she was warmly received by the Turkish Emperor at the famous Dolma Bache Palace. The Sultan then personally escorted the Begum to meet the Sultana, passing through labyrinthine corridors that were manned by eunuchs. There came a point where even the eunuchs were not allowed and were replaced by female guards. Eventually, they reached the Sultana's harem. The Sultana received the Begum with much affection, the Emperor interpreting for the Begum from Persian into Turkish. After a while, the Sultan withdrew and the Sultana then asked the Begum to remove her veil and kissed her on both cheeks. They spoke warmly to each other with the Sultana's daughter interpreting the Begum's English into Turkish.

Before Sultan Jahan left Turkey, she received the most unexpected and precious gift, one that she cherished all her life and that became the Bhopal royal family's proudest possession. Though Sultan Jahan has not mentioned in her memoirs the background to the Ottoman Sultan's gift, reliable sources confirm that Sultan Mehmet Reshad decided to decorate the Begum with Turkey's highest award. Sultan Jahan thanked the Emperor, stating that before accepting the honour she would need to obtain clearance from the British government. The British Ambassador in Istanbul referred the matter to London and received a reply which stated that only the British government could confer awards on its subjects and that the Begum should decline the honour. This response disappointed the Begum and the Turkish emperor was incensed at Britain's affront to him. He then decided to confer an even greater honour on the Begum by giving her a gift of the Prophet's hair – a rare relic that the Ottoman Sultans had preserved with loving care. In her memoirs, Sultan Jahan probably omitted mention of this incident in order not to offend the British government. A devout Muslim, she was overwhelmed by the Emperor's gesture. She immediately commissioned her accompanying Minister to take charge of the holy relic, not to part with it for a moment and to proceed to Cairo where she would join him on the return journey. The holy relic became one of Bhopal's proudest possessions and was kept in a special room by the Begum and by her successor, to be displayed once a year, on the Prophet's birthday.

After a week's stay, Sultan Jahan left Turkey and stayed in Budapest for a few days before proceeding to Rome, Venice and Florence. Maimoona Sultan records in her travel diary that Venice had never seen a horse and that its nearest supplier of milk was five miles away. In Florence, the Begum visited the famous galleries and, being an artist herself, appreciated the beautiful works of art in the Italian museums. In the same city, the Begum's party saw from their hotel balcony uniformed Italian soldiers, marching through the town singing patriotic songs. The Begum was informed that the soldiers were being sent to the Turkish front to fight. Maimoona records that the Italians did not appear very enthusiastic, barely reflecting the nationalist fervour normally found at times of war.

While in Florence, Sultan Jahan received a telegram from Nasrullah informing her that the plague had again struck Bhopal. The Begum decided immediately to cut short her stay in Europe and took a small ship from Brindisi to Alexandria. There was a four-day wait in Egypt for the next ship to sail from Port Said, during which the Begum visited Cairo, the Khedive placing his special saloon at her disposal. In Cairo, the Begum met her old friend Lord Kitchener, who insisted on entertaining her. She also gave Al Azhar University a handsome donation. Meanwhile, more telegrams arrived from Bhopal stating that panic had gripped the state and an average of 150 deaths a day were taking place. Sultan Jahan could not wait for the return journey to begin and set sail on board SS *Mantua*, arriving back in Bombay with the Prophet's hair on 22 October, exactly six months after embarking on her voyage to Europe. Sultan Jahan went straight from the quayside to the railway station in Bombay to catch the train to Bhopal, ordering the cancellation of a ceremonial welcome that was planned for her. So ended a momentous voyage of discovery to Europe. Sultan Jahan returned to Bhopal to give moral support to her beleaguered people and to launch, with renewed vigour, her campaign not only to educate, emancipate and enlighten the people of Bhopal but also to carry the torch to the Muslims of India, especially its women.

Sultan Jahan and women's emancipation

Soon after Sultan Jahan's return to Bhopal, she was invited to the Imperial Durbar held in Delhi on 12 December 1911. The durbar was attended by King George V and Queen Mary and was the only occasion when the British monarch visited India as Emperor. The glittering ceremonies were full of pomp and pageantry, held in the presence of all the maharajas, nawabs and their consorts. Grand festivities and ceremonials were held in Delhi with durbars, garden parties, parades, exhibitions and investitures. Sultan Jahan met the King and Queen for the third time since she became ruler and received awards for herself and for Obaidullah Khan who led the Bhopal Lancers in an impressive march past. She also mingled with bejewelled and resplendent ranis from other princely states. Perhaps the most significant honour – one that was not bestowed on Sultan Jahan, but truly earned by her for her services to promote education – was the invitation to preside over the All-India Women's Conference on Educational Reform. The Begum gave a stirring address which was followed by speeches from Mrs Sarojini Naidu and Mrs Sarala Devi Chaudhrani. Sultan Jahan appreciated Mrs Naidu's contribution, but was critical of Mrs Sarala Devi wading into political issues which Sultan Jahan felt were out of place at an education conference.

On her return from the Coronation Durbar, Sultan Jahan immersed herself in promoting her grand design of supporting Muslim education and enlightenment. She wrote pamphlets on the subject and went to Calcutta to seek advice and support from Lady Hardinge, the Viceroy's wife. Sultan Jahan encouraged research among renowned Islamic scholars and provided support to Islamic educational and religious institutions. Maulana Shibli Naumani's famous book on the life of the Holy Prophet, *Seerat-un-Nabi*, was completed as a result of support from the Begum of Bhopal, a fact that was recognized by Maulana Suleiman Nadvi in his foreword to the book. Sultan Jahan had already gathered around her educated women from all parts of India who were leading figures in the emancipation of Indian women. They included Abroo Begum and Fatma Begum, Maulana Abul Kalam Azad's widowed sisters,

Atiya Fyzee, a renowned painter, and the brilliant Mrs Sarojini Naidu. Sultan Jahan was nominated the first Chancellor of the Aligarh Muslim University by Lord Chelmsford, Viceroy of India. Thereafter, the University itself elected her for another two successive terms, a unique achievement for a Muslim woman. The following extract from her autobiography[1] indicates Sultan Jahan's concern for education:

> As my readers can imagine, it was both a trouble and a grief to me that out of all my subjects, 660,961 in number, I was unable to find a single one who was a graduate of a university; and this in spite of the fact that, in my mother's reign, the state had offered free grants to any students who were willing to continue their studies after completing the primary course. Even in the city itself, although there was a High School maintained at considerable cost to the state, there were not two dozen persons who had passed the Matriculation examination.
>
> But it was the backwardness of the upper classes, particularly of the jagirdars and others in receipt of large pensions, that I viewed with the deepest concern. The prejudice which these people displayed against modern education was far stronger than that of any other class of the population; while their bigoted adherence to worn-out customs and ideas, their indolence, and their reckless extravagance on the occasion of marriages and other festivals, was exercising a most baleful influence on the social life of the state.

After her return from Europe in 1911, Sultan Jahan Begum's educational and social campaign for women's emancipation moved out of the Bhopal–Aligarh syndrome to an all-India canvas. She participated in the Mohammedan Education Conference and became the founding President of the All-India Muslim Ladies Conference in 1914. This conference supported girls' education and raising the age of marriage, but discouraged the abandonment of purdah. Over a period of time, the modernist views of the Conference began to carry greater weight on issues such as the banning of polygamy. Bhopal was the venue of the All-India Muslim Ladies Conference in 1918 during which there was animated debate between the younger modernists and the older traditionalists favoured by the Begum. In 1928, Sultan Jahan attended the All-India Women's Conference on Educational Reform. By then at the age of 70, her stance on purdah had mellowed. At the Conference, she advocated a lessening of purdah restriction, greater focus of work on under-privileged women and a style of education less geared to domestic concerns. In the same year, Sultan Jahan Begum took the symbolic and historic step of coming out of purdah.[2]

Bhopal, the Khilafat Movement and the First World War

By now, the war clouds that Sultan Jahan had glimpsed in Italy when she saw Italian soldiers moving reluctantly to the Turkish front, were looming large over Europe. When war broke out in 1914, Britain looked to India to provide manpower and assistance for the war effort. The

---

[1] *An Account of My Life*.
[2] Siobhan Hurley, *Emergence of Muslim Women: Bhopal 1901–30*.

princely states were regarded as the most willing supporters of the British, particularly as, in the regions under direct British rule, a groundswell of anti-colonial fervour was beginning to take shape under the guidance of the new generation of political leaders, like Gokhale, Motilal Nehru, Gandhi, Jinnah and Sarojini Naidu who called for independence from colonial rule.

Bhopal would normally be regarded by the British as in the forefront of those states that would loyally support the British in their war effort. After all, Bhopal's Victoria Lancers had been offered by Shahjehan Begum to fight on behalf of the British against the Russians in 1890s. There was a problem, however, in the present case because of the Turkish factor. The Indian Muslims had long been ardent admirers of the Turkish Empire even when it was degenerate and decaying. Somehow, after the decline and fall of its own Moghul Empire the Indian Muslim transferred his visions of lost glory and grandeur to Turkey. The rulers of Bhopal were particularly beholden to the Turkish Emperor because of Turkish support during the pilgrimages of Sikandar Begum and Sultan Jahan. The gift of the holy hair to Sultan Jahan by the Ottoman Emperor had sealed the unity between Bhopal and Turkey. With Britain and Turkey on opposing sides, Bhopal's loyalty to the Allied cause could not be taken for granted. Accordingly, instead of relying blindfold on Bhopal's support for their war effort, the British scrutinized Bhopal with a magnifying glass to see if it veered in sympathy towards the Turks.

By 1910, 'Little Hamid' had enrolled in the famous Muslim University at Aligarh; this represented an historic step for the Bhopal royal family as he was the first of its members to be given a formal university education. Apart from special arrangements for his accommodation, Hamidullah was treated like any other student, including being 'ragged' as a freshman. He made his mark as an outstanding sportsman, a capable student and a natural leader of men. Soon, the short, stocky but handsome prince had gathered around him a group of young Aligarh students who were academically high achievers and politically aware. Many of these Aligarh compatriots were later to end up in Bhopal.

Half-way through his college education, Hamid was allowed conjugal rights with his child bride Maimoona Sultan. He was 18 years old and Maimoona barely 12! On 28 August 1913, Maimoona gave birth to the first of her three daughters – Abida Sultaan – who was followed by Sajida Sultan on 4 August 1915 and Rabia Sultan on 21 November 1916.

At Aligarh, two main issues absorbed the Muslim student body. The first was a deeply emotional but vaguely focused solidarity with the Turkish people. At the time, Turkey was seen as an enemy by Britain and ended up opposing the Allies in the First World War. Eventually, the Ottoman Emperor was vilified and deposed which led to the rise of the Khilafat Movement among the Muslims of India. This movement, which called for the restoration of the Ottoman Sultanate, was as much anti-British as it was based on nostalgia for the glory that the Indian Muslim had lost with the fall of the Moghul Empire. A similar fate was now being dealt to the magnificent Ottoman Empire. Therefore, decadent or otherwise, a surge of sympathy and support welled up among the Muslims of India in favour of the Turkish Emperor. Paradoxically, the Turks were themselves to throw off the decaying weal of the Ottomans and to re-emerge, vibrant and successful, under Mustapha Kemal, a republican and anti-monarchist reformer.

Hamid and his Aligarh friends became deeply embroiled in the Khilafat Movement whose leaders, Maulana Mohammad Ali, and his brother, Shaukat Ali, were frequent visitors to Bhopal as the young prince's guests. Even the Begum felt sympathetic towards the Khilafat Movement, partly because her favourite son had espoused their cause and partly out of a spiritual commitment to pan-Islamism and because of her memories of the affectionate treatment that the Turks had accorded to her during her pilgrimage and subsequent visit to Turkey. A constant reminder of this bond of affection between Bhopal and the Turkish Sultanate was the custody of the Prophet's hair which was kept in a separate, guarded chamber in the Begum's palace.

Delicate warnings were conveyed by British officials to the Begum about the company that Hamid kept and about his political inclinations, but the Begum could see no wrong in her youngest son and was almost as much under his spell as Shahjehan had been under Siddiq Hassan's.[1] She paid little heed to these warnings, but reaffirmed her loyal support for the British imperial power by providing troops, cavalry and guns from Bhopal to the Allied war effort, on condition that they were not used in the Turkish theatre of operations. The Bhopal military contingent fought with the Allies in France and Mesopotamia. In fact the heir apparent accompanied the troops as far as Aden where he fell ill and had to be evacuated home. The Begums also raised £330,000 as a contribution from Bhopal to the Allied war effort.

By the time Hamid graduated from Aligarh in 1915, the war was at its height and the Khilafat Movement in full swing. The Congress Party under Gandhi and Nehru was engaged in galvanizing educated Indians into supporting the independence movement while Mohammad Ali Jinnah was beginning to channel Indian Muslims in a similar direction. On returning to Bhopal from Aligarh, Hamid was given the special responsibility of acting as Chief Secretary to the Begum. Being educated, democratically inclined, a renowned sportsman with a polo handicap of nine and a fearless shikari, Hamidullah was emerging as an outstanding figure whose prowess was beginning to spread beyond Bhopal. Moreover, his wife, Maimoona was accomplished, graceful and urbane, moving easily in British circles as well as in Sultan Jahan's conservative, oriental household. They made an impressive modern couple. Hamid gradually arrogated executive power to himself and began inducting his Aligarh friends into important positions in Bhopal. He accompanied his mother as Chief Adviser to frequent meetings of the Chamber of Princes where he cut a dashing figure with his sporting prowess and his articulate expression of political ideas. Sultan Jahan gave Hamid full latitude

---

[1] AGG Oswald Bosanquet's report to the Viceroy Lord Elgin dated 17 January 1915, India Office Records.

which led to increasing signs of friction between the households of the two older brothers and Hamidullah. Even the Bhopali public began resenting the influx of 'Aligarh outsiders' to posts that had traditionally been held by Bhopalis themselves. British intelligence reports continued to question Hamidullah's loyalties due to his involvement with the Khilafat Movement and his association with anti-colonial activists in Aligarh.

The mild, obedient heir apparent's resentment towards his mother was expressed by Nasrullah withdrawing himself for months to his jagir. However, his two sons, Habibullah and the epileptic Rafiqullah, were less restrained and openly expressed their opposition to Hamidullah's growing influence. General Obaidullah – General Saheb as he was known – was of a different mettle. Mercurial of mood and frequently breathing fire, he would express his anger volubly by throwing fits of temper, stopping just short of insubordination to his mother. These were troubling times for Sultan Jahan who discerned a Jalalabadi hand behind the distancing of her two older sons from herself and Hamid. The beginnings of a rift emerged between the Jalalabadi families that included the descendants of Sultan Doulah and of Umrao Doulah, linked by Chanda Bi's daughters, and Sultan Jahan's supporters comprising the old Barru-kat Pathans.

Immediately after the war, India's independence movement gathered momentum and was matched by an increasingly violent and nervous response from the British. There were a number of incidents, notably the slaughter on 13 April 1919 of unarmed Sikhs in Amritsar by General Dyer's troops. The massacre sent waves of shock and horror across the Sub-Continent, fuelling the call for the British to 'quit India'. The British resisted these forces through numerous political stratagems, one of which was to attempt to divide the religious communities and set them up against each other. Bhopal remained relatively quiet during this period, enthusiastically celebrating the Turkish recovery of Smyrna (Izmir) and playing host to the Prince of Wales (subsequently Edward VIII and Duke of Windsor) who came to Bhopal in 1922 for a tiger shoot.

Except during the period of Siddiq Hassan's Wahabi oppression, Bhopal had been a haven of Hindu–Muslim tolerance and harmony. Sultan Jahan with her modern, liberal ideals had allowed a measure of democratic representation with the result that Bhopal began to witness the rise of Hindu representation in the lower and middle strata of society. Accordingly, the Congress Party began to make in-roads into Bhopal's power structure, sending alarm signals to the Muslim gentry that had dominated Bhopal's political structure. These elements blamed the Begum and especially her educated, democratically inclined son Hamidullah for the emergence of Hindu-based democratic power in Bhopal.

Meanwhile, at home, Sultan Jahan's domestic problems began to grow with the widening rift between Hamid and his older brothers. Sultan Jahan openly aligned herself with Hamid and, though the veneer of cordiality and respect was maintained by the two older sons, their Jalalabadi women presided over an undercurrent of hostility against the

Begum, her playboy son and his westernized 'Pathan' wife. They sneered at Maimoona playing Dvorak and Chopin on the piano, her garden parties for British memsahebs, her smoking scented Balkan Sobranie cigarettes in long cigarette holders, her speaking in French and her friendship with the likes of Sarojini Naidu. They mocked her first-generation Pathan family and laughed at their men who wore the loose baggy shalwar, considered an exclusively women's dress in Bhopal, calling them the *ghagra paltan* (the shabby shalwar platoon). They looked down on Hamid's daughters, calling them 'dark, ugly tomboys' compared to their fair, effete, doe-eyed children brought up in the orthodox feudal tradition. Sultan Jahan had indeed taken over the complete upbringing and education of Hamidullah's daughters as Maimoona Sultan was considered too young to fulfil the responsibilities of a mother. The three girls were also to straddle both cultures – Islamic and western – and they too were taught to be better in every respect than their male cousins. So Sultan Jahan encouraged them to ride, swim, shoot, hunt and cycle. They studied the Quran and Hadith and were given a thorough western education by British governesses and tutors until they were old enough to go to school. Sultan Jahan opened a girls' school in the palace premises so that her granddaughters were given a proper education and also learnt to mix with girls from other Bhopal families.

Bhopal's cultural landscape

By 1923, Sultan Jahan had ruled Bhopal for 22 years. Except for the friction between her own household and that of her two older sons, Sultan Jahan's achievements in the educated humanitarian and cultural fields had placed Bhopal at the pinnacle of well-governed, enlightened and forward-looking states of India. Among her most notable achievements were the opening of schools, colleges, technical institutions, hospitals and medical centres – both western and *unani* (oriental) – in towns as well as in the villages. She had set up a High Court and a police training institute; electricity, clean water, telephones and motor cars were increasingly being made available, and reforms in the land settlement, postal, communications and financial sectors had seen rapid development in the revenue and state finances. Some industrial units were set up in the state and Bhopal continued to be a haven of tolerance and harmony between the Hindu and Muslim communities. Bhopal in 1923, therefore, presented a stable, settled and contented society, flourishing under the benign and enlightened leadership of an exceptionally able ruler.

Over the years, Bhopal had also developed its special culture, influenced by a century of women's rule and their deliberate emphasis on simple living, justice and caring governance. Bhopal's dress was singular, the fashion set by the ruling family themselves. The men wore a *safa* (turban) for a head-dress as it was considered improper to go around bare-headed. These safas were four to six metres long and tied in the

Rajputana style. Traditionally, each major household selected a particular colour and distinct style in tying its turban. Sultan Jahan selected turquoise as the colour of her household and at ceremonial occasions her entourage consisted of men dressed in white sherwanis and turquoise safas. With the passage of time, the common folk in the street soon took to the Turkish cap as a cheaper and less cumbersome alternative to the safa. This was a fashion that was started after Sultan Jahan's return from Turkey in 1911. Up to the time of Bhopal's merger with the Indian Union, Bhopalis, especially the Muslims, wore the soft, dark red Turkish cap with a black tassel (in contrast with the hard, bright red Turkish cap worn in Egypt or Bahawalpur). For formal occasions, men wore sherwanis with white cotton pyjamas that were neither too tightly fitted (like the *choori-dar* pyjama of United Provinces) nor too loose (like the flabby, Allahabad-style pyjama). The shalwar prevalent today in Pakistan was worn only by women in the home. The Hindu community wore the *dhoti*[1] at home, but wore pyjamas with Jodhpur-style coats outside and on formal occasions. As a head-dress they too wore safas but not the Turkish cap. Instead they wore the white, boat-like Nehru cap.

The Bhopali women also adopted a distinctive dress which was graceful and elegant. It consisted of a Turkish-style *kurta* (shirt) that flared in a circle flowing down from a tight fitting waist. The kurta was made of the finest cloth, often bordered with golden and silver linings. In addition, Bhopali women carried a dopatta that measured 4½ metres elegantly carried across the body and over the shoulder. These dresses were sewn by special seamstresses and dyed to matching and contrasting colours with the pyjamas. Unlike the men, women wore tight, calf-hugging pyjamas made from rich coloured material. At the time, every young girl was taught to stitch her own under-garments as it was considered immodest to have them sewn or even washed by women outside the family.

As Bhopal's ambience, throughout its history, was Spartan, frugal and simple, the Begums deliberately encouraged simplicity of dress and life-style so that it was unfashionable to be ostentatious or extravagant in dress, jewellery or entertainment. However, for special occasions like durbars, weddings, nashras and official ceremonies, the simplicity was temporarily set aside and Bhopal's gentry would adorn themselves with glittering jewellery, gorgeous dresses and ceremonial festivity that was typical of the princely states. For these special occasions, the men wore *sehlas* for their head-dress. These were turbans made of heavy, brocade material, often with a bejewelled *kalghi* at the front of the turban. The gorgeous brocade sherwanis would have buttons cast in diamonds, rubies or emeralds and ceremonial swords or scimitars would be carried in the hand. Women would on such occasions cover themselves with jewellery, literally from head to foot, starting with diamond or emerald *tikas* on the forehead, huge earrings and nose pins. The Begums would

---

[1] A dhoti is a piece of cloth – usually muslin – wrapped round the waist, covering the legs. It is worn by Hindu men.

cover their necks with beautiful pearl necklaces and wore brooches, necklaces, armlets, bangles and rings descending to their ankles, so that nearly every part of the body was adorned with exquisite jewellery. Part of dressing-up would also involve bathing in scented baths and wearing pungent, oriental perfumes. The younger girls would have their hands and feet dyed in intricate patterns with henna.

In the field of literature, Bhopal's special culture produced its own accent in spoken Urdu and Hindustani and a lexicon of words that are typically Bhopali and barely understood in other parts of India. Bhopal produced its erudite scholars, poets and religious philosophers, but typical of Bhopal was the tradition of non-Muslims writing Urdu and Farsi prose and poetry. Shahzad Masih, the Bourbon, was a poet who wrote under the *nom de plume* of Fitrat. There were also settlers of Portuguese extraction who composed in Urdu poetry so that Bhopal's Urdu and Farsi literati included the somewhat incongruous names of Hakeem Ilyas De Silva, Thomas Batista and a lady named Flora Sakis. It was a measure of Bhopal's tolerant society that these wandering foreigners not only settled in Bhopal, but integrated sufficiently to become part of its literary landscape.

Bhopal's cultural scene was also dominated by sport. Shikar, especially big game, was abundantly available in Bhopal and was a pastime for most people who could afford to maintain a gun. Because of the abundance of big game, Bhopal often had an edge over other princely states who vied with each other to ensure that their visiting dignitaries went home with at least a tiger bagged in a shikar. The Prince of Wales (later Edward VIII) visited Bhopal in 1922 and was able to bag three tigers during his shikar safaris. The following description from the London *Times* gives an apt description of the Prince of Wales's visit to Bhopal:

> After lunching with the General Officer Commanding, the Prince played polo, and left by train at 6 o'clock for Bhopal. We arrived here this morning in bracing cold weather. The Prince was received at the station by the Begum, with whom were the heir apparent, the Nawab, and her two other sons, as well as two young princes, sons of the Nawab, and a glittering group of Bhopal chiefs and nobles. Outside the station were seven state elephants and an escort of the State cavalry.

> A more splendid spectacle was seen later when the Prince returned to make a formal visit to the Begum at the Palace. No Durbar we have seen presented a more gorgeous scene. The Prince and her Highness were seated on thrones of turquoise blue gold, in a hall of white marble with arches picked out in gold. The whole floor was covered with very costly carpets of wonderful hues of crimson, scarlet, rose, and sea green, all sumptuously gold embroidered. The princes, officers, State, and other dignitaries were all rightly dressed with turquoise blue pugaris. Turquoise blue was again in the pennons and standards, and in a balcony behind the thrones were the three tiny granddaughters of the Begum, the children of her third son, who is Chief Secretary, dressed in turquoise blue. Turquoise blue is Bhopal's Royal colour, and the effect of the pale blue with the white marble frame to the mass of lovely colours of the carpets, and the costumes mingled with the heavy gold, was very fine.

The Begum, who on each appearance has been veiled in a light blue Burqa, is a good deal shorter than the Prince, but has all the dignity which we British know well can be associated with a Sovereign lady, regardless of stature. There is to be a state banquet at the Palace tonight. Tomorrow morning the Prince goes into camp for shooting, and will not return till the 7th, when we leave for Gwalior.

Prince of Wales's Camp, Bhopal, February 6

The Prince of Wales, with a small party of his staff, went by special train on Sunday afternoon to a shooting camp at Kachnaria, where he will engage in big game hunting until Tuesday morning. — Reuters.

February 7. The Prince of Wales returned to Bhopal from Kachnaria this afternoon. The Royal party of seven guns bagged three tigers, one panther, 11 sambhar, one cheetah, and two nilgais.

This afternoon the Prince attended an American polo tournament, and, after dining quietly at the Lal Kothi Palace, left for Gwalior, without ceremony.

— Reuters.

Apart from shikar, Bhopal was famous for polo – Hamidullah having an outstanding nine-goal handicap – and for field hockey which, somehow, caught the imagination of the common man. Bhopal became famous as a home of hockey with the legendary Bhopal Wanderers winning every major tournament in India. By 1923, the Begum had also built a yacht club and sailing had become a fascinating sport for the gentry while the townsfolk sat crouched around the lake-side, placing bets on the boats racing in the regattas.

Thus, in 1923, 200 years after Dost Mohammad Khan had founded the state, Bhopal presented a picture of a settled, well-governed, fair and tolerant society. But around the corner were tragedy and crisis that were to send Bhopal suddenly into a dangerous tail-spin.

8

The Bhopal Succession Case[1]

1924 – The year of crisis and tragedy

The dawning of 1924 saw the beginning of a year that plunged Bhopal again into tragedy and high drama. At the time, the rift between the Begum and her two older sons had continued to widen as Little Hamid was being given more control over governance and was virtually ruling the state. Family relationships, however, remained superficially cordial with only the Jalalabadi women showing a disrespectful arrogance towards the Begum, openly announcing that the 'old woman' was now 65 years old and the heir apparent would soon be Nawab when the Jalalabadis would rule the roost and put the arrogant, whipper-snapper Hamid and his 'Kharya' (a derogatory term for Pashto-speaking Pathans) family in their place.

By this time, General Obaidullah's psychological condition had deteriorated sharply. He was given to extremely volatile temper tantrums during which he showed unbelievable cruelty to all around him and especially to his grown-up children. Mispronouncing a Quranic word would set him off into ferocious beatings of his children and it was known that he would have them stripped and lash them personally with his leather belt. General Saheb was, therefore, feared wherever he went, even in his mother's household. In 1923, General Obaidullah's eldest son Wahid was married, rather secretively and unceremoniously, to an attractive young girl from the Bhopal gentry. Her name was Sheher Bano. Wagging tongues in the palaces spread the rumour that Wahid had made Sheher Bano pregnant, leading to a shotgun wedding. General Saheb was furious with his son and daughter-in-law and both were given horrendous treatment at Shamla Kothi. Sheher Bano became a nervous wreck, miscarried and died six months after her marriage. Wahid, who was known to be flogged regularly by his father, could not take it any more and committed suicide by shooting himself in the

---

[1] The memoranda, notings on file, reports, telegrams and letters referred to in this chapter are drawn from records available in the India Office Library.

temple. These tragic events were the beginning of Sultan Jahan's year of personal tragedy.

On 24 March 1924, General Obaidullah died of cancer – an illness that he had concealed until its final stages and the news of his death, therefore, came as a shock. By summer 1924, it was evident that Sultan Jahan's eldest son and heir apparent, Nasrullah, was also dying of advanced diabetes. This was the time that Reginald Glancy, the British Resident, alerted the Viceroy in Delhi that should Nasrullah die, a battle of succession for the Bhopal masnad was likely as the Begum was bound to favour her surviving son, Hamidullah, while Nasrullah's eldest son, Habibullah, was expected to claim the title according to the law of primogeniture.

Glancy's fears came true on 3 September 1924 when Nasrullah died. By then, Bhopal was dividing itself, again, into two camps. Habibullah was supported by his family and the Jalalabadi clan that had married into the Baqi-khels, while Sultan Jahan was supported by the Shahzada-khel (Maimoona Sultan's clan) who did not have much influence in Bhopal and the die-hard Barru-kat Bhopalis who had always been loyal to their ruler. A large number of Bhopalis sat on the fence to see which way the tide turned. Some leading Bhopal families decided, as a double insurance, to align some family members to the Begum's camp while others were told to side with Habibullah.

Nasrullah's death had seen Sultan Jahan's cup of tragedy spill over. She had lost a sister, a husband, a grandson, a granddaughter and four of her five grown-up children in her life. As the tragedy sunk deep into her well of resilience, the drama of the battle for succession began to unfold. Sultan Jahan felt that Allah had ordained that, almost by a miracle, her youngest and favourite son Hamidullah should guide the destiny of Bhopal after her. Accordingly, she launched herself into securing his succession to the Bhopal masnad with a single-minded and obsessive determination. The Bhopal succession issue became one of the most complex, fascinating and dramatic events in the history of all the Indian princely states. It was a complicated legal conundrum, a murderous family feud and a political thriller all rolled into one. Its repercussions were felt by all the princely states of India and went far beyond the Viceroy's Council in India, landing on the table of the British Cabinet and in the lap of King George V himself. The entire story of the battle of succession, therefore, needs to be disentangled chronologically, step by step.

The competing claims to succession

Immediately after Nasrullah's burial, the knives were out and the battle for succession was on. Sultan Jahan hastily consulted lawyers, advisers and loyalists and, ten days after the heir apparent's death, shot off three letters to King George V, the Secretary of State for India and the Resident informing them that she had decided to 'appoint' Hamidullah as her successor in accordance with Muslim law. The critical paragraph of Sultan Jahan's letter to the Secretary of State runs as follows:

> My only surviving son Nawabzada Mohamed Hamidullah Khan is now my sole heir according to Islamic Law, which, being the personal law of the ruling family, has always been the principal factor in governing inheritance and succession in this State. I have consequently appointed him as my successor and heir apparent, and addressed a request to His Excellency the Viceroy to give formal recognition to this decision.

Glancy described the timing of the letters as showing 'indecent haste'. Habibullah also fired off his claim to succession so that both parties had taken up positions in their trenches in anticipation of a protracted war.

In a nutshell and over-simplifying an extremely complex legal issue, Habibullah's case rested on the relatively straightforward claim of primogeniture, recognized by the British in matters relating to succession. Primogeniture had also been adopted in a number of princely states, both Muslim and Hindu, particularly since the Mutiny in 1857.

The Begum's case in favour of Hamidullah was more complex. It rested on a combination of the following considerations:

1. The Begum's right to nominate a successor
2. Muslim law which considered a surviving son to have a superior claim over a grandson from a pre-deceased elder son
3. Precedent in Muslim states favouring a son over a grandson
4. Hamidullah being 'more capable' than Habibullah and the Bhopal public's 'preference' for him
5. The 1818 treaty between Bhopal and the East India Company
6. The 1862 Canning Sanad – given by Viceroy Lord Canning to Sikandar Begum.[1]

In their reports to Delhi, Glancy and Jelf, the Political Agent, analysed the competing claims, taking into consideration precedents quoted by both parties, particularly those relating to Muslim princely states. They also dug deep into Bhopal's history to discover analogies that could assist Delhi in making a final judgement. It was evident from their analyses that there could be no clear-cut decision in favour of either contestant and that both sides had weighty legal arguments in their favour. They concluded that the legal issue of succession was balanced on a knife-edge. Glancy and Jelf came out in favour of Hamidullah, giving greater weight to political over legal considerations. They argued that a decision in favour of Habibullah would play havoc in Bhopal's political and social balance. They advised that, if Delhi decided in favour of Habibullah, the decision should not be revealed until after the Begum's death. Glancy ended his letter with the following warning:

> Unless we wish to face a storm for no reason, I believe we shall be well advised to recognise Hamidullah Khan.

---

[1] The operative paragraph of the Canning Sanad granted to Sikandar Begum on 11 March 1862 reads as follows: 'Her Majesty being desirous that the governments of several Princes and Chiefs of India who now govern their own territories should be perpetuated and that the representation and dignity of their houses should be continued; I hereby, in fulfilment of this desire, convey to you the assurance that, on failure of natural heirs, any succession to the government of your State which may be legitimate according to Muhammadan Law will be upheld.' Signed Canning.

In Delhi, the Viceroy's legal and political advisers, J.P. Thompson, K.S. Fitze and G.D. Ogilvie, recorded in their preliminary assessments long, erudite dissertations on the merits of both cases. Laws, history, custom and precedents were analysed in great depth before arriving at conclusions. Tupper's famous legal treatise on state succession in India[1] was minutely studied and extensively quoted by the Viceroy's staff who were conscious of the fact that, in deciding the issue of succession in princely states, they were required to play a judicial as well as a political role. Since the law and precedent gave no clear pointers in either direction, the Bhopal case was fraught with sensitivity, particularly as all the Indian princely states eagerly awaited what would be a landmark decision from the Viceroy.

Arguments in favour of primogeniture

As a starting point, the Viceroy's legal and political advisers began their rationalization of the case on Habibullah's claim, based on primogeniture. They examined precedents among the Muslim princely states and found that primogeniture had been increasingly accepted as the overriding criterion for succession. In a similar case to that of Bhopal, the case of Bahawalpur (1897) and Dugri, a small Muslim principality, primogeniture had been recognized. The Viceroy's advisers concluded that primogeniture should prevail unless other laws and customs specifically negated this principle. Ogilvie, quoting from Tupper's treatise, *Political Practice in Indian States* (Volume II, Chapter 11), stated in his note:

> In Mohammadan as in Hindu houses, primogeniture is the ordinary rule of succession to Chiefships. But this rule is not absolutely binding on the Government in all cases. For instance a departure from it might be warranted by proved incapacity to rule on the part of the heir, by previous proceedings on the part of the Government or by the general expectation and family and public feeling in the state combining in support of some other candidate.

Ogilvie goes on to quote the Secretary of State's verdict in the Bahawalpur case of 1897 as follows:

> The principle of primogeniture determines the succession in Muhammadan States, but the successor must be fit to rule.

From these precedents, Ogilvie adduced the following principles on the application of the law of primogeniture:

1. Primogeniture is the rule that has been followed almost invariably in Muhammadan successions, since the Muhammadan States came into political relations with the British Government, but

2. this rule is not absolute, and

---

[1] *Political Practice in Indian States.*

3. considerations such as family and public feeling and the preservation of peace and tranquillity are allowed some weight.

To this reasoning, J.P. Thompson, the Viceroy's Political Adviser, agreed, stating in his note of 29 September 1924:

> The Secretary of State in the correspondence regarding Adoption Sanads (Canning Sanads) definitely declared in favour of primogeniture where there were direct heirs to a Muhammadan Chiefship.

The Begum's case

Basing themselves on the contention that primogeniture would apply provided other laws did not over-ride the principle, Fitze, Ogilvie and Thompson proceeded to examine if the Begum could establish a superior claim on the basis of Muslim law, precedent and custom. For a start, they immediately dismissed the Begum's arguments that Hamidullah was 'more capable and more popular' than Habibullah. They recorded that since Hamidullah was the Begum's favourite son, her judgement was prejudiced and could not be relied upon. As regards his popularity, the Begum's opinion was also highly subjective. Moreover, Habibullah had been doing his homework and a long telegram had been received by the Viceroy from the 'representatives of the Bhopal public' who criticized Hamidullah and expressed their support for Habibullah. The Viceroy's advisers concluded that both candidates were fit to succeed, clearly inclining in favour of Habib because of Hamidullah's 'Aligarh connections'. Ogilvie undermined the Begum's contention in the following terms:

> For several years the Begum has been entirely dominated by him (Hamidullah) and has given him an absolutely free hand in State affairs. His energy and capacity are admitted, but I believe there is very little ground for asserting that they have been used in the interests of the State. On the contrary it is generally believed that the administration has deteriorated to a marked extent, that such reforms as have been introduced are of the nature of camouflage and that large sums have been squandered in personal extravagances; and as regards the relations of the State with the Paramount Power, I do not think that any loyal and impartial person who has been in touch with Bhopal during recent years would be found to deny that these have undergone a very marked change for the worse. Arrogant and unjustifiable demands are frequently put forward, friction with the Political Agent has been going on to an extent hitherto unknown, notorious extremists who are proclaimed enemies of the British Government are frequently received in Bhopal as honoured guests, and a host of minor undesirables each with his C.I.D. dossier in the Province of his origin, are establishing themselves in the State, largely as the result of Hamidullah Khan's connection with Aligarh.

Examining the remaining elements of the Begum's case, the Viceroy's advisers recorded that the Begum had no right to nominate or appoint an heir. They quoted precedents from other states requiring the British Government's prior approval and dismissed the Begum's argument that Nasrullah and she, herself, had been nominated heir apparent by the rulers with British concurrence. Sultan Jahan had also quoted the case of Nazar Mohammad Khan succeeding Wazir, even though he was the younger son. British advisers argued that Nazar's appointment was exceptional in that Bhopal faced a critical situation from its neighbours and that Amir, his elder brother, had been regarded as entirely unsuitable to rule because of 'vicious traits' in his character. Amir had voluntarily withdrawn his claim and Nazar had been approved by consensus. They argued that Nasrullah and Sultan Jahan had been 'proposed' not nominated as heir apparent and the British government had approved. There was, thus, no right to nominate. Ogilvie made the following comment:

> Her Highness's claim on this point cannot be accepted. As pointed out in paragraph 5 of my previous note, it is a cardinal principle that the recognition or selection of a successor to any chiefship is an Act of State and the British Government do not recognise the right of a Ruling Prince to select a successor and then to ask for recognition merely as a matter of routine. The previous procedure in the Bhopal family itself is quite clear. Her Highness the Begum in 1901 merely expressed her desire that her eldest son should be recognised as her successor. She did not present the Government of India with a fait accompli as she has done on the present occasion. Again in the case of Her present Highness, her mother when she succeeded in 1868 merely expressed 'the earnest desire' that Sultan Jahan should be recognised as her heir.

On the issue of Muslim law prevailing over the British law of primogeniture, the Viceroy's advisers felt that the Begum had not established that Muslim law actually prevailed in Bhopal's state succession. They stated that if Muslim law had prevailed, the Begums, themselves, would not have been rulers. Secondly, it was evident that the Muslim law of inheritance did not apply in the case of Muslim 'regality'. They concluded that no clear-cut Muslim law relating to Muslim regality had been established and that precedents, though having gone both ways, were more inclined to accept primogeniture than the principle of *Mustajirul-ars*[1] in Islamic law.

Thus, on the basic issue of primogeniture versus Muslim law, the Delhi bureaucrats came out heavily in favour of primogeniture. Unfortunately for the Begum, the cases that she quoted in Hamidullah's favour boomeranged on her. She quoted Tonk where a son had been accepted in preference to a grandson from a deceased elder brother, only to be informed by the British that the real reason for the son's succession was that the grandson had been illegitimate! Similarly, in the case of Khairpur, it was found that the presence of a grandson from an elder deceased son was not known to the British and when the discovery was made, 20 years later, it was too late to make the correction. In the case of Bahawalpur in 1850, the British were unable to exercise authority in the Punjab region because of the Sikh War. Once the British gained control of the region, they upheld primogeniture in the subsequent Bahawalpur case of 1897. In all three cases quoted by the Begum, the

---

[1] The Mustajirul-ars in Muslim inheritance law pronounces that the children of a pre-deceased heir are not able to claim the inheritance that would otherwise be due to the deceased.

British were able to prove that primogeniture rather than Muslim law had been upheld.

The Viceroy's advisers considered that the Begum's strongest point was her reference to the Canning Sanads. Viceroy Lord Canning had in the years between 1858 and 1862 signed sanads with a number of princely states, both Muslim and Hindu, that regulated succession. The Canning Sanad signed with Sikandar Begum in 1862 read as follows:

> Her Majesty being desirous that the governments of the several Princes and Chiefs of India who now govern their own territories should be perpetuated, and that the representation and dignity of their Houses should be continued; I hereby, in fulfilment of this desire, convey to you the assurance that, on failure of natural heirs, any succession to the government of your State which may be legitimate according to Muhammadan Law will be upheld.
>
> Be assured that nothing shall disturb the engagement thus made to you so long as your House is loyal to the Crown, and faithful to the conditions of the Treaties, Grants or Engagements which record its obligations to the British Government.

The Begum had quoted the Canning Sanad as justifying her right to appoint an heir apparent from among competing claims by heirs. The Viceroy's advisers, however, interpreted the Canning Sanad in the opposite way. They felt that the right of nomination existed only if no direct, lineal heirs existed. They argued that, in the Bhopal case, several direct and lineal heirs did exist and hence the Canning Sanad confirmed the right of primogeniture. K.S. Fitze recorded as follows:

> The real grounds are simple enough and any disposition to conceal them or to substitute others as more politic can only lead to the undermining of our authority in the exercise of the all important function of determining disputed successions in Indian States.

After a thorough examination of the competing claims, Fitze and Ogilvie sent up their advice to Thompson who endorsed their opinion, favouring Habibullah. Before placing the note before the Viceroy, Lord Reading, Thompson recorded as follows:

> There can be no doubt that the Begum has no right to select her heir.
>
> It is not clear what the Begum means by saying that the Islamic Law applied to the case.
>
> The position that succession to Muhammadan Chiefships where there are lineal heirs does not pass according to Muhammadan Law is apparently well established, though no doubt the Government of India would be prepared to take special customs into account.
>
> The Secretary of State in the correspondence regarding Adoption Sanads definitely declared in favour of primogeniture where there were direct heirs to a Muhammadan Chiefship.

A preliminary examination of the case by the Viceroy's staff clearly upheld Habibullah's right to succeed. Only Glancy, the Resident, favoured the Begum's claim on political grounds. On receiving the file, the Viceroy Lord Reading temporized. He asked Thompson to instruct the Resident to find out from the Begum what she meant by invoking Muslim law as she had not established her case by quoting relevant laws or precedents. Thompson recorded the following comment after the Viceroy had seen the note prepared by his advisers on 30 September 1924:

> His Excellency approves of the action proposed, i.e. asking Agent to the Governor-General officially for his opinion and instructing him to ascertain what foundation there is for the Begum's statement that Islamic Law is the chief factor governing inheritance in Bhopal.

Thus, another, more detailed examination was set in motion as a result of the Viceroy's comments.

By the end of September 1924, leaks from Delhi had indicated that the case was going badly for the Begum. In fact, she had been poorly advised and her case had not been effectively researched. Her advisers had quoted precedents that could easily be torn to shreds. For instance, she had quoted precedents that boomeranged against her claims. She had not realized that, by invoking Muslim laws, she was handling a double-edged sword that could be used against her. She had written letters to the King and the Viceroy full of cringing bathos that better advice would have warned her would cut no ice. She did not even realize that by over-eulogizing her son's character as 'the more capable and popular figure', she was creating a wall of antipathy in Delhi towards him. News from Delhi sent a wave of concern through the Begum's entourage and, conversely, cheered Habibullah's Jalalabadi supporters. The Begum began to lose her cool and reported disobedience from Habibullah because he had 'raced off in a motor car to Lahore to watch a wrestling match'! She also issued eviction orders against Habibullah's tutor, a quixotic and eccentric Englishman called Arnold who was the progeny of a famous father, Sir Edwin Arnold, who had served in the jungles of Malaya and had bigamously married his native cook. The British began to have increasing concerns about the Begum's mental state, concerns which were confirmed when she informed Glancy that she would abdicate if the case went against her. Glancy's initial fears of Bhopal being convulsed if the case went against the Begum were beginning to ring true.

By November 1924, Habibullah and his Jalalabadi coterie of uncles and young cousins had begun to scent victory and went a little wild. One of his young Jalalabadi uncles, Mahfooz Ali Khan, went to England and became infatuated with a tea-dance waitress at London's famous Trocadero restaurant. Mahfooz married this dazzling Cockney blonde, called Marjorie, and brought her to sleepy, traditional, rural Bhopal. There Marjorie, who enjoyed the good life, soon left Mahfooz grovelling in the dust while his richer and more powerful relatives vied with each other to take her on midnight shikar jaunts. Marjorie Memsaheb, as she was known – who was not at all like the prissy, prim colonial-type memsahebs known to Bhopal – created havoc in Bhopal's society as a sort of brazen beauty queen. This annoyed the austere Begum though she secretly enjoyed the Jalalabadi boys fighting over the 'Trocadero Tart'.

Between September and December 1924, the Viceroy's staff completed their review of the Bhopal succession by examining precedent, Muslim law and the implications of the Canning Sanad in greater detail. If anything, the verdict now in favour of Habibullah was even more emphatic than at the earlier review. On 20 December, Colonel S.B. Patterson (who had temporarily replaced Thompson) recorded the following advice to the Viceroy:

> It appears to me that there is nothing in the present case to justify our departing from the accepted policy. The evidence in regard to Sahibzada Habibullah Khan, Her Highness the Begum's grandson, does not show any actual incapacity to rule, rather the contrary, and I cannot but think that to depart from the rule of primogeniture and to accept the nomination of Nawabzada Hamidullah Khan because of a storm which might arise if Her Highness's wishes are not acceded to would be regarded as a policy of concession to clamour which would have widespread and undesirable results and would engender a feeling of insecurity among Indian Princes and their progeny.

The Begum's case was demolished by the Viceroy's advisers who had made a deep and careful study of all the relevant factors. But the Viceroy, Lord Reading, was still not convinced of their arguments. On 24 December 1924 he recorded as follows on the file:

> I am not quite satisfied that all relevant facts necessary to arrive at a decision have yet been ascertained. Without in slightest degree wishing to indicate a decision I may reach, I cannot but think that we should attempt to arrive at better knowledge of successions in other Muhammadan States, such as, for example; Rampur, Tonk, Palanpur, Malerkotla, Junagadh, Bahawalpur, etc. In any event, the decision in this case must have an important influence upon future practice among Muhammadan States in similar or analogous questions of succession. I agree with Mr Glancy at least to this extent that the Government of India should not pronounce an ex-cathedra decision whether in favour of or adverse to Her Highness's claim without making exhaustive searches into available records and collecting together all possible material to assist conclusions.
>
> Until this information has been obtained I do not propose to make further observations on the case.

Back went the case for a third time to the Viceroy's advisers; they returned to the drawing board, this time seeking advice from all those AGGs that had dealt with Muslim states and their succession, including Hyderabad, Bahawalpur, Khairpur, Rampur, Tonk, Malerkotla, Junagadh, Janjira and Savanur, to name only a few.

The Viceroy's advisers took another three months to delve deeper into practice in Muslim States. They also analysed again the Begum's claim that Muslim law had always applied in Bhopal and found that the rationalization proffered by the Begum, based on family precedents, not only unsound but rebounding adversely on her case. Fitze recorded the following comment on the Begum's latest representation:

> It is very clear that by thus attracting closer attention to the history of her own family from 1816–1844, Her Highness has done very ill service to her own cause.

Finally, on 10 March 1925 submitting the case for the third time to the Viceroy, Colonel Patterson confirmed his earlier recommendation in favour of Habibullah in the following words:

> Further perusal and close study of this case leads me to the conclusion that it would be most dangerous to depart from our accepted policy that, in Muhammadan, as in Hindu houses, primogeniture is the ordinary rule and to admit Her Highness's contention that in the presence of lineal heirs a Ruler has any right of selection. Any such departure or admission would create a feeling of grave unrest in the families of Ruling Princes. I adhere to the views expressed in my note dated the 20th December 1924.

Lord Reading now had to make a final decision. He kept the file with him for a month, consulting Glancy again before recording his comments in writing. On 10 April 1925, the Viceroy recorded his verdict, supporting the advice tendered by his staff. The operative paragraph of Lord Reading's note read as follows:

> I can find no ground in all the material submitted to me, which I have carefully studied, for Her Highness's contention that Hamidullah should succeed. I come to the conclusion that the law of primogeniture should be applied and that the heir apparent is the elder son of the deceased Nawab, the eldest grandson of Her Highness.

The Viceroy's comments, along with the document prepared by his staff, were then circulated to the seven-member Viceroy's Council, comprising three Indians (two Hindus, one Muslim) and four Britons. On 13 May 1925, the Council confirmed the Viceroy's recommendations, the Chairman, B.N. Sarma, recording laconically, 'I am sorry for the Begum, but Fiat Justitia.'

The die was cast. The Begum's case had been rejected, her goose cooked.

Meanwhile, both the Begum and Habibullah had their informers hovering around the Secretariat in Delhi. The Begum soon found out that the case had gone against her. She charged out of her thicket like a wounded tigress to fiercely lobby every influential person that she could approach. These included fellow princes, the Aga Khan, British civil servants, her own ulema, jagirdars and gentry whom she began to browbeat into supporting Hamidullah. The opposing camp, sensing victory, also redoubled their efforts and found that a number of persons sitting on the fence were coming down in their favour. The rift in Bhopal became a chasm with ugly rumours of dark intrigues and planned assassinations. The Begum again told Glancy that she would abdicate if the verdict went against her and stormed into the Viceroy's lodge in Delhi in an effort to press Hamidullah's case.

Eventually, the only concession given to her by the Viceroy, who acknowledged her deep loyalty to the British Crown, was that the Bhopal succession would not be decided in Delhi and was sufficiently important to be referred to London.

Verdict of the memorandum of 21 May

After the Council's decision, a memorandum was prepared, stating the arguments for and against the Begum's claim. In a detailed analysis of the case, the 21 May memorandum, signed by the Viceroy, arrived at the following conclusion:

> To sum up, we find that Her Highness the Begum of Bhopal has no valid title to the right which she has assumed in regard to the nomination of her successor. And in all the voluminous material which we have carefully studied for a proper appreciation of the case we have been unable to find anything which would establish Her Highness's contention that Nawabzada Muhammad Hamidullah Khan should succeed her. We have come to the conclusion that the Law of Primogeniture should be applied, and that the heir apparent is the elder son of the deceased Nawab Sir Muhammad Nasrullah Khan. Neither in the history of Tonk, nor of Khairpur, nor of Bahawalpur, nor of Hyderabad can we find any sufficient precedent for Her Highness's claim. The action taken in regard to all those States had its own special explanation, and, singularly or collectively, those precedents are, in our judgement, wholly insufficient to warrant a departure from the primary policy of following the Law of Primogeniture. Neither have we been able to find any justification for Her Highness's contention regarding the alleged regulation of successions in the Bhopal family by Islamic Law.

The memorandum alluded to the possibility of consulting the Muslim princely states, but decided against it on the grounds that some of these princes would sell their opinion to the highest bidder! The memorandum played down the adverse political impact of the decision that Glancy had considered vital. It also decided not to recommend a deeper study of Islamic law as it considered that Bhopal's succession had never been decided on the basis of Islamic law. The memorandum recognized that the decision would be devastating personally for the Begum and felt that while the government decision should be conveyed to the two major contenders it should not be made public until after the Begum's death.

The memorandum's verdict was a killer blow to the Begum. She was devastated, considering it a betrayal of her deep loyalty to the British Crown. She almost lost her composure and dignity as she floundered around India, seeking support for her cause which for all practical purposes had been lost. Sultan Jahan was, however, a fighter with a never-say-die motto. She was not prepared to accept the Viceroy's recommendation which would almost certainly be endorsed by the British Cabinet in London. She would fight to the last, try to find a chink in the Viceroy's armour and seek additional points on which to rebuild her case that had been torn to shreds by the Viceroy's advisers.

Sultan Jahan began knocking at every door while Bhopal, for the first time in her 25-year reign, saw itself divided again between family contenders and power slipping away from the Begum. The Jalalabadi women became more arrogant and contemptuous of Her Highness and even the state Qazi, who would normally obey the ruler on such a sensitive issue, declined to give a clear-cut fatwa in favour of Hamidullah, implying that Nasrullah may have pre-deceased his mother but not his father which in accordance with Islamic law was the predominant factor. These were the signs of changing times and loyalties. Reassured by Lord Reading's commitment that no final decision would be made until the British government approved the memorandum in London, Sultan Jahan decided to proceed to London to personally plead her case with the British government and with King George V.

The Begum proceeds to England

Sultan Jahan made quick preparations for her journey to England and boarded the SS *Kaiser-e-Hind* in September 1925, accompanied by her son, her three granddaughters, her nephews (Obaidullah Khan's sons) in order to keep them away from mischief, the usual retinue of ministers, relatives, household staff, and the inevitable jars of pickles and spices.

In England, the Begum initially rented a house at 29 Portman Square and then moved to a large estate in Wimbledon – Belmont House – and laid siege to important Cabinet ministers and members of the royal family. She pleaded her case from a legal, political and emotional point of view, quoting her family's loyalty to the British Crown dating back to General Goddard, the 1818 treaty and the 1857 Mutiny. The Begum was fighting a battle that was almost lost, but her tenacity, her passion and her pleading left all her interlocutors if not impressed, deeply moved by her arguments. Young Hamidullah also helped his cause by cutting the figure of an educated, intelligent sportsman whose prowess at polo had no peer in England. Thus the talk at polo tournaments, garden parties and the salons of Britain's powerful aristocracy began building up in favour of the loyal Begum and her 'educated' debonair, sporting son who had received a decoration for his effort in the war, rubbing out some of the imagery of an anti-British pro-Turkish rebel.

The Secretary of State for India, Lord Birkenhead, also received the Begum, gave her a patient hearing and promised only that she would be informed in advance of the government's decision. An amusing episode relates to his return call on the Begum when the Begum's ministers, English butler, liveried footmen and servants decked in ceremonial costumes and turbans awaited the noble Lord's limousine. At the appointed hour, a rather scruffy-looking man with an umbrella, wearing an unironed suit and soiled shoes, walked past the liveried footmen and was stopped at the main entrance by Her Highness's butler, Badcock. "Ey, you sir,' said Badcock. 'You will 'ave to wait as we are waiting for 'is lordship Lord Birkenhead's limousine.' 'But I am Lord Birkenhead,' replied the scruffy intruder. 'I came by bus'!

Throughout England's bleak winter of 1925–26, long after the allure of England's social round had faded and the Begum's stock of spices and pickles was depleted, the Begum stuck it out, facing the bitter cold and dampness in pursuit of the only aim left in her life. She refused to lift the siege on Britain's fort and hammered away at all and sundry in her broken English, astounding Lady Reading, the Viceroy's wife, who was in England and had called on the Begum, by referring to Lord Reading as 'a great liar'. Seeing Lady Reading change colour, horrified by the Begum's calumny against her husband, Maimoona Sultan quickly intervened and explained that her mother-in-law was praising Lord Reading's qualities as a 'great lawyer'.

The Begum made her round of calls on British royalty, presenting to the young Duke of York (later King George VI) and the Duchess a ceremonial offering of *chatti*[1] on the birth of their daughter Elizabeth (later Queen Elizabeth II). The Begum's granddaughters were also photographed in the British press selling poppies in the streets of London for Armistice Day, dressed in a strange hybrid of Scottish and Muslim dress that the Begum had contrived!

Eventually, King George V and Queen Mary received the loyal Begum at Buckingham Palace. Before the audience, the Begum was politely reminded that, unlike herself, King George was a constitutional monarch and all decisions were made by the British Cabinet. Sultan Jahan made her solemn entrance into the King's chamber, dressed in a burqa. George V received her warmly as they had met several times and Sultan Jahan was clearly a favourite with British royalty. Sultan Jahan presented her salaam and took off her veil to underline her warm, long-standing relations with the British monarch.

Sultan Jahan initially met the King alone.[2] After basic courtesies, she launched herself into a tirade of bathos, loyalty and pleading for justice. King George was sympathetic, but explained that, unlike the Begum, he was only a constitutional monarch. Sultan Jahan refused to accept, responding that the British monarchy had always sustained the women rulers of Bhopal. She reminded His Majesty that women's rule in Bhopal had only been possible because of Queen Victoria's support. She had been like a mother to the Begums and her grandson could not turn away Queen Victoria's 'daughter'. After all, Queen Victoria had also been a constitutional monarch, but had exerted great influence. George V could surely do the same. With this emotional and heart-rending appeal, Sultan Jahan burst into tears and fainted! This led to consternation in the King's chamber and Queen Mary appeared, calling for smelling salts and water to help the Begum recover her composure. Undoubtedly, the scene was embarrassing, but it also created a deep feeling of sympathy for the loyal, venerable and dignified Begum who had pleaded her case so movingly to the King.

Sultan Jahan believed that she had convinced George V – and certainly Queen Mary – that regardless of constitutional constraints, the loyal Begum's case carried weight. She felt sure that the British monarch sympathized with her and would help her cause. It is possible that King George mentioned the issue to Prime Minister Baldwin and to Lord Birkenhead. In any case, political decisions in Britain often crystallize in the corridors of power, in the cigar-filled libraries of London clubs, at country-house fox hunts and at polo matches. It is certain that the Begum's cause, so emotionally and tenaciously pleaded at Buckingham

---

[1] Chatti is a traditional Muslim ceremony in which, on the sixth day after the birth of an heir, family members carry gifts to the parents' household.
[2] This account is based on tapes recorded by Princess Abida Sultaan.

Palace, reverberated around these political watering-holes where men of power and influence gathered and discussed issues of importance.

Unknown to the Begum, the first dent in the Viceroy's 21 May memorandum was made in July 1925 when Sir Arthur Hertzel, Under Secretary to the Secretary of State for India in London, questioned the basis on which Delhi's legal foundations had been built in favour of Habibullah. Hertzel's letter to Delhi stated as follows:

> It is, I think, important that this question should be treated from the outset as one, not of law, but of policy. There is no Muhammadan law of succession to regalities, and though the Government of India seem to me to have established that the Paramount Power took the Muhammadan law of succession to private property as a guide in dealing with State successions, I very much doubt whether they are right in saying (paragraph 25) that 'in the later rulings it assumed the importance of a principle which was binding in itself'. Isolated dicta supporting this view can no doubt be quoted. But my belief is that what was always uppermost in the mind of the Company was policy. What policy required was a peaceful succession with a reasonable amount of good government in the State concerned; and in the conditions existing in India in the first half of the 19th century this was more likely to be secured by the application of the analogy of Muhammadan law, because it would usually set upon the masnad an older man who would, generally speaking, be more capable of undertaking the administration, and who would in all events be more established in popular estimation. Thus policy and law went hand in hand, but I doubt if the Company ever hesitated to set law aside in succession cases if policy required it; and this habit of mind was carried on into the early days of Crown Government.
>
> The Government of India seem to me to have established beyond all reasonable doubt that if this case had arisen in 1850 or even in 1860 it would have been decided in favour of the son as against the grandson.

Hertzel's letter was immediately followed up by Lord Birkenhead's telegram to the Viceroy on 22 July, calling for a re-examination of the case. Clearly, the India Office in London was not convinced by the rationalization made by the Viceroy's Office in its 21 May memorandum. Thus, London pressurized Delhi to re-examine the case.

Deferring to Birkenhead, Reading sent the case back, a fourth time, to his advisers for further scrutiny, referring specially to Hertzel's comments regarding pre-Mutiny practice in Muslim states and the need for a deeper legal examination of the Canning Sanads. On 26 July 1925, Lord Reading, who was in London at the time, sent the following telegram to his staff in Delhi:

> I have examined again the case relating to the Bhopal succession by light of the documents in the India Office. The matter will need to be examined further by the Government of India, particularly in reference to the Hyderabad case. In order to avoid delay it would be well for the Political Secretary himself to examine the case before my return.

J.P. Thompson, Ogilvie and Fitze dutifully obeyed and yet another round of examination of laws, customs, treaties etc was carried out. Pre-Mutiny precedents that had been glossed over were brought out and practice in all Muslim states – ranging from Egypt to Iran – examined in minute detail.

The India Office's reservations on the Viceroy's recommendations contained in the 21 May memorandum were based on two broad factors. First, that too great an emphasis had been laid on legalistic issues against the weight of government policy. Hertzel quoted Lord Salisbury's famous comment:

> I have no doubt the law of this despatch [i.e. the draft before him] – if law be applicable – is accurate. But I dread the assumption that law is to be our main guide.

Secondly, the India Office in London felt that the Viceroy's staff had not adequately researched custom, precedents and laws in pre-Mutiny times which the India Office considered relevant. In short, the India Office was not convinced of the rationale behind the Viceroy's recommendations and began bombarding Delhi with legal and other opinions that favoured contrary conclusions. Probably, during Lord Reading's visit to London, the groundswell of sympathy in favour of the Begum in the corridors of power was conveyed to the Viceroy so that, on his return to Delhi, he had made up his mind to review his earlier conclusions.

In Delhi, Thompson and his colleagues stubbornly held on to their earlier conclusions and on 14 November 1925 Thompson recorded the following recommendations to the Viceroy:

> That the Muhammadans themselves did not consider the rules of the Civil Law applicable to Principalities and that their practice was nomination.
>
> That we abandoned nomination and without inquiry applied to Principalities the principle of the Civil Law, that sons exclude grandsons.
>
> That Lord Canning proposed to restore nomination.
>
> That the Secretary of State accepted his proposal subject to primogeniture among lineal descendants.
>
> That primogeniture was meant in the English sense and has been so interpreted ever since, and
>
> That primogeniture in the English sense should govern the present case.

But by December 1925, the India Office's legal torpedoes from London had holed the Viceroy's ship in Delhi. On 24 December, Reading overruled Thompson and reversed his earlier decision. In a humiliating telegram sent on Christmas Day 1925, Lord Reading virtually ate humble pie and acknowledged that his earlier conclusions contained in the 21 May memorandum were wrong and that fresh recommendations were being sent to Lord Birkenhead. Lord Reading's telegram read as follows:

> Unless you see any objection we desire to withdraw our despatch (Secret Political) No. 7 of 21st May 1925 (Serial No. 11). Fresh material of relevance in the Bhopal succession case was brought to our notice in July last in circumstances of which you are aware. The examination of documents relating to the pre-mutiny period, which resulted as a consequence, has now convinced us that the conclusions previously submitted by us to you in May last cannot be

sustained in the light of the evidence now available. We regret that these documents were not before us when the case was examined last spring. Our researches were in fact confined in the main to the past history of the dynasties which are still in existence and to accessions which have occurred since the Indian Mutiny.

Subsequent information has shown us that we attached undue importance to the years subsequent to the issue of the Canning Sanads and we concentrated on these documents and on decisions of later date because they appeared to us to mark a new period in connection with the principles of recognition of succession in Indian States. Had we not confined ourselves to events subsequent to the time when the British government directly assumed the administration of India we should have recognised the force of the precedents antecedent to that period in shaping and interpreting subsequent policy.

Please telegraph if you agree to withdrawal of May despatch (Serial No. 11). A fresh despatch is being drafted.

London immediately agreed to the withdrawal of the 21 May memorandum. A second memorandum, drafted by Lord Reading himself, supported Hamidullah's claim and was signed by the Viceroy's Council on 14 January 1926.

Comparison of first and second memorandums

Rarely if ever had the British government in India reversed itself on a decision of such importance. Within seven months of the first (21 May) memorandum, the Viceroy had proffered legal arguments justifying a 180-degree turn in the second (14 January) memorandum. A comparison of the two memorandums illustrates how the case turned on vital issues.

Both memorandums began with the following seven points put forward in the Begum's case:

1. Her Highness claims, within certain limits, the right to nominate her successor. In support of this claim she has attached to her will a fatwa of the Ulama of Bhopal.

2. The nomination is justifiable in view of Nawabzada Muhammad Hamidullah Khan's local popularity, personal qualities, and administrative experience.

3. It is argued that, under Article IX of the Bhopal Treaty of 1818, the British Government are debarred from introducing their jurisdiction into the State in any manner and that consequently it would be a breach of a Treaty obligation to insist on the application of the English law of primogeniture in the matter of successions in the ruling family.

4. Reference is made to the modern policy of the Government of India regarding recognition of successions in Indian States. In particular, a quotation is made from the Government of India's Resolution in the Foreign and Political Department, No. 426-R, dated the 29th October 1920, regarding the procedure for debarring from the succession any member of

a ruling family, who, according to the law and custom of his State, is entitled to succeed.

5   It is stated that Islamic Law and practice has been the chief factor in governing inheritance in the ruling family of Bhopal since the foundation of the State.

6   Further arguments are based on the wording of the Adoption (Canning) Sanad granted to the Ruler of Bhopal in 1860.

7   It is stated that Nawabzada Muhammad Hamidullah Khan is the only possible heir under Islamic Law and practice, which is only possible heir under Islamic Law and practice, which is applicable to all Muhammadan States. In particular, Her Highness has made references to alleged analogies in the Muhammadan States of Tonk and Bahawalpur.

Both memorandums summarily dismissed items 2, 3, 4 and 5 as follows:

Personal popularity and public approval

We are unable to admit the relevancy of any personal considerations in the present controversy. We propose in this despatch to refrain from any comparison of the personal merits of the two candidates for the succession. We think it sufficient to observe that we are satisfied that neither could be passed over on the ground of unfitness for the responsibilities of Rulership. Nor do we accept at their face value Her Highness's protestations regarding the popularity of her youngest son and the universal local desire for his succession. In our opinion it would be impossible to obtain any reliable indication of local public opinion on this point so long as Her Highness is alive and her powers as Ruler remain, as they are at present, vested in Nawabzada Muhammad Hamidullah Khan.

Treaty

We are quite unable to admit that Article IX of the Treaty of 1818 has any bearing on the question now under discussion.

1920 Resolution

Nor does it appear to us that Her Highness's reference to the wording of Foreign and Political Department Resolution of the 29th October 1920 is deserving of serious consideration.

Muhammadan Law

Throughout the whole of the tangled history of successions in Bhopal we have found no reference or appeal in the official correspondence to the principles of the Muhammadan Civil Law.

The issues on which the case turned were: primogeniture versus nomination, the implications of customary law and the interpretation of the Canning Sanad.

Primogeniture versus nomination

Referring to the substantive arguments made by the Begum, the first memorandum had built a strong case in favour of Habibullah on the principle of primogeniture. The second memorandum weakened this premise by reasoning that the term primogeniture, as applied in British law, was never actually introduced in India as a policy. It was accepted as part of Hindu and Muslim customary law, usually confirming decisions based on local and customary law. The second memorandum states as follows:

> When Sir C. Wood stated that where there were direct heirs there should be no departure from the policy of recognising the claims of primogeniture, it appears to us that he referred to an existing policy and we cannot think that he intended to convey a desire to change it. The policy then in force, as we have shown, was the recognition of a son in preference to the son of a predeceased elder son.
>
> As the tone of his statement shows, in our opinion, that he had no intention of changing established principles in the case of lineal heirs, the probabilities appear to us in favour of his having used the word 'primogeniture' in its restricted sense only.

The first memorandum had dismissed the right of nomination by a ruler. The second memorandum, however, found that the right of nomination had existed in Muslim regalities. Research that arrived at this conclusion went deep into Muslim history covering the Egyptian, Turkish, Persian, Moghul and other Muslim dynasties of India. The second memorandum concluded that a limited right of nomination had existed with Muslim regalities and had, in fact, been exercised in the history of the Bhopal dynasty. The limitations to nomination were that of public approval, acceptance by religious leaders (ulema) and fitness to govern. Accordingly, the second memorandum accepted the Begum's limited right to nominate a successor. The second memorandum states as follows:

> It seems to us proved beyond possibility of doubt that in India the custom was:
>
> 1 nomination by the Ruler, and
>
> 2 confirmation or nomination by the Nobles and principal officers of the States.

Muslim law and custom

The Viceroy's staff and the first memorandum had dismissed the application of Muslim law of inheritance applying in the case of regalities. Even the second memorandum stated that the Begum had failed to establish her claim based on Muslim law. However, the second memorandum departed from the reasoning of the first by referring to succession cases before the Mutiny. In reviewing these cases dating back several centuries, the second memorandum established that in Muslim regalities, analogies with Muslim civil law led to Muslim regalities favouring a son over a grandson from a deceased son. The following extract from the second memorandum illustrates:

Further, we consider it fully established that the practice in regard to succession was independent of the Civil Law, and that in making nominations the choice of the Ruler and the Nobles was not fettered by anything corresponding to the rule of the Civil Law which denies the right of representation to a grandson so long as any sons survive.

The field of selection was limited to the members of the Royal family, descendants were preferred to collaterals, and, as between sons, there was a strong feeling in favour of the eldest.

Our conclusion that the true Muslim practice in India was nomination receives religious support from *fatwas* pronounced by doctors of the faith of Islam on two widely separate occasions during the British period.

The Canning Sanads

The first memorandum concluded that the Canning Sanads upheld the right of primogeniture. The second memorandum opposed this conclusion based on research relating to the pre-Mutiny period, on the grounds that the term 'Muhammadan Law' used in the Canning Sanad was unfortunate (since there is no Muslim law for regalities) and actually meant Muhammadan custom. Accordingly, the Canning Sanads were deemed to uphold Muslim customary law, based on the analogy of the Muslim law of inheritance that gave preference to sons over grandsons in succession cases and accepted the limited right of nomination. The following extract refers:

> Further it is a just inference from both the rulings that the reference Meaning of the term 'Muhammadan Law' in the Sanads to Muhammadan Law is to succession. The reference is in fact to that system of selective nomination, which Lord Canning had rightly discerned to have been the traditional practice and on which he laid so much stress.

Final conclusion

The second memorandum then came to the following final conclusion of this historic case:

> After mature consideration it appears to us from the material before us that the proper conclusion is that the important precedents of the first half of the last century establish the practice of recognition by the British Government of a son in preference to the son of a predeceased elder son in succession to a throne in Muslim States in India. It does not appear to us that this practice was altered by Sir C. Wood's pronouncement. We do not hold that the slight tendency in later years towards acceptance of the idea of succession by primogeniture in the English sense has affected the application of the principle which has guided the British Government since the beginning of the 19th century. Nor do we find in the present case any sufficient reason or grounds of policy for departing from these precedents. It is true that in many of the cases referred to in Appendix A to Annexure VII, more especially during the early years of our ascendancy in this country, the decisions in succession cases were dictated by reasons of State rather than by definite principles. But in the present case and at the present time there are no reasons of State

which would justify us in following the later tendency in preference to the series of earlier rulings. As a result, we hold that Nawabzada Hamidullah Khan should be recognised as the heir to the masnad of Bhopal.

His children will not by this recognition be placed in any better position than that enjoyed by the offspring of Nawab Nasrullah Khan during the lifetime of their father, and should Hamidullah die before the termination of Her Highness's Rule, the senior surviving grandson of the Begum would become the heir.

As soon as the second memorandum was received in London, Lord Birkenhead recorded the following minutes to the Cabinet on 2 February 1926:

This matter presents great difficulty. Indeed, if the Government of India, on a further reference to them had sent the matter back reaffirming their opinion, though I was by no means satisfied with many of the reasons upon which they founded themselves, I should on the whole have recommended an adherence to their view. The matter is, however, complicated by the fact that the Government of India has very elaborately re-examined the question; that the Viceroy has given his own personal attention to the matter; and that his Government now recommends that the claim of the Begum be allowed. Whatever criticism the arguments relied upon in India may invite, the fact of their conclusion, after reconsideration, is a formidable one. I am not disposed to interfere with it on a matter which I admit to be both difficult and disputable, but which I think can be recommended by stronger arguments than those in India have employed.

By this time, the tension in Wimbledon was unbearable as the Begum's spies had informed her that a glimmer of hope could be seen and that the Viceroy's earlier recommendation might be reversed. In Bhopal, Habibullah's informers had given him the bad news so that the victory flags that had almost been unfurled were folded up again. Glancy reported that Habibullah was threatening suicide. Fence-sitting Bhopalis who had jumped on to Habibullah's side were busy climbing back and the jagirdars and ulema who had earlier defied the Begum were beginning to show solidarity with her, issuing fatwas and statements in her favour. In London, doctors reported that the Begum's heart condition was being affected by the tension.

On 12 February 1926, Lord Birkenhead obtained Cabinet approval on the second memorandum in favour of Hamidullah's succession and quietly informed the Begum of the British government's decision. The relief and subsequent joy at Belmont House knew no bounds. The remaining weeks were taken up in ironing out the repercussions of the decision as a legal precedent on other princely states, and on Habibullah and his family. The announcement was made formally by the Viceroy, on 20 March 1926 as follows:

The Government of India have for some time past had under consideration representations from Her Highness, the Begum of Bhopal, in regard to Her Highness's desire that her only surviving son should be recognised as her heir to the exclusion of the sons of her elder deceased sons. Those representations have necessitated prolonged and exhaustive researches into history and precedents, as the result of which Her Highness has now been informed by

His Excellency the Viceroy, through the Secretary of State for India, who is in full concurrence with the decision, that the Government of India are prepared to recognise her only surviving son, Nawabzada Haji Muhammad Hamidullah Khan, CSI., CVO., as heir apparent to the masnad of Bhopal. In making this communication to Her Highness, it has been explained that decision is based on certain rulings of the Government of India in a number of analogous cases of succession in Muhammadan States which occurred during the nineteenth century and on the view that, in the absence of any local custom to the contrary, the rule then followed is applicable to the succession in Bhopal in the present circumstances.

Subsequently, the Viceroy recorded a most acerbic and admonitory note to his subordinates (Thompson, Patterson, Ogilvie and Fitze) for not researching the issue in sufficient depth and for failure to give correct advice. Lord Reading noted:

It is of the greatest importance that a request for formal orders should never be submitted to the Viceroy until full and exhaustive search into precedents has been made, and especially in succession cases. In the present case, when it was originally submitted to me, I had some doubt regarding the adequacy of the examination of past records and I sent the case back for further investigation. It is very unfortunate and regrettable that I was not then informed of the limited character of the search that had been made, but, on the contrary, I was unintentionally led to believe that no further precedents were available. Had I then been informed that the inquiry had begun only at the Mutiny period I should have directed further examination and the Government of India would have been saved from the unpleasant position that ensued when I was confronted at the India Office with cases which were directly relevant and had been decided in the first fifty-odd years of the 19th century but had never been brought to my notice. In consequence of the further search by the Political Department, which I then directed, the first Despatch was withdrawn at Government of India's request and with the assent of the Secretary of State and another Despatch of later date was forwarded.

I accept the very proper expressions of regret of Colonel Patterson who was at the time in question officiating as Political Secretary, Mr Thompson being absent on leave by reasons of ill health. The incident is now closed.

While the rationale for the British government decision to over-rule the Viceroy needed to be expressed on legal grounds, it was evident that the political implications of the Bhopal succession had been given special importance. In a nutshell, while Glancy and the India Office in London placed greater weight on political factors, the Viceroy's Office in Delhi saw the succession essentially in legal terms. It will never be known if the Begum's hysterical scene at Buckingham Palace and her constant lobbying of important personages in London during her six-month stay in Belmont House tilted the balance in her favour. Certainly, if Sultan Jahan had not arrived in London, the Viceroy's initial advice in favour of Habibullah might well have prevailed.

Sultan Jahan's abdication

On 29 April 1926, while still in London, Sultan Jahan informed the Secretary of State for India, Lord Stamfordham, that she was abdicating in favour of her son, a decision that stupefied the British ministers. There was another flurry of legal controversy in the Viceroy's Secretariat questioning the Begum's right to abdicate and pointing out that in the event of Hamidullah, the proposed Nawab, pre-decreasing her, the children from the older sons, Nasrullah and Obaidullah, would take precedence over Hamidullah's children. The British noted that young Hamidullah had nearly died of a broken neck in a polo accident and, being a fearless shikari, had survived several narrow escapes in the jungle with charging tigers. The Begum again refused to accept the Viceroy's contention that abdication was not legally acceptable. Practical considerations again prevailed and the British gave in, accepting on 17 May 1926 that Sultan Jahan's abdication was legal and that Hamidullah would be recognized as Nawab. Meanwhile, Habibullah left Bhopal for Poona, vowing never to return. There, he went to the dogs under the influence of assorted scoundrels who told him that they could get the British decision reversed – for a price. Habibullah lost money, became an inveterate gambler and debauchee who eventually fell under the spell of a prostitute called Nawab Jan whom he married.

On his return to Bhopal, Nawab Hamidullah Khan was recognized by the Viceroy as the 13th Nawab of Bhopal in a durbar held on 29 June 1926. The drama of the Bhopal Succession Case did not quite end with Sultan Jahan's triumph, her subsequent abdication and the installation of Hamidullah as the Nawab of Bhopal. The Viceroy's staff had, rightly, raised the issue of succession in case Hamidullah died before the Begum. Moreover, Hamidullah had three daughters and were he to die, would his eldest daughter succeed or would the gaddi pass to one of the male children of Nasrullah or even Obaidullah?

Legally, if Hamidullah were to pre-decease the Begum, the second memorandum's final paragraph clearly established that Habibullah would succeed as Nawab. Sultan Jahan and Hamidullah realized that this situation was fraught with the danger of Hamidullah being assassinated. They hastened to close off this possibility by urging the Viceroy to declare Hamidullah's eldest daughter as heir apparent. In fact, assassination attempts were made on Hamidullah that were, rightly or wrongly, laid at Habibullah's door. They led to an atmosphere of high tension in Bhopal with Sultan Jahan imagining hired assassins ready to pounce on Hamidullah from behind every bush.

The British soon recognized that allowing the situation to drift was an incentive to assassination and instability. Lord Irwin, who had replaced Lord Reading as Viceroy, urged his staff to resolve the matter quickly by agreeing to Sultan Jahan and Hamidullah's request to recognize Abida Sultaan as heir apparent.

Here, another legal conundrum delayed Abida's recognition as heir apparent. The Nawab was still only 30 years old and his wife, Maimoona Sultan, 25. They could have more children and in the event of the birth of a son, would he not become the heir apparent? The Viceroy's staff, therefore, argued against declaring Abida heir apparent.

On this issue, there arose an interesting difference of opinion between Sultan Jahan and Hamidullah. The old Begum maintained that Abida should be declared heir apparent regardless of the possibility of a son being born. She argued that 107 years of women's rule in Bhopal had established that women could rule at least as effectively as men and that, according to established tradition in the Bhopal family, the eldest child, male or female, should be recognized, provided, of course, she was fit to rule. Sultan Jahan harked back particularly to her grandmother Sikandar's golden reign and to her personality. In fact, Sultan Jahan had completely taken over Abida's upbringing and had attempted to cast her in Sikandar's mould. Accordingly, Sultan Jahan wanted Abida to be declared, unconditionally, as heir apparent.

Hamidullah took a more orthodox line. He pressed the Viceroy hard to appoint Abida, as heir, for political reasons. He wanted the line of succession to be clarified and for the assassination syndrome to be banished for good. He was not insistent, however, on Abida having a superior claim in case a son was born. That bridge would be crossed when they came to it. For the present, stability and common sense required that the British government accept Abida as heir if not as heir apparent! The British government agreed to Hamidullah's pragmatic approach and after several formulae had been drafted and rejected, Lord Irwin the Viceroy made the formal announcement at a banquet in Bhopal on 15 March 1928. Abida Sultaan was thus declared heir apparent about two years after Hamidullah was recognized as ruler. History had repeated itself in Bhopal as Sultan Jahan was also declared heir apparent at the age of ten when her mother was young and able to have more children.

Sultan Jahan was now content and at peace. She had achieved the near miracle of having the Viceroy's decision on the succession case reversed. Her favourite son who could have never hoped to be Nawab was formally recognized as ruler and his opponents and potential assassins left grovelling in the dust by the British government's decision to recognize Abida as heir. After four years of turmoil, uncertainty and high drama, Bhopal was at peace again. For the first time in five generations and in 107 years, the ruler was a male, claiming to rule not through marriage but as a direct heir in the line of succession. Surprisingly, the chapters on women's rule in Bhopal were not closing because the next generation after Hamidullah was again all girls!

After her abdication, Sultan Jahan dedicated herself to two objectives. The first was the moulding of her eldest granddaughter Abida into a personality that would rule Bhopal in the manner of preceding Begums. The child was given a harsh apprenticeship in learning the Quran's Urdu translation by heart, Farsi, Hadith and English. She was encouraged to ride, shoot, swim, drive, play all the manly sports like hockey, tennis, squash and go out big-game hunting. In fact, Abida and her sisters engaged in the rough sports of bicycle polo and roller-hockey! Her second objective was to continue her crusade for the emancipation of Muslim women in India, Dramatically discarding purdah in 1928 at the age of 70, Sultan Jahan urged Muslim women to follow her example and to seek enlightenment through education emancipation and assertion of their rights.

In May 1930 Sultan Jahan was advised gall-bladder surgery. The operation was not a success. As she lay dying on her bed in the palace, her favourite granddaughter, Abida Sultaan, sat grieving silently in a corner of the darkened room. The doctors had forbidden Sultan Jahan water and her lips were parched as she lay comatose in deathly silence. Abida recalls that Sultan Jahan stirred but unable to speak beckoned her with her eyes. Abida approached her and held her hand. 'Pani' ('Water') she whispered imploringly. Abida knew she was not allowed water but she also knew that 'Sarkar Amman' was dying. She brought a cup of water to her beloved grandmother who sipped from it. Then she blessed the child with her eyes and whispered, 'God bless you – may He protect you forever'. Sultan Jahan never opened her eyes again.

Sultan Jahan – An assessment

Unquestionably Sultan Jahan was a towering personality of her times. Each preceding Begum had left her personal imprint on the history of Bhopal. Qudsia had wrested power in a man's world and had proven the case that a woman could rule successfully. Sikandar had been an outstandingly able ruler in the most turbulent times. Shahjehan was a builder, a poetess and full of panache. But Sultan Jahan not only brought integrity and fair governance, she also had the vision to modernize, emancipate and educate the people of Bhopal and the women of India.

Sultan Jahan's personality was cast in steel. She was devout, just, tenacious and ascetic. Her early life had been hard, replete with personal tragedy and immense deprivation suffered at the hands of her mother and stepfather. It was typical of Sultan Jahan's gracious nature and traditional obedience that, in her autobiography, she has nothing but praise and understanding for her mother.

Sultan Jahan was a visionary and modernizer who broke with tradition to have her son educated at a university. She educated her little daughter-in-law and her granddaughter so that they were not only steeped in the Quran and Hadith, but also learnt English, French and to play Chopin on the piano. The learning of the martial arts for the girls – marksmanship, swimming, riding – was also an essential part of the role of complete woman that Sultan Jahan had conceived for girls in her family. Her contribution to education and the emancipation of women has been recorded in several books on Sultan Jahan, but her struggle for women's rights is not so well documented. It is specially interesting to note that in 1927, Sultan Jahan favoured the recognition of a daughter as heir apparent, even if a son were to have been born to Nawab Hamidullah Khan later. These are concepts that even in modern European regalities are not accepted though there is now a serious debate in

Europe that, in future, a female heir should have equal rights with a male. Sultan Jahan advocated this concept 70 years ago!

Sultan Jahan's 25-year reign was one of enlightenment and stability for Bhopal. Though personally set in a traditional, conservative, Islamic mould, Sultan Jahan was a far-sighted ruler who moved with the times, pointing the way towards education, emancipation and fair governance. During her quarter-century rule she presided over a contented, well-administered and loyal people who saw in Sultan Jahan a mother-figure who was principled, caring, devout and fair.

At a personal level, Sultan Jahan suffered the ultimate pain of losing four grown-up children and a grandson during her lifetime. Added to these tragedies was the humiliation and tension that she withstood from her mother and Siddiq Hassan. These experiences hardened her so that she developed a cussed obstinacy, a fierce determination and a never-say-die attitude to life which saw her, for instance, achieve an incredible victory in the succession case when all seemed lost.

Sultan Jahan's greatest contribution was in leading the women of Bhopal – and indeed of India – towards education and progress. Her pioneering efforts were recognized by her election as Chancellor of Aligarh University and Chairperson of the All-India Women's Conference on Educational Reform. Her progressive, liberal ideals allowed limited democratic reforms and numerous changes in the legal, judicial and administrative system to ensure justice and fair play for her people. Roads, bridges, waterworks, communications were improved and in the first decade of the twentieth century, Bhopal saw the arrival of the first motor car and the advent of electricity and the telephone.

Two criticisms relating to Sultan Jahan appear valid. First, she appeared to overstate her loyalty to the British paramount power so that she appeared to cringe and grovel before British royalty and the Viceroy. This fawning obsequiousness was probably embarrassing to British rulers who had seen earlier Begums underline their loyalty with dignity and sometimes – as in the case of Qudsia and Shahjehan – even cross swords with them. However, when it came to the crunch – as in the succession case – Sultan Jahan was capable of fighting the Viceroy to the bitter end with no holds barred.

The second criticism relates to Sultan Jahan's favouritism towards her youngest son, Hamidullah. From the day Hamidullah was born, he was the apple of Sultan Jahan's eye. As he grew older, her blind devotion towards him became almost obsessive. Eventually, she handed over the running of the state to him even in the lifetimes of her older sons Nasrullah, the heir apparent, and Obaidullah. This favouritism led to schisms in Bhopal and could have permanently damaged Sultan Jahan if the Viceroy's initial recommendation on the succession case had been accepted.

Considering all factors, when Sultan Jahan abdicated, she could look back on a reign of enlightenment and progress. Bhopal was solvent, well administered and stable. Tolerance and harmony existed between Hindus and Muslims, each being free to develop their own culture and religious beliefs. Bhopal was also a bastion of Muslim culture and encouraged a democratic spirit so that poets, democrats and anti-colonial politicians gathered and flourished in the state. Like her grandmother and idol, Sikandar Begum, Sultan Jahan's rule had been the age of emancipation in Bhopal – its second golden reign.

9

The Begums – A final assessment

Why no male rulers?

The first question relating to the Begums of Bhopal invariably asks how, in a traditional Muslim society, four women rulers governed Bhopal for 107 years and, if Mamola Bai is included, as she should be, 157 years of its 241-year history.

The easy answer to this question is that there was no male issue in the direct line of succession for three generations after Qudsia was recognized as Regent in 1819. Qudsia became a widow at 19, having produced an only daughter, Sikandar. Qudsia miscarried her second child soon after her husband's accident and, true to pristine Afghan tradition, never thought of remarrying. Sikandar lived only briefly with her husband, Jahangir, from whom she later separated. Their union produced an only daughter, Shahjehan, who had two daughters from her first husband, Umrao Doulah, the younger dying of small-pox at the age of five, again leaving an only daughter – Sultan Jahan – in the direct line of succession. Sultan Jahan was, therefore, the first ruler in four generations to give birth to a male heir.

This simple answer suggesting a smooth, uncontested succession of women rulers due to the absence of male heirs is, however, far removed from the reality. In fact, the first two Begums – Qudsia and Sikandar – wrested power from male contenders who subsequently resorted to violent and unrelenting campaigns to oust the Begums. They based their claims on legitimacy and on Islamic tenets militating against women's rule. Surprisingly, the British hierarchy supported the men against the Begums until after the Mutiny in 1857.

The first salvo in favour of women's rule in Bhopal was fired on 13 November 1819 by Qudsia after the sudden death of her husband, Nawab Nazar Mohammad Khan. Qudsia's coup d'état was daringly conceived and brilliantly executed. She devised a 'consensus formula' claiming the gaddi for her 15-month-old daughter Sikandar with herself as Regent and promising to hand over the reins of power on Sikandar's marriage to a cousin. At the time of Nazar's death, several male descendants of Dost's family had better legal claims to mount the masnad. First, Nawab Ghous Mohammad Khan, Qudsia's father, was still alive and had never been formally divested of his title even though Wazir and Nazar had been recognized as de facto rulers. In any case, Ghous had two sons, Moiz and Faujdar, who could legitimately claim superior title to Qudsia, their real sister. The second claimant to succeed Nazar was his elder brother Amir who had earlier been bypassed by general family consensus. Now that Nazar was dead, Amir put forward his claim as Wazir's sole heir. Qudsia's dramatic intervention that carried the day against these competing claims was audaciously executed with the help of the Loyal Quartet, headed by Shahzad Masih. The state Qazi and Mufti, having earlier been appointed by male rulers, gave verdicts that Islam did not prevent women's rule and in a manoeuvre worthy of Machiavelli, word was discreetly passed around that any heir pressing his claim against the agreed formula would automatically attract the suspicion of having had Nazar assassinated! The formula was thus approved by the family caucus with the British having no option but to go along.

Subsequently, Qudsia and Sikandar faced a succession of attempts by Amir and his family to supplant the Begums. These attempts took the form of intrigues, armed revolts, assassination attempts and pitched battles in which the Begums usually had the better of their male opponents. Eventually, the British intervened and insisted on a hand over of power to Sikandar's consort, Jahangir, who proved an abject failure as Nawab.

After Jahangir's death, the claims of the male heirs weakened, especially as the robust and dynamic Sikandar was the sole unifying heir to the Wazir and Ghous branches of Dost's dynasty. She had also produced an heir, Shahjehan, born from the union between herself and Jahangir, the two principal pretenders to the gaddi during Qudsia's Regency. There could be no doubt, therefore, about Shahjehan's legitimacy to succeed.

The British, however, continued to oppose women's rule and first bypassed both Qudsia and Sikandar as Regent in favour of Qudsia's brother, Faujdar. Furthermore, they insisted on implementing the same formula for Shahjehan that had been such an abject failure in the case of Sikandar, that of the infanta's consort assuming full executive powers as Nawab on marriage.[1]

Through force of personality, public support and a demonstration of governing capability, Sikandar was able to ride off the worthless Faujdar as Regent, the British meekly accepting that Sikandar was fully capable of governing the state on behalf of her daughter. Sikandar then proved herself an outstandingly capable ruler, eventually gaining from the British her daughter's right to rule as Begum even after marriage, and subsequently for Sikandar to be recognized as ruler in her own right.

Fortunately, by then Victoria was Queen of England and it was generally recognized by the people of Bhopal and even by the British that

---

[1] Letter from Secretary of State T.H. Maddock to Political Agent L. Wilkinson dated 24 May 1641, India Office Records.

women's rule was entirely acceptable. Therefore, in Bhopal, it was not simply the accident of female heirs being in the direct line of succession, but in the case of the first two Begums, Qudsia and Sikandar, they actually wrested power from male contenders and managed to withstand the onslaughts by male contestants and the British government to unseat the Begums.

After the 1857 Mutiny, Shahjehan and Sultan Jahan's successions were essentially legal with no male claimant in sight. By then, Queen Victoria was established as Empress of India and Britain's reservations to women's rule in Bhopal had changed from opposition to approval. In fact, Shahjehan's attempts to hand over real power to her second husband were regarded with deep concern by the British, a marked contrast to pre-Victorian times when they insisted that the husbands of Sikandar and Shahjehan should be recognized as rulers of the state.

Reasons for the success of the Begums' rule in Bhopal

The second question relating to the Begums is how they managed to rule so successfully over a substantially Hindu population, surrounded as they were by powerful, predatory neighbours. How did the Begums, particularly the earlier ones, including Mamola Bai, manage to navigate Bhopal's destinies with such success across these turbulent seas?

By the mid-eighteenth century, the Moghul Empire had collapsed, unleashing destructive forces across India. The Begums' success in retaining Bhopal's independence against the onslaughts of powerful neighbours is, therefore, all the more extraordinary. Sometimes this independence was barely visible, like a lamp that is turned down to shed a bare glimmer of light. But the flame that was lit by Dost never went out and was ready to shine brightly again when Bhopal's fortunes revived. By the time Shahjehan and Sultan Jahan ascended the masnad, the British Raj dominated a stable and settled India with Bhopal figuring as a favoured jewel in the British Crown. What were their qualities and characteristics that led to Bhopal staying afloat in these dangerous times?

The first of these qualities was a woman's instinct to hold and preserve what she owns. A woman conserves, husbands and protects her belongings; a man explores, hunts, and expands, often risking what he holds. A woman looks at weakness as well as strength; a man often overestimates his strength and underplays his weakness. Generally, women tend to be far-sighted, men live with the times. These feminine qualities guided Bhopal's destiny for almost a century after Dost's death. It was Mamola who advised ceding territory and forts to the powerful Nizam and Peshwa in order to preserve the kernel of her state. It was she who sent tributes of cash, elephants, cavalry and expensive gifts to the Moghul Court, the Nizam and the Marhatta overlords to keep Bhopal's nose above water. It was Mamola Bai who had the far-sight to welcome General Goddard, thereby gaining for Bhopal the strategic support of the rising power in India. Sikandar Begum's help to the British during the

Mutiny was similarly aimed at preserving her state. Given the fact that Bhopal was surrounded by more powerful, irredentist neighbours, the Begums' close relationship with the British must be seen as part of wise and astute statecraft rather than an excessive subservience to the British Crown. Women's rule, therefore, helped to preserve Bhopal, often at the cost of territory and finance. It is likely that if men had ruled, they would have fought gallantly and with immense bravado, but would have lost the state!

Secondly, except for Shahjehan, the Begums achieved public respect and widespread acceptability from their subjects due to their qualities of personal integrity, their humane and fair treatment of Hindu and Muslim communities and a dedicated commitment to good governance and emancipation. Gradually the Begums' rule saw Bhopal emerge as a haven of Hindu–Muslim harmony, of economic and social advancement, of a just and benign rule. The Begums themselves were upright and of high moral character, living simple lives, shorn of the excesses, quirks and kinky eccentricities normally associated with princely states. The only exception to these pious, ascetic Begums was Shahjehan whose feminine *joie de vivre* brought colour and panache to the austere social landscape of Bhopal.

The character pattern of the Bhopal Begums

What were the character moulds that made the Begums such outstanding rulers? How did they cultivate qualities that saw them lead their men by example, to establish control over the state and to create an aura of moral authority over their people? In short, as women brought up in the traditional Muslim family environment, how did the Begums of Bhopal assert their authority in a male dominated society? Before answering this question, it needs to be noted that, apart from the four Begums, Bhopal's history is littered with examples of its women playing dominant roles, beginning with Fatah Bibi and followed by the remarkable Mamola Bai, both born Rajput Hindus but converts to Islam. Then there were Kamlapati, the supremely beautiful Gond-rani who initially gifted Bhopal to Dost for saving her honour, Bahu Begum, Faiz's widow, who ran a parallel government to Hayat's for many years, Moti Begum, Hayat's spirited sister, who refused to surrender Islamnagar to the treacherous Murid, Asmat Begum, Hayat's beautiful wife whose influence on her husband was likened to Nur Jahan's on Jahangir, and Zeenat Begum, Ghous's wife, who played an heroic role in rallying the women of Bhopal during the siege.

It is difficult to put forward a political or sociological explanation for the grit, assertiveness and truculence normally found in Bhopali women. Part of the explanation lies in the Barru-kat Pathans of Bhopal acquiring a siege mentality, surrounded as they were by hostile neighbours and having settled amidst a population that was predominantly non-Muslim. Everyone, including the women, had to pull their weight to survive. Moreover, with the collapse of Moghul authority, the security normally available to the Muslim settler had evaporated. This mentality probably helped mould the Bhopali female character. Secondly, the example of Bhopal's leading women during the early days of the state probably inspired other women of Bhopal. Mamola Bai, Qudsia and Sikandar became early, character-forming role models. In every household, women saw their rulers dominate the men which made them strike similar attitudes in their own domains.

Thirdly, Malwa had been influenced by the Pindaras. They were marauding brigands who were basically land pirates, operating from the jungles of Malwa. The Pindaras were mainly Muslim Pathans and, being mostly wanderers, their women travelled on horseback with their menfolk. They helped their men in attacking and looting villages and towns so that, in time, the Pindara women became excellent riders, experienced fighters and adept at using weapons. The Pindara women also claimed their rights in sharing the booty and became assertive, robust and politically conscious. This Amazonic tradition in the Pindara women probably rubbed off on to the Pathan settler women of Bhopal, making them unusually aggressive and dominant.

With the exception of Shahjehan, the Begums of Bhopal shared similar character traits. All the Begums, except Shahjehan, shunned the glamour and pomp normally associated with princely states. They lived simply, wore plain clothes, were pious Muslims and led by example. Qudsia would be so meticulous in separating state finances from personal expenditure that she would sell simple handicrafts made by elderly retainers in her palace and live on the income of this cottage industry. Qudsia paid for Bhopal's waterworks system from her private funds and forbade her successors from charging a water tax on the people. She also contributed from her personal funds to the building of the state railway. Sultan Jahan was equally conscientious about state and personal funds, transparently demonstrating to her public how revenues to the state were being spent on public welfare. Sikandar was an outstanding ruler, less frugal than her mother and granddaughter, but not a spendthrift. She was the first to formally divide state from private finances, replace Persian with Urdu as the official language and introduce far-reaching reforms in the administrative and educational sectors.

Shahjehan was formed in a different character mould. She was generous, a lover of the arts and music, a poetess and a great builder. She was extravagant and profligate, spending vast sums of state money on festivity, celebrations and pomp. For instance, completion of her Taj Mahal palace was celebrated with rejoicing over two years. Towards the end of her life, when she suffered the humiliation of her husband being deposed and the anguish of losing her favourite grandchild, Shahjehan probably took to drinking wine. Unlike all the other Begums of Bhopal, Shahjehan was feminine, attractive and flirtatious, though once she had found her real love in life, she stood by him with tenacious devotion, even after his death. Shahjehan was not a gifted administrator but introduced a *joie de vivre* in Bhopal that had until her reign been lacking. The music, the shikar, the midnight picnics, the mujras, the never-ending festivity were all frowned upon by her Wahabi husband, but Bhopal knew *la dolce vita* only during Shahjehan's rule. When she died, the treasury was bare and Bhopal's society sinking fast in the quicksand of degeneration and decay.

Mother-daughter relations

Mother-daughter relations were complex and never easy during four successive generations of women rulers. In assessing these relations, it must first be recognized that, during that period, a daughter brought up in a conservative Islamic family was expected to demonstrate unstinting, submissive obedience to her mother. This deference was doubly reinforced when the mother happened to be the ruler of the state to whom everyone – nobles, courtiers, family members and the general public – were expected to offer their complete obeisance.

Qudsia, who had brought up Sikandar to resist the inevitable contest for power from her male relatives, was perhaps closest of all the Begums to her daughter. Sikandar gave Qudsia her total reverence, never being seated in her mother's presence, even when Sikandar was the all-powerful Begum. Qudsia and Sikandar also lived through the harshest times, facing repeated onslaughts from Amir and his sons and also from Wilkinson. Differences and tension did, however, emerge between Qudsia and Sikandar. The first occasion was when Sikandar, clearly enamoured of her consort Jahangir, favoured the transfer of power to him in accordance with the pledge made by her mother 16 years earlier. Jahangir's attempted murder of his wife put an end to Sikandar's 'romantic folly' and a contrite daughter joined Qudsia in exile. Subdued tension between Qudsia and Sikandar also emerged when, after Jahangir's death, Qudsia, though only 45 years old and a proven success as Regent, was bypassed by the British, and first Faujdar and later Sikandar were appointed Regent. Qudsia initially sulked for a while, but later gave her full support to Sikandar as Regent and Begum of Bhopal. The third time that differences emerged between Qudsia and Sikandar was when Qudsia began supporting the rebels during the Mutiny. By then, Sikandar was fully in command and quickly brought her mother into line by firmly explaining the repercussions of her capricious action. Qudsia obeyed the ruler and thereafter mother and daughter enjoyed close, respectful relations. It is interesting to note that, contrary to the custom of the time, Qudsia did not bring up the first born granddaughter in her house and that Shahjehan grew up in her mother Sikandar's household.

The relationship between Sikandar and Shahjehan began to fray as Shahjehan achieved adolescence and formed a character mould that was diametrically opposite to her mother's fierce, dominating, masculine and overbearing personality. Perhaps Sikandar was too engrossed in the affairs of state to engage in bringing up her only daughter who developed into an entirely feminine, coquettish and rather spoilt personality. Shahjehan must have realized that she was, after all, the titular Begum while her mother ruled in her name, as Regent. Shahjehan gave to her mother the superficial obedience of an oriental daughter and constantly refers to her mother in her autobiography as 'my sainted mother', but in effect they were poles apart. At a critical moment, Shahjehan abdicated in her mother's favour, but shortly afterwards she was forced into a marriage with an older man who had been twice married already. She was also cast aside as caretaker ruler when Sikandar left for Hajj, leaving her Chief Minister and not her designated heir apparent in charge of the state. Moreover, as soon as Sultan Jahan was born, Sikandar turned all her love and attention to bringing up her granddaughter. By the time Sikandar died, Shahjehan's marriage had broken down and she was living life in her own feisty, hedonistic style that was scorned by Sikandar and by her even more ascetic grandmother, Qudsia.

On Sikandar's death, Shahjehan's relations with her grandmother were frosty. Shahjehan's marriage with Siddiq Hassan worsened this relationship so that it became positively acrimonious. A virtual undeclared war existed between Qudsia's and Shahjehan's households with the Begum adopting an irreverent, insulting attitude to her grandmother.

On Sikandar's death, the 10-year-old Sultan Jahan went to live with her mother. She found the ambience in her mother's house to be disconcertingly lax, almost immoral, which led to subdued friction between mother and daughter until they both married, Shahjehan for the second time. Thereafter, mother–daughter relations degenerated gradually into an unbridgeable chasm, probably exacerbated by the ambitious, covetous attitudes of both husbands. During the last 14 years of Shahjehan's reign, the Begum refused to meet her daughter, even on her deathbed when Sultan Jahan visited her to beg forgiveness.

Unlike the three other Begums who were basically one-dimensional characters, Shahjehan was a complex, almost contrary personality. From her early youth it was evident that she did not fit into the ascetic and Spartan life-style of her mother and grandmother with whom she developed grating, difficult relationships. Sikandar was clearly disappointed with her daughter's comportment. All this after Shahjehan had voluntarily abdicated in her mother's favour. With Qudsia, Shahjehan Begum developed an antagonistic relationship that deteriorated with the passage of time. However, it was with her only surviving daughter, Sultan Jahan, that Shahjehan spent the best part of her life in inimical and hostile confrontation. Family annals and British accounts of Shahjehan's life tend to place the blame for these family tensions on Shahjehan, whose devotion to her second husband was seen as the major reason for these schisms. This criticism of Shahjehan's personality may have been overplayed, especially as some of the opprobrium placed at her door may have been due to the goading of her ambitious son-in-law, Sultan Doulah, and to the British government's blind opposition to everything that Siddiq Hassan stood for.

By the time Shahjehan was half-way through her reign, it was evident that her immediate family, her daughter and grandmother, had drifted away from the circle of mutual affection. Shahjehan had by then lost hope of producing a son from Siddiq Hassan and, though she remained loyal to him till his death, it placed a heavy premium on Shahjehan's relations with her immediate family and her loyalty to the British imperial power. Her personal relations with Siddiq Hassan had also deteriorated. Thus Shahjehan stood alone, unloved by her immediate family and resented by the British and her own public due to the arrogance and political activity of her husband.

In this barren, emotional wasteland, there appeared only one person – her granddaughter Bilqis Jahan – on whom Shahjehan could pour out all the love and affection that had been bottled up inside this passionate, artistic and humane woman. Bilqis was the only link left between herself and her daughter and it is to her immense credit that, despite the tension between the two households, Shahjehan insisted that Bilqis visit her mother daily before returning home to her doting grandmother. How far can one give credence to the view held that Shahjehan planned to break her daughter's engagement with Sultan Doulah and supplant him with Siddiq's elder, already-married stepson, remains a question mark as Sultan Jahan may well have been influenced by vicious palace intrigues that tended to play on mother–daughter antagonisms. Even more incredible were the rumours that Shahjehan intended to marry Bilqis to her younger stepson, who was also married. Clearly the decision by Sultan Jahan to suddenly prevent Bilqis from returning to her grandmother's palace devastated the lonely Begum who was denied the proximity of the only person that she genuinely loved. Predictably, Shahjehan went mad with anger and wanted the Political Agent to declare war on Sultan Jahan to wrest her beloved granddaughter back to her fold. Shahjehan never forgave her daughter for this act, not even on her deathbed, especially as Bilqis died soon afterwards, pining away for her grandmother. Sultan Jahan's action in keeping Bilqis in her household was deeply insensitive and the reasons given for this act not entirely convincing. At least part of the blame for the stand-off between Shahjehan and Sultan Jahan must therefore be placed at Sultan Jahan's door.

An abiding and attractive trait in the characters of both women was that, in their autobiographies, neither recorded the slightest criticism of their respective mothers with whom each had a difficult, tense relationship. This was due to the reverence and obedience that a Muslim woman was expected to show to a mother. Shahjehan always referred to Sikandar as 'my sainted mother', praising her reforms, her achievements and her personality. On the other hand, Siddiq Hassan had, in a public durbar, referred to Sikandar's reign as oppressive, draconian and the darkest period in Bhopal's history. Shahjehan never gave the slightest hint of such criticism in her autobiography. Similarly, Sultan Jahan was full of praise and admiration for her mother, placing all the blame for her profligate, 'disloyal' rule on Siddiq Hassan. In fact Shahjehan, despite her devotion to Siddiq Hassan, remained loyal to the British Crown, though spirited and full of bristling indignation against Sir Lepel Griffin whom she blamed personally for the woes that she and her husband faced at the hands of the British. The record of her last meeting with Sir Lepel Griffin is a classic encounter between a defiant woman ruler standing up to her perceived tormentor. Unquestionably, the Begum emerges the victor in this extraordinary verbal duel.

Thus, while it is true that Shahjehan had many weaknesses of character – she was hedonistic, profligate, passionate, stubborn to the point of cussedness, she imbibed alcohol, the cardinal sin in the eyes of Bhopal's Afghan gentry, and was on bad terms with her immediate family – she was also a remarkably spirited woman. She was a great builder, a poetess, a patron of the arts, liberal and humane. She was also a reasonably able ruler and cannot be blamed entirely for family tensions. She was loyal and proud of Bhopal's traditions, giving its society an ambience that was liberal, tolerant, fair and stable. Shahjehan, both as a person and ruler, deserves to be reappraised in a better light than has been the case so far.

The Begums' consorts

The attitude of the four Begums to their husbands followed differing patterns. However, Sir Lepel Griffin's likening of the Begums of Bhopal to Queen Joan of Naples or Catherine the Great of Russia, suggesting sexual licentiousness, is not borne out by facts. No doubt, Shahjehan was emotionally wayward and sensual. Sikandar was no prude. Qudsia and Sultan Jahan were absolute puritans who did not consider remarrying despite losing their husbands when they began ruling the state. Qudsia was devoted to her husband and his accidental death left her a widow at 19. Her husband's loyal friend, Shahzad Masih, stood by Qudsia through the most difficult times and it has been suggested, somewhat maliciously, that the Bourbon aristocrat and Qudsia were romantically linked. However, Qudsia's life-long character traits and indeed Shahzad Masih's devotion to the Bhopal family, indicate that their relationship was platonic. Sikandar, true to her full-blooded personality, was a romantic character. Her husband, Jahangir, was her rival and enemy who had tried to assassinate her. She fought him during the day and loved him for his virile, personal qualities at night. The union was totally bizarre, but their mutual affection was apparent from the dying Jahangir's last letter to Sikandar in which he professed his love for her and blamed his family for their separation.

Shahjehan was not enamoured of her first husband, Umrao Doulah, whom she was forced to marry. It is obvious that she was unfaithful to him and enjoyed the attention of several men until Siddiq Hassan won her over, heart and soul. In fact, Umrao Doulah formally sought a separation from Shahjehan that was refused by Sikandar. Thereafter, Shahjehan remained constant and faithful to her second husband till long after his death. Somewhat intriguing is the triangular relationship between Zakia, Siddiq's first wife and daughter of Maulvi Jamaluddin, and Shahjehan. Despite sharing the same husband, Zakia and Shahjehan were close – Zakia helping to soothe the conjugal ties between her husband and Shahjehan whenever there was a row between them. Zakia was clearly far-sighted and managed to secure the financial future of her children through this benevolent attitude towards Shahjehan. To outsiders, this strange *ménage à trois* between Zakia, Siddiq and Shahjehan epitomized *les liaisons dangereuses* of Shahjehan's court.

Sultan Jahan was a prude from childhood to death bed. Like a true Muslim oriental wife, there was only one man in her life, her childhood companion and eventual husband, Ahmad Ali Khan (Sultan Doulah). There was not a breath of scandal in her life, nor was she seen by family and the public as anything but a pious and morally chaste mother figure. Shahjehan, in one of her malicious asides regarding her daughter's character, did suggest that Sultan Jahan, before she married, was playing off Yasin, a cousin, against Ahmad Ali, but this accusation is totally out of character and probably born out of the jealousy and malice that Shahjehan held towards Sultan Jahan. In fact, Sikandar wanted her granddaughter to select her own husband and she was encouraged to include boys from good families in her chaperoned play group. From the first day, Sultan Jahan was set on marrying Ahmad Ali Khan whom, she blushingly confessed to her granddaughter, was the only man in her life.

Thus, except for Shahjehan, a streak of chastity and Puritanism ran through the character mould of the Begums of Bhopal, the first and last Begums setting the tone of high integrity and spotless chastity for Bhopal's royal family.

The Begums and Islam

The attitude of the Begums towards Islam was an important influence on Bhopal's public life and its social ambience. Even before Qudsia, Bhopal's rulers had inclined towards respecting Islamic tenets with deep reverence. Mamola Bai, a converted Muslim, set the tone by her humane, devout and mosque-building rule of nearly half a century. Pir Ghous Gailani had referred to her as 'the second Rabia Basri' and another saint, Shah Ali Shah, had remarked, 'What is my life worth, when she [Mamola Bai] gives succour and hope to lakhs of Muslims?' Mamola Bai's stepson, Faiz, was a religious recluse who was recognized for his saintly character far beyond the state of Bhopal. Generally, therefore, Bhopal's rulers were devout Muslims, veering towards the orthodox, pristine standards of orthodox Islam of the Deoband school.

For the Begums to govern a state while observing purdah posed special problems. It is evident that Mamola Bai did not observe purdah, but was accepted as a dedicated Muslim. Qudsia was brought up in purdah and was a particularly devout Muslim. She not only prayed five times a day as required in Islam, but offered the midnight tahajjud prayer which is voluntary and observed only by the most pious Muslims. When Qudsia became Regent, she learnt the martial arts of fencing, archery and riding. On some occasions, she rode out to lead her troops. After a few years as ruler and despite her deep commitment to Islam, Qudsia discarded purdah. She reasoned that Islam did not make purdah or covering the face obligatory and, in order to rule effectively, purdah needed to be discarded.

Qudsia's influence and attitude towards purdah rubbed off on her daughter and granddaughter who were also expected to rule. Neither Sikandar nor Shahjehan observed purdah, until Shahjehan was pushed behind the veil by Siddiq Hassan at the age of 32. Sikandar was also a practising Muslim, but religion was not as deep an influence in her personal life as it was for Qudsia and later for Sultan Jahan. Sikandar's devotion to Islam was personal as well as part of statecraft. She became the first ruler from the Sub-Continent to perform the pilgrimage to Makkah and persuaded the British to re-open the famous Juma Masjid in Delhi which they had seized after the Mutiny. Sikandar went down on her knees and personally washed the floors of the Juma Masjid courtyard. Sikandar was never in purdah. She was open-faced to her subjects and wore the veil only when outside the state and when meeting 'strangers'. The same was the case with Shahjehan until her second husband prevailed on her to adopt purdah.

Unlike her mother, grandmother or her daughter, Shahjehan was not devout. Her contribution to Islam was in the building of beautiful mosques like the Taj-ul-Masjid and her support for shrines. Muslim art and calligraphy also flourished in Bhopal during her 33-year reign. For a Bhopal ruler, Shahjehan did the unpardonable – imbibe alcohol – defiantly contemptuous of her husband's strict Wahabism.[1]

Sultan Jahan's contribution to the Islamic ethos and culture of Bhopal was the most profound. Herself a pious, committed Muslim, she reversed the liberal and easy-going tradition set by her mother and brought Bhopal back to its simple, Spartan, ascetic way of living. She then launched a crusade for education and women's emancipation which saw her elected Chancellor of Aligarh University for three terms and preside over the All-India Women's Conference on Educational Reform. She also wrote numerous books, articles and pamphlets on education. Sultan Jahan's contribution to arousing Muslim women to the call of education was profound. Sultan Jahan had been brought up not to observe purdah by Sikandar, but after her mother had been pushed into purdah, she was obliged to follow suit. When Sultan Jahan became ruler, she continued to observe purdah. She wore the burqa when travelling abroad and even on ceremonial occasions like the Coronation and the Viceroy's durbar.

Unlike her mother, Sultan Jahan was not a scholar nor had she literary pretensions, but she was a prolific writer of books, pamphlets and essays on subjects ranging between her memoirs, a history of her forebears, education for women, religious subjects like the values of purdah and the comportment of Muslim women. She even wrote a book on her favourite recipes which became a best-seller.

Sultan Jahan was deeply set in her religious ways, but she was wise and far-sighted enough to recognize the need to adjust to the change of times. She formally discarded the burqa in 1928, at the age of 70, two years after her abdication. She reasoned that she had to set the example

---

[1] AGG Sir Lepel Griffin's report to Secretary of State Henry Durand dated 22 September 1885, India Office Records.

for Muslim women and that she could not ask the younger generation to carry forward the torch of education and emancipation from purdah. Thus a lifetime's habit was abandoned by Sultan Jahan at the age of 70, two years before she died.

The Begums and the British Raj

The Begums' relations with the British East India Company and subsequently with the British paramount power form an essential part of the history of Bhopal. The first linkage dates back to 1778 when Mamola Bai provided help and succour to General Goddard during his historic march from Calcutta to Bombay. The initiative for this far-sighted act came from Mamola Bai and set the seal on Bhopal's close relationship with the British. General Goddard was highly appreciative of Bhopal's help and from that point onwards Wazir and his son Nazar consolidated this relationship by helping the British to suppress the Pindaras. Britain and Bhopal needed each other. They had common opponents – the Marhattas and, to a lesser extent, the Rajputs – who vied for control of Malwa. The 1818 treaty between the Viceroy and Nazar, became a landmark in British–Bhopal ties, forming the bedrock of the close relationship between them.

Nazar's sudden death saw a twist in Britain's relationship with Bhopal. Britain opposed women's rule – Qudsia being Regent – and insisted on the handover of power to Qudsia's teenage son-in-law, Munir, later replaced by his half-brother Jahangir. This insistence was based more on political than legal considerations and the British went to great lengths to ensure that Jahangir, a mediocre, pleasure-loving, degenerate, should mount the masnad of Bhopal occupied by a competent, devout and popular woman ruler. In fact the transfer of authority was insisted upon by the British even after Jahangir's forces had been defeated by the Begum's at Ashta.

Some chroniclers explain this excessive bias by Britain against women's rule as being due to the Political Agent Wilkinson's personal predilection against women. It is said that he fell for the good life offered by Jahangir and his family, thereby ranging himself against Qudsia and Sikandar. There are unsubstantiated stories of Wilkinson enjoying himself on shikar and all the earthy pleasures that are associated with it. The fact that Wilkinson was prejudiced against the Bhopal women is borne out by his own admission that Jahangir's seven-year degenerate reign had seen Bhopal descend into lawlessness, corruption and mismanagement. Wilkinson was eventually forced to issue a warning to Jahangir, telling him that his misrule had made Bhopal's public disaffected with him. Wilkinson's bias was also discernible when he gave Jahangir an 11-gun salute when he escaped to Sehore from house-arrest in Bhopal and finally from the following extract of his report to the Resident just before Jahangir's death, in which he paints Qudsia in particular, and also Sikandar, in excessively negative colours:

> The Nawab's death without heirs would immediately awake their [the Begums'] ill-concealed ambitions and hopes. The Sikandar Begum would at once claim the exercise of power, not only because she is the daughter of the old Nawab [Nazar] but also because she is the widow of the present Nawab [Jehangir] and the mother of his daughter [Shahjehan]. She even now affects to deem her exclusion from power as an act of oppression and as being, she maintains, in violation of that article of the Treaty which guarantees the succession to the offspring of the Nawab Nazar Muhammad. The old Begum, with all her affectation of plainness and simplicity of manners, has her share of love of power, and she might embarrass the superior rights of her daughter by her folly, caprice and jealousy.

Wilkinson's personal bias against women's rule at the time does not offer the only explanation for Britain's negative attitude. In fact, the British hierarchy in Delhi fully supported Wilkinson's approach. Long after Wilkinson's death in 1841 and when Shahjehan was installed as ruler in 1845, the British continued to insist that, on marriage, her consort would take over as ruler. It was only after Queen Victoria had firmly entrenched herself on the throne and Sikandar had made an issue of the right of women to rule that the British relented and agreed that Shahjehan and not her husband would rule in her own right. Immediately after this decision, Sikandar claimed that if Shahjehan's right to rule could be recognized, why was she denied the same right? The British found themselves embarrassed and completely stumped for an argument, especially as Sikandar had passed the litmus test of loyalty by helping the British during the critical days of the Mutiny. The only argument that the British could fall back on was that they had acknowledged Shahjehan to be the ruler and could not withdraw recognition. Shahjehan then obliged by abdicating in favour of her mother and saving Britain's embarrassment. Sir Richmond Shakespear, the Resident, who spearheaded negotiations on behalf of the British with Sikandar Begum described Shahjehan's unique gesture in a report sent to the Viceroy (see Appendix 9).

Britain's relations with Qudsia were coloured by the personal antipathy between Wilkinson and herself. Qudsia was, however, wise enough to realize that she needed the British to protect Bhopal's independence. She therefore continued on the path that Mamola, Wazir and Nazar had chosen. Her personal relations with Wilkinson were bitter and led to Qudsia taking an acerbic view of the British in general, especially during the Indian Mutiny when she found herself in sympathy with the rebels.

Sikandar, on the other hand, saw Britain's support as vital, not only in safeguarding Bhopal from outside threats, but also in supporting her to govern the state effectively. Administrative reforms, roads, railways, communications and education could be achieved quicker and more effectively with British support. Accordingly, Sikandar decided to give her full and loyal support to the British.

The real test of loyalty came during the Indian Mutiny which, in British eyes, was failed by most ruling princes and passed, with flying colours, by the woman ruler of Bhopal. From 1857 onwards, Bhopal held a special position based on proven loyalty. Added to this favourable facet was the fact that Bhopal was ruled with admirable and enlightened governance by its women rulers. Thus the wheel had turned full circle from Wilkinson's times, when the British actively opposed women's rule, to Sikandar's reign in which she was the *vedette célèbre* at all the gatherings of the princes, such as the Viceroy's durbars.

Shahjehan who succeeded Sikandar was carried along by the momentum of Bhopal's loyalty during the Mutiny. After Shahjehan married Siddiq Hassan, however, the British began to experience difficulties with the Begum. She went into purdah and handed over governance to Siddiq Hassan, which would not have worried the British were it not for the fact that Siddiq was seen as an anti-British militant fundamentalist. Bhopal's administration also became increasingly corrupt and personalized. Shahjehan constantly defended her husband and began a series of clashes with Sir Lepel Griffin, the Resident, who eventually humiliated Siddiq Hassan in public by divesting him of his title. Surprisingly, despite the bitter stand-off with Griffin, Shahjehan's loyalty to the British Crown was never questioned. Nor did Shahjehan allow what she regarded as a gross injustice to her husband to colour her attitude towards the British establishment. After Siddiq's death and Griffin's transfer, personal cordiality was restored between the Begum and the new Resident and also with the Viceroy, Lord Landsdowne, who was obviously much taken by Shahjehan's flirtatious welcome to him in Bhopal.

Of the four Begums, Sultan Jahan was the most loyal to the British Crown. Deeply influenced by her grandmother during childhood, Sultan Jahan saw British support sustain her in her long, bitter rift with her mother and stepfather. This support of theirs for the under-dog clearly influenced Sultan Jahan in favour of British fair play and justice so that she became a confirmed loyalist and a personal supporter of the British royal family. The death of Queen Victoria affected Sultan Jahan deeply and in her greatest moment of crisis – Hamidullah's succession – Sultan Jahan went to Buckingham Palace to personally ring the bell of justice, drawing on every drop of goodwill that she had built up over the years with the British monarchy.

Sultan Jahan's loyalty to the British Crown came under pressure on two counts. First, her university-educated son developed close relations at Aligarh with young Muslim supporters of the pro-Turkish Khilafat Movement, notably the brothers Mohammad Ali and Shaukat Ali. This movement was seen by the British as not simply pro-Turkish, but also nationalist and anti-colonial. At Aligarh, Hamidullah also became acquainted with players on the purely nationalist, anti-British front who were making their impact across India as members of the Congress Party and the Muslim League. The Viceroy and his representatives began warning Sultan Jahan Begum about her favourite son's association with anti-British elements that was filling his dossier with negative comments. Sultan Jahan denied these accusations, particularly that of Hamidullah financially supporting these movements, but privately attempted to rein in Hamidullah's enthusiasm and association with the nationalists.

At the time, the groundswell of nationalist feeling was beginning to rise with Gokhale, Gandhi, Nehru and Jinnah taking up cudgels against British Raj. This groundswell was not so prominent in the princely states, but Sultan Jahan had to tread carefully in demonstrating her loyalty to the British Crown because she was also aware of her favourite son's interest and dabbling in pro-Turkish and anti-colonial politics.

The Begum's second dilemma related to her personal relationship with the Ottoman Turks. Her grandmother had been royally received and protected by the Ottoman Sultan Abdul Aziz during her famous pilgrimage to Makkah in 1864. Sultan Jahan had been similarly welcomed by Sultan Abdul Hamid II during her Hajj in 1903 and later in 1911, when she visited Istanbul and received the priceless gift of the Prophet's hair from Sultan Mehmet Resat. Hence her close relations, with the Turks stood in the way of Bhopal's support for the British war effort when the Turks and the British were on opposite sides during the First World War. Sultan Jahan eventually supported Britain's war effort by providing funds and a contingent from the Bhopal army to fight on behalf of the Allies, but not against the Turks. However, Bhopal's pro-Turkish inclinations were manifested when the Begum ordered the lighting up of the city and a famous display of fireworks to celebrate the capture of Smyrna from the Greeks in 1923. Like her grandmother, Sultan Jahan managed to play on both sides of the fence while demonstrating her basic loyalty to the British.

Thus all four Begums saw the political need to maintain close relations with the British. Qudsia was not personally loyal to the British, but Sikandar, Shahjehan and Sultan Jahan were not only loyal but regarded the British royal family with an almost filial affection, engendered by the fact that, had it not been for Queen Victoria, Bhopal might not have seen the rule of four Begums, lasting for over a century.

Indian history is littered with instances of imposing women personalities ruling through sons, brothers or husbands. Occasionally, as in the case of Begum Samru, Tarabai, the Jhansi-ki-Rani or Ahlya Bai they assumed de facto up-front command of their principalities. Bhopal was unique, however, in that it saw the rule of four Begums over a period of 107 years, governing in their formal, legal right as heads of state. Only the current monarchy of Holland approaches such an extraordinary record.

Today, as Bhopal assumes its new role as Madhya Pradesh's capital, the images of its 250-year history begin to fade, like glittering stars, overtaken by the onset of dawn. The places of historical interest lie mostly in ruins with the Indian government able to preserve only a few historic monuments. The Fatahgarh Fort was demolished and an ugly market built on its grounds. Some of the fort's ramparts remain, as does also the neglected tomb of Dost and Fatah Bibi. Islamnagar Fort is being maintained by the Indian government, but not the mazar of Yar Mohammad Khan, which decays untended and can only be approached by hacking through brambles and bushes. The tombs of other rulers lie in similar stages of neglect. The Raisen Fort has been maintained but, alas, Ginnor and Chowkigarh – immense, impregnable fortresses that have played a dramatic part in Bhopal's history – are in total decay. The mosques are generally in good order thanks to public support, but no such sustenance has been possible for the beautiful palaces. The magnificent Taj Mahal has recently been abandoned as unsafe and stands in complete ruins. The palaces Gohar Mahal, Shish Mahal, Sadar Manzil, Shaukat Mahal and even Qasri-Sultani are in varying stages of crumbling decay – fading silhouettes of a glorious history.

Epilogue

From 1926 until the state's final merger with India in 1949,[1] Nawab Hamidullah Khan continued the enlightened, democratic and fair rule that he inherited from his mother. Hamidullah inducted a number of distinguished advisers into his Cabinet, mainly from outside Bhopal. These included Shoaib Qureshi, Khundkar Fazle-Haider, Salamuddin, Ali Haider Abbassi, Sir Liaquat Hayat, Sir Joseph Bhore, Sir Ross Massood, Hassan Mohammad Hayat, Ustad Wazir, Mohammad Akram and several others. Among his advisers were Chaudhri Khaliquzzaman, Abdur Rahman Siddiqui, Allama Iqbal, Chaudhri Zafrullah Khan and some British officers with outstanding records like the police chief, Freddy Young, and General Toogood. In consonance with his liberal, democratic upbringing, Hamidullah encouraged the democratic process which, sometimes to his discomfort, led to the rise of a strident Congress leadership in which Shankar Dayal Sharma (later President of India) played a leading role.

The Nawab was also renowned in India as a sportsman. He was an outstanding polo player with a nine-goal handicap and a fearless, crack-shot hunter who frequently went after tigers on foot because he wanted the beast 'to have a fair chance'. He was also a leading social figure as he and the regal, urbane Maimoona Sultan made a handsome couple. Late in life, around 1948, Nawab Hamidullah Khan married again, to Aftab Jahan, daughter of one of Bhopal's gentry. He had three daughters from Maimoona Sultan, the eldest of whom – Abida Sultaan – was appointed heir apparent in 1928.

In pre-independence India, Nawab Hamidullah Khan became an important political figure. As an educated, articulate and politically aware prince, he became Chancellor of the Chamber of Princes and engaged in negotiations with the British and also with Congress and the Muslim League. Hamidullah attempted, as Chancellor of the Chamber of Princes, to create a Third Force by unifying the major princely states into a common front. There was, however, no basic unity between these states and, given an element of mistrust towards a Muslim Chancellor, the Indian Home Minister, Vallabhai Patel, and his deputy, V.P. Menon, were

---

[1] A stand-still agreement was signed with the Indian Union on the eve of independence on 15 August 1947.

able to negotiate merger agreements individually and separately with the princely states.

The Nawab's initiative, however, found a positive echo with Mr Jinnah, the leader of the Muslim League, with whom he established a relationship of confidence. The Nawab of Bhopal had been a financial benefactor of the Muslim League since his Aligarh days and became a supporter of Jinnah's concept of Pakistan. Eventually, it was Hamidullah who persuaded Mahatma Gandhi to publicly accept the concept of the Muslim League representing the Muslims of India in a statement which Mr Gandhi later admitted was 'an Himalayan blunder'! Nawab Hamidullah Khan of Bhopal thus played a significant role in the evolution of post-independence Pakistan.

Bhopal, like Hyderabad, was landlocked and completely surrounded by territory constituting the Indian Union. Its population, also like Hyderabad, was predominantly Hindu. On the other hand, Kashmir and some other princely states in Rajputana and Kathiawar were located on the borders of Pakistan and India. Briefly, the rulers of these states attempted to gain special advantages by negotiating with the new independent governments of Pakistan and India. Hyderabad resisted for a few days in an attempt to remain quasi-independent, but was taken over by force. The case of Kashmir, tragically, remains unresolved even today – a festering sore between Pakistan and India.

Seeing the writing on the wall and with no Hyderabad-style *folies de grandeur*, Hamidullah signed a stand-still agreement with the Indian government a few days before independence. This was followed on 30 May 1949 by a merger agreement. Unlike Hyderabad, Kashmir or Junagadh, Bhopal's merger into the Indian Union was peaceful, Hamidullah ceding through the pen suzerainty that Dost had won by the sword, 240 years earlier.

After partition Bhopal was, even in those volatile turbulent times, a haven of peace where large numbers of Muslims from neighbouring areas fled for safety. On 1 November 1956, Bhopal was made the capital of Madhya Pradesh, the new Indian state, in preference to the competing claims of Indore and Gwalior, two larger cities and traditional Marhatta strongholds. Bhopal today has grown into a large sprawling city with an expanded industrial base. Made infamous by the gas leak disaster from the Union Carbide Chemical Factory on 2 December 1984, Bhopal retains its distinctive image of a Muslim culture, its tradition of communal harmony and its special significance as a cross-road between India's east and west, north and south. Gone, alas, are the magnificent shikargahs where big game of every kind could be found in abundance. Gone also are the state's traditions and sense of history that gave Bhopal its special character.

After partition Mr Jinnah, who knew he was seriously ill, persuaded the Nawab of Bhopal to emigrate to Pakistan, probably to replace him as Governor-General. However, political developments in Pakistan took a different turn after Quaid-e-Azam's death, discouraging Nawab Hamidullah Khan from transferring to Karachi. As late as 1955, however, Nawab Hamidullah Khan told the author, his grandson, that he still intended coming to Pakistan. Again, political circumstances in Pakistan and fading health prevented him from doing so.

Heir apparent Abida Sultaan married Nawab Sarwar Ali Khan of neighbouring Kurwai in 1933, but separated from him after a year, taking custody of her only son – Shaharyar Mohammad Khan, the author. Nawab Sarwar Ali Khan married a second time with Abida's approval. She never sought a divorce. Abida retained her title of heir apparent until the state's merger in 1949. Shaharyar was sent to a military boarding school, the Royal Indian Military College at Dehra Dun, and completed his education in England with an honours degree in law from Cambridge University.

Before the Second World War Abida Sultaan, who had been brought up by her grandmother, Sultan Jahan, to follow in the footsteps of Sikandar Begum, took over the onus of running the state on behalf of her father who was, by then, playing a role on a broader political canvas. Abida was tough, sporting, headstrong and principled – modelling herself on Sikandar Begum, her great-great-grandmother. She too was a fearless crackshot (having bagged 72 tigers) and an outstanding sportswoman, playing polo, bicycle polo, hockey (with men), cricket, squash and inventing roller-hockey which she played on the hallowed marble floors of Minto Hall. She became All-India Women's Squash Champion in 1948 – the only time she competed – and also learned to fly a plane, being the second Muslim woman in South Asia to be given a pilot's licence. Tennis, swimming and sailing were other sports that Abida pursued. She was also an accomplished musician, an expert on the harmonium, but also adept at playing the sitar, tabla and piano. She is a devout Muslim who knows the *lafzi-tarjuma* (the word-for-word Urdu translation) of the Quran by heart and is a fervent supporter of a liberal, tolerant Islam that she fears has been hijacked by illiterate and politically motivated mullahs.

Abida Sultaan, who had been her father's greatest support, confidante and favourite, fell out with him over his second marriage. She resented being ordered to pay obeisance to a new Begum after her mother had been a dutiful consort for 45 years. In 1949, without telling anyone, Abida Sultaan took the train to Bombay and next day boarded the ship for London as the first step to migration to Pakistan. She took only her personal jewellery and left behind a palace, servants, jagirs, shikargahs, an arsenal of rifles, furniture, ceremonial artefacts, cars and her beloved polo ponies. She emigrated to Pakistan in 1950, driving a jeep station wagon across from Europe, to engage actively in political life. She remains the only senior member of a major Indian Muslim princely state to have emigrated to Pakistan. All the remaining members of Bhopal's ruling family stayed behind in India.

Abida Sultaan sold her jewellery and with these funds financed her emigration to Pakistan and her son's education at Cambridge University, her father having stopped all financial support to her. For eight years, she lived without electricity in a small house in Malir on the outskirts of Karachi that she built for herself. The stand-off with her father was complete and was never bridged. Abida was appointed Pakistan's

Ambassador to Brazil and was a member of Pakistan's delegation to the UN in 1954 and also to China where she met Mao Tse-tung, Chou En-lai and engaged in a famous shooting competition with Marshal Ho Lung, the Chinese Defence Minister. But diplomatic life did not suit her. Abida Sultaan then entered the rough and tumble of politics and became Miss Fatimah Jinnah's principal supporter when the Quaid's sister stood against Ayub Khan in the presidential election of 1964. Abida Sultaan was subsequently elected President of the Karachi Council Muslim League.

On 4 February 1960 Nawab Hamidullah Khan died of a heart attack in Bhopal. Abida, a Pakistan national, attended the funeral in Bhopal. After the funeral, the emotional crowds of Bhopal clamoured for their former heir apparent to 'return home'. Shortly afterwards, at a fateful meeting with President Ayub Khan, the Pakistan President informed the princess that if she wished to go back to her home and heritage in Bhopal she could do so, knowing that her credentials as a Pakistani would never be questioned. Abida replied, 'I have made my choice for Pakistan. If it was a question of palaces, money or a life of leisure, I would never have come to Pakistan in the first place. I shall always be a Pakistani. But I do not want to stand in the way of my son – he is 26 – a member of the Pakistan Foreign Service. Maybe he wants to return to his heritage.' The son also declined.

In 1962, Abida's second sister, Sajida Sultan, who married the famous cricketer the Nawab of Pataudi Senior, was recognized as the titular ruler of Bhopal. She lived mainly in Delhi, paying visits to Bhopal with her son, Nawab Mansoor Ali Khan of Pataudi, also a famous cricketer. Maimoona Sultan died in 1982. Abida Sultaan and her son, who is married with four children, live in the same house in Malir which Abida built with the sale of her jewellery. In 1987, Shaharyar was appointed Pakistan's High Commissioner to the Court of St James and he was Pakistan's Foreign Secretary between 1990 and 1994. After retiring, he was appointed the UN Secretary-General's Special Representative for Rwanda, and in 1999 was brought out of retirement to be nominated Pakistan's Ambassador to France.

At partition, a number of Bhopalis emigrated to Pakistan and achieved distinction in their adopted country. The most prominent among these émigrés is Dr Abdul Qadeer Khan, the nuclear scientist who is the father of Pakistan's nuclear programme. Dr Qadeer, despite his status as a national hero, retains his humility, sense of humour and a deep reverence to his Barru-kat family roots of Bhopal. In the military sector, General Latif Khan and General Abdul Hamid Khan rose to the top of their profession. Admiral Saeed Mohammad Khan was Commander-in-Chief of the Pakistan Navy and was appointed Ambassador to Holland. In the diplomatic field, Mr Mohammad Ikramullah was Pakistan's first Foreign Secretary and later High Commissioner to the Court of St James. His youngest daughter is HRH Princess Sarvath, married to HRH Prince El-Hassan Bin Tallal of Jordan. Sultan Mohammad Khan rose to the heights in the Pakistan Foreign Service, being an outstanding Ambassador to China, the USA and Japan, and serving as Foreign

Secretary. Anwar Kamal, great-grandson of Umrao Doulah, has also served with distinction as Pakistan's High Commissioner to Bangladesh and is currently Ambassador to Egypt. Direct descendants of Dost Mohammad Khan have emigrated to Pakistan, notably Brigadier Ghazanfar Mohammad Khan and Sardar Aslam Mohammad Khan. In the field of sports, Bhopal was famous as a breeding ground for hockey players. Shakoor, Muneer and Maulana Bunney were household figures in pre-independence India. After partition, Bhopal's youngsters were prominent in Pakistan's Olympic team – notably Anwar Ahmad Khan, Latif-ur-Rehman and Habib-ur-Rehman.

Among the well-known women from Bhopal who settled in Pakistan were Umrao Doulah's granddaughter, Munawwar Jahan, who married the Nawab of Junagadh. Her son, who succeeded him as Nawab, married Umrao Doulah's great-granddaughter, the current dowager Begum of Junagadh. Maimoona Sultan Begum's niece, Shahzadi Farhat Sultan, married Pakistan's renowned Commander-in-Chief of the Air Force, Air Marshal Nur Khan. In the field of education and culture, the Arabic scholars and sisters Ruqayya and Atiya bint Khalil Arab – the latter currently Professor of Arabic at Karachi University – are recognized for their contribution in the field of literature and scholarship.

A large colony of Bhopalis live in Pakistan, mainly in Karachi; they speak with their distinctive Bhopali accents, their women are still aggressive, tough and resplendent in their Bhopali dress and above all they are proud of the heritage and tradition that Bhopal has given them.

Appendix 1

Confusion on dates of birth and death of Dost and Yar

Basically, there are two sets of conflicting dates of birth and death of the first three nawabs of Bhopal. The Begums, their commissioned state historians and some chroniclers who have obviously taken the Begums' dates as conclusive (for convenience called the First Group) maintain that Dost arrived in India around 1708 (i.e. after Aurangzeb's death) and died in 1740 at the age of 66. They state that Yar was 18 years old when, in 1740, he became Nawab (indicating a date of birth in 1722), that he ruled for 15 years and died in 1755 when his 11-year-old son Faiz took over as the third Nawab (indicating that he was born around 1744).

British, Rajput, Marhatta and some Bhopali historians (for convenience called the Second Group) maintain that Dost arrived in India before Aurangzeb's death (i.e. around the turn of the century), enlisted in Aurangzeb's army around 1704 and was assigned to Malwa when Aurangzeb died in 1707. The Second Group records Dost's death in 1728 and Yar taking over as second Nawab at the age of 18, which would indicate that he was born around 1710. They maintain that Yar died in 1742 when his 11-year-old son, Faiz, became third Nawab, which would indicate that he was born around 1731.

Both groups agree that Yar was 18 and Faiz 11 years old when they became rulers. They also agree that Dost took on the lease of Berasia in 1709, that Yar was handed over to the Nizam as hostage in 1724 and that Faiz died in 1777 when he was succeeded by his brother, Hayat, as the fourth Nawab. The two groups differ on Dost and Yar's dates of birth and death and on the date of Yar's successor. The First Group's contention is based on the plaque at Dost's grave which indicates his dates of birth and death. The Second Group's dates are based on numerous Marhatta, Rajput and British documents including treaties, firmans and general records that show Yar Mohammad Khan as the Nawab of Bhopal between 1728 and 1742 and Faiz as Nawab from 1742 to 1777. Clearly Yar could not have been Nawab between 1728 and 1740 if Dost had been alive.

After careful scrutiny of the records and analysis of the events of the period, the author has come to the conclusion that the dates proffered by the Second Group are more reliable for the following reasons:

a It is evident that the Begums in writing and commissioning the history of Bhopal were highly inaccurate in their recall of dates. This may have been due to three sets of calendars being quoted by them – the Gregorian, the Hijri (AH) and the Fasli (based on crop harvests). For instance, Shahjehan Begum's *History of Bhopal* begins with the sentence 'Dost Mohammad Khan emigrated to Hindustan in the beginning of the reign of Bahadur Shah in 1120 AH i.e.

1716 AD'. This statement is factually incorrect on several counts: 1120 AH does not correspond to AD 1716 and Bahadur Shah had died in 1712!

b The plaque on Dost's grave does not date back to the time of his burial and is not inscribed on its headstone but on a plaque outside the monument. The plaque is written in English. It was obviously placed at his mazar long after his burial. The plaque cannot, therefore, be treated as indicating authentic dates of birth and death.

c The First Group's dates envisage Dost's first child – Yar – to have been born around 1722, as he was stated to be 18 on succeeding Dost. This means that Dost was 46 years old before he began fathering the first of his 11 children. This would seem much too late for a virile, robust man who had already married at least twice before 1709.

d It is highly unlikely that in 1724 the Nizam would have accepted as hostage a two-year-old (as Yar would have been according to the First Group's dates). It is far more likely that Yar was around 14 years old when the Nizam returned with him to Hyderabad (Second Group dates). It follows that Yar, at the age of 18, succeeded Dost on his death in 1728. Moreover, Yar remained in Hyderabad for about four years (Second Group) and not 16 years (First Group).

e Dost took on the lease of Berasia in 1709. According to the dates recorded by the First Group the following events would have occurred in the two-year period between Dost's arrival in India (i.e. after 1707) and the lease of Berasia (1709) a) enlisting in the Moghul army, b) being assigned to Malwa, c) serving at least four different masters, d) establishing a relationship of trust with the Raja of Mangalgarh and after his death with the Dowager Rani and e) marrying Fatah Bibi. It is highly unlikely that so many events could have been compressed into such a short period! A far more likely scenario is, as suggested by the Second Group, that Dost enlisted in Aurangzeb's army in 1704–5, gradually earned his spurs, found himself in Malwa in early 1707 at the time of Aurangzeb's death and, over a two-year period, established himself in Malwa before taking on the lease of Berasia.

f There is no reason to doubt authentic Rajput, Marhatta and British records indicating that Yar was Nawab from 1728–44 (i.e. that Dost died in 1728) and that Faiz succeeded Yar in 1742.

g Dost's diary (*roznamcha*) contradicts the First Group's dates.

h Dost's date of birth is not known, but assertions that he was 66 at the time of his death are probably inaccurate. It is likely that he was in his 50s when he died in March 1728. He is therefore likely to have been born around 1672.

Taking all factors into consideration, the author is convinced that the Second Group's dates are correct and that the Begums miscalculated the dates of their ancestors and had the wrong dates inscribed on the plaque outside Dost's tomb. These dates were also perpetuated by state archivists acting under the directions of the Begums. The First Group's dates do not stand up to the test of historical scrutiny and it is interesting to note that even Nawab Hamidullah Khan has confirmed Dost Mohammad Khan's death to have taken place in 1728, thereby contradicting the chronicles recorded by his immediate ancestors.

Appendix 2

Gonds and Bhils

The Gonds and Bhils were the indigenous people of Malwa. They were Dravidians and the original inhabitants of the region. The Gonds were mainly peasants while the Bhils were hunters. Even before the arrival of Muslim invaders in the eleventh century, non-Muslim Aryans – Rajputs, Marhattas etc – had dominated the region. The Gonds had their own language and were idol-worshippers. Initially they were distinct from Hindus but, over the centuries, were absorbed into the Hindu mainstream. A gond-raja was the warlord of the local population of Gonds and Bhils.

The Dravidian Gonds preferred to maintain their distinction from the Aryan Hindus, particularly from the Brahmins. They were meat-eaters, had their own traditions and were ethnically different from the succeeding layers of Aryan settlers, both Hindu and Muslim, who had driven them southwards into central India and the deep south.

Successive Bhopal rulers recognized the separate culture of the Gonds, their loyalty and their contribution to the economic and social development of Bhopal. The famous forts of Ginnor and Chowkigarh were initially constructed by the Gonds. Kamlapati was a famous gond-rani who built a seven-storey palace in Bhopal that still overlooks the lake. Nawab Hayat Mohammad Khan adopted two Gond boys, Faulad Khan and Chottey Khan, both of whom became Dewans. The Begums granted large jagirs to the senior Gond families, who still retain property rights to these estates.

Appendix 3

The Orakzai Pathans Their origins

The origins of the great Pathan warrior tribes that straddle today's Afghanistan and Pakistan's North-West Frontier are shrouded in a haze that merges legend into history. The Pathans date back to pre-Islamic times and are generally regarded as Aryans who moved eastwards from Arabia and central Asia towards Persia and Afghanistan. Sir Olaf Caroe traces the origins of the Orakzai tribe to Karlanr who was the fourth progenitor of the famous Pathan tribes. The first three were all sons of Qais. The eldest, Sarbanr, was the ancestor of the Yusafzais, the Durranis and the Tarins among others. The second son, Bitan, headed the Ghilzais, Lodis and Suris whose dynasties ruled over northern India before the Moghuls. The third, Ghurghusht, was the ancestor of the Kakars and Jadoons. Karlanr was not one of Qais's sons (some say he was a son of Ghurghusht), but was a figurehead of the time whose tribal offspring included the Gorran, Orakzai, Afridi, Khattak, Mahsud and Bangash.

The Orakzai were mainly Sunni and settled in the Tirah Valley which lies in Pakistan's tribal area. They moved from Persia to Afghanistan sometime in the seventh century. Each tribe was divided into clans – khels – who took their names after a family stalwart. Dost Mohammad Khan was an Orakzai who belonged to the Mirazi-khel. Other clans of the same tribe were the Jalal-khel of Lohari where Dost initially stayed in India; it was from the Jalal-khel that Ahmad Khan (Sultan Doulah) was selected by Sikandar Begum as her granddaughter's consort; the Mishti-khel comprising Bhopal's most loyal commanders including Bakhshi Bahadur Mohammad Khan and his son Sardar Baqi Mohammad Khan (Umrao Doulah); and the Feroze-khel who settled in the neighbouring state of Kurwai.

There is a genealogical table of the Orakzai-Bhopal family on p 262.

Appendix 4

The Pindaras

The Pindaras were armed freebooters or land pirates that emerged out of the chaos and lawlessness following Aurangzeb's death in 1707. The Pindaras began operating in the central and northern provinces of India drawing their support from disbanded armies of Pathan and Marhatta chieftains. Ganging together in search of loot and plunder, they marauded across the central region on horseback with their women and families in tow, a menace to settled societies. With the passing years, the Pindaras grew in military strength and had to be taken head on by the major states, some – like Bhopal – buying them off, others – like Gwalior and the British – engaging in battle. Eventually, Sir Barry Close undertook a major campaign to suppress them which was assisted by Nazar Mohammad Khan. The Pindaras were defeated and their Afghan leader settled in the state of Tonk. The Marhatta leader, Chitu, escaped into the jungles where he was conveniently eaten by a tiger.

Appendix 5

The Bourbon family tree

Charles de Bourbon de Navarre
↓
Jean-Philippe married Juliana Mascrenhas
↓
Seville married Miss Allemaine
↓
Alexandre married Miss Robertson
↓
Anthony married A Muslim lady
↓
Francis I married An American lady
↓
Francis II married Miss de Silva
↓
Salvador I married Miss Brevette
↓
Salvador II married Miss Thome
(Inayat Masih)
↓
Balthazar married Miss Isabella Stone (Sarkar Dulhan)
(Shahzad Masih)

Appendix 6

Treaty between the British East India Company and the Nawab of Bhopal, Raisen, 8 March 1818

There shall be perpetual friendship, alliance, and unity of interests between the Honourable the East India Company and the Nawab of Bhopal, his heirs and successors; and the friends and enemies of one party shall be the friends and enemies of both.

The British Government engages to guarantee and protect the principality and territory of Bhopal against all enemies.

The Nawab of Bhopal and his heirs and successors will act in subordinate cooperation with the British Government, and acknowledge its supremacy, and will not have any connection with other chiefs and States.

The Nawab and his heirs and successors will not enter into negotiation with any chief or State without the knowledge and sanction of the British Government. But their usual amicable correspondence with friends and relations, and necessary correspondence with neighbouring zamindars and managers on matters of small importance shall continue.

The Nawab and his heirs and successors will not commit aggression on any one. If by accident disputes arise with any one, they shall be submitted to the arbitration and award of the British Government.

The State of Bhopal shall furnish a contingent of six hundred (600) horse and four hundred (400) infantry for the service of the British Government. Whenever required, and when necessary, the whole of the Bhopal forces shall join the British army, excepting such a portion as may be necessary for the internal administration of the country.

The British troops are to be at all times admitted into the Bhopal territory, the commanding officers of such troops using their utmost endeavours to prevent injury to the crops or other damages, and if necessary shall cantoon there; in which event the Nawab engages for himself, his heirs and successors, on application to that effect to cede to the British Government to serve as a depot the fort of Nuzzurghur or of Gulgaon with ground to the distance of 2,000 yards all round the fort.

The Nawab; his heirs and successors, will afford every facility to the British troops in obtaining supplies; and all articles of supply required for them shall be purchased in and pass through the Nawab's territory free of duty.

The Nawab and his heirs and successors shall remain absolute rulers of their country, and the jurisdiction of the British Government shall not in any manner be introduced into the principality.

The Nawab having exerted himself and employed the resources of his government with zeal and fidelity in the late service against the Pindaries, the British Government, in order to make its approbation of his conduct, and to enable him to maintain the stipulated contingent, hereby grants to the Nawab, his heirs and successors in perpetuity the five mahals of Ashta, Sehawur, Sehore, Doraha, and Debipura to be held by them in exclusive authority.

This treaty, consisting of eleven articles, having been concluded at Raisen, and signed and sealed by Captain Stewart and by Kurrim Muhammad Khan Bahadoor, and by Shahzad Massi Sahib. Captain Stewart engages to obtain the ratification of the Governor-General within three weeks from this date; and Kurrim Muhammad Khan and Shahzad Massi engage to obtain the ratification of the Nawab Nazar Muhammad Khan in two days.

Appendix 7

Nawab Nazar Mohammad Khan's death at Islamnagar

Political Agent, Major Henley's report to the Secretary of State[1]

On the 11th instant [11 November 1819] about sunset, the Raneeji, widow of Wazir Muhammad, came to Islamnagar for the purpose of inviting the Begum, wife of the Nawab, to an entertainment prepared on the occasion of concluding the marriage contract of her daughter, the Nawab's sister. On her arrival, the Nawab who was sitting in a separate Bungalow [*Mahal*] was summoned to give his assent to the proposed visit to Bhopal. He presently arose and went towards the Mahal.

According to Kalloo Khidmatgar (personal servant), 'On his master rising to go towards the Mahal, he called for a pistol[2] which he was in the habit of carrying about with him, he [Kalloo] accordingly brought the pistol from another room and gave it to the Nawab, just as was entering the Mahal. At this moment, he heard the Nawab call to Faujdar, brother to the Begum, to come and taking his hand went in with him.'

According to Sawal, an Useel, the female attendant of Nazar Muhammad Khan's daughter, Sikandar Begum, 'On Nawab's coming to the Mahal, he asked for his daughter who was brought to him and taking her in his arms began to caress her. He then called for a *paun* [betel leaf] and sat down on a low Hindostani cot laying his sword by his side and still having his daughter in his arms. That as it was becoming dark she [the Useel] brought a light and afterwards went for the *Oogaldan* [spitoon] which is used in chewing paun. While she was searching for it, the Begum, the Nawab's wife, called for some water but for her [the Useel] not being at hand to bring it (she) went for it herself. At this moment, she heard the report of the pistol and returning to the Nawab saw him fallen back on the cot as she thought in a swoon with a wound at his right ear. Her daughter had fallen from his arms on the ground. The boy Faujdar had come in with the Nawab but at the moment of her return she did not perceive him or any one else

---

[1] Major Henley reached Islamnager on 20 November 1819. His report to the Secretary of State is included in the Foreign Department Political Consultation records dated 1 January 1820 in the Indian National Archives. Qudsia Begum became Regent on 14 November 1819.
[2] The pistol was a gift from General Adams to Nawab Nazar Mohammad Khan.

there. Afterwards the Begum and the Ranee [the Nawab's stepmother] who had been in the cook-room at a distance came in and also Bakshi Bahadur Muhammad Khan. On the latter feeling the Nawab he fell on the ground and burst into loud lamentation. It was then only they knew the Nawab was dead.'

Bakshi Bahadur Muhammad Khan stated he was sitting in the Kutcherry about 30 paces from the Mahal and hearing the report of the pistol from thence, his mind misgave him that something was wrong and he immediately ran to the door when finding the Begum and the Ranee there he called to them for God's sake to remove and went in. He there saw the Nawab expiring on the cot, motionless and insense. The pistol was lying on the ground. The Nawab had not taken off his shoes so short was the interval from his coming in. On Bakshi Bahadur Muhammad Khan's first reaching the door of the Mahal, he saw Faujdar Khan crying who told him the Nawab had been struck by a pistol and on being afterwards questioned added, the Nawab, after playing with the pistol and showing it to his daughter laid it down besides him when it went off he knew not how. Seeing the Nawab's hair burning he endeavoured to put it out but afterwards on the blood appearing he ran out fearing it would be said he had fired the pistol. Bakshi Bahadur Muhammad Khan and Jamal Muhammad Khan immediately searched the Mahal to detect any person who might be concealed there but found no one.

Hakim Shahzad Masih stated that he immediately repaired to Islamnagar on hearing of this event. On taking the pistol and putting his finger into the barrel, he found it had evidently been recently fired. On examining the wound it appeared the discharge had been so near as to burn the side of the face and set fire to the hair. The ball had struck the tip of the right ear and passing through the neck in somewhat below a horizontal direction standing backwards, had penetrated deep in the opposite wall. He also observed that in the posture the Nawab had been sitting, there was no door or entrance behind him.

Faujdar Muhammad Khan had also repeated to Hakim Shahzad Masih, the same as to the discharge of the pistol which he had given to Bakshi Bahadur Muhammad Khan.

In addition to the above, the following were the observations and remarks communicated by the principal friends and dependants of Nazar Muhammad Khan:

'The child Faujdar Khan had been seen to handle the pistol when sitting by the Nawab who had on such occasions, taken it from him. He was moreover just of that height that a pistol discharged from his hand would strike the temple when standing by the side of the Nawab sitting on the cot.'

It can be concluded that Nazar Muhammad Khan's death was due to the accidental discharge of the pistol by Faujdar Muhammad Khan. No preplan to kill Nazar Muhammad Khan seemed to have been arranged. After his death nobody came forward as claimant of the throne.

Appendix 8

The relationship between Qudsia Begum and Shahzad Masih

Vitold de Golish, a French traveller and author of books on the Indian princely states, records that Shahzad Masih and the young Regent, Qudsia, became lovers soon after the young widow assumed powers as Regent. He states that Shahzad Masih, who was Prime Minister and Qudsia's most loyal adviser, initially used to meet Qudsia across a purdah curtain. One day, he was summoned by the Regent and met her face to face. The screen had been removed and the Regent was dressed in a transparent chemise. Shahzad Masih left the room in consternation but found himself consumed with passion and love for the young Regent to the extent that he could not sleep all night. Clearly, the Regent had demonstrated her own feelings towards him and unable to contain his latent love for the Begum which was obviously requited, the two began a romantic liaison that led to trysts in country estates and shikargahs.

After a while, the scandal of the romance between Qudsia and Shahzad Masih could not be suppressed and began to reverberate around Bhopal's court circles. In order to scotch these scandals, Qudsia advised Shahzad Masih to find himself a European wife. Shahzad Masih duly obeyed the Regent and found himself a young English bride in Delhi, Isabella Stone, the daughter of an English nobleman who returned to Bhopal and bore Shahzad two children – Salvador and Maria. Isabella was given the title of 'Sarkar Dulhan' and unexpectedly struck up a warm friendship with Qudsia. Shahzad Masih died in 1829 – apparently poisoned by Afghan nobles in the court – but Sarkar Dulhan stayed on in Bhopal and built a Catholic cemetery, school and church which survive to this day. Sarkar Dulhan remained loyal to Qudsia and was given a large jagir and income, so that the Bourbon family prospered in Bhopal during the reigns of Qudsia and Sikandar Begum. A downturn in their fortunes came during Shahjehan Begum's rule when her consort, Nawab Siddiq Hassan – a bigoted Wahabi – persecuted the Christian Bourbons.

Vitold de Golish's description of a romantic liaison between Shahzad Masih and Qudsia Begum is based on the verbal account of the surviving head of the Bourbon family in Bhopal. De Golish is not a historian and visited Bhopal as a journalist/traveller for a few days only. His account of Bhopal's history is full of errors and exaggerations which casts doubt on the veracity of his contention that Shahzad Masih and Qudsia were lovers. For example, his Bourbon informer states that the last Nawab of Bhopal had two daughters. In fact, he had three.

Also, that their husbands had 'conspired with the Pakistan government' which led to their losing credibility with India. This assertion is also false as the elder daughter – Princess Abida Sultaan – had been separated from her husband since 1935 and the younger daughter's husband – the Nawab of Pataudi Senior – had never been in bad odour with the government of India. Moreover, the photograph in de Golish's book claiming to be the 'Bourbon Palace' is, in fact, the Ahmadabad Palace.

These inaccuracies suggest that de Golish's description of Qudsia's regency is speculative and based on the fertile imagination of his informants. It is true, however, that Shahzad Masih demonstrated extraordinary loyalty and personal devotion to Qudsia Begum throughout her regency until his death. He risked his life and family honour to defend Qudsia against repeated onslaughts from male opponents. In today's world, such devotion can only be explained in terms of a profound love between man and woman. In those chivalrous times, it was also possible to explain the extraordinary commitment as loyalty between subject and ruler, especially as Qudsia was the widow of Shahzad Masih's dearest friend.

Appendix 9

Sir Richmond Shakespear's report to the Governor-General after meeting Sikandar Begum[1]

During my third visit to the Secunder Begum, I had a private audience with Her Highness at which Captain Hutchinson was the only other person present.

I told the Lady that I was sorry to hear from Captain Hutchinson that she was still dissatisfied, although the Government had ruled that authority was to rest in her hands during her life. She replied that she considered the Rank as well as the authority belonged to her by inheritance and that she could not understand upon what grounds her daughter was granted supremacy over her. I urged that the wish of our Government had always been to obtain a male successor to Nuzzur Mahomed, that therefore, when she was a child, we had ruled that the nearest blood relation should be married to her, and that, when we found that the only child born of the marriage was a daughter, that we had ruled that her daughter should marry the nearest male relative of Nuzzur Mahomed's family.

Her Highness, immediately, replied that she understood thoroughly what was the intention of the British Government; but that, as our plans had failed in obtaining a male heir to Nuzzur Mahomed, she considered that our selecting his granddaughter in preference to herself (who was his daughter) was a direct and serious injury to herself. I remarked that though I had read the correspondence I had failed to notice any objections urged by Her Highness when the orders of Government were issued. That on the death of her Father in 1819 it was ruled that her cousin Moonur (Munir) Mahomed Khan should be the Ruler, that, on his abdicating the succession was ruled to rest with his brother the Nawab Jehanzeer Mohamed Khan, after his marriage to Her Highness that she was at that time of seventeen years of age. Again at the death of her husband it was ruled that the husband of her daughter the Shahjehan Begum should be the Chief of Bhopal.

Also at the marriage of her daughter it was ruled that as the husband was not of the family of Nuzzur Mahomed Khan therefore the succession to the Goddee [gaddi] should rest with the Shahjehan Begum herself.

That during all these discussions I could not discover that Her Highness had ever advanced her own claim to succeed in person.

---

[1] AGG Sir Richmond Shakespear's letter to Secretary of State Mr Cecil Beadon dated 14 December 1859, India Office Records, L/145/10/1114.

She assured me that she had written to Captain Cunningham and appealed to me, whether it was just that her daughter should be Queen while she herself was living.

I confessed that it did appear that she had some cause for complaint, but I expressed my surprise that one who had shown such great proof of intellect should herself raise obstacles to a very simple mode of attaining her wishes. That, if she would only allow me to speak to her daughter on this subject, I felt sure of her consenting.

To this the Secunder Begum replied very quickly but very firmly No, I will not be indebted to my daughter for that which is assuredly my own right by inheritance.

I pointed out that the orders of the Government of India were clear and conclusive against Her Highness' wishes and I was told that she was well aware of this, and that she had long since made up her mind to appeal to the authorities in England. That she was so certain of success that she would not wish to be under obligation to her daughter.

The above conversation took place late on Saturday evening and on Monday morning the 12th instant I sent Captain Hutchinson to the Secunder Begum to say that, after mature consideration I had decided that it was my duty to speak to the Shahjehan Begum for two reasons.

That I was convinced that the Shahjehan Begum would raise no objection, for, if she did so, they might prejudice her own claim, when her daughter the Sultan Jahan Begum became of age.

I was convinced that the reply of the Home Authorities (even if favourable to Her Highness) would direct, as a preliminary measure, the Shahjehan Begum being consulted.

In reply to this message I was informed by the Secunder Begum that, Her Highness would no longer object to my speaking to Her daughter.

On the evening of the 12th instant, I accordingly had an interview with the Shahjehan Begum at which Captain Hutchinson was the only other person present.

On my praising her filial conduct in having herself proposed that her Mother should continue to be Regent during her life, she replied immediately, 'Of course, she is the superior and I am her heir'.

I remarked that the present arrangement was only regarding the authority in the State and I asked whether she entertained the same feeling regarding the rank? She immediately replied, 'Yes, my mother is the superior and I am her heir'. I remarked that I thought it would be for the good of herself and her house generally, if the question was put in a clear and formal light and I asked whether she had any objection, when replying to my Khureeta regarding authority, to make a request on her own part, that both rank and authority should rest with the Secunder Begum during her life.

Appendix 10

Meeting between Shahjehan Begum and Sir Lepel Griffin[1]

Translation of notes of a dialogue between Sir Lepel Griffin, British Resident (R), and Shahjehan Begum (B). The Taj Mahal, 9 a.m., 21 January 1888.

R. - You seem to be annoyed with me.
B - You are an officer of high rank, how can I be annoyed with you?
R. - Since my departure to England, the Government has been repeatedly abused by the Press.
B. - Have I been abusing the Government? You can question the editors, and inquire into the matter.
R. - I do not want to inquire. I hold proofs – the State papers.
B. - You have proofs – well and good, and you have also authority to inflict punishment. But may I ask, who causes articles to be written against me in the vernacular and English papers in India, and also in the newspapers in England?
R. - The articles written against you do not give any dates, nor do they refer to any State paper. But the articles against the Government are written at the instigation of your husband.
B. - You had better bring an action against the editors, and they will furnish proofs.
R. - I will not prosecute any editor, but you may do it if you like.
B. - As the Government has granted liberty to the Press, I have no right to prosecute any editor.
R. - I have to speak to you about another matter. Siddiq Hassan practises sorcery, and does the dirty work both of Hindus and Mussulmen.
B. - Siddiq Hassan, a Wahabee and sorcerer! A Wahabee can never be a sorcerer. You may make any inquiry you like.
R. - The death of Bilqis was caused by the Black Art.
B. - What could be gained by the death of Bilqis?
R. - You call your husband a Wahabee.
B. - You call him so. But a Wahabee does not practise sorcery.
R. - A Sorcerer is an infidel, but the British Government does not take cognizance of such matters. I have another important case. I believe you

---

[1] The record of the meeting held at Taj Mahal Palace on 21 January 1888 is contained in *Appeal and Correspondence* by Shahjehan Begum, a private publication with no date.

	know that it is a serious offence to bribe the Political Agent or the Resident.
B. -	I have never offered a bribe to any person.
R. -	I have proofs.
	[*Reads a letter written by Col. Wylie to the following effect:*]
	'The State vakil met me at the Sehore Garden, and told me that the Bhopal State would make good the loss of pay which I had incurred on account of my transfer from Jhalwar.'
B. -	The vakil is a fool. He might have said so of his own accord; I never told him to say anything of the kind.
R. -	The vakil sits outside. I shall record his statement after confronting him with Colonel Wylie. Siddiq Hassan, if not you, might have instructed him.
B. -	No person ever goes near Siddiq Hassan.
R. -	You don't know. People come to him.
B. -	I and Siddiq Hassan are now almost in prison. False reports are spread about him to ruin him. You may, if you choose, banish him, and we will both leave this country.
R. -	I don't say any such thing, but I shall report him to the Government. I will expel him from Bhopal, but not you.
B. -	You may do so, but I will accompany him wherever he goes.
R. -	As you like, but I can't say so. I know Siddiq Hassan is sitting behind the screen and is overhearing us.
B. -	Come in and see.
R. -	I don't want to see. But why are you talking out loud? Your husband may overhear us.
B. -	Siddiq Hassan is not here.
R. -	You are a party to the bribery case. After Wylie flatly refused, you made friends with Mrs Wylie and presented a gold jewel.
B. -	Of course, I gave Mrs Wylie a jewel as a present, and in token of friendship. It is not of much value. I send presents also to Mrs Ward – looking glass, & c.
R. -	Ward is in your service. You may give him ten lacs if you choose.
B. -	My mother, the Nawab Secunder Begum, used to give such presents.
R. -	Those days are now gone by, and all is changed. Government officers commit an offence if they accept bribes.
B. -	Of course, I know that, but I gave a present.
R. -	If Wylie accepts a present worth 300 rupees, you will give him three lacs hereafter.
B. -	I have not yet offered any bribe.
R. -	I know well that you remitted money to the Foreign Office, but the Officials there are not open to bribes. He who offers bribes is robbed by his own servants.
B. -	You can inquire at the Post Office and find out the numbers of the notes sent.
R. -	I have found all out. Why will you not settle the disputes with your daughter? She is on the right side. You had better pay her what is due, and pass an order to that effect.
B. -	I will not do so.
R. -	Why? Why will you not agree?
B. -	She is disobedient.
R. -	She is not. She demands her right. I have seen no proofs of her disobedience. Be kind and become reconciled to her.
B. -	Colonel Bannerman made the terms, but the settlement fell through.
R. -	What were the terms?

APPENDIX 10

B. - I agreed to what Colonel Bannerman dictated, but my daughter would not agree. She apprehended that I would take back Bilqis, but I had no such intention. I asked my daughter to see me frequently along with Bilqis.

R. - It would have been hard for your daughter to wean away Bilqis from you.

B. - My heart has been already wounded. I will not come to terms.

R. - Why are you not kind to your daughter? You are sensible, but you are not just to your own child. The days of Secundar Begum are over. The Sultan Jahan cannot stand the treatment which you experienced at the hands of your mother. You must pay the money.

B. - You are a Government officer. You may order Colonel Ward, and he will obey you, but I will never consent to it.

R. - When will you send a reply to my Khurita?

B. - Within eight or ten days.

R. - The matter is simple, two days will suffice.

B. - I am not feeling well, I cannot therefore send a reply in two days.

R. - This is no proper excuse. You must send a reply sharp. You must sanction the payment of money.

B. - I have already given you my reply. You may do anything you like, but I will never agree to it.

R. - But you have paid Yasin.

B. - I carried out your orders.

R. - I never passed any order. I gave you advice.

B. - I have got a copy of your final order.

R. - And in the same way you can pay your daughter.

B. - You may do anything you like.

R. - Will you agree to it?

B. - No, I will not.

R. - Why? Your objections are not good. Everyone sympathises with Sultan Jahan. The Viceroy will compel you to pay it.

B. - Your order will suffice. Why should you trouble the Viceroy to pass any order?

R. - Why will you not agree to the proposal?

B. - As you are not open to reason, you may do as you like.

R. - You are both sensible and intelligent, but you are almost in a prison on account of the PURDAH.

B. - I am not the only one in this position. Sultan Jahan is in the same predicament, and so are all Mussulman ladies.

R. - You are a Ruler. You are as intelligent as your mother, but she was strong and you are weak.

B. - The question of purdah is of no importance. The administration is a different thing altogether. I quite concur with you when you say that a change has come upon the present time. In those days my mother was advised by the Agent to retire behind the purdah, whereas you are advising me to give it up.

R. - You are a Ruler, and should not be pent up behind the purdah.

B. - Sultan Jahan, my heir apparent, will follow in my wake.
[*After keeping quite quiet for a few minutes, the Resident said in a very quiet tone:*]

R. - I beg of you, with my clasped hands, to agree to the terms.

B. - I beg of you, with my clasped hands, to excuse me. I will not agree. You may pass any order you like.
[*The same question was repeated and the same reply given. The Resident rose to depart.*]

R. -   You should think over the matter until the evening, and then agree to what I say.
[*The Begum gave the same reply as above.*]

Bibliography

General

Bayly, Professor C.A., *Rulers, Townsmen and Bazaars 1770–1870* (Delhi: Oxford University Press, 1992)
Burgess, James, *Chronology of Modern India* (Edinburgh: Al-Biruni, 1913; Lahore, 1975)
Caroe, Sir Olaf, *The Pathans* (Karachi: Oxford University Press, 1983)
Jacobson, Doranne, *Purdah in the Palace – The Begums of Bhopal* (South Asia Institute, Columbia University, 1982)
Singh, K. Natwar, *Maharaja Suraj Mal* (Delhi: BI Publications, 1981)

Chapter 1

Dost's life

Ali, Allama Abid Wajdi-al-Husseini, *Tarikh-e-Riasat Bhopal* (Bhopal Book House, 1957), Chapter 1
Ali, Luard and Kudrat, *State Gazetteer – Bhopal* (Calcutta: Government Printing Press, 1907)
Chishti, Wahajuddin, *Begmat-e-Bhopal* (Karachi: Qudsia Printers, 1981), chapter on Bhopal
Dirafshe-Shaukat [History of Bhopal in verse] (1894), original available in India Office Library
Dost Mohammad Khan, *Dost's Diary (Roznamcha)*,[1] serialized in the Urdu journal *Shola-e-Hayat* (Bhopal, 1962)
Hamid, Dr Razia and Rafat Sultan (eds), *Nuqoosh-e-Bhopal* (Bhopal: Babul Uloom, 1986), Chapter 4 on history of Bhopal, Chapter 8 on Kamlapati
Malhotra, O.P, *History of Bhopal (1707–1818)* (unpublished thesis, Vikram University, Ujjain), Chapter 1

---

[1] Dost Mohammad Khan's diary (*Roznamcha*), edited by Dewan Bijjey Ram, was one of the documents that was kept in the custody of successive rulers of Bhopal. The author's mother, Princess Abida Sultaan, recalls that her grandmother, Sultan Jahan Begum, used to annually bring out the diary from her personal safe and show it to close members of the family. Extracts of the diary were serialized in the Urdu journal *Shola-e-Hayat* in 1962. Princess Abida Sultaan considers the reproduction to be authentic. Regrettably the original diary has not been traceable since the death of Nawab Hamidullah Khan in 1960, not even in the Indian National Archives.

Shahjehan Begum, *History of Bhopal (Taj-ul-Iqbal)* (Calcutta: Thacker-Spink & Co., 1876), Part I, Chapter 1

Tayyaba Bi, *Tarikh-e-Farman-ravanyan-e-Bhopal* (Karachi, 1977), chapter on Dost Mohammad Khan

Zuberi, Mohammad Amin, *Begmat-e-Bhopal* (Bhopal: Hamidi Arts Press, 1918), Part I

History of Malwa and India

Dodwell, W.H., *The Cambridge History of India*, Vol IV (New Delhi: C. Chand & Co., 1963)

Gascoigne, Bamber, *The Great Moghuls* (London: Jonathan Cape, 1971)

Gordon, Stewart, *Marhattas, Marauders and State Formation in Eighteenth Century India* (Delhi: Oxford University Press, 1994), Chapter 3

Hough, Maj. William, *A Brief History of the Bhopal Principality of Central India* (Calcutta: Baptist Mission Press, 1845)

Keay, John, *The Honourable Company* (New York: Macmillan, 1994), Part III, Chapters 11–13

Malcolm, Sir John, *A Memoir of Central India* (Gannon, 1972)

Sarkar, Sir Jadunath, *Fall of the Moghul Empire*, Vols I–II (New Delhi: Orient Longman, 1950)

Sinh, Raghubir, *Malwa in Transition* (Bombay: D.B. Taraporevale and Sons, 1936), Chapters 3–7

—— *Indian States and the New Regime* (Bombay: D.B. Taraporevale and Sons, 1938)

Tod, James, *Annals and Antiquities of Rajeshtan* (Calcutta, 1898)

Chapter 2

Mamola Bai and the Bhopal Nawabs

Ali, Allama Abid Wajdi-al-Husseini, *Tarikh-e-Riasat Bhopal* (Bhopal Book House, 1957), Chapters 2–5

Ali, Luard and Kudrat, *State Gazetteer – Bhopal* (Calcutta: Government Printing Press, 1907)

Chishti, Wahajuddin, *Begmat-e-Bhopal* (Karachi: Qudsia Printers, 1981), chapter on Mamola Bai

Dirafshe-Shaukat [History of Bhopal in verse] (1894), original available in India Office Library

Hamid, Dr Razia and Rafat Sultan (eds), *Nuqoosh-e-Bhopal* (Bhopal: Babul Uloom, 1986), chapter on history of Bhopal

Hough, Maj. William, *A Brief History of the Bhopal Principality of Central India* (Calcutta: Baptist Mission Press, 1845)

Khan, Hamidullah, *Bhopal State – Its Ruler and Method of Administration* (Bhopal: Times of India Press, 1932)

Malcolm, Sir John, *A Memoir of Central India* (Gannon, 1972)

Malhotra, O.P, *History of Bhopal* (1707–1818) (unpublished thesis, Vikram University, Ujjain), Chapter 2

Shahjehan Begum, *History of Bhopal (Taj-ul-Iqbal)* (Calcutta: Thacker-Spink & Co., 1876), Chapters 2–5

Sultan Jahan Begum, *Tazkirat-e-Baqi* (Calcutta: Thacker Press, 1929), Chapter 1, Parts III–IV

Tayyaba Bi, *Tarikh-e-Farman-ravanyan-e-Bhopal* (Karachi, 1977), chapter on Yar, Faiz, Hayat and Ghous

Zuberi, Mohammad Amin, *Begmat-e-Bhopal* (Bhopal: Hamidi Arts Press, 1918), Part I

History of Malwa and India

Dodwell, W.H., *The Cambridge History of India*, Vol V (New Delhi: C. Chand & Co., 1963), Chapters 4–23 and 31–2

Gascoigne, Bamber, *The Great Moghuls* (London: Jonathan Cape, 1971)

Gordon, Stewart, *Marhattas, Marauders and State Formation in Eighteenth Century India* (Delhi: Oxford University Press, 1994), Chapter 2

Hussain, Iqbal, *Rise and Decline of Ruheila Chieftains in 18th Century India* (Delhi: Oxford University Press, 1994), Chapters 6 and 8

Keay, John, *The Honourable Company* (New York: Macmillan, 1994), Part III, Chapters 13–18

Sarkar, Sir Jadunath, *Fall of the Moghul Empire*, Vols III–IV (New Delhi: Orient Longman, 1950)

Singh, K. Natwar, *Maharaja Suraj Mal* (Delhi: BI Publications, 1981), Chapter 7

Sinh, Raghubir, *Malwa in Transition* (Bombay: D.B. Taraporevale and Sons, 1936), Chapters 3–8

—— *Indian States and the New Regime* (Bombay: D.B. Taraporevale and Sons, 1938)

Tod, James, *Annals and Antiquities of Rajeshtan* (Calcutta, 1898)

Chapter 3

Wazir and Nazar's life

Ali, Allama Abid Wajdi-al-Husseini, *Tarikh-e-Riasat Bhopal* (Bhopal Book House, 1957), Chapters 6–7

Ali, Luard and Kudrat, *State Gazetteer – Bhopal* (Calcutta: Government Printing Press, 1907)

British India Office Records (IOR)

Chishti, Wahajuddin, *Begmat-e-Bhopal* (Karachi: Qudsia Printers, 1981), chapter on Wazir

Gordon, Stewart, *Marhattas, Marauders and State Formation in Eighteenth Century India* (Delhi: Oxford University Press, 1992), Chapter 2

Hamid, Dr Razia and Rafat Sultan (eds), *Nuqoosh-e-Bhopal* (Bhopal: Babul Uloom, 1986), chapter on Wazir

Hough, Maj. William, *A Brief History of the Bhopal Principality of Central India* (Calcutta: Baptist Mission Press, 1845)

Khan, Hamidullah, *Bhopal State – Its Ruler and Method of Administration* (Bhopal: Times of India Press, 1932)

Malcolm, Sir John, *A Memoir of Central India* (Gannon, 1972)

Malhotra, O.P., *History of Bhopal (1707–1818)* (unpublished thesis, Vikram University, Ujjain), Chapters 4 and 5

Shahjehan Begum, *History of Bhopal (Taj-ul-Iqbal)* (Calcutta: Thacker-Spink & Co., 1876), Chapter 6, Part I

Sultan Jahan Begum, *Tazkirat-e-Baqi* (Calcutta: Thacker Press, 1929), Chapter 1

Tayyaba Bi, *Tarikh-e-Farman-ravanyan-e-Bhopal* (Karachi, 1977), chapter on Siege of Bhopal

Zuberi, Mohammad Amin, *Begmat-e-Bhopal* (Bhopal: Hamidi Arts Press, 1918), Part I
—— *History of Bhopal* (Books for Libraries Press, 1922)

The Bourbons of Bhopal

British India Office Records (IOR)
Diver, Maud, *Royal India* (Freeport, New York: Libraries Press, 1942)
Golish, Vitold de, *Splendeur et Crépuscule des Maharajahs* (Paris: Hachette, 1963), chapter on Bhopal
Hamid, Dr Razia and Rafat Sultan (eds), *Nuqoosh-e-Bhopal* (Bhopal: Babul Uloom, 1986), chapter on the Bourbons
Kincaid, C.A., 'Bourbons of Bhopal', *Illustrated Weekly of India*, 1 September 1946
Malhotra, O.P., *History of Bhopal (1707–1818)* (unpublished thesis, Vikram University, Ujjain), Chapters 4 and 5
Rizvi, Dr Salim H., *Bhopal's Role in Urdu Culture* (Bhopal: Alvi Press, 1965), Chapters 2 and 4
Sultan Jahan Begum, *Tazkirat-e-Baqi* (Calcutta: Thacker Press, 1929)

The Mishti-khels

Sultan Jahan Begum, *An Account of My Life* (London: John Murray, 1910), Vol I
—— *Tazkirat-e-Baqi* (Calcutta: Thacker Press, 1929)
Tayyaba Bi, *Tarikh-e-Farman-ravanyan-e-Bhopal* (Karachi, 1977)

Chapter 4

Qudsia Begum's life

Ali, Allama Abid Wajdi-al-Husseini, *Begmat-e-Bhopal* (Bhopal Book House, 1957), Chapters 8 and 9
Chishti, Wahajuddin, *Begmat-e-Bhopal* (Karachi: Qudsia Printers, 1981), chapter on Qudsia
Shahjehan Begum, *History of Bhopal (Taj-ul-Iqbal)* (Calcutta: Thacker-Spink & Co., 1876, Part 1, Chapters 7–8
Sultan Jahan Begum, *An Account of My Life* (London: John Murray, 1910), Vol I
—— *Hayat-e-Qudsi* (Calcutta: Thacker-Spink & Co.,1909)
Tayyaba Bi, *Tarikh-e-Farman-ravanyan-e-Bhopal* (Karachi, 1977), chapter on Qudsia
Zuberi, Mohammad Amin, *Begmat-e-Bhopal* (Bhopal: Hamidi Arts Press, 1918)
—— *History of Bhopal* (Books for Libraries Press, 1922)

Chapter 5

Sikandar Begum's life

A woman of no importance, *Joys of Life* (London: John Murray, 1926), Chapter 5
Ali, Allama Abid Wajdi-al-Husseini, *Begmat-e-Bhopal* (Bhopal Book House, 1957), Chapter 10

Ali, Luard and Kudrat, *State Gazetteer – Bhopal* (Calcutta: Government Printing Press, 1907)
British India Office Records (IOR)
Chishti, Wahajuddin, *Begmat-e-Bhopal* (Karachi: Qudsia Printers, 1981), chapter on Sikandar Begum
Hamid, Dr Razia and Rafat Sultan (eds), *Nuqoosh-e-Bhopal* (Bhopal: Babul Uloom, 1986), chapter on Sikandar Begum
Shahjehan Begum, *History of Bhopal (Taj-ul-Iqbal)* (Calcutta: Thacker-Spink & Co., 1876), Part II
Sultan Jahan Begum, *An Account of My Life* (London: John Murray, 1910), Vol I, Chapters 2–4
—— *Tazkirat-e-Baqi* (Calcutta: Thacker Press, 1929), Chapter 1
—— *Hayat-e-Sikandari* (Daftar Tarikh, 1930)
Tayyaba Bi, *Tarikh-e-Farman-ravanyan-e-Bhopal* (Karachi, 1977), chapter on Sikandar Begum
Zuberi, Mohammad Amin, *Begmat-e-Bhopal* (Bhopal: Hamidi Arts Press, 1918)
—— *History of Bhopal* (Books for Libraries Press, 1922)

The Indian Mutiny

Bhopal and the Indian Mutiny, Indian National Archives
Bhopali, Asadullah Khan, *Sipahi Bahadur* (Delhi: Nice Printing Press, 1994)
Hamid, Dr Razia and Rafat Sultan (eds), *Nuqoosh-e-Bhopal* (Bhopal: Babul Uloom, 1986), chapter on Mutiny
Sultan Jahan Begum, *Tazkirat-e-Baqi* (Calcutta: Thacker Press, 1929), Chapter 2

Sikandar Begum's pilgrimage to Makkah

du Gaury, Gerald, *Rulers of Mecca* (AMS Press, 1954)
Sikandar Begum, *Pilgrimage to Makkah* (London: Thacker and Spink, 1906)

Chapter 6

Shahjehan Begum's life

A woman of no importance, *Joys of Life* (London: John Murray, 1926), Chapter 6
Princess Abida Sultaan, Recordings and Tapes[1]
Ali, Allama Abid Wajdi-al-Husseini, *Tarikh-e-Riasat Bhopal* (Bhopal Book House, 1957)
Ali, Luard and Kudrat, *State Gazetteer – Bhopal* (Calcutta: Government Printing Press, 1907)
British India Office Records (IOR)
Chishti, Wahajuddin, *Begmat-e-Bhopal* (Karachi: Qudsia Printers, 1981), chapter on Shahjehan Begum

---

[1] The author's mother, Princess Abida Sultaan, has recorded her memoirs on tape. She recalls the first-hand accounts of events from the days of Sikandar Begum's rule as conveyed to her by her grandmother, Sultan Jahan Begum, and numerous relatives, state officials and domestic retainers who had served with the former Begums. For instance, Shahjehan Begum's Personal Secretary, Hameed Ali Khan, rose to the level of Under-Secretary in the Deori Khas (Personal Office) which was controlled by Princess Abida Sultaan as heir apparent.

Shahjehan Begum, *History of Bhopal (Taj-ul-Iqbal)* (Calcutta: Thacker-Spink & Co., 1876), Part III, Chapters 2–4
—— *Appeal and Correspondence* (privately published)
Sultan Jahan Begum, *An Account of My Life* (London: John Murray, 1910), Vol I, Chapters 7, 9 and 13
—— *Hayat-e-Shahjehani* (Bombay: Times Press, 1929)
—— *Tazkirat-e-Baqi* (Calcutta: Thacker Press, 1929), Chapter 2
Tayyaba Bi, *Tarikh-e-Farman-ravanyan-e-Bhopal* (Karachi, 1977), chapter on Shahjehan Begum
Zuberi, Mohammad Amin, *Begmat-e-Bhopal* (Bhopal: Hamidi Arts Press, 1918), Part I

Defence of Siddiq Hassan

Princess Abida Sultaan, *Recordings and Tapes*
British India Office Records (IOR)
Hamid-Bhopal, Dr Razia, *Nawab Siddiq Hassan Khan* (Bhopal: Babul Uloom, 1983)
Saeedullah, *Life and Works of Siddiq Hassan Khan* (Lahore: Mohammad Ashraf, 1973)
Shahjehan Begum, *Appeal and Correspondence* (privately published)
Siddiq Hassan, *Defence* (Calcutta: Bannerjee/Chatterjee, 1888)
Sultan Jahan Begum, *An Account of My Life* (London: John Murray, 1910), Vol I, Chapters 7, 9 and 13

Chapter 7

A woman of no importance, *Joys of Life* (London: John Murray, 1926), Chapter 8
Ali, Allama Abid Wajdi-al-Husseini, *Tarikh-e-Riasat Bhopal* (Bhopal Book House, 1957), Chapter 12
Ali, Luard and Kudrat, *State Gazetteer – Bhopal* (Calcutta: Government Printing Press, 1907)
Chishti, Wahajuddin, *Begmat-e-Bhopal* (Karachi: Qudsia Printers, 1981), chapter on Sultan Jahan
Freely, John, *Inside the Seraglio* (London: Viking, 1999), Chapters 17 and 18
Hamid, Dr Razia and Rafat Sultan (eds), *Nuqoosh-e-Bhopal* (Bhopal: Babul Uloom, 1986), chapters on Sultan Jahan, jewellery and costumes, and buildings
Khan, Hamidullah, *Bhopal State – Its Ruler and Method of Administration* (Bhopal: Times of India Press, 1932)
Maimoona Sultan, *A Trip to Europe* (Bhopal: Gulshan-e-Alam, 1913)
Rizvi, Dr Salim H., *Bhopal's role in Urdu Culture* (Bhopal: Alvi Press, 1965)
Sultan Jahan Begum, *The Story of a Pilgrimage to Hijaz* (Calcutta: Thacker-Spink & Co., 1909)
—— *An Account of My Life* (London: John Murray, 1910), Vol I, Chapters 2 and 3
Tayyaba Bi, *Tarikh-e-Farman-ravanyan-e-Bhopal* (Karachi, 1977), chapter on Sultan Jahan
Zuberi, Mohammad Amin, *Begmat-e-Bhopal* (Bhopal: Hamidi Arts Press, 1918), Part II

Chapter 8

Princess Abida Sultaan, *Recordings and Tapes*
British India Office Records (IOR)
Hurley, Siobhan, *Emergence of Muslim Women: Bhopal 1901–30*, PhD thesis (London: SOAS, 1996)
Sultan Jahan Begum, *An Account of My Life* (London: John Murray, 1910), Vol III

Bhopal rulers and British officials

Ruler	Governor-General/Viceroy	Agent of Governor-General/ Resident	Political Agent
1744–77 Faiz Mohammad Khan	1772– Warren Hastings		
1777–1807 Hayat Mohammad Khan	1786– Marquess Cornwallis 1793– Sir John Shore, Lord Teignmouth 1798– Earl of Mornington, Marquess Wellesley 1805 Marquess Cornwallis		
1807 Ghous Mohammad Khan	1807– Earl of Minto		
1807–16 Wazir Mohammad Khan	1814– Earl of Moira, Marquess of Hastings		
1816–19 Nazar Mohammad Khan			1818– W. Henley
1819–37 Qudsia Begum	1823– Earl Amherst 1828– Lord William Bentinck 1835– Earl of Auckland	Mr Meade	1824– T.H. Maddocks 1828– Capt. N. Aloes 1834– L. Wilkinson

1837–44 Jahangir Mohammad Khan

1844–68 Sikandar Begum

1868–1901 Shahjehan Begum

1901–26 Sultan Jahan Begum

1842– Earl of Ellenborough

1844– Viscount Hardinge
1848– Marquess of Dalhousie
1856– Earl Canning
1862– Earl of Elgin
1863– Lord Lawrence

1869– Earl of Mayo
1872– Earl of Northbrook
1876– Earl of Lytton
1880– Marquess of Ripon
1884– Marquess of Dufferin
1888– Marquess of Lansdowne
1894– Earl of Elgin
1899– Marquess Curzon

1905– Earl of Minto
1910– Lord Hardinge of Penshurst
1916– Viscount Chelmsford
1921– Marquess of Reading
1926– Lord Irwin, Earl of Halifax

1854– Sir Robert Hamilton
1859– Sir Richmond Shakespear
1861– Sir Richard Meade

1869– Sir Henry Daly
1881– Sir Lepel Griffin
1888– Mr F. Henvey
1890– Mr R. Crosthwaite
1894– Sir David Barr
1900– Mr C.S. Bayley

1905– Col. Hugh Daly
1910– Mr M.F. O'Dwyer
1912– Mr A.L.P. Tucker
1914– Mr R.R. Glancy

1842– H.W. Trevelyan

1847– J.D. Cunningham
1850– Maj. H.M. Durand
1854– W.F. Eden
1859– Maj. McMullin
1861– A.R.E. Hutchinson
1863– J.W. Willoughby Osborne

1869– Col. E. Thomson
1874– Col. W. Kincaid
1887– Maj.-Gen. H. Wylie
1891– Lt.-Col. J. Meade
1896– Lt.-Col. J. Newmarch
1900– J. Lang

1903– Maj. L. Impey
1904– Maj. J. Manners-Smith
1906– Lt. Col. J.R.C. Calvin
1908– Maj. S.F. Bayley
1911– P.T.A. Spence
1913– W.S. Davis
1920– Col. C.E. Luard
1923– L.M. Crumpt
1925– A.R. Jelf

GENEALOGICAL TREE: ORAKZAI PATHANS OF TIRAH

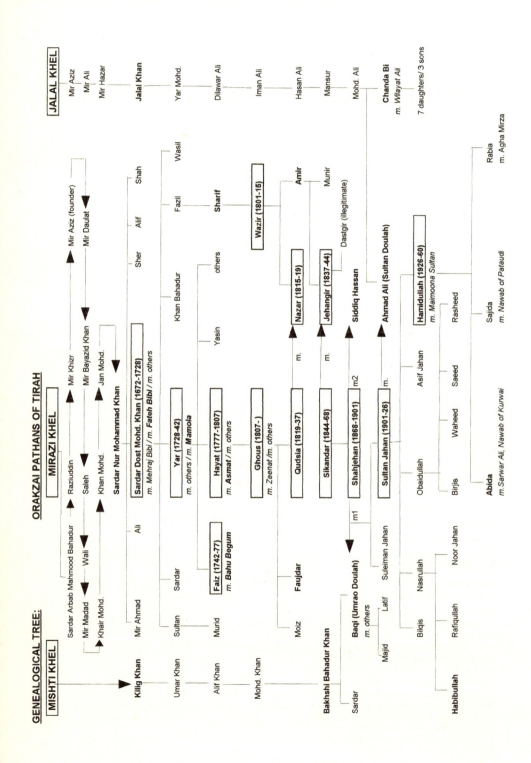

Reigns of Bhopal rulers

Age		Reign
Dost Mohammad Khan b.c.1672 – d.1728 aged 56	Founder and first Nawab	c.1709–28
Yar Mohammad Khan b.c.1709 – d.1742 aged 33	Second Nawab	1728–43
Faiz Mohammad Khan[1] b.1731 – d.1777 aged 46	Third Nawab	1744–77
Hayat Mohammad Khan[1] b.1735 – d.1807 aged 72	Fourth Nawab	1777–1807
Ghous Mohammad Khan[2] b.1767 – d.1827 aged 60	Fifth Nawab and titular Ruler	1807
Wazir Mohammad Khan[2] b.1766 – d.1816 aged 50	Sixth Ruler	1807–16
Nazar Mohammad Khan b.1791 – d.1819 aged 28	Seventh Nawab	1816–19
Qudsia Begum[3] b.1801 – d.1881 aged 80	Regent and eighth Ruler	1819–37
Jahangir Mohammad Khan b.1816 – d.1844 aged 28	Ninth Nawab	1837–44
Sikandar Begum b.1816 – d.1868 aged 50	Regent and tenth Ruler	1844–68
Shahjehan Begum b.1838 – d.1901 aged 63	Eleventh Ruler	1868–1901
Sultan Jahan Begum b.1858 – d.1930 aged 72	Twelfth Ruler	1901–26
Hamidullah Khan b.1895 – d.1960 aged 65	Thirteenth Ruler	1926–60[4]

[1] Mamola Bai (c.1720–95) exercised executive authority during the rule of her stepsons Faiz and Hayat.
[2] Wazir exercised gradual, de facto rule over Bhopal from the 1797s till his death in 1816. He did not claim the title of Nawab during this period. Hayat and Ghous were titular rulers, though they intermittently exercised executive authority. After the Siege of Bhopal (1812–13), Ghous was pensioned off and did not contest Nazar's succession as Bhopal's seventh Nawab.
[3] Qudsia Begum exercised all powers of a ruler in her capacity as Regent. It was agreed by family consensus that her only daughter's consort would succeed as ruler, on maturity. The British authorities insisted on implementing this agreement by first placing her cousin, Munir, on the masnad and subsequently replacing him with his brother, Jahangir.
[4] The state of Bhopal was merged into the Indian Union in 1949. Hamidullah remained titular Nawab until his death in 1960.

Glossary

akhara	wrestling pit
alap	opening stanza of a raga
amil	manager or administrator
ashrafi	gold coin
azan	Muslim call to prayer
baksheesh	gratuity
begum	Muslim princess, lady of rank
bimbashi	officer
booa	senior maidservant
burqa	tent-like garment, worn by women observing purdah
chapati	Indian flat bread
chauth	Marhatta tax equivalent to a quarter of revenue
chehlum	fortieth day of mourning
deorhi	estate
dewan	senior minister, head of administration
dholak	cylindrical drum
dhoti	loin-cloth worn by Hindu men on lower part of the body
Diwali	Hindu festival of lights
doli	palanquin
dopatta	long scarf worn across body by women
durbar	royal court, formal assembly
Eid	Muslim festival after Ramadhan and to commemorate Abraham's sacrifice
farangi	foreigner
fatwa	religious ruling or edict
firman	order issued by ruler
gadda-nashini	coronation; literally, ascending the throne
gaddi	throne
gao-takya	large, cylindrical cushion or pillow
Hafiz-e-Quran	someone who has learnt entire text of Quran by heart
hakeem	oriental doctor
Holi	Hindu festival held in Spring
huqqa/hookah	water-based tobacco-pipe
imam	religious leader, cleric
imli	tamarind
itr	oriental perfume
jagir	hereditary estate or fief
jagirdar	grantee of hereditary estate or fief
jawan	soldier
jehad	call for religious war
kalghi	jewelled crest worn on turban

GLOSSARY

kamdar	comptroller or manager
kathak	North Indian dance
kharita	formal letter to or from a ruler
khillat	robe of honour worn at ceremonial occasion
khula	divorce
khutba	Friday sermon
killedar	fort commander
kucheri	open-house meeting
kurta	shirt
lakh	unit of 100,000
madar-ul-maham	chief minister or prime minister
madrasa	school
mahawat	elephant-keeper or rider
mansabdar	person with official Moghul rank
masnad	ceremonial carpet usually signifying ascension of the throne; alternatively, seats of honour
maund	40 seers; one seer is approximately 0.88 kg
mazar	tomb of an eminent Muslim
mir-munshi	chief clerk
muafidar	freeholder
mufti	official interpreter of Islamic theology
mujra	performance by dancing girls
mukhtar	guardian
mushuk	water-carrier made from cowhide
mustajir	lease-holder
mustajiri	lease-holding
nan	circular baked bread
nan-bai	roadside baker
nashra	ceremony signifying completion of first reading of Quran
nazim	salaried administrator of district
nazrana	ritual gift
nikah	Muslim marriage contract
nilgai	blue bull – Indian equivalent of African kudu
paan	betel leaf
pandit	Hindu theology teacher
panj-hazari	military officer commanding 5000 troops
pargana	administrative division
pari	fairy
Peshwa	Chief Executive in Marhatta hierarchy
pir	religious leader, Muslim saint
qazi	Islamic law dispenser, judge
raj	rule, reign
rakhi	cotton bracelet
rani	Hindu queen
riasat	state
roznamcha	diary
rubats	lodging houses for pilgrims
rukhsat	marriage celebration signifying completion of wedding ceremonies
safa	turban
salaam	formal salutation
sambar	Indian elk
sanad	grant, potent or deed conferring rights or title
sanyasi	Hindu soothsayer, astrologist
sardar	clan chief

sari	traditional Indian dress worn by women
seer	approximately 0.88 kg
sehla	brocade turban
sehri	pre-dawn meal before beginning fast
serai	wayside inn
shalwar	baggy trousers
shamiana	large ceremonial tent
shariat	Islamic law
sherwani	formal dress, similar to frock-coat
shikar	hunting safari
shikargah	hunting lodge or preserve
soyem	mourning ceremony
stupa	dome
sufi	Islamic mystic
syce	groom
tahajjud	voluntary midnight prayer
tahajjud-guzar	one who offers up the voluntary midnight prayer
tahsil	district
talwar	sword or scimitar
tekri	hillock
thakur	term of respect for Rajput landlord of lower status than rulers
thana	compound
tika	jewelled crest worn on forehead
top-khana	arsenal for cannons; hence artillery in the context of regiments
ulema	learned religious Muslim clerics
urs	annual religious festival
vakil	representative, attorney
waqf	grant of land for religious or charitable purposes
yaddasht	memorandum
zamindar	land-owner, squire
zenana	women's quarters
zilla	small administrative district

Index

Abbassi, Ali Haider 230
Abdul Hamid, Sultan, Ottoman Emperor 161, 163
Abdul Jabbar Khan 155
Abdul Latif Khan 136
Abdullah Ibn Muhammad Ibn Aun, Sheikh, Sherif of Makkah 109, 110–11
Abida Sultaan: born 181; education 184, 210; accompanies Sultan Jahan to England to plead Hamidullah's case 199; made heir apparent 209–10; at Sultan Jahan's deathbed 211; marriage 232; runs Bhopal on Hamidullah's behalf 232; sporting prowess 232; life in Pakistan 232, 233
Abroo Begum 179
Afghanistan 1–2; *see also* Ahmad Shah Abdali
Aftab Jahan 230
Ahliya Bai 39, 48
Ahmad Ali Khan (Sultan Doulah), Sultan Jahan's husband: character 150; brought to Bhopal 115–16; wedding 128–9; verbally attacked by Syed Siddiq Hassan 131; dies 157
Ahmad Shah Abdali 36, 37, 38
Ahmed Effendi 163
Akbar the Great, Moghul Emperor 6, 61, 62
Akram, Mohammad 230
Alam Shah 16
Alamgir II, Moghul Emperor 35
Alexandra, Queen 176
Ali, Maulana Mohammad 182
Ali, Shaukat 182
Ali Hassan 138
Ali Yamani Beg 163

Alif Khan 65
Aligarh University 152, 180, 181–2
Amir Khan 47
Amir Mohammad Khan, Wazir's son: character 66; claims throne on Nazar's death 70; bought off by Qudsia 71; plots against Qudsia 75–6, 79, 81; seeks British support for Jahangir 80; plots to assassinate Sikandar 82–3; claims throne for himself 84; dies 85
Amritsar massacre 183
Anand Singh Solanki, Raja 10
Anwar Ahmad Khan 234
Aqil Mohammad Khan, Dost's brother 11, 26, 31
army in Bhopal: Chottey Khan's reforms 46; Sikandar's reforms 91
arts 151–2
Asad Ali, Hakim 58–9
Asad Ali Khan: plots with Amir 70, 75–6, 81; made Dewan 82; claims throne for Dastgir 84; banished 85
Asif Jahan 129, 144
Aslam Mohammad Khan, Sardar 234
Asmat, Hayat's wife 48, 49–50
Atiya Fyzee 180
Auckland, Earl of 80–1
Aun-ur Rafiq Ibn Abdullah Ibn Aun, Sherif of Makkah 161–2, 163, 164, 166, 167–8
Aurangzeb, Moghul Emperor 4–5, 6; meets Dost 7–8; dies 9
Ayesha, Hazrat 73
Ayub Khan 233
Azim-us-Shan 18

Bahadur Mohammad Khan, Bakhshi: background 65; Siege of Bhopal 55, 66; supports Nazar's accession 67; negotiates treaty with British 68; support for Qudsia 71, 75; retires from power with Qudsia 82, 86; dies 93
Bahadur Shah, Moghul Emperor 17–18
Bahu Begum, Faiz's wife 39–40, 42–3
Baji Rao, Peshwa 21; allies himself to the Nizam 25; struggles for Malwa 31; invades Bhopal 32, 33; dies 33
Bala Rao Anglia 50
Balaji Rao II: succeeds as Peshwa 33; signs treaty with Yar 33; signs treaty with Faiz 35; dies 38
Balaji Rao Viswanath 21
Baqi Mohammad Khan, Bakhshi (Umrao Doulah), Shahjehan's husband: character 75; strength 97; support for Sikandar 65–6; marriage to Shahjehan 95–7; Indian Mutiny 98–9; accompanies Sikandar on travels 105–8; relations with Shahjehan 114; dies 115
Bedar Bakht 9
Bentinck, Lord William Henry Cavendish 78
Berasia 11, 98, 99, 105
Bhils ix, 237
Bhilsa Fort 35
Bhoj, Raja ix
Bhopal: dress 184–6; literature 185; sport 186–7; early history ix–x; village gifted to Dost 17; early eighteenth century 22; development in eighteenth century 23–4; territory ceded to the Nizam 25; cultural life under Dost 25–6; Dost's governance 28–9; struggles with Marhattas 32, 33, 35, 39, 48, 52, 53, 59; Chottey Khan's governance 41–2, 46; Mamola Bai's governance 47; Murid's governance 49; summary of governance between Dost and Wazir 51; Wazir's governance 52, 60; 1818 treaty with British 68, 241–2; Qudsia's governance 74, 87; Jahangir's governance 82, 85; Sikandar's governance 91–4, 118; Indian Mutiny 98–102; annexes Berasia 105; Shahjehan's governance 133, 143–4, 151–3; famine 144; railway built 144; Sultan Jahan's governance 155–6, 171–3, 212–13; plague 178; contribution to First World War 180–1, 182; relations with Turkey 181–2; Congress Party makes in-roads 183, 184; Hamidullah's governance 230; recent history 231; present-day appearance 228–9
Bhopal, Siege of (1812–13) 54–8, 63
Bhore, Sir Joseph 230
big game hunting 186–7; Sikandar's prowess 91; Nasrullah's prowess 160, 161; Hamidullah's prowess 230; Abida's prowess 232
Bijjeh Ram: made Dewan 23–4; support for Yar's claim to throne 30; support for Faiz's claim to throne 34; Barru-kat Pathan resentment of 37; dies 38
Bilqis Jahan: birth 129; adopted by Shahjehan 130; entertained by Lady Durand 140; dies 138–40
Birjis Jahan 161
Birkenhead, Lord Frederick Edwin Smith 199, 201, 207
Bitan 238
Bourbon, Alexandre de 62
Bourbon, Balthazar de 60, 62; relations with Qudsia 63, 64, 88–9, 245–6; relations with Nazar 63, 67; Nazar's death 244; marriage 64; negotiates treaty with British 68; support for Qudsia 71, 74–5; puts down Munir's revolt 75–6; dies 77
Bourbon, Salvador de 60, 62–4
Bourbon, Sebastian de 64
Bourbon de Navarre, Jean-Philippe de 60–1
Bourbon family 60–5; family tree 240
British: situation in India in seventeenth century 5; situation in India in eighteenth century 22; growth in strength in India in eighteenth century 36; Goddard's march across India 40–1; Wazir negotiates with 52, 54; relations with Wazir 59–60;

INDEX

relations with Nazar 67–9; 1818 treaty with Bhopal 241–2; approve Sikandar's and Munir's succession 72; support for Qudsia 76; support for Jahangir 78, 80, 81; support for Faujdar 85; relations with Qudsia 87–8; power in India in mid-nineteenth century 93–4; support for Shahjehan 95, 96; Indian Mutiny 97–102; announce Sultan Jahan as heir apparent 119–20; award GCSI to Shahjehan 123; give titles to Syed Siddiq Hassan 126; replace Syed Siddiq Hassan with Colonel Ward 134–8; lobbied by Shahjehan about Syed Siddiq Hassan 140–2; return full executive authority to Shahjehan 142–3; attitude to Syed Siddiq Hassan 146–7; award GCIE to Sultan Jahan 173; give awards to Sultan Jahan and Obaidullah 179; warn Sultan Jahan about Hamidullah's behaviour 182; reaction to independence movement 183; decide who should succeed Sultan Jahan 189–208; make Abida heir apparent 210; relations with Begums 225–8
Brook, Colonel 137
Bunney, Maulana 234
Burhanpur, Battle of (1720) 24

Canning, Charles John, Earl 105, 106; Canning Sanad 190, 194, 206
Chanda Bi 115, 116
Chauhan, Narsingh Rao 12
Chelmsford, Frederick John Napier Thesiger, Viscount 180
Chitu 239
Chottey Khan: appointed Chief Minister 41; governance of Bhopal 41–2; support for Hayat at Battle of Phanda 43; increasing power 43–4; dies 44
Chou En-lai 233
Close, Sir Barry 59, 239
Connaught, Lord 159
Cook, David 74, 158, 159
costume *see* dress

Cunningham, J.D. 84, 90
currency 92, 133
Curzon, Lady 173
Curzon, George Nathaniel, Marquess 143, 159, 173

Daly, Sir Henry 150, 153
Damaji Gaekwad 37, 38
Dane, Colonel 141
Dastgir Mohammad Khan 84
de Golish, Vitold 245–6
Delhi, seventeenth century 5–6
Dilawar Ali Khan 24
Diye Bahadur 10, 12–13
Dost Mohammad Khan: character 12; appearance 26; background and education 1; sets off for India 2; sojourn in Jalalabad 2–3; sojourn in Delhi 4–7; early days in Moghul army 7; presented to Aurangzeb 7–8; assigned to Malwa 8; heads mercenary band 9–10; leases Berasia 11; brings kinsmen to join him 11; consolidation of domain 12–14; gains Bhopal village 15–17; captures Ginnor Fort 17; benefits from strife in Moghul Empire 21–2; becomes Nawab 22; qualities as ruler 23; strife with the Nizam 24–5; truce with the Nizam 25; religious devotion 25, 26, 27; children 26; dies 26; author's assessment 26–9; tomb 228; dates of birth and death 235–7
dress: seventeenth century 5–6; use of muslin 8; Bhopal 184–6
Dufferin, Marquess of 134
Durand, Colonel H.M., later Sir Henry 100–1, 134–5
Durand, Lady 140

East India Company *see* British
education: Sikandar's reforms 92; Shahjehan's reforms 151; Sultan Jahan's reforms 172, 173, 179–80, 212
Edward VIII, King 183, 186–7
Eid 6
El-Hassan Bin Tallal, Prince 233
Elgin, Earl of 143
Elizabeth II, Queen 200

Faiz Mohammad Khan, Yar's son: birth and parentage 31; proclaimed Nawab 34; appearance and character 34; makes treaty with Marhattas 35; refuses support to Marhattas against Ahmad Shah 37, 38; dies 39–40
famine 144
Farooq, Mohammad 10, 14–15
Farrukhsiyar, Moghul Emperor 18
Fatah Bibi, Dost's wife 10, 22–3, 26, 27, 28; tomb 228
Fatahgarh Fort 23, 34, 50
Fatma Begum 179
Faujdar Mohammad Khan, Qudsia's brother: shoots Nazar 69, 243–4; Qudsia takes into her care 71; proclaimed Regent 85; resigns 86; accompanies Sikandar on pilgrimage to Makkah 109
Fazil Mohammad Khan 98, 99
Fazle-Haider, Khundkar 230
Filoze, Jean Baptiste 60, 63–4
First World War, Bhopal's contribution 180–1, 182
Fitze, K.S. 191, 192, 194, 196–7, 208
Florence 178

Gailani, Pir Ghous Ahmed Shah 47
Gandhi, Mohandas Karamchand, Mahatma 181, 182, 231
George V, King: visits India 173–4; coronation 176; receives Sultan Jahan 176; attends Imperial Durbar 179; Sultan Jahan asks for help in Bhopal Succession Case 189, 200
George VI, King 200
Ghansi Ram 39
Ghazanfar Mohammad Khan, Brigadier 234
Ghous Mohammad Khan, Hayat's son: character, marriage and children 48; accused of Asmat's murder 50; treacherous dealings with Gwalior and Nagpur 52, 53; succeeds to throne 53; banished 53; given safe passage from Bhopal during siege 55; pensioned off 58; position during Nazar's reign 67–8; position upon Nazar's death 70
Ghurghusht 238

Ginnor Fort 16, 17
Glancy, Reginald 189, 190, 194
Goddard, General Thomas 40–1
Gohar Ara *see* Qudsia Begum
Gonds ix, 237
Griffin, Sir Lepel: supports wedding of Shahjehan and Syed Siddiq Hassan 124–5; proceeds against Syed Siddiq Hassan 134–6, 137, 140–1, 249–52; Shahjehan's attitude toward 148–9; behaviour toward Shahjehan and Syed Siddiq Hassan assessed 149–50
Gulab Khwajah 49, 50
gun salutes, Indian states 106

Habib-ur-Rehman 234
Habibullah Khan, Nasrullah's son: born 161; resentment of Hamidullah 183; claims throne 190; Bhopal Succession Case 192, 194 195–6, 197–8, 202–3, 206–8; his reaction 207, 209
Hamid Khan, General Abdul 233
Hamidullah Khan, 'Little Hamid': birth 129, 144; goes to Shahjehan's deathbed 144, 145; trained in governance by Sultan Jahan 156; Sultan Jahan's preference for 161, 212; accompanies Sultan Jahan on pilgrimage to Makkah 162; education 169, 170–1, 181; marriage 168–70; accompanies Sultan Jahan on visit to Europe 174; children 181; involvement in Khilafat Movement 181–2; made Chief Secretary by Sultan Jahan 182; sporting prowess 187, 230; Bhopal Succession Case 189–208; becomes Nawab 209; has Abida made his heir 209–10; governance 230; political influence 230–1; dies 233
Hamilton, R.C. 84
Hardinge, Lady 179
Hayat, Hassan Mohammad 230
Hayat, Sir Liaquat 230
Hayat Mohammad Khan, Yar's son: proclaimed Nawab 40; absence from battlefield at Phanda 43; attitude to Chottey Khan 43–4; cedes territory to Marhattas 48;

appoints Murid as Chief Minister 41; summons Wazir to put down Murid 50; appoints Wazir Dewan and Commander-in-Chief 52; dies 53
health: Sikandar's reforms 92; Sultan Jahan's reforms 172
Henley, Major W. 69, 70, 72, 243–4
Henvey, Francis 141
Hertzel, Sir Arthur 201, 202
Hilmi Effendi 164, 165
Himmat Rai 48
Hinduism: Hindu culture in seventeenth century 6; see also Eid
Ho Lung, Marshal 233
hockey 187, 232, 234
Holkar, Malhar Rao 37, 38, 39
Hoshang Alap Khan ix

Ibrahim Khan Gardi 37
Ikramullah, Mohammad 233
Imtiaz Ali, Munshi 142
Inayat Masih see Bourbon, Salvador de
independence movement 181–3, 231
Indian Mutiny (1857) 97–102
Iqbal, Allama 230
Irwin, Lord 210
Islam: Hajj ceremony 111; Muslim culture in seventeenth century 5–6; women's right to rule 72–3; Dost's religious devotion 25–6, 29; Faiz's religious devotion 34–5; Begums' attitude 223–5; relic of Prophet given to Sultan Jahan 178; see also Makkah; purdah; Wahabism
Islamnagar 12, 22
Istanbul 177
Izzat Khan 39

Jagua Bapu 55, 57
Jahandar Shah, Moghul Emperor 18
Jahangir Mohammad Khan, Sikandar's husband: appearance and character 79, 82; betrothed 76; meets with Lord Bentinck 78; marriage 80; revolt against Qudsia 81; crowned Nawab 82; attempts to assassinate Sikandar 82–3; dies 84; author's assessment 85

Jai Kunwar see Taj Bibi
Jai Singh 33
Jalal Khan 2–3
Jamali, Mullah 4, 7
Jamaluddin, Maulvi: made Dewan 93; accompanies Sikandar on pilgrimage to Makkah 109, 110; Sultan Jahan's tutor 113; employs Syed Siddiq Hassan 122; ousted from power 127; dies 133
Jeddah 109
Jelf, A.R. 190
Jhansi-ki-rani 99–100
Jinnah, Fatimah 233
Jinnah, Mohammad Ali 181, 182, 231
Juma Masjid 107

Kalka Binda 120
Kamal, Anwar 234
Kamlapati, Rani 15–17
Karam Mohammad Khan, Mian 70, 71, 74, 78
Karlanr 238
Kashko Khan 7
Kessari Lall 39
Khalil Arab, Atiya bint 234
Khalil Arab, Ruqayya bint 234
Khaliquzzaman, Chaudhri 230
Khandwa, Battle of (1720) 24
Khilafat Movement 181–2
Khushwakt Rai, Raja: support for Qudsia 70, 71, 74, 81; made Dewan 86, 93
Kincaid, Colonel 150
Kishan Maharaj 120, 152
Kitchener, Lord 173, 178
Kuli Khan 58
Kunwar Sardar Bai, Dost's wife 27

Lang, J. 154, 155
Lansdowne, Henry Charles Keith Petty Fitzmaurice, Marquess of 142, 143
Latif Khan, General 233
Latif-ur-Rehman 234
law and order: Chottey Khan's reforms 41–2; Qudsia's reforms 87; Sikandar's reforms 92–3; Shajehan's reforms 123; Sultan Jahan's reforms 184
literature 151, 152, 186

MacWatt, Colonel 162, 163, 164

MacWatt, Mrs 163
Maddocks, Thomas Henry 76
Madelena of Ethiopia 61
Madhav Rao 38, 39
Mahavir 98, 99
Mahfooz Ali Khan 195
Maimoona Sultan, Hamidullah's wife: relationship to Ahmad Shah Abdali 38; brought back to Bhopal 169–70; education 170; accompanies Sultan Jahan on visit to Europe 174–5, 177, 178; children 181; culture 182, 184; accompanies Sultan Jahan to England to plead Hamidullah's case 199, 200; dies 233
Makkah: Sikandar's pilgrimage to 108–14; Sultan Jahan's pilgrimage to 161–8
Malwa: early history ix; seventeenth century 8–9; strife during collapse of Moghul Empire 9, 21–2; Nizam establishes control 24–5; development during eighteenth century 28; strife after collapse of Moghul Empire 31
Mamola Bai, Yar's wife: origins 31; childlessness 31; religious devotion 31–2; influence at Yar's court 31; support for Faiz's claim to throne 34; governs on behalf of Faiz 35; Barru-kat Pathan resentment of 37; proclaims Hayat Nawab 40; relations with British 41, 66; welcomes Bourbons to Bhopal 62; appoints Chottey Khan as Chief Minister 41; dies 44; author's assessment 44–7
Mangalgarh 10, 14
Mansoor Ali Khan 233
Mao Tse-tung 233
Marhattas: revolt against Moghul Empire 5; aspirations to Malwa 8, 9, 21, 31; aspirations to India 20–1; gain supremacy in Bhopal 32; campaign in Bhopal during Faiz's reign 35; dominate north of India 35–6; struggles with Afghans 37; defeat at Battle of Panipat 37–8; regroup after Panipat 39; ceded territory by Hayat 48; attempt to take over Bhopal 52–8; return territory to Bhopal 59

Marjorie Memsaheb 195–6
Marseilles 174–5
Mary, Queen: visits India 173–4; receives Sultan Jahan 176; attends Imperial Durbar 179; audience with Sultan Jahan re succession 200
'Maryam the Sorceress of Ethiopia' 61
Mascrenhas, Maria and Juliana 61–2
Massood, Sir Ross 230
McNaughten, Charles 81
Meade, Colonel Malcolm 154, 155
Mecca see Makkah
Mehmet Reshad, Sultan, Ottoman Emperor 177–8
Mehraj Bibi, Dost's wife 2, 11, 27
Menon, V.P. 230–1
Minto, Earl of 59
Mir Fazlullah 7
Moghul Court 19, 21, 29
Moghul Empire: scope at zenith 1; signs of decline 4–5; collapse 9; strife after Aurangzeb's death 17–19; terminal decline in strength 35–6; see also Delhi
Mohammad, Prophet (Pbuh) 178
Mohammad Hamidullah Khan see Hamidullah Khan, 'Little Hamid'
Mohammad Khan 65
Mohammad Khan, Ustad 120
Mohammad Moazzam, Qazi 23
Mohammad Nasrullah Khan see Nasrullah Khan
Mohammad Obaidullah Khan see Obaidullah Khan
Mohammad Saleh Maulvi 11
Mohammad Shah, Moghul Emperor 18, 24, 29
Mohammadi Begum 115, 116
Moiz Mohammad Khan, Ghous's grandson 70, 71; part in Siege of Bhopal 57; Indian Mutiny 101–2; accompanies Sikandar on pilgrimage to Makkah 109
Moti Begum 50
Munawwar Jahan, Amir's wife 70
Munawwar Jahan, Baqi Mohammad Khan's granddaughter 234
Muneer 234
Munir Mohammad Khan, Amir's son: to be betrothed to Sikandar 71; made Nawab 72; plots

against Qudsia 75–6; set aside 76
Murid Mohammad Khan 49–51
muslin 8
Mustan Shah, Pir 57

Nadir Shah 33
Naidu, Mrs Sarojini 180, 181
Nasrullah Khan, Sultan Jahan's son: birth 129; trained in governance by Sultan Jahan 156; marriage 157–8; education and character 160–1; children 161; left in charge in Sultan Jahan's absence 162, 174; greets Sultan Jahan on return from pilgrimage 168; resentment of Hamidullah 183–4; dies 189
Nawal Shah 17
Nazar Mohammad Khan: relations with Balthazar de Bourbon 64; character 66–7; succeeds to throne 67; relations with British 67–9; dies 69; his will 71; Henley's report of his death 243–4
Nehru, Motilal 181, 182
Nizam-ul-Mulk, Chin-Qilich Khan, Asaf Jah 19–20; aspirations to Malwa 21; ambushed by Dilawar Ali Khan 24; establishes control of Malwa 24–5; care of Yar 30; struggles for Malwa 31; invades Bhopal 32; decline and death 36
Nizam Shah 15, 16
Nur Khan, Air Marshal 234
Nur Mohammad Khan, Dost's father: joins Dost in Berasia 11; dies 14
Nurul Hassan 127

Obaidullah Khan, Sultan Jahan's son: birth 129; trained in governance by Sultan Jahan 156; marriage 157–8; at Edward VII's coronation durbar 159; education and character 160, 161; children 161; accompanies Sultan Jahan on pilgrimage to Makkah 162, 164–5; heads Maimoona Sultan's wedding party 169–70; Prince of Wales's visit to India 173; heart problems 174; accompanies Sultan Jahan on visit to Europe 174, 175; receives award at Imperial Durbar 179; resentment of Hamidullah 183–4; psychological condition 188; dies 189
Ogilvie, G.D. 191, 192, 193, 194, 208
Omar Effendi 163
opium 123
Orakzai Pathans 1, 238, 262

Pakistan, creation of 231
Panipat, Battle of (1761) 37–8
Parason, Battle of 12
Parliament: introduced in Bhopal by Sikandar 92; Sultan Jahan revives 172
Patel, Vallabhai 230–1
Patterson, Colonel S.B. 196, 197, 208
Payne, C.H. 170
Phanda, Battle of (1787) 43
Pindaras 44, 239; relations with Wazir 59, 60; relations with Nazar 68; character of Pindara women 218
polo 187
postal service 92, 123
purdah 77–8, 91

Qadeer Khan, Dr Abdul 233
Qaisar Dulhan, Obaidullah's wife 157, 158
Qandhari Khan 169
qawwali 5
Qudsia Begum: character 73; parentage 48; part in Siege of Bhopal 55, 56; relations with Balthazar de Bourbon 63, 64, 65, 88–9, 245–6; relations with Sarkar Dulhan 64; marriage 67; becomes Regent 71–3; governance 74; Munir's revolt 75–6; emerges from purdah 77–8; delays handover of power 78–81; retires to Islamnagar 82, 83; attempts to have Jahangir set aside 83–4; relations with Sikandar 86, 90–1, 219; withdraws from power 91; Indian Mutiny 99, 101–2; accompanies Sikandar on pilgrimage to Makkah 109–10; relations with Syed Siddiq Hassan 125–6; relations with Shahjehan 126–7; not invited to Sultan Jahan's wedding 128;

support for Sultan Jahan 130;
support for railway 144, 153;
religious devotion 223; relations
with British 226; dies 133;
author's assessment 86–9, 218,
222
Qureshi, Shoaib 230

Rabia Sultan 181, 184, 199
Rafiqullah Khan 183
Raghib Bey 177
Raghunath Rao 39
railways in Bhopal 74, 93, 144,
152–3
Raisen Fort 35
Rajputs: revolt against Moghul
Empire 5; aspirations to Malwa
8, 9, 20, 21, 33; attitude to war
12; relations with Dost 12–13;
decline in power 36
Rani-jee, Wazir's wife 66
Reading, Lady 199–200
Reading, Rufus Daniel Isaacs,
Marquess of: hesitates in Bhopal
Succession Case 194–5, 196;
decides in favour of Habibullah
197; refers case to London 197;
pressurized by London to re-
open case 201–2; decides in
favour of Hamidullah 202–3;
reprimands staff for poor advice
208
Redhill 175
Rhaghuji Bhonsle 53
Rose, Sir Hugh 99
Rustam Ali Sirhindi 26

Sadar Mohammad Khan 34, 65, 75
Sadiq Ali 53, 55, 57
sailing 187
Saeed Mohammad Khan, Admiral
233
Sajida Sultan 181, 184, 199, 233
Salamuddin 230
Saleha Begum see Bahu Begum
Sarbanr 238
Sarkar Dulhan 64, 77, 133
Sarma, B.N. 197
Sarvath, Princess 233
Sarwar Ali Khan, Abida's husband
232
Sayyed Abdullah Barha 14; power-
broker behind Moghul throne
18; relationship with the Nizam
19–20, 24

Sayyed Hussain Ali Barha: life
saved by Dost 13–14; power-
broker behind Moghul throne
18; relationship with the Nizam
19–20, 24; death 29
Scindia, Daulat Rao 35, 48, 52, 59
Scindia, Jankoji 37, 38
Scindia, Mahadji 39, 48
Sehore, Indian Mutiny 98, 99
Sepoys' Revolt, 1857 see Indian
Mutiny (1857)
Shah Alam II, Moghul Emperor 38
Shah Ali Shah 45–6
Shaharyar Dulhan, Nasrullah's wife
157, 158, 164, 169, 174
Shaharyar Mohammad Khan,
Abida's son 232, 233
Shahjehan Begum: character 120;
born 83; proclaimed ruler by
British 85; education and
appearance 94; marriege to Baqi
Mohammad Khan 95–7, 114;
gives birth to Sultan Jahan 102;
abdicates 102–4, 248;
accompanies Sikandar on
travels 105–8; relations with
Sikandar 112, 219; succeeds to
the throne 119; falls in love with
Syed Siddiq Hassan 122; early
years of reign 122–4; relations
with Sultan Jahan 124, 129,
130, 148, 150, 220–1; marries
Syed Siddiq Hassan 124–6;
relations with Qudsia 126–7;
invested with GCSI 129;
attempts to have more children
129–30; rift with Sultan Jahan
131–3; reforms 133; supports
Syed Siddiq Hassan to British
134–7, 140–2, 249–52; attitude
to Syed Siddiq Hassan 148–9;
relations with Bilqis 138–9, 142;
resumes full executive authority
142; attitude to religion 142,
224; relations with British 227;
relations with Bourbon family
64; latter years of reign 143–4;
dies 144–6; author's assessment
151–3, 218–19, 222
Shahu 20, 21
Shahkarkhelda, Battle of (1724) 25
Shahzad Masih see Bourbon,
Balthazar de
Shakespear, Sir Richmond 103–4,
247–8

INDEX

Shakoor 234
Shareef Mohammad Khan, Dost's grandson 42, 43
Sharma, Shankar Dayal 230
Sheher Bano 188
Shibli Naumani, Maulana 179
Siddiqui, Abdur Rahman 230
Sikandar Begum: character 78–9, 90, 91; made ruler 71; betrothed to Jahangir 76; education 78–9; marriage 80; relations with Wilkinson 82; Jahangir's assassination attempt 82–3; cares for dying Jahangir 84; made Shahjehan's guardian 85; becomes Regent 86, 90; relations with Qudsia 86, 219; governance 91–4; claims throne for Shahjehan 94–5; finds husband for Shahjehan 95–6; relations with Shahjehan 219; Indian Mutiny 98–102; made Regent for life 102–4, 247–8; travels 105–8, 159; relations with British 106, 226–7; pilgrimage to Makkah 108–13; relations with Sultan Jahan 112–14; arranges Sultan Jahan's marriage 115–16; employs Syed Siddiq Hassan 122; religious devotion 224; dies 116; author's assessment 116, 218, 222
Sivaji 20
Soliman the Magnificent, Sultan, Ottoman Emperor 61
sport 186–7
Stamfordham, Lord 209
Stone, Isabella see Sarkar Dulhan
Sudashiv Bhau 36, 37–8
Suleiman Beg 109
Suleiman Effendi 163
Sultan, Shahzadi Farhat 234
Sultan Doulah see Ahmad Ali Khan
Sultan Jahan Begum: character 155, 159, 172–3; born 102; relations with Sikandar 112–14; Sikandar chooses her husband 115–16; made heir apparent 119–20; education 123; relations with Shahjehan 124, 129, 130–3, 148, 150, 220–1; marriage and children 127–9, 144; attempts reconciliation with Shahjehan 138–9, 144–6; attitude to Syed Siddiq Hassan 147; succeeds to throne 154; governance 155–6, 171–3, 184; arranges sons' marriages 157–8; husband's death 157; attends ceremonials 158–60, 173–4, 179; pilgrimage to Makkah 161–8; arranges Hamidullah's marriage 168–70; educates Hamidullah and Maimoona Sultan 170–1; visits Europe 174–9; given relic of the Prophet 178; support for education and women's emancipation 179–80, 210–11; relations with Bourbon family 64, 65; sympathy for Khilafat Movement 182; gives power to Hamidullah 182; educates granddaughters 184, 210; Bhopal Succession Case 189–208; abdicates 209; support for Abida as heir apparent 210; religious devotion 224–5; relations with British 227–8; relations with Turkey 228; dies 211; author's assessment 211–13, 223
Sultan Mohammad Khan, Dost's son 30, 31, 34
Sultan Mohammad Khan 233
Suraj Mal Jat 37
Syed Ahmad Shahid 121
Syed Awlad Hassan 121
Syed Siddiq Hassan: background 120–1; comes to Bhopal 121–2; marries Shahjehan 124–6; given titles by British 126; involvement in Sultan Jahan's marriage 127–8; attempts to gain control of state 130–3; deposed by British 134–8; Shahjehan seeks to clear his name 140–2; dies 141; posthumously resumes title of Nawab 142; author's assessment 146–51
Syed Waliullah 121

Taj Bibi, Dost's wife 27
Tara Bai 20
Tardi Beg 7
Thompson, J.P. 191, 192, 194, 202, 208
Toogood, General 230
trade 42
Trevelyan, Henry 84

Turkey: Maimoona Sultan's description 177; relations with Bhopal 161, 163, 177–8, 181–2

Umar Khan 65
Umrao Doulah see Baqi Mohammad Khan, Bakhshi

Venice 178
Vishvas Rao 37, 38

Wahabism 121
Wahid-uz-Zafar Khan, Obaidullah's son 188–9
Wali Shah 98, 99
Ward, Colonel C.H.E. 137, 138, 142
Wasil Mohammad Khan, Dost's son 35, 42
water 74
Wazir, Ustad 230
Wazir Mohammad Khan: support for Shareef 43; returns from exile 48–9; puts down Murid 50–1; appointed Dewan and Commander-in-Chief 52; banished by Ghous 53; struggles with Marhattas 53–4; Siege of Bhopal 55, 56, 57, 58; relations with British 59–60; relations with Pindaras 60; relations with Bourbons 63; comparison with Dost 66; marriage and children 66; author's assessment 58–60
wildlife 8, 176

Wilkinson, Lancelot: character 76–7; becomes Political Agent 77; insists on Qudsia's handover of power 79–80; support for Jahangir 81, 84; relations with Sikandar 82; attitude to women 225–6
Willoughby Osborne, Captain John William 125
Windsor, Duke of see Edward VIII
women: education 92, 172; emancipation 179–80, 210–11, 212; purdah 77–8, 91; right to rule 72–3
Wyndham, Mr 154

Yar Mohammad Khan, Dost's son: parentage 27; given to the Nizam as hostage 25; life as hostage 30; becomes Nawab 30–1; marriage and children 31; makes treaties with Marhattas 32, 33; dies 34; tomb 228; dates of birth and death 235–7
Yasin Mohammad Khan, Yar's son 39
York, Duke and Duchess of 200
Young, Freddy 230

Zafrullah Khan, Chaudhri 230
Zakia, Syed Siddiq Hassan's first wife 122, 124, 129, 130
Zeenat Begum, Ghous's wife 48, 55, 56, 57; role model for Qudsia 73–4